SCREENING ETHNICITY

CINEMATOGRAPHIC REPRESENTATIONS OF ITALIAN AMERICANS IN THE UNITED STATES

edited by

ANNA CAMAITI HOSTERT

ANTHONY JULIAN TAMBURRI

BORDIGHERA PRESS

Library of Congress Cataloging-in-Publication Data

Camaiti Hostert, Anna and Anthony Julian Tamburri.

Screening ethnicity : cinematographic representations of Italian Americans in the United States / edited by Anna Camaiti Hostert, Anthony Julian Tamburri.
p. cm. -- (VIA folios ; 30)
Includes bibliographical references and index.
ISBN 1-884419-53-4 (alk. paper)
1. Italian Americans in motion pictures. 2. Motion pictures--United States.
I. Hostert, Anna Camaiti. II. Tamburri, Anthony Julian. III. Series.

PN1995.9.I73 S38 2002
791.43'6520351--dc21

2002071744

Printed in the United States.

Published by
BORDIGHERA PRESS
Department of Languages & Linguistics
Florida Atlantic University
777 Glades Road
Boca Raton, FL 33431

VIA FOLIOS 30
ISBN 1-884419-53-4

TABLE OF CONTENTS

SCREENING ETHNICITY

CINEMATOGRAPHIC REPRESENTATIONS OF ITALIAN AMERICANS IN THE UNITED STATES

edited by

ANNA CAMAITI HOSTERT
ANTHONY JULIAN TAMBURRI

WHY THIS BOOK
AN INTRODUCTION

When we first felt the necessity and desire to put together this book, we were confronted with the issue of what it means to be Italian American, especially in this post-millennial era of the decidedly hyphenated;[1] from two different roads, similar conclusions were reached. The predominant, Italian experience of one co-editor, who came to study in the United States, having remained for well over a decade before returning again to Italy on a more permanent basis, is keenly mirrored by her co-editor. He, in turn, born and raised in the United States in an Italian family – and having earned a graduate degree in Italy – now returns consistently to Italy, while living and working in the United States. We, these two editors, also realized then, and have since affirmed, that the manner in which we have and continue to live this experience – indeed still and always in progress – is surely tied also to difference. Impossible to ignore, it is a difference based in both sexuality and gender that, while may very well constitute an element of specificity, does not by any means signal separation.

Assembled by way of a constant open channel across the Atlantic, this book represents structurally the possibility of a dialogue between two countries and two cultures intimately intertwined the one with the other, though physically thousands of miles apart. The choice of Italian, Italian/American,[2] and American scholars – some may indeed question the validity of these distinctions today – seemed all the more logical at this new *fin de siècle*. Their respective analyses and points of view certainly examine a complex reception of origins and belongings. And in so doing, we came to realize how these various aspects and characteristics of the filmmakers are articulated, as for example in the cases of De Palma and Tarantino, avoiding every attempt of assimilation, of marginalized separatism,

---

[1] For a discussion on the notion of *italianità* and Italian Americans, see Tamburri, Giordano, Gardaphè, "Introduction," *From the Margin: Writings in Italian Americana,* eds. Anthony Julian Tamburri, Paolo A. Giordano, and Fred L. Gardaphé (West Lafayette, IN: Purdue UP, 2000, 2ⁿᵈ edition).

[2] With regard to the use of the slash instead of the hyphen, see Anthony Julian Tamburri, *To Hyphenate Or Not To Hyphenate. The Italian/American Writer: An* Other *American.* Montreal: Guernica Editions, 1991.

or of pride in ethnic purity. They are figures of rootlessness, of hybridity or contamination, which is, in effect, that which defines cinema, as Bazin tells us[3] – figures and attitudes that are indeed the very substance of this collection in the various forms of cinematographic representations of Italian Americans. It is the other from itself, the body of the other, that is incorporated into the language and visual narrative forms of the directors studied herein. Thus, the identity of the various characters loses ethnic consistency and alters the process of vision, dispossessing it of the univocality that only a single point of view claims as representative.

This constant switch from one country to the other, from one language to the other, from one culture to the other, from one body of images to the other, constitutes the mobile *trait d'union* of an ever-open dialogue full of continual surprises, especially in a Benjaminian sense. It is a dialogue, namely, that unites us within a constant form of bewilderment, leading us off the beaten paths and into an undefined space, which constitutes not only those non-places of our own situation, but also those cinematographic spaces that the filmmakers in this volume choose in order to tell their stories.

Originally, these are stories of emigration, of miserable conditions often due to marginalization and alienation of those who have lost their own geo-cultural coordinates – their own roots – and ultimately try to insert themselves in a new society very much different from their own. One result is that they have also lost their personal abilities of expression and communication. In particular, the contradiction between the private dominance of an "ethnic" tradition based on religious and family values – often distorted and practiced to extremes – and the public subalternity of marginalized individuals deprived of their original forms of expression reaches its climax in the stories by Scorsese and Coppola, the first to speak – indeed, *to shout out loud* – of their roots while feeling at the same time fully American.[4] Beside an affectionate declaration of one's

---

[3] See Andrè Bazin, *What is Cinema?* (Berkeley: U California P, 1967).
[4] We underscore *shout out loud* for the simple fact that these two especially were artistically involved with their ethnicity from the earliest years of their carriers. It is by no means far-fetched to state that both directors had their first taste of great success with those films in which their Italian American-ness lies at the very base, films such as *The Godfather* (1972) and *Mean Streets* (1973).

own origins, there is no true pride of belonging; rather, one perceives a suffering denial of interior clashes of rootlessness and a constant condition of the outsider, which, with these directors, becomes one of the predominant characteristics of narrativity of *auteur* American cinema.

The result is an acquisition of a perennial tone of *dislocated* stories whose protagonists are, without any solution toward continuity, strangers not only to the *to and fro* of the dominant culture but indeed, and not on rare occasions, also to themselves. All the essays in this volume emphasize an aspect of <u>unconnected alterity</u> on the part of the directors and their creations – that is, their films and the protagonists of their stories – as well as a continuous hybridity with the other, be this other the dominant culture or other subaltern cultures. It is indeed the accentuation of this aspect that structurally represents and allows for the cinematic vision that has changed the films' basic texture and essence, thus changing the way of making and viewing cinema.

•

With regard to essays and articles, there are indeed many and, to be sure, most acute in their respective analysis. However, when one looks at the number of book-length studies, the terrain is indeed most barren;[5] and in this regard only three titles come to mind. In 1998 Paola Casella's *Hollywood Italian* appeared.[6] Chock full of paper – 549 pages – but lean on rigorous analysis,[7] this book

---

[5] What we mean by book-length study here is that type of general analysis by one author on Italian/American cinema, be that study either of a particular theme or more general in scope. This said, books such as *Coppola*, *Francis Ford Coppola: A Filmmaker's Life*, *Scorsese on Scorsese*, *Martin Scorsese: Interviews*, *The Cinema of Martin Scorsese*, or other studies on single directors are not included in this sense.

[6] Paola Casella, *Hollywood Italian: gli italiani nell'America di celluloide* (Milan: Baldini & Castoldi, 1998).

[7] Lacking in this book are bibliographic references to the more fundamental studies on Italian/American cinema. In the section of the bibliography dedicated to the "history of cinema," eight essays are included, and only two have appeared in scholarly journals. Missing, for example, are some significant essays such as those by Ben Lawton, a keen reader of both the Italian and Italian/American visual text, such "*Taxi Driver*: 'New Hybrid Film' or 'Liberated Cinema?'" *Italian Americana* 5.2 (1979): 238-48; "America Through Italian/American Eyes: Dream or Nightmare?" *From the Margin: Writings in Italian Americana* ed. Anthony Julian Tamburri, Paolo A. Giordano, and Fred L. Gardaphé (West Lafayette, IN: Purdue UP, 1991), 397–429; "*Impressioni d'America*: Italia—>America: Italians; Americans; ItalianAmericans; Italian>/<Americans Giacosa's Voyage of Discovery of

is better viewed as a type of film encyclopaedia, not a keen and penetrating study of Italian/American cinema and the various people – characters and actors – who populate these films. This book is divided into sections that consist of a series of chapters and sub-chapters dedicated to many films; and each section is introduced by a small chapter dedicated to history in general as well as the more specific film history pertinent to that section. *Hollywood Italian*, therefore, is better shelved among those reference books that have as their primary goal the offering of basic information about the subject at hand – to furnish the naïve reader,[8] that is, with a first introduction to the world of cinema populated by Italians and Italian Americans.

We would be remiss not to mention a few of the infelicities of *Hollywood Italian*. Two of the more debatable points are: (a) In discussing Al Pacino, for example, we read: "Il suo talento di attore, come era già successo a molti interpreti di origine italiana, da Sinatra alla Magnani, è stato in qualche modo sminuito dalla definizione di 'naturale': 'E' un animale istintivo', ha detto ad esempio di lui Sidney Lumet, il regista di Serpico" (310-11); and nothing follows this quote vis-à-vis Lumet's opinion. We might ask, as a reaction to what we read followed by no editorial comment, if such use of the adjective "istintivo" should be perceived as a negative comment: the jury, for sure, is out. Secondly, we might question the use of the phrase "di origine italiana" used to describe both Sinatra and Magnani; the first United-States born and socialized in North America, the second Italian-born and socialized in Italy. A connection of sorts between two such representatives of these two cultures surely exists, as we so imply in the first part of this introduction; however, such an expansive use of the phrase "di origine italiana" surely warrants some sort of explanation outlining both the similarities and differences the author perceives. (b) Another infelicity, in our opinion, is the author's characterization of Joe Mantegna; she writes: "Fra i primi attori italo-americani – nono-

---

Self/Other," *DIFFERENTIA, review of italian thought* 6/7 (Spring/Autumn 1994): 99–118; and "What Is ItalianAmerican Cinema?" *Voices in Italian Americana* 6.1 (1995): 27-51.

[8] By "naïve reader," we refer to that concept of general reader as opposed to the more specialist reader discussed by theorists such as Seymour Chatman, Umberto Eco, Gerard Genette, Wolfgang Iser, and the like.

stante l'aspetto etnico – il più affermato è Joe Mantegna, che negli anni ottanta è emerso come protagonista, e talvolta persino come eroe romantico" (382). First of all, so it would seem, one might wonder how, after more than 350 pages in which the names of Pacino and De Niro often appear, one readily makes the above-mentioned declaration. Indeed, in his own right, Mantegna is a most accomplished actor. However, it seems most difficult to place him at the same level with, and we use Lumet's term in the most flattering sense possible, a "natural," as one might consider both De Niro and Pacino. Secondly, what exactly is the meaning of the phrase, seemingly articulated *en passant,* "nonostante l'aspetto etni-co"? Is not this book also about Italian Americans who by definition within the greater semiotics of the United States also signifies ethnic? Yes, we know, a rhetorical question indeed.

Our second title worth mentioning is by Lee Lourdeaux, *Italian and Irish Filmmakers in America: Ford, Capra, Coppola, and Scorsese,*[9] a more satisfying book than the first, overall, which discusses three Italian/American directors and one of the greatest Irish/American directors. This first chapter dedicated to Ford serves as wonderful point of comparison between the two ethnic groups, especially with regard to Frank Capra as a sort of bridge between the two groups.[10] Lourdeaux prefaces his discussion of the four directors with a type of history of film imagery in the silent movie and, more specifically, in the films of D.W. Griffith. In his discussion of the four directors, Lourdeaux wishes to underscore the importance of their ethnic heritage and their Catholicism in their films, and rightly so, perhaps. But the westerns by John Ford and the comedies by Frank Capra seem less of a fit in his overall interpretative scheme than do the films by Coppola and Scorsese. *A Hole in the Head,* for example, a film which John Paul Russo dis-

[9] Lee Lourdeaux, *Italian and Irish Filmmakers in America: Ford, Capra, Coppola, and Scorsese* (Philadelphia: Temple UP, 1990).
[10] As in Casella's bibliography, here, too, some fundamental essays seem to be missing. In addition to those we mentioned in note 5, we would include the following two for sure on Coppola and Scorsese: Robert Casillo, "Catholicism and Violence in the Films of Martin Scorsese," *Support and Struggle: Italians and Italian Americans in a Comparative Perspective.* Ed. Joseph L. Tropea *et al.* (Staten Island, NY: AIHA, 1986), 283–304; and John Paul Russo, "The Hidden Godfather: Plenitude and Absence in Francis Ford Coppola's *Godfather I* and *II,*" *Support and Struggle: Italians and Italian Americans in a Comparative Perspective.* Ed. Joseph L. Tropea *et al.* (Staten Island, NY: AIHA, 1986), 255–81.

cusses in his contribution to our collection – indeed, the first true analysis of the film – is only mentioned in the last four lines of the chapter dedicated to Capra. Russo, instead, convinces us of both the historical and artistic significance of this film not only in the history of Capra's movies but also within a more general discourse of Italian/American and United States cinema.

The third title that comes to mind is undoubtedly the most satisfying of the three, and it is, instead of a book in the technical sense, a very long chapter that is in its own right comparable to the length of anything we would readily consider a book. This essay by Pellegrino D'Acierno, "Cinema Paradiso: The Italian American Presence in American Cinema,"[11] is an excellent reading, in the form of an historical analysis, of the cultural phenomenon of Italian/American cinema, which includes a markedly ample bibliography.

Only three titles of a general nature surely signals a critical gap yet to be filled surrounding a greater discourse on Italian/American cinema. Why such a gap, one might ask, may be due to a more general notion of cultural inferiority, when until approximately twenty-five ago, Italian/American culture did not enjoy the cultural significance it does today. Then, the so-called dominant culture did not direct its attention that often toward those cultural productions, visual and written, that we readily associate as Italian/American. Namely, those works that had not yet received the cultural value – from those who were in the decision-making position – to be able to cross over the threshold that provided access to the reigning cultural-artistic world.[12]

---

[11] Pellegrino D'Acierno, ed. *The Italian American Heritage. A Companion to Literature and Arts* (New York: Garland Publishing, Inc., 1999), 563-690.

[12] There are at least two important historical moments in this regard: (a) the publications of: [1] Rose Basile Green's *The Italian-American Novel: A Document of the Interaction of Two Cultures* (Madison, NJ: Fairleigh Dickinson UP, 1974), and [2] the inaugural issue of *Italian Americana* (1974). (b) The publications of: [1] Helen Barolini's anthology, *The Dream Book. An Anthology of Italian-American Women Writing* (New York: Schocken, 1985, now available from Syracuse University Press, 2000), [2] the resumption of *Italian Americana* (1990) and the inaugural issue of *Voices in Italian Americana* (1990), and [3] the publication of *From The Margin: Writings in Italian Americana* (1991). Subsequently, publications on literary studies especially have increased by more than thirty books – authored and edited – in the last ten years.

The overall purpose of this collection is to cross finally that threshold, now open to the critical world of visual Italian America. Secondly, by gathering an array of critical voices from various perspectives and hermeneutico-semiotic specificities, we hope to contribute to a growing critical discourse on Italian/American culture in general and, with specific regard to cinema, to the equally nascent discourse on Italian/American visuality. There is without doubt a debt we all owe to those who have helped furrow this path from an editorial point of view. Fairleigh Dickinson University Press, Purdue University Press, Guernica Editions, Duke University, and SUNY Press, to name a few, have already led the way, running certain risks by publishing the works they did – both creative and critical – which ultimately opened new paths, and which we now find less overrun by the metaphorical scrub-brushes. Secondly, we would be remiss not to mention the intellectual foresight of Luca Sossella in his publication of the Italian version of this collection, which creates for the first time an intellectually rigorous meeting point, as we mentioned at the outset, of Italian, American, and Italian/American voices; a space in which diverse viewpoints were born on different semiotic shores, which nicely emulate to a certain degree that kaleidoscopic mosaic that is – still – the United States.

In closing, we need to mention the superb editorial and production assistance of two indispensable people. Natalia Giannini spent innumerable hours copy-editing and proofing the essays, as well as enhancing and compiling the final indexes. Deborah Starewich, in turn, added her usual touches of excellence in the final stages of pagination and cover design. To both of them we owe an immense debt.

Anna Camaiti Hostert
Roma, Italia
Anthony Julian Tamburri
Boca Raton, Florida, USA
March 2002

Specific Themes, Multiple Voices

GREY SHADES, BLACK TONES
ITALIAN AMERICANS, RACE AND RACISM IN AMERICAN FILM

Francesca Canadé Sautman
CUNY GRADUATE CENTER

> ...–yes, I tell you
> Italians owned Britain
> And Hannibal blackened the earth from the Alps to the Adriatic
> Roman blood sickles like the blood of an African people
> So where is true history written
> Except in the poems?...
> Audre Lorde, "On my way out I passed over you and the Verrazano Bridge,"
> *Our Dead Behind Us*

> [Coffy to Italian gangster Vitroni]: "...Are you sure you're not a little bit
> Black?..."
> *Coffy,* (Jack Hill, 1973,)

I. *Italian American Ethnicity and the "Scramble for Whiteness"*

The late 19th-century immigration wave brought Italians in large numbers to the shores of the United States, sailing to a place with a firmly entrenched system of well-honed racial discrimination, maintained through a virulent discourse about race. They were to fit into that discourse as abjectified other, becoming a category of not-fully-white, or imperfect whites. For Matthew Frye Jacobson, they were among the "probationary white races of the nineteenth century" (57). David Roediger refers to such ethnic groups as "not yet white" (1994), and Robert Orsi speaks of "in-between peoples" (1992). In a more vulgar form, this status was starkly rendered by a famous exchange between a journalist and a construction boss in the 1890s; to the question "Is an Italian a white man?" the employer responded: "No sir, an Italian is a Dago" (Jacobson, 56).

Images of Italian Americans[1] in contemporary American film function as sites for the inscription of explosive or socially unac-

---

[1] The question of terminology in referring to people of Italian descent has been discussed by others; does one refer to Italians, or to Italian Americans, does one use a hyphen, or a slash

ceptable racial discourses; as such, they engage critically the problematics of how "whiteness" has been constructed and embraced. The tense relationship between racial and ethnic identities, and the ways they intersect with other identitarian planes, such as class, gender, and sexuality,[2] are fundamental to the representation of Italian Americans in popular media. In the history of European immigrant communities, racial identity – buying into "whiteness," as opposed to being inflected towards or into "blackness" – stands in obdurate contrast to ethnic identity – rejecting mainstream hegemonic cultural practices in favor of ancestral, allogenous ones. This complex array of identity possibilities implies yet two other quandaries. First, recognizing that "ancestral, traditional" ethnicities are, more often than not, invented and reinterpreted (Sollors, Di Leonardo, Fischer); and secondly, acknowledging that the very choice between poles of identity, electing to define oneself as white or not, are the hallmark of white power and privilege itself, and are denied to non-whites. Another way of formulating the distinction, by contrasting visual and verbal, is offered by Suzanne Yang: "Ethnicity – and why not say *versus race?* – is a way of contrasting two approaches to alterity. I would like to start by aligning *race* with a visible otherness in the scopic dimension, using the term *ethnicity* to designate an otherness in the acoustic field of verbal phenomena."(139) And Patricia Williams offers this challenging remark: "...if the "underclass" is a way of unnaming the poor, "whiteness" is a way of not naming ethnicity" (258).

"Whiteness" is at first circumscribed by two extremes: a white supremacist endorsement of whiteness as a superior identity that perceives itself as "under siege," as Giroux points out; and a critical stance that equates being white with power and oppression of others. Henry Giroux has eloquently argued for a third dimension as well, based on efforts to examine "whiteness" critically, to determine "how whiteness as a racial identity is experienced, repro-

---

(Tamburri, 1989)? I have adopted a convention here of using "Italian" to refer to people who immigrated from Italy or to characters thus identified in a given text, and Italian American without hyphen or slash for people born here of Italian descent. I use the generic "Italian" when both groups are being referred to together.

[2] Such analysis remains relatively rare with respect to Italian Americans; for an essay that does make these links, Tamburri (1999).

duced, and addressed by the diverse men and women who identify with its common sense assumptions and values" (1998, 46).

Italian Americans in contemporary American culture, especially film, raise specific problems in the "reading of race." The racially hegemonic inflects in particular ways "...the ethical and racial dilemmas that animate the larger racial and social landscape" (Giroux 1997, 307). Italian Americans forcefully interrogate these very dilemmas, sometimes in spite of the filmmakers' intentions. Simply put, Italian Americans are presumed by themselves and much of society to be "white"; yet the experience of early Italian immigrants in this country called that denomination into question. The Italian immigrants of the 1890s and even 1910s and 1920s were not considered "really" white, and if not actually black, shaded to black, bringing the white identity of their descendants under suspicion, marked with sequels and residues of earlier marginalization. Thus, one has to ask, how does a group who has not been "really white," and continues to carry that stigma in various forms of representation, go about acquiring a "white identity"? How indeed, since, as David Roediger reminds us, there was a claim to ethnicity by European immigrants that did not preclude simultaneous investment in the ideology of white supremacy.[3] Or, again, how does such a group give purchase to white identity, even as it claims to maintain its own, separate, uncompromising, ethnic/national identity? In how much actual *work*, in what kinds of social practices does this group have to engage to effect, and make effective, its exclusion of non-whites?

Film plays a decisive role in answering these types of questions and in racial acculturation today. The affirmation of a certain version of ethnic and cultural identity, based on invention and nostalgia, sustains a cinematic narrative in which the tragic, the fateful, the weight of centuries of custom and belief, are mobilized to legitimize racial exclusion, and deployed to give immutable foundations to ethnic identity.[4] If ethnicity is, as Michael Fischer sug-

---

[3] David Roediger (1994, 181-98).
[4] Building on the work of feminist sociology and anthropology, I have discussed this phenomenon at some length in my essay "Women of the Shadows" (1994).

gested, constantly "reinvented and reinterpreted,"[5] film participates and is complicit in the play between reinvention and reaffirmation of tradition, between creativity and repetition, between self-affirming cultural strategies and subservient ones, that generate complex discursive and visual narratives on the screen.

Historically, the dangerous "middle ground" occupied by immigrants of dubious whiteness could be severely aggravated in more racially hierarchical surroundings. In regions of the South, such as Louisiana in the 1890s, Italians were perceived as not looking and not acting white. They accepted economic occupations usually reserved to Blacks, such as farm labor and small tenancy, lived, worked side by side with Blacks, and also fraternized and intermarried with them, and as well, supported republican and populist political candidates rather than the "white" worthies. Thus, "they occupied a racial middle ground within the otherwise unforgiving caste system of white-over-black" (Jacobson 57). The lynchings in New Orleans[6] underscored how much the fate of poor Italians in this country might become a reflection of that of Blacks, and intertwine with it. This incident, and a series of legal issues around immigration and naturalization in the first decades of the century, as Jacobson suggests, point to a process in which "unsure whites" are not always "whitened" by the presence of nonwhite Others in a given locale, for people who were actually entering the country as "free white persons," "could also lose that status by their association with nonwhite groups. This was precisely the case with Italians in New Orleans" (Jacobson, 57). Following the lynchings, the press, including the *New York Times*, extolled the actions of the lynch-mob. Popular fiction also took up the narrative as a discourse on racial difference and supremacy; in April 1891, an issue of the *New York Detective Library* carried a story on "The New Orleans Mafia: Or, Chief Hennessy Avenged," stating: "Like the Negro, the

---

[5] Fischer (1986, 207) remarks in particular: "Transference, the return of the repressed in new forms, and repetitions with their distortions are all mechanisms through which ethnicity is generated." Essay quoted in relation to Italian American identity by Gardaphè (1996).

[6] This is the most famous, and most commented-on case of Italians being lynched, but by no means the only one. Gallo mentions the 1874 riots and killings in the coal fields (111), an 1886 lynching in Vicksburg, Miss. (112), four lynchings near Seattle in 1892 and four more in Oklahoma that same year (113); this violence continued between 1900 and 1929: in Tampa, in 1910, two Italians taken in custody were lynched, and two more in Johnson City, Illinois, in 1914 (119).

favorite weapon of the Sicilian is the razor," and attributing to Sicilians a bloody-minded disposition greater than among other Mediterraneans (Jacobson, 60-61). The proximity of Italians to Black Americans was not only denoted by the construction of their racial history, but invoked to further their status as marginalized others, and feared as a catalyst to the disorderly expression of this moral and social otherness. Thus, a 1925 study of immigrants and the justice system concluded that Italians "were by nature emotional and demonstrative," and "should not be allowed to drift into racial communities [ghettoes], forming habits of thought...that are limited and warped" (Jacobson, 62). Legally, the middle ground was fully inscribed with the contradictions of the American system, between democracy and racial terror, between systems of exclusion and the rhetoric of the melting pot, between citizenship and being outside of society. Thus, Jacobson remarks, in the 1910s and 1920s, during a period of "volatile racial meanings," Jews, Italians, Celts, and Slavs, "were becoming less and less white in debates over who should be allowed to disembark on American shores, and yet were becoming whiter and whiter in debates over who should be granted the full rights of citizenship" (75).

A recent film, *Vendetta* (1999), attempts to convey these subtle inflections of race, ethnicity, and citizenship around the New Orleans lynchings, but does so rather poorly. Problems start with the sensationalist title, for a "vendetta" implies a dispute between equal rivals, and it highlights the conflict between Matranga and Provenzano, rather than the power differentials that made Italians in New Orleans non-citizens and non-whites at once. Here, Blacks are counter-posited to Italian Americans and racist whites as the third category, but in the most perfunctory way, with a few black characters lost in the mass of whites. The young hero-narrator encounters a black sharecropper who seems amused and bewildered by the Italian's efforts to buy vegetables, as if greengrocery were a concept alien to Blacks. Eventually he brings his own wares to the Italian market, and seems inordinately enthused by the sale. This is a recognizable cinematic cliché: black people are expected to show disproportionate gratitude and love at the smallest recognition by whites, who remain indifferent towards them. During the trial, Blacks are merely the victims of the white racist establishment that extorts false testimony out of them, until one, still grateful over his fruits, changes at the least minute at great risk to himself. He then disappears from the narrative and we have no idea of what the consequences might be. Black characters are only go-betweens that allow the Italians more depth. They serve the purpose of underlining the Italians' abjection and poverty, saying for instance that they would not work for as little as the "Dagoes."[7] The complexity of that statement – Italians are foreigners, thus cheaper, but they still have the historical potential to become white – is never explored. The narrator himself never recognizes blackness discursively: only the image and the narrative encode the situation of racial hierarchy and oppression under which Black Americans lived. At the same time, the various forms of exclusion Italians face are only sketched out so that racist oppression can gather pitch exclusively in the framing and lynchings. Indeed, an exposition of the actual structures of racism experienced by Italians in 1890s New Orleans would not be possible without bringing in serious reflection simultaneously on the status of Blacks. As well, since all those lynched were men, this gives the film an easy pretext to not present Italian women at all, except in picturesque glimpses, as frightened and suffering black-clad victims, while the blonde Irish lass is given more focus, albeit a predictable one.

Indeed, Italians, as reviled as they were, were *not* Black. Their history did not derive from the brutal legacy of slavery, but from other, less devastating forms of human exploitation, and it is disingenuous to attempt claims to "parity in oppression." Italians could remain, in spite of it all, connected, through recent memory, familial ties, personal narratives, or economics, to the European land of origin they had left under duress, but had not been ripped away from to be cast off to the oceans in chains.[8] Similarities there were, but differences as well, the most crucial being that the door to whiteness remained ajar for them eventually to push open. In their

---

[7] Relations between Blacks and Italians in Louisiana at the time, the perception of Italians by Blacks as "docile whites" used as a wedge against them, and the place of Italians in the fruit business, from garden growers and peddlers to various levels of activity in the port, are discussed by Gallo (117-19).

[8] For one of the richest, most complex, explorations of an Italian immigrant community, its new ties and political relations (around anti-fascism) with the Old Country, see Mormino and Pozzetta.

new land, even as "imperfect whites," or "whites in the making," they nevertheless had the option to negotiate themselves into that place of relative power and privilege – whiteness, like other European immigrant groups.

Economic deprivation, even poverty, labor strife, employment discrimination, bias attacks on the street, ostracism, cultural prejudice were the lot of people of Italian descent through the 1920s and 30s.[9] In the 40s and 50s, they were still a blue-collar population, living in separate areas (the "gray" neighborhoods of the 1950s Midwest), on the front lines of labor struggles, allied with other minority groups, especially Jews, and sometimes Blacks. But realignments were also taking place early. In the 1943 Detroit riots, in which whites and Blacks were violently pitted against each other, Italians had become just another group of whites.[10] During this period of intense racial attacks, from March to December 1943, there were 242 incidents of black-white conflicts in 47 cities, and 145 interracial committees for unity had formed, mostly in the North. Blacks, Italians and Jews were starting to be caught in the nets of racial contradictions that would bear poisoned fruit in the next generations. For instance, the journal *Race Relations* noted a case of "interminority" strife in which a Jewish landlord allowed Blacks to move in his buildings and was met by fierce resistance by Italians residents (Jacobson 113-14). In the 60s, change occurred more drastically; Black Americans began to rise in mass against segregation, and eventually against grinding poverty, social humiliation, and police violence, this resistance culminating in the urban uprisings of the late 60s. Howard Winant has suggested that "...by the 1960s white ethnicity was in serious decline," and that, reacting as embattled and displaced by the limited victories of the Civil Rights Movement, most whites, unable both to revert to old-style white supremacy, or to commit themselves to a new kind of politics welded by common working-class interests, "were ripe for conversion to neo-conservative racial ideology..." (103). As communities, notwithstanding their individual roles, Italians began to fill a different kind of social space: now Anthony Imperiale and his

---

[9] See Gallo, LaGumina, McLaughlin, Mangione and Morreale, Rolle, and Starr.

[10] On Detroit see also Domenic J. Capeci.

ilk were patrolling Newark to fend off the "Black menace," local gangs in neighborhoods like East New York were fighting Black youth.[11] And so it went: Gravesend, Howard Beach, Bensonhurst, when, in the political landscape of New York City, the public drama of racism was played out with the murder of Yusuf Hawkins and the heinous role readily attributed by the media to Italian Americans as a block.[12] For Italian Americans, that gradual acceptance into whiteness of former white immigrant communities referred to by David Roediger as "buying into whiteness," or acquiring "the wages of whiteness," seemed complete.[13] They were no longer "Wops" and "Dagoes," and had bought into the American racial "dream." Indeed, film has given its own interpretation of the Italian role as an intermediary, even contradictory, category, not white enough but not dark enough – and not Black, especially. It has problematized this position to varying degrees, mostly, through the mobilization and manipulation of recognizable but unquestioned racial categories, images and themes, within diverse narrative economies. At the same time, for the most part, these films have also allowed a screaming silence on matters of racial oppression to resonate across the screen.

II. *Italians in Film: Race Riot*

In the year 2000, lingering questions remain. In the 1920s, most Americans could have named Sacco and Vanzetti as the most publicly known Italian Americans; gradually this spot was reserved for an assortment of historical gangster figures. Today, sadly, the most likely candidate would be Tony Soprano! And this is no quip,

[11] My colleague George Yúdice provided me with this information: growing up in East New York in the late 60s and early 70s, he encountered gangs of Italian American youth organized against Blacks with the acronym Sponge, meaning "Society for the prevention of niggers (sic) getting everything."

[12] See John De Santis. Public discourse around Bensonhurst was obfuscated by a clear desire both from media and some civil rights groups to totally obliterate the oppositional voices of those Italian Americans who denounced racism and participated in demonstrations. Albeit a small number, they were erased because their presence was too unsettling for the construction of Italians as violent, lower-class racists. It was socially and politically important to maintain that reading, and groups like Italian Americans against Racism could not be *authorized* to speak.

[13] Roediger (1991), asserts: "The pleasures of whiteness could function as a 'wage' for white workers. That is, status and privilege conferred by race could be used to make up for alienating and exploitative class relationships" (13).

for the "middle ground" of Italian immigrants perseveres in the construction of Italian Americans, caught in the double bind of an invented ethnicity foisted on them by the mainstream, and internalized, digested and taken on by themselves. Indeed, Italian Americans are not just passive recipients of a mainstream plot: they can exercise agency, choose their own images,[14] their historical traces, their cultural identifications, and create a different discourse, particularly through film. Yet, this is impossible as a "community," because as in other ethnoracial groups, there is no real community, just one invented to speak hegemonically for its members. There is no single, cohesive, shared set of values and beliefs, even if there is a socially and politically conservative discourse that wishes itself all-encompassing, and is given license by society's mainstream culture to dictate what it means to be "Italian American." Mayor Giuliani's attempt to organize tours of mob sites for tourists visiting New York powerfully illustrates the limits and double standards of conservative ethnic discourse. In that version of ethnicity, gangsters can find a niche, but neither radical activists and labor organizers, nor lesbian and gay writers and other public figures, nor people of mixed non-white parentage whose ethnic ancestry complicates the "purity" of Italian American purchase into whiteness.[15]

Even though the fates of Italian Americans became more in tune with the dominant social and political discourse since the

---

[14] This is what Abel Ferrara attempts in his films on gangters and hoods. However, without "footnotes," the greater public may read such films as acquiescence. Ferrara, for instance, establishes some clear distinctions about what he is trying to say and how it is perceived in an interview given to *Le Monde* (Blumenfeld, 1996). He states in particular that he refuses to use the term "Mafia," that it is a slur, "like [saying] nigger, chink, kike. I am insulted by the use of that term."

[15] Yet, a myriad of initiatives and individuals point to the unwillingness of outsiders within the "imagined community," to accept that status and just hand over to conservatives the cultural control of their representation. Among vast numbers of possible examples, we might consider the scholarship of historians like Gary Mormino, or anthropologist Micaela Di Leonardo, or literary critics Mary Jo Bona and Edvige Giunta. The cultural and political work of IAMUS, of the BASIL collective published in *Sinister Wisdom*, of the poetry anthologies of Mary Mazziotti Gillan. Among writers the work of Pietro di Donato, more recently, Dodici Azpadu, Rachel Guido de Vries, Paul Mariani, or Robert Viscusi. Among musicians, the work of composer John Corigliano, and in the realm of pop, Louis Prima's transcultural music, or the contemporary blue-collar lesbian singer Ani Di Franco. My ongoing preparation of a documentary on "Queer Italian America" and its relationship to working-class Italian American culture, presented at several CUNY campuses in 1995, was met with a preemptive strike at one to ban me from speaking: the words "queer" and "Italian American" together were too "offensive" to some.

1960s, they gradually but ungracefully slid into the mainstream at a very high price. The trade-off was to swallow their continued caricature as vulgar, violent and vicious, albeit fascinating, mobsters and low-lives, providing movie-going audiences with the voyeuristic pleasures of witnessing unbridled culturally permitted cruelty and rage. From being dealt terror on the street and on the job, Italians had become entrusted with dealing out terror, on the screen. This relentless stereotyping and appropriation by Anglo-dominated cinematic culture as icons of ethnic, class, and sexual desire and repulsion continues unabated. Further, through the violence attributed to them, Italian Americans have begun to function as the unwittingly annexed harbingers of a thinly veiled form of racial terror.[16] No other group of "white ethnics" has been subjected to such a sinister reputation, built so systematically, so *canonically* through popular culture, not even Jews or Poles, even as their economic fortunes were improving.[17] It is this system of representation, a stolen identity, that defines being Italian American in contemporary U.S. society, not the particulars of Italian American social life. It is not through food, nor hair color, nor alleged cultural behaviors, that Italian Americans occupy a special place in American culture, but through a type of split identity, and the abjectified image that sticks to their skin and is *authorized* in our culture. On the one hand, it still bespeaks inferior or picturesque ethnoracial traits, while on the other, Italian Americans occupy an increasingly affluent and powerful social and political position, which, nonetheless, remains powerless to undo that image. This means that in the realm of *representation* Italian Americans still inhabit the racial "middle ground," as an in-between culture that is racially, politically, and sexually explosive and inferior, translated on the screen through a consistent syntax of otherness. Neither fact nor fury, neither statistics nor discursive sophistication can seriously damage this well entrenched construction. Bombarded with

[16] The terror I speak of here is the one defined by bell hooks in her critique of white assumptions about culture: whites need, among other things, she says, to understand that they represent a form of racial terror for most black people (*Reel to Real*).

[17] This is certainly not to say that no whites have been caricatured equally, but not "white ethnics"; poor whites, associated with semi-rural cultures, have, on the other hand, been mercilessly ridiculed and lambasted. See Patricia Williams's perceptive and generous analysis of the "white trash" theme in American culture.

the constant reinvention of their own ethnicity, Italian Americans too often end up accepting the view that this really is their culture. The compensation is that they get to be white – more or less.

Stereotyping of Italian Americans in American film has been sufficiently commented on in general terms to not warrant further discussion here.[18] My intent is to focus on aspects of American film's discourse on race through the theme of Italian American identity. In this paradigm, Italian Americans on screen are not only racialized in predictable ways, but they actually become the vectors of the very dreaded subject of race, one at once avoided and central in American culture.[19] Through the screen representations of Italian Americans, some of society's most prevalent fears and agonistic performances about race can be enacted, in ways that no other ethnic group could elicit – and truly, literally, *make licit.* Through their construction as racial signifiers, Italian Americans become the means of authorizing public discourse about race, even in its most unsavory renditions, such as the repeated use of racial slurs (Bogle) or expressing openly discriminatory intent towards people of color. They are made to give voice to the racist pulsations of U.S. society,[20] in particular about black people and the fact of *Being Black* in our society. There is no end to the media-generated definition of what it means to be "Italian," what constitutes Italian American culture, which of its traits and manifestations are culturally writable and readable, and among these, the axiomatic racism of Italians ranks high.[21] A recent example among many: in writing on the film *Restaurant*, Joe Morgenstern, reviewer for the priceless *Wall Street Journal*, describes the hero, Chris Calloway, as the "rebellious son of a racist Italian father." The trouble here is that the hero is Irish and has no Italians in his ancestry mentioned anywhere in the

[18] See Golden (1980), Cortès, De Stefano, Woll (all 1987), Canadé Sautman (1994),Tomasulo (1996).

[19] In a much more eloquent manner, Winant thus describes this centrality of race: "The racial struggles at the heart of U.S. society, the racial *projects* whose clash and clangor leap off the pages of today's headlines as they have for centuries, have created the politics and culture of today" (87).

[20] A good example is provided by a mediocre farce, *Spike of Bensonhurst*, directed and partially written by Paul Morrissey, who must have thought his homophobic and racist (in all directions) portrayal of a young hood "straightening out" Red Hook funny and even transgressive.

[21] See Barolini's essay on her unsuccessful struggles with the *New York Times* to correct their article on absent Italian American writers, a view promoted by Gay Talese.

script. A second problem is that his rebellion consists merely in dating two black women, while eventually hurling the ultimate racist slur at a black youth, in anger – the film seriously tries to establish distinctions allowing for certain whites to use the term "jokingly" in certain contexts. Such journalistic drivel makes clear both the limits placed on Italian American interactions with race and on the acceptable level of racial integration for the white mainstream.

Yet, film functions as a multi-layered text, and as such, provides avenues for resistant or at least complicating readings, in which the connective tissue of hegemonic racial discourse begins to rend and tear. For example, the screen stereotyping of Italian Americans can produce its own fault lines through certain constructions of masculinity that are inseparable from ethnic invention.[22] These assert normative values through screen violence and ridicule, and by defining Italian American working-class life as crude and devoid of moral boundaries. At the same time, whether the screenplay writers will it that way or not, these particular views of masculinity often reveal themselves as fragile and on the verge of cracking. In her analysis of Black film and Blacks in film, cultural critic bell hooks underscored how much the function of women remains scopic rather than discursive (197-213). The negotiation of racial images and ideology in films about Italian Americans has, for a long time, reproduced that separation. For instance, in Abel Ferrara's *China Girl*, and in Robert de Niro's *Bronx Tale*, racial conflict is addressed through the attraction of a male (Italian) to a female of another group (Chinese, Black) attacked and excluded by the particular Italian community on-screen. This device appears to create critical distance from one's own community, but it is paired with an elision of Italian American women from this "new" imagined community. Within the specific discourse of masculinity inherent to ethnic representation, women are unproblematically constructed as mere commodities, apparently confirming an all-powerful male control of change, as if Italian women were inherently conservative and atavistic. In this system, while women

---

[22] See Uebels and McDowell for two fine critical discussions of the link between masculinity and race.

are passive accretions, albeit useful legitimizing forces in the racial order, they fade into oblivion once it is changed. The reverse scenario attempted by Spike Lee (*Jungle Fever*) still avoided difficult issues by erasing the possibility of love, except once again, between an Italian man and a Black woman. Thus, in much of the film production concerning Italian Americans, Italian women often become in their very bodies the objects of a negativizing, abjectifying gaze.[23] It is Spike Lee's unique contribution that, in *Summer of Sam*, he avoided that stereotypical set-up, and in fact, turned it around, as we shall see below.

A little-known satirical film made by Danny De Vito, *The Ratings Game* (1984), offers an almost revolutionary reading of the "middle ground" of race. The film depicts the role of Italian Americans in the film industry, with De Vito's character as an entrepreneur fed up with its ethnic segregation and Wasp-down control, who tries to sell some particularly outrageous screenplays to movie moguls. De Vito tackles Wasp control of television subject matter with a bitter sarcasm that is quite surprising. The scripts written by the trucking boss are his answer to the mogul's rejection who exclaims, without joking: "Jews, Italians, Spicks? We don't want that. Don't you have Nazis?" De Vito's screenplays are virulent and warped reversals of the usual stereotypes. Italians are supposed to be gangsters? In a road piece called "Nunzio's girls," the trucker-would-be-screenplay-writer creates a character of a pimp dressed in the kind of flashy clothing that was associated with procurers in the films of the 1970s. Italians are obsessed with affirming whiteness? His entrepreneur creates a cartoon called "The Gumbas," celebrating bookie lore, in which all the characters sing in Neapolitan dialect, have kinky hair, and are painted in very dark hues, just a few shades away from black, and are thus, literally "people of color." The Jewish-Italian connection is affirmed, in opposition to "*amazzacristo*" clichés with his marriage – fictional and actual – to a clever but homely Jewish girl. The sarcastic humor in this farce is so potentially disturbing, that it has been completely ignored by critics. De Vito's star role in a gangster film by Brian De

---

[23] See a more detailed analysis of this point in Canadé Sautman.

Palma (another race provocateur),[24] broached a few similar themes. In *Wise Guys*, an Italian gangster and his Jewish buddy, in the name of their personal and business alliance (to set up an Italian-Jewish deli) wreak havoc in a Newark-based mob. De Vito's unique contribution to the representation of Italian-ness, whiteness, and race is not acknowledged, possibly because not accompanied by hails of bullets, pools of blood, degraded women, and pretensions to making ethnic stereotyping into gut-wrenching "Southern Italian tragedy."

Not surprisingly, Black American cinema has grappled with these issues in most interesting ways. In particular, it has interrogated and destabilized Italian American identity as a conduit for whiteness, as incorporated in a "universal" transparent norm. Thus, the tight relationship between "Blackness" and "Italian-ness," as a shaky modality of "white," has been brought up almost allegorically by a small group of "Black" works of very uneven aesthetic and value. Paradigmatic may seem the appearance in Mario Van Pebbles' *New Jack City* (1991) of a scruffy street-wise Italian-American cop who expounds racist ideas but also identifies with a black crack addict ("I was Pooky," he says). It may be, more than a pat attempt at refocusing the racial lines of the film, a metaphor for the cinematic presence of Blacks and Italian Americans, marked, with both groups, by a focus on violence, sexual intemperance, and outlaw status. The stark similarities between Van Peebles' film and Abel Ferrara's *King of New York* are another piece in that puzzle. In an interview, in fact, Ferrara confirmed that race/ism is an important consideration in his films, for instance in *King of New York*, with his "multicultural" perception of the New York street, his acknowledgment of police violence and with the metaphoric use of the rap song at the end with the chorus "Am I Black enough?" (Smith).

Films made by Black directors, or for a Black audience, in which gangster themes and biases appear perpetuate familiar cliches. Yet, caricatures and slurs may then be imbedded in a dis-

---

[24] One of Brian de Palma's early films, *Hi, Mom!* (1970) is renowned for its outrageous treatment of racial relations, including a performance in "whiteface" by a black militant theater troupe. The film was co-written by De Palma and Charles Hirsch and starred Robert de Niro. Generally speaking, de Palma's work includes as many political films as the better-known horror and thriller movies (see White).

course that is oppositional because it is the harsh hegemony of whiteness that is being contested, and accessed through stock Italian American characters. Black film heroes confront militantly racist discourse about blackness by "writing back/Black," with derogatory representations of whites and whiteness. By leveling them in particular at racist Italian/Italian Americans, they may end up calling into question the integrity of whiteness itself. Such is the scene in *Coffy* alluded to at the beginning of this essay, or the confrontation of Shaft and the mobster in the village *caffè*, or Mookie telling Pino in *Do the Right Thing* that he secretly wants to be black, or a character in *Jungle Fever* being told that his Sicilian mother has African blood. In these scenes, black voices destabilize the hierarchical design of whiteness, show its fragility and flawed underpinnings. By challenging the white status of some of its members, questioning their supremacist claims, and reminding them of a painful history they would like to forget, they state that such ethnic Americans are actually "other than white" and thus darker than most. In this sense, these films do not merely deride Italian American pretenses at white supremacy; they also reappropriate them as tools to undermine the virulently oppressive structure of whiteness itself.

The commercial nature of films like *Coffy* or *Shaft* is misleading. As George Lipsitz points out in discussing genre, "Filmmakers from aggrieved racial communities": "…often [they] find it necessary to displace the conservative effects of previous representations, not just by adding on new racial characters or settings but by using race as a way of disrupting and restructuring genre conventions themselves" (210). *Coffy's* mediocre technical quality, and its screenplay loaded with laughable cliches of all types, carried off by a radiant Pam Grier, should not mask some of its incisive digs at the racial fabric of US society and its apparent contradictions. Coffy's adversaries are equally black and white, but while the former exploit or betray her, the latter assault her and the black community directly, both verbally and physically. In one scene between Coffy and the cruel gangster Vitroni, the play on race, sex, power, and subjugation is quite explicit, as Vitroni heaps racist abuse on her, and she follows her comment about his putative black ancestry with a "give me your precious white body" that is heavily sarcastic rather than playful. In fact, the entire scene is not about sex but race war.

Shaft came out in 1971 and was a considerable box office success. Directed by Gordon Parks, it has been traditionally labeled "blaxploitation,"[25] although its director, a noted photojournalist of Sub-Saharan descent, who worked as a photographer for *Life* from the 40s to the 60s, actually has a honorable record as a filmmaker.[26] *Shaft* pits the suave black private eye against the local hoods, and then an Italian mob that moves into New York to wrest business from black gangsters. It espouses seventies black nationalist rhetoric – through the members of the militant organization – but also shows Shaft's complicit relations with a few whites.[27] The choices as well as the inversion of the rapport are very interesting, especially for that period. Discounting the white woman fling – presented as obligé trophy – these associations are with the Italian American detective Vic, and the underground doctor Sam, apparently coded as Jewish. There is also the ethnically ambiguous character of the bantering gay bartender in the village – played by a Hispanic actor – treated with remarkable ease and lack of hostility. In all cases, against the traditional, stereotypical role of black people – including black men –[28] seeking to please whites, to serve them, and protect them when they are in trouble, all of these characters work for or around Shaft (Vic Androzzi is a sidekick who brings out Shaft's own clever investigative tactics). But direct comments on race take place in the interactions with the mob. In a brief but revealing scene, Shaft sits and orders an espresso in the Greenwich Village caffè Reggio, while waiting to meet a mobster. There is an intricate exchange between him and a red-haired waitress over lemon peel in the coffee – the little strip of lemon peel that is the

[25] For a current reevaluation of "Blaxploitation," see for instance the introduction to the blaxploitation.com site, and essays by Nicky Baxter and Jim Morton.

[26] His filmography includes: *The Learning Tree* (1969) about growing up Black in the early part of the century; it was selected in 1989 by the US library of Congress to be among the first 25 films to be preserved in the National Film Registry for all time. It was followed by *Shaft* in 1971, *Shaft's Big Score* in 1972, *Super Cops*, a comedy, in 1974, a film on the life of Leadbelly in 1976, and *Solomon Northrup's Odyssey* (also known as *Half Slave, Half Free*) in 1984, a highly praised film for TV that has been shown in public school classrooms to teach about slavery. He was also a composer for several of his films, an actor (voice role in a 1992 TV film on Lincoln), and wrote both the screenplay and the novel for *The Learning Tree*.

[27] On the original *Shaft*'s place in blaxploitation, see online essay by Colm.

[28] bell hooks, "Doing it for Daddy," (*Reel to Real*).

ethnic marker of a true Italian-style espresso. It seems that she does not take it seriously –she is probably Irish – and neglects to bring it to him, assuming, that he, a black man, would not want it. His reaction ("let it go") is correctly read by the waitress to imply that he does expect it after all, so she apologizes and brings it. This brief instant in the movie is actually rich with ethnic meaning, which in this scene and the following one, will center around food items. Shaft's treatment of the coffee garnish, and the waitress's hesitant, repeatedly corrected readings, reflect the possibility of his belonging, through food customs, to a group from which he is clearly excluded, or possibly, the fragile frontier that separates that group from him, regardless of its own claims. When the mobster arrives, well dressed and swarthy, he addresses Shaft "I am looking for the nigger [sic] Shaft." The hero responds by aptly turning the whiteness tables around, responding "you just found him [pause] Wop!" The pause unquestionably marks the purposeful "writing back" of the ethnic slur, the carefully poised arrow, as opposed to the "naturalized" response of the bone racist. Then Shaft takes the offensive, adding insult to injury by amiably proposing an espresso, and adding "maybe they'll put a little garlic in it, that would be nice...." The foray of ethnoracial insults continues with the mobster's reference to fried chicken. All in all, this spectacle of racist jokes could be merely intended to amuse a very low level of spectator. Yet, it may also force the limits of racial construction, deflate the expectation of supremacy enjoyed by one group, and confronts it to the vulnerable, endangered status it occupies in the social experience of another.

It is easy to bemoan anti-Italian stereotyping as the key to these scenes and not hear the ethnic "mixing-up" that takes place here. It would also be quite a contextual error. While *Shaft* and other films of the genre were clearly directed at black audiences, and reproduced more or less what was assumed they wanted to hear, it is of interest to know that their producers were often white. In *Coffy*'s case, the link is even clearer: not only *Coffy*, but the entire series of "blaxploitation" Pam Grier vehicles directed by Jack Hill,[29]

---

[29] Jack Hill is a former apprentice to Roger Corman who studied at UCLA with Coppola. His filmography includes "blaxploitation" classics *Foxy Brown* (1974) and *The Big Doll*

had as one of its producers an Italian filmographer, Salvatore Billitteri.[30]

III. *Spike Lee's* Summer of Sam*: Border Wars*

These racial border raids (Paulin) have been conducted with no
greater skill and persistence, however, than by Spike Lee, through
three movies that address relations between Italian Americans and
Blacks (*Do the Right Thing, Jungle Fever,* and *Summer of Sam.*) And
before anyone simply tosses Spike Lee in the cinematic refuse can
of Italian-haters, it is important to take a closer look at what he has
said himself on the subject, and on the place of Italian-ness in his
discourse on race. Indeed, in interviews, Lee has outlined his long-
standing interest in establishing a discourse of racial history in
which Blacks and Italians are brought together. He has visited Italy
a number of times, and has spoken of his interest in things Italian,
confiding his perplexity at the level of violence between Blacks and
Italian Americans, although they look so much alike... (Moneta
7).[31] If all this does not clear the stereotyping charge, one can simply answer that his script was co-written with two Italian American
writers – one of whom, Michael Imperioli, turned out later to be
one of the main actors in the *Sopranos* – and that should not make
the film any more stereotypical or objectionable than one written
exclusively by an Italian American, and focusing exclusively on
gangsters, such as *The Godfather* or *Goodfellas.* The harsh criticism
leveled at Spike Lee for his Italian-themed movies just might instead raise once more the tired question "Who speaks? Who has the
right to speak?"[32]

House [also known as *Women in Cages* or *Women's Penitentiary*] (1971). A brief assessment of
Hill's place in the genre is found in Lumholdt's online entry.

[30] Salvatore Billitteri began his career in Italy in the 1950s, working on Italian horror films
and peplums. In 1969 he produced *De Sade* (dir. Cy Enfield), was post-production
supervisor for *Boxcar Bertha* (1972; Scorsese) *Voodoo Girl/Sugar Hill* (1974; Paul Maslansky),
Rape Squad (1974), *Foxy Brown* (1974; dir. Jack Hill), *Wild Party* (1975), *Sheba, Baby*
(1975; William Girdler), *Cooley High* (1975; Michael Schultz), and producer of many films
based on H. G. Wells.

[31] "Cè un qualcosa tra italoamericani e neri che fa in modo che le cose finiscono sempre in
violenza. Questo è strano perché la Sicilia non è molto distante dall'Africa e molti italiani
hanno la pelle scura. Se chiudo gli occhi quando sono in Italia, mi sembra di star tra neri.
Ma forse è proprio per questo che esplode tutta questa violenza...."

[32] bell hooks has commented that the right of white male filmmakers to speak of all white or
people of color subjects is not questioned, but "however, when a black filmmaker, or for that

Further, one might remark that it becomes impossible to analyze the complex levels of discourse on race that some films provide if one stops short as soon as the look at ethnicity fails to promote the blandest version of "positive." Homi Bhabha's discussion of race and representation underlines the need to move away from the first level of seeking positive identifications and engage what the particular representation offers for reflection, the deeper levels that disturb and challenge (66-84).

At least in *Summer of Sam*,[33] everyone is not a gangster, even if there are some gangsters. *Summer of Sam*'s neighborhood boys are not very bright, to say the least, and that may be upsetting to some. But the girls in the hood are, in their own way, and in ways that deflect the standard diet of misused Italian American women, which may indeed be comforting to many of us, satiated with such pathetic images. The boys are a ludicrous bunch of rejects who apparently never work – contradicting Eddie Sabbatini's statement that everyone should work, for "only Niggers and Spicks [sic] do not work" – sell dope, shoot up, chase and beat up unwanted visitors to "their neighborhood." They range from a cringing junkie, to the useless enforcers, and the leader, low-level dope seller Joe T who keeps his friends suitably supplied and stoned out of their minds. They all report to Luigi, the local mob boss. Their political consciousness is limited to objecting to slurs to themselves, as when Ruby is delivered by a date who calls her a "dago wop skank, " or viciously beating up a drunk Irish kid who called them "Dagos."

These boys are oafish but dangerous. Their system for identifying suspects and going after them is idiotic, yet terrifying. The list of misfits tossed together – from Ritchie, because of his punk

---

matter any filmmaker of color, makes a work that focuses solely on subjects exclusively black, or white, they are asked by critics and their audiences to justify their choices and to assume political accountability for the quality of their representations" (69).

[33] Spike Lee's *Summer of Sam* has been both attacked and praised by reviewers, with objections raised in particular to the stereotyping of Italian Americans. See for instance *Time Magazine* July 5, 1999, 154.1, Richard Corliss, "Bronx Bull," who asserts that he is "dead serious in his ethnic stereotyping," and shares responsibility for this "ethnic defamation" with actor and playwright Victor Colicchio and Michael Imperioli. *The Nation* (Stuart Klawan, "Spike's Season") July 2, 1999 gave it a completely positive assessment. About equal time for both viewpoints can be accessed through the internet database us.imdb.com. keyword, *Summer of Sam*.

hairdo and increasingly disturbing homosexuality, to the priest because of his reputed mishandling of boys, to the long-haired cab driver because he is a Vietnam vet, and to Reggie Jackson because of the 44 on his shirt and he is black – outline the contour of an ideology of exclusion. The realization that a "*mulignan*" could be Son of Sam after all, since he is "invisible" and no one thought of that before, is given as proof of likely guilt. And this is profound in spite of itself. Invisibility is the trademark of the killer, the protective stance sought by his would-be victims, and the status of people of color in this all-white enclave. These invisibilities are allegorical of the hoodlums' own invisibility, the transparency of their wretched, wasted lives – rendered in the middle of the movie by a haunting and lyrical montage that interrupts its affirmed narrative style – and the normalizing position they assume for themselves, although, clearly, society views them as quaint ethnics (as evidenced by Vinnie and Dionna being picked as party-goers outside of Club 51).

The women have no time for all this nonsense. They are either working long hours, alone like Gloria, or with a parent like Dionna, or struggling to get a job, like Ruby. And discrimination works at all sorts of levels: labeled "not a nice girl," Ruby finds herself the object of general disregard. Harassment and demeaning treatment are Ruby's daily diet, including from her half-brother. Disrespected, she fights back: when the guys make fun of her and tell her that she "knows how to suck," she shoots back: "I learned from your mother, dick." Gloria also responds in kind: when Vinnie breaks down and starts to scream at her although she is his employer at the hair salon – in his eyes just a woman to lay – she tries to regain control to the end of the argument; and failing that, she still has the last words (" fuck *me* Vinnie? I'm going to *fuck you!*" And she does). And in contrast to the abjectifying portrayal of so many Italian American women in film, Spike Lee directed his actresses to express glowing beauty on the screen; neither overweight nor dowdy, Dionna (Mira Sorvino) and Gloria (Bebe Neuwirth) have lithe bodies and wear outrageously sexy clothing. Ruby (Jennifer Esposito) exudes a fuller, complex sensuality as she gradually modifies her look in stages, from naïve neighborhood cheap girl, to do-good seducer, to a fierce-sounding punk rocker who sings Son of Sam's words, a powerful metaphor of her own disempowerment and new self.

The representation of Italian Americans in this film remains ambiguous but self-reflective. The filmmaker mirrors his own representational system in allusions, hard to miss, to a strong subtext of Italian American presence in iconic American films. This is a kind of back-handed homage to Italian American screen presence through the cinematographic intertext, such as *Saturday Night Fever* and the *Godfather*. *Saturday Night Fever*, an important film about working-class Italian Americans,[34] is referenced at the beginning of the movie in the dance scene between Vinnie and Dionna, and in the farcical scene between Vinnie and Dionna's cousin when he jumps out of the car with his pants around his ankles and his behind showing. The *Godfather* remains also in the background, with the highly satirical scene of Don Luigi and his henchmen at Dionna's father's restaurant being visited by the cops. Familiar cliches are given a light twist that deflates their pretensions: "your father is a great man," Luigi says to Dionna as she delivers the veal. Luigi speaks literally like a godfather, when he reproaches the young cop from the neighborhood, whom he "treated [you] like a son" for not asking for his blessing when he became a cop. He then whispers to him in dialect, concluding: "non preocupate, ci penso io, figleddu."

The actual Son of Sam killed a number of people, mostly women, but, by no means were they all Italian American or killed in one single neighborhood. Spike Lee's choice of making those murdered mostly Italian American and setting the reactions to the murders in an insular Italian American neighborhood of the Bronx, can be seen as brilliant. It allows him to explore the way race, ethnic identity, and fear play out in a contained setting that is being threatened by undisclosed outside forces. And there is another reason why this choice of the neighborhood seems terribly significant. The killer was a young man by the name of David Berkowitz, whose jet black hair, soft face, and sweet smile made him look like "a nice Jewish kid from the Bronx." But Berkowitz was an adopted

---

[34] See Peter Gard Steven's thesis.

child, and his real name was Italian, Richard Falco (Abrahamsen 12-17).

Being outside one's community rather than included, or seeking to go out of it and come back, but being rejected, or leaving it of one's own will, belonging nowhere, are all overarching themes of this film. They are drawn in a parallel with the comment by the black woman community organizer speaking on the "darker perspective." The mainstream media has to go outside, to the margin, the "black neighborhood" where Son of Sam would be "taken care of" to get that perspective; and it sends a black reporter (Spike Lee) who is treated like an outsider himself in that community. The woman organizer implied that the request from the journalist is silly, then says "I thank God (three times) it is a *white* man who kills all of these *white* people, because if it were a *Black* man killing all these white people, there would be the biggest race riot ever in the city of New York." But the small Bronx community kills itself, with dope, economic stagnation, hate, while it acts out its fears of outsiders. Ritchie's status is chosen as an act of rebellion, but it is ambiguous, because he still wants to fit back in, live in the neighborhood, in his mother's house, and go to the punk clubs. Ritchie is in effect the individual struggling against the community invention of identity; the irony is that his rebellion is superficial, but that he is nearly killed over it, that his difference stands out disproportionately for all sorts of other differences.

Race is a fore-grounding element, swathed in visibility/invisibility. Specifically, Spike Lee resorts to devices such as having the "young girls with dark hair," as one of the father's puts it, stalked by the killer, suddenly rush to have it dyed blonde. This enables the inscription of resistant voices around hair and masquerade, as is the case of Dionna, who refuses the change and only wears a wig to please her father, referring to it disparagingly as "the Barbie doll thing." Later, Gloria, the hair salon owner with an independent mind about everything, also insists on keeping her long dark hair intact. Ruby does go for blonde, but she also changes to a punk rock identity, foregoing the narrowly defined script originally written for her in her immediate social environment. Never has the old cliché "blondes have more fun" been underlined with more sarcastic glee, touching upon a raw nerve in the cultural experience of many Italian American women who have for generations straightened, blown out, and dyed their hair in efforts, conscious or not, to look "less ethnic."

One of the director's most amazing talents is his gift for using actors, even sometimes against his own inclinations.[35] The choice of mild-mannered, wise-man Ben Gazzara to play the local don gives richly complex inflections to the mob figure. But most outstanding is his use of John Leguizamo, a great actor and solo performer of Colombian descent. The actor's performance of Vinnie is remarkable in every detail, but at least as important is his jarring casting as an Italian American: there is no way that Vinnie can truly be a "white Italian" with Leguizamo's look, and the actor's presence on the screen is a constant reminder of Lee's unequivocal position about the dubious whiteness of Italians, their unclaimed "darker perspective," and their problematic inscription in the ideology of whiteness. As in *Jungle Fever,* with the character of the neighborhood racist who is incensed by his Sicilian origins being chalked up to black (and looks racially mixed), this is a strong statement on the director's part.

Spike Lee's merciless look at gender and at the construction of masculinity is another agent of ethnic destabilization that works oddly, given the theme of male sexual profligacy, to the women's advantage. This is achieved through a skillful counterpoint of the film's flagrant, flamboyant sexuality of many types, and the careful undermining of the claims to normative manhood made by most of the male characters, but especially that of Vinnie. This incurable Bronx playboy says that he cannot be a whore unlike women, simply, as a self-evident truth, "because I am a man," and he *believes* in marriage. But he is a hairdresser, an ambiguous profession, who gets his ass pinched by women customers; he is constantly in a state of panic about Son of Sam; he loses out – discursively and logistically – in his argument with Dionna, as even the car is hers and he can't order her out of it; he completely falls apart; and, ultimately,

---

[35] See discussion in bell hooks on his conflicts with Annabella Sciorra. Perhaps Lee is sexist; but the actress *did* prevail and play the character as she wished after all ("Critical Contestations," 185-86). In the same volume by bell hooks, another essay praises Spike Lee for delivering an unconventional feminist-inflected film text with *Girl 6* ("Good Girls Look the Other Way").

he betrays his best friend in the most ignominious manner. In the end, the kiss and praise, "That's my man" from a blonde matronly woman to Luigi during the street feast he organized to control the neighborhood – the idea would be brilliant if the threat were real and it did not have such blatant racist content – takes on bitter historical irony. In this self-protecting neighborhood, only the mobster with men who obey his orders can really "be a man." The others are underlings, losers, and fools who eventually run from the other "man" in the story, Ritchie's stepfather, a bookie and gambler who threatens to shoot his aggressors. This economy of masculinities speaks volumes to the particular history of Italian American communities.[36]

Homosexuality is the second front in this major onslaught on conventional views of masculinity that are usually interwoven with hierarchical, supremacist views of ethnoracial identity. Among the boys at the waterfront, Bobbie Del Fiore is a queen par excellence. He can joke around with them as the "44 caliber queer," and although he may get slightly roughed up if he strays over the line, he is defended by his group. When he is really beaten up by another group of young males, "his" boys come to the rescue and fiercely trash the offenders. As Ritchie is becoming gradually more suspect, Bobbie sides with the boys in the hood against the outcast whose ambiguous homosexuality – he fights and conceals it, with the disclaimer: "so you think I'm a fucking homo?" – is considered much more unacceptable than Bobby's public one. His clothes and hair, which do not fit the neighborhood ethos, and his insertion in a shady sexual underworld, acting in porn flicks and performing male dancing, are more dangerous than Bobby's behavior; and the latter's blowing the whistle on him – an accusation by a bona fide homosexual – clinches his fate.

Sex and race mix in an explosive scene when Dionna and Vinnie settle accounts after the orgy at Plato's Retreat. He blames her for having experienced pleasure, at least partially, with women, calling her "you stupid lesbian fucking whore," provoked most

---

[36] See Abel Ferrara's comment, in lieu of the volumes of social history one could adduce, that his father and family were hoods "and so what?", and that his father did these things for a while, then stopped, "and all his friends did the same thing, we were Italians, we lived in the Bronx, what else could we do?" (Blumenfeld).

likely by his realization that his very normative and patriarchal sex with her is a total failure. Dionna loses her usual meek little girl voice and retorts: "You are a faggot fucking hairdresser,... a linguini dick motherfucker." She then threatens – they are lost in the middle of nowhere – to offer herself to the first black man who passes by ("Do you want to watch while I have a big black dick up my ass?"). The threat, confronting Vinnie with the likelihood of his passivity as a reflection of his failure with her, fits with the exchange of mutual accusations of homosexuality (dyke, slut/fucking faggot, pansy, hairdresser). Dionna's repeated threat to await the arrival of "a soul brother" and the promise of "... a big black dick" constitute her supreme insult to a devirilized Vinnie, taunted through the racial stereotype of the exacerbated virility of black men and the availability of out of control white women (she shouts "free pussy here!").

Race remains the main cipher of the entire movie. But what is remarkable is the way it interweaves Black-ness and Italian-ness. Reggie Jackson appears midstream and then remains a leitmotiv, the visible reminder of the gradual implosion of white supremacist myths about Blacks. The last moment of the film, before Breslin gives his New York yarn, is of Reggie Jackson winning the game against the Dodgers and waving to the crowd. Another important figure is Luigi, the gangster, a twist on traditional film portrayals. Approached by the cops for help, Luigi responds with bitter sarcasm: "Last night in Harlem your people and the colored, how many of each other did you kill, 8, or 20? And how many Saturday night? Why don't you ask me who killed them? Not enough press in it, not enough coverage?" This is one of the two most politically charged statements on race and violence in the entire film, and it is Luigi who makes them. Subtly, Spike Lee shows how such inklings of understanding can turn into their opposite. We move on to the power outage, then the riot. This is a crucial scene visually. Indeed, the riot (an actual event), with its famous "it feels like Christmas in July" quote, with Blacks and Puerto Ricans rebelling by looting in a festive atmosphere, contrasts with the orderly, fascistic organizing of the white ethnic neighborhood, enforced by the baseball bat. Then, Luigi and his men change their outlook: the rebellion of black and brown people scares them, the language becomes supremacist, his guys talk about "the nigger and spicks [sic]... who give the cops a handful." They actually repeat the slurs like a chant, concluding that they need to protect the neighborhood against non-white intruders at least as much as against the Son of Sam. The neighborhood is closed off by his orders, resulting in vigilante actions, as their search for Son of Sam and assaults on people who are "other" easily merge: a driver who got lost is taken out of his car and beaten up simply for speaking Spanish and being unknown.

Stuart Hall has proposed to read ethnicity to create a "new ethnicity," separated from "the traditional moorings of nationalism, racism, colonialism, and the state." As a referent for "acknowledging 'the place of history, language, and culture in the construction of subjectivity and identity" (Giroux 1997, 311) he provides a "theoretical language for racializing whiteness without essentializing it."[37] The otherness of "white" Italians in film provides, in spite of itself, such a de-essentializing. While the cultural marginalization of Italians is adduced and exploited by run-of-the-mill commercial filmmaking, many Italian American filmmakers (Scorsese, Ferrara) have tried to reinvent these stereotypes, sometimes successfully, sometimes not, but with the avowed project of recreating the Italian American world of their childhood, viewed through contemporary lenses, and affirming difference from the Anglo-white mainstream. Black-audience films scraped at the well-polished surface of whiteness and gloated over its cracks. And in Spike Lee's films, the completely problematic historical claims to whiteness status by blue-collar Italian American communities is deftly modulated across the screen. As in most deconstructive tasks, we find that such readings can, in effect, produce resistant discourses on race. Spike Lee in particular offered a shimmering palimpsest – aesthetically reproduced in the films' very particular cinematography – which eloquently showed the chaos, fear, and implosion of belief through the heavy coats of cliches, stereotypes, stock scenes, and characters, reworking and dis-articulating both "whiteness" and Black-Italian inter-weavings.

[37] For Spike Lee's deessentializing texts, see Diana R. Paulin.

FILMOGRAPHY

A Bronx Tale. Dir. Robert de Niro. Screenplay by Robert de Niro and Chazz Palmintieri. HBO, 1993.

China Girl. Dir. Abel Ferrara. Screenplay by Nicholas St-John. Vestron, 1987.

Coffy. Dir. Jack Hill. Screenplay by and Produced by Samuel Z. Arkoff, Salvatore Billitteri, Robert Papazian. Orion, 1973.

Do the Right Thing. Dir. Spike Lee. Screenplay by Spike Lee. MCA, 1989.

The Godfather. I (1972). II (1974). III (1991). Dir. Francis Ford Coppola. Screenplay by Mario Puzo and Francis Ford Coppola. Paramount.

Jungle Fever. Dir. Spike Lee. Screenplay by Spike Lee. MCA/Universal, 1991.

King of New York. Dir. Abel Ferrara. Screenplay by Nicholas St-John. Avid, 1990.

The Mogul/The Ratings Game. Dir. Danny De Vito. Screenplay by Michael Barrie and Jim Mulholland. Showtime, 1984.

New Jack City. Dir. Mario Van Peebles. Screenplay by Thomas Lee Wright and Barry Michael Cooper. Warner, 1991.

Saturday Night Fever. Dir. John Badham. Screenplay by Norman Wexler, Story by Nick Cohn. Paramount, 1977.

Shaft. Dir. Gordon Parks. Screenplay by Ernest Tidyman and John D.F. Black. MGM/UA, 1971.

Spike of Bensonhurst. Dir. Paul Morrissey. Screenplay by Alan Bowne and Paul Morrissey. FilmDallas, 1988.

Summer of Sam. Dir. Spike Lee. Screenplay by Spike Lee with Victor Colicchio and Michael Imperoli. Touchstone, 1998.

Vendetta. Dir. Nicholas Meyer. Screenplay by Timothy Prager. Prod. Gary Lucchesi. HBO, 1999.

Wise Guys. Dir. Brian de Palma. Screenplay by George Gallo. MGM/UA, 1986.

WORKS CITED

Abrahamsen, David. *Confessions of Son of Sam*. New York: Columbia UP, 1985.

Barolini, Helen. "The Case of the Missing Italian American Writers." *Chiaroscuro: Essays of Identity*. Madison: U of Wisconsin P, 1999. 124-31.

Barrett, James, and David Roediger. "In-between Peoples: Race, Nationality and the New Immigrant Working Class," *Journal of American Ethnic History*, (Spring1997): 3-44.

Baxter, Nicky. "Sweet's Back Again." *Metro: Silicon Valley's Weekly Newspaper*, (Nov. 9-15, 1995): www.metroactive.com/papers/metro/11.09.95/blax-9545.html.

Bhabha, Homi K. "The Other Question: Stereotype, Discrimination and the Discourse of Colonialism." *The Location of Culture*. London and New York: Routledge, 1994. 66-84.

Blaxploitation.com. "Introduction." Blaxploitation.com/st-intro.html. 5 pp.

Blumenfeld, Samuel. "Abel Ferrara, réalisateur: 'les bandits du film ressemblent à mon père'" (Interview with Abel Ferrara). *Le Monde* (November 28, 1996): 28.

Bogle, Donald. *Blacks in American Film and Television: An Encyclopedia*. New York: Garland, 1988.

Canadé Sautman, Francesca. "Women of the Shadows: Italian American Women, Ethnicity and Racism in American Cinema." *Differentia* 6/7 (Spring/Autumn 1994): 219-46.

Capeci, Domenic J. *Race Relations in Wartime Detroit: The Sojourner Truth Housing Controversy of 1942*. Philadelphia: Temple UP, 1984.

Colm. "Blaxploitation". *Blackvoices*. blackvoices.com/feature/blk-history-98/blaxploitation/shaft.

Corliss, Richard. "Bronx Bull." *Time Magazine* 154.1 (July 5, 1999): 75.

Cortès, Carlos. "Italian-Americans in Film." *Melus*, 14.3-4 (Fall-Winter 1987): 107-26.

De Santis, John. *For the Color of His Skin: The Murder of Yusuf Hawkins and the Trial of Bensonhurst*. New York: Pharos Books, 1991.

De Stefano, George. "Italian-Americans: Family Lies." *Film Comment* 23 (August 1987): 22-24.

Di Leonardo, Micaela. *The Varieties of Ethnic Experience: Kinship, Class and Gender Among California Italian Americans*. Ithaca, N.Y.: Cornell UP, 1984.

Fischer, Michael. "Ethnicity and the Post-Modern Roots of Memory." *Writing Culture: The Poetics and Politics of Ethnography*. Ed. James Cliford and G. E. Marcus. Berkeley: U of California P, 1986. 194-233.

Gallo, Patrick. *Old Bread, New Wine: A Portrait of the Italian-Americans*. Chicago: Nelson-Hall, 1981.

Gardaphè, Fred. *Italian Signs, American Streets: The End of Italian American Representation*. Durham, NC: Duke UP, 1996.

Giroux, Henry. "White Noise: Toward a Pedagogy of Whiteness." Myrsiades and Myrsiades 42-76.

———. "Racial Politics and the Pedagogy of Whiteness." *Whiteness: A Critical Reader*. Ed. Mike Hill. New York: New York UP, 1997. 294-315.

Golden, Daniel Sembroff. "The Fate of La Famiglia: Italian Images in American Film." *The Kaleidoscopic Lens: How Hollywood Views Ethnic Groups.* Ed. Randall M. Miller. Englewood, N.J.: Jerome S. Ozer, 1980. 73-97.

hooks, bell. "Good Girls Look the Other Way." *Reel to Real: Race, Sex, and Class at the Movies.* New York: Routledge, 1996. 10-19.

_____. "Artistic Integrity: Race and Accountability." *Reel to Real.* 68-82.

_____. "Critical Contestations: A Conversation with AJ (Arthur Jaffa)." *Reel to Real.* 171-96.

_____. "The Oppositional Gaze: Black Female Spectators." *Reel to Real.* 197-213."

Jacobson, Matthew Frye. *Whiteness of A Different Color: European Immigrants and the Alchemy of Race.* Cambridge, Mass., London: Harvard UP, 1998.

LaGumina, Salvatore, ed. *Wop! A Documentary History of Anti-Italian Discrimination in the U.S.* San Francisco: Straight Arrow Books, 1973.

Lipsitz, George. "Genre Anxiety and Racial Representation in 1970s Cinema." *Refiguring American Film Genres.* Ed. Nick Browne. Berkeley, Los Angeles, London: U of California P, 1998. 208-32.

Lubiano, Wahneema, ed. *The House that Race Built.* New York: Vintage, 1998.

Lumholdt, Jan. "Jack Hill: Utskälld och kulturförklavnd regissör." *Magasin Defekt.* Defekt.com (SW).

Mangione, Jerre Gerlando and Ben Morreale. *La Storia: Five Centuries of the Italian American Experience.* New York: Harper Collins, 1992.

McDowell, Deborah E. "Pecs and Reps: Muscling in on Race and the Subject of Masculinities." Stecopoulos and Uebel 361-85.

McLaughlin, Virginia Ians. *Family and Community: Italian Immigrants in Buffalo, 1880-1930.* Ithaca, NY: Cornell UP, 1977.

Moneta, Fernanda. *Spike Lee.* Milano: Il Castoro, 1998.

Morgenstern, Joe. "Restaurant (Review)." *Wall Street Journal* (2-4-2000): W1.

Mormino, Gary and George E. Pozzetta. *The Immigrant World of Ybor City: Italians and their Latin Neighbors in Tampa, 1885-1985.* Urbana: U of Illinois P, 1987.

Morton, Jim. "Am I Black Enough for You?" *Popvoid.* Popvoid.com/pages/Blax/Blax1.html.

Myrsiades, Kostas and Linda Myrsiades, ed. *Race-ing Representation: Voice, History, and Sexuality.* Lanham, Md.: Rowman and Littlefield, 1998.

Orsi, Robert. "The Religious Boundaries of an In-between People: Street Feste and the Problem of the Dark-Skinned Other in Italian Harlem, 1920-1990." *American Quarterly* 44.3 (Sept. 1992): 313-47.

Paulin, Diana R. "De-essentializing Interracial Representations: Black and White Border-Crossings in Spike Lee's *Jungle Fever* and Octavia Butler's *Kindred.*" *Cultural Critique* 36 (Spring 1997): 165-93.

Roediger, David. *The Wages of Whiteness: Race and the Making of the American Working Class.* New York: Verso, 1991.

_____. *Towards the Abolition of Whiteness.* London: Verso, 1994. 181-98.

Rolle, Andrew. *The Italian Americans: Troubled Roots.* New York: Free Press, 1980.

Smith, Gavin. "Moon in the Gutter: Interview with Abel Ferrara." *Film Comment* 26 (July-Aug 1990): 40-46.

Sollors, Werner. *The Invention of Ethnicity.* New York: Oxford UP, 1989.

Starr, Dennis J. *The Italians of New Jersey.* Newark: New Jersey Historical Society, 1985.

Stecopoulos, Harry and Michael Uebel, ed. *Race and the Subject of Masculinities.* Durham and London: Duke UP, 1997.

Steven, Peter Gard. *Hollywood's Depiction of the Working Class from 1970 to 1981: A Marxist Analysis.* Thesis. Northwestern University, 1982.

Tamburri, Anthony Julian. "To Hyphenate or not to Hyphenate: The Italian/American Writer and *Italianità.*" *Italian Journal* 3.5 (1989): 37-42.

_____. "Black and White, *Scungilli* and *Cannoli*: Ethnicity and Sexuality in *Nunzio's Second Cousin.*" *Adjusting Sites: New Essays in Italian American Studies.* Ed. William Boelhower and Rocco Pallone. Stony Brook, NY: Forum Italicum, 1999. 183-99.

Tomasulo, Frank P. "Italian-Americans in the Hollywood Cinema: Filmmakers, Characters, Audiences." *VIA* 7.1 (1996): 65-72.

Uebel, Michael. "Men in Color: Introducing Race and the Subject of Masculinities." Stecopoulos and Uebel 1-16.

White, Armand. "Brian de Palma: Political Filmmaker." *Film Comment* (May-June 1991): 72-78.

Williams, Patricia. "The Ethnic Scarring of American Whiteness." Lubiano 253-63.

Willis, Sharon. "Tell the Right Story: Spike Lee and the Politics of Representation Style." *High Contrast: Race and Gender in Contemporary Hollywood Film.* Durham and London: Duke UP, 1997. 158-88.

Winant, Howard. "Racial Dualism at Century's End." Lubiano 87-115.

Woll, Allan C. *Ethnic and Racial Images in American Film and Television.* New York: Garland, 1987.

Yang, Suzanne. "A Question of Accent: Ethnicity and Transference," *The Psycho-analysis of Race*. Ed. Christopher Lane. New York: Columbia UP, 1998. 139-53.

THE ITALIAN MOTHER
THE WILD WOMAN WITHIN

Dawn Esposito
ST. JOHN'S UNIVERSITY

Images of Italian Americans in the cinema are initially not hard to catalogue. Godfathers and their faithful soldiers engaged in vendettas, and neighborhood studs out on a Saturday night enable the spectator to vicariously participate in a macho identity involving conquest and transgression. It would not be inappropriate for the woman spectator to wonder just where she fits in this patriarchal space. Helpful to her ruminations is a focus on the word patriarchal; it leads her to the realization that she's likely to be the wife and mother. But what does that mean? What are the parameters of her representation? Would she, should she want the experience even if it is only a vicarious one? Can she find an alternative space for herself? This article will address the representation of the mother, the point of entry into the space of femininity, the space offered to women spectators in the cinematic address. Each spectator must assess the desirability of this space for herself. This analysis seeks to make it critically visible so that her choice can be an informed one. It intends to reveal the parameters of ideology "a system of representations by which we imagine the world as it is" (Althusser 233).

A woman's inscription into patriarchy and her allegiance to what Teresa de Lauretis (1984) has named the "sex-gender system," relationships of power predicated on the oppression of women, requires the repression of mother-love. This is accomplished through socialization into the Symbolic, the domain of ideological representations, the domain of literary and cinematic texts. It is within the Symbolic that the "family romance," a term employed by Marianne Hirsh (1989) to describe "the story we tell ourselves about the social and psychological reality of the family in which we find ourselves" (9), gets enacted over and over again.

Hirsch's influential book, *The Mother Daughter Plot* (1989), concerns itself with the representation of the mother and the family romance in literary works of fiction by women writers within the realist, modernist and postmodernist genres. She notes that there is a "slow emergence of maternal speech from silence" (36), a movement from repression, maternal anger, and absence characteristic of realist fiction of the Victorian period, to a valuation of maternal presence that is nonetheless "always in danger of being replaced by paternal heritage" (117) in modernist fiction. The importance of paternal heritage is persistent until the feminist novels of the 1970s in which a return to the pre-Oedipal, preverbal moment of connection with the mother is explored and a "more or less successful displacement of fathers and other males from the feminist family romance" occurs (130). Hirsch constructs a continuum of maternal representation that can be used to analyze all forms of texts. Movie screenplays, sometimes original and sometimes adaptations of novels provide fertile ground for such a project.

Hirsch notes that maternal repression takes a number of maternal representational forms "from dead mothers ... trivialized comic mothers ... the malevolent yet inconsequential mother ... and ineffectual, silenced mothers" (44). That these forms help produce and maintain a patriarchal, male-centered consciousness in women spectators seems indisputable. They are forms that the spectator of films of Italian ethnicity knows all too well. From the dead mother depicted in *Fatso*, who continues to harm her son from her grave, to the shrill disembodied voice of the mother in *MAC*, to the silent Mrs. Vito Corleone in *The Godfather* who births murderous sons, the woman spectator is inculcated into a family romance that marginalizes the mother and positions the father and or his sons as central. These representational forms close off the possibility of resisting readings by the woman spectator who is predisposed to looking for the mother and through her, herself. As Hirsch notes, the mother surfaces as a potential object of identification in feminist works of fiction; can she be found in the mainstream cinema?

A sociologically informed answer to that question begins with the concept of ideology formulated by Althusser (1977). The cinema constitutes an ideological apparatus by definition committed to reproducing an image of the social world that serves the interest of the dominant power structure. It has a hegemonic function: to enlist the support of individuals who are not themselves supported by that system. In a patriarchy, this means enlisting women into the Freudian family romance interpolating or hailing them into the positions of wife and mother. The intended impact on consciousness is to normalize the woman into her own oppression critical to which is her acceptance of the supremacy of men. The movie *Moonstruck* (1987), directed by Norman Jewison with a screenplay by John Patrick Shanley, rich with details of *italianità* or things Italian, is an excellent example of the hegemonic family romance (Bona, 1999). The relationship between the mother and daughter, Loretta is loving but secondary. The narrative revolves around women's relationships to men.

Loretta Castorini is an old-worldly, dour looking woman of 37 who has "bad luck." Her first husband, whom she loved, was killed by a bus, a tragedy she blames on their having had a civil marriage ceremony at City Hall rather than "a wedding in a church with a big reception after." Her plans to change her luck embody the hegemonic script for women. At the movie's opening, she becomes engaged to Johnny Cammarere who is about to fly to Palermo to be at his dying mother's bedside. The first person Loretta shares her news with is her father Cosmo. He suggests that they wake her mother Rose to tell her. Rose asks Loretta if she loves Johnny; when she says no Rose replies "good because if you do they drive you crazy because they know they can." It is clear from the narrative that Rose deeply loves her husband but his fear-of-death life crisis has sent him out of her bed and to another woman's arms. She wants to spare her daughter the pain she now endures. Rose and Loretta share the desire to remain living in the same house together after the wedding. The tendency in modernist fiction by women, identified by Hirsch (67), of retaining maternal presence, centrality and thereby a connection to the past, is jeopardized by the father's dislike of Johnny. The spectator recognizes that this is an insertion of patriarchal authority.

Loretta, in preparation for the wedding is instructed by Johnny to find his brother Ronnie and settle the "bad blood" between them. Ronnie is an angry, irrational man who blames his brother for causing him to have "no life." Loretta, displaying the traits desirable in women in the patriarchal imagination, cooks him a rare steak "to feed his blood" and listens to his tale of woe. She calls him an animal, "a wolf who had to chew off his own hand" because he was engaged to the wrong woman. She, "the bride with no head," in no time at all is overcome by passionate desire for him. As he sweeps her up and carries her off to bed, the woman spectator hears Loretta say, "I was dead ... take your revenge out on me, leave nothing left for (Johnny)." The spectator watches true love unfold before her. Loretta is transformed. She consents to accompany Ronnie to the opera. Intended as a farewell gesture, it rather is a very hot date for which she sheds her dark, drab clothes and graying hair. Her body, having met its purpose in Ronnie has come alive.

One of the four encounters between mother and daughter included in the narrative takes place in a church. Loretta has confessed her "sin" with Ronnie; her mother that her husband is having an affair. Loretta leaves her mother in the church, uncomforted; the bond between them is clearly mediated by their relationship to men. When leaving the opera house, Loretta sees her father with his other woman. Noticing she's not with Johnny, he calls her a *puttana*, a whore; she wants to know what that makes him. They agree to not be certain that they were there at all; they both "don't know what they're seeing."

While the rest of her family is at the opera, Rose goes to dinner alone in a neighborhood restaurant. She invites a man who has just had a glass of wine thrown in his face by his much younger date to join her. She comments that he doesn't know himself. She lets him walk her home but tells him, "I can't invite you in because I'm married. I know who I am." The message is clear; she's someone's wife. It does not come as a surprise that she intends to reclaim her husband.

The culminating scene of the movie opens on the morning after the opera. Loretta and Ronnie, proudly wearing the "love-bites" on their necks that signify their connection wait at her family's breakfast table for Johnny, who has returned to tell Loretta that he can not marry her. Rose uses the opportunity to tell her husband that she wants him to stop seeing the other woman. He initially feigns resistance explaining that "a man understands one day that his life is built on nothing." His response challenges the significance of her presence in his life and that of the family's. She will not let it go unanswered. Rose's reply is simple, "your life is not built on nothing, ti amo, (I love you)." The line is said to Cosmo but the female spectator knows it is intended for her. The mother is delineating the daughter's part in the family romance. She is to love the man so that he can be. Loretta will restore Ronnie to life. The camera, in its closing shot lingers on the photo of an old, married, ancestral couple hanging on the wall. It signifies the continuum that moves through Rose and Cosmo to Loretta and Ronnie to the spectator trembling in the dark.

The hegemonic, ideological thrust of the cinema demonstrated in *Moonstruck* and countless other movies severely limits the potential for resisting spectatorship. Yet a few movies do get made that make resistance possible. *Angie* (1994) a film directed by Martha Coolidge with a screenplay by Todd Graff based on the novel *Angie, I Say* by Avra Wing, is one such movie.

The film's narrative revolves around a woman in her late twenties in the midst of questioning everything about her life. Angie is raised by her Italian father and Irish stepmother Kathy. Angie's birthmother, an "Italian from Texas" has been absent since Angie was seven. Angie thinks she simply ran away; twenty years later she still does not know why. Angie's only real memory of interaction with her mother is a poignant one. In the midst of being questioned by intrusive Aunts who want to know what three-year-old Angie is going to do with her life, her mother recognizes her confusion and fear. She sweeps Angie in her arms and utters the only words attributed to her in the narrative, "some stories don't fit inside a person's mouth; some stories just have to tell themselves." Angie cherishes a photo commemorating the moment. A short time after, her mother, "a free-spirit who danced in the snow until her lips were blue," disappears from her life; yet Angie is preoccupied with her. The narrative suggests two possible points of association for the spectator. It signifies maternal silence, absence, and possible death, attributes Hirsch relates to repression, while at the same time "including the maternal in a position of centrality through its "focus on her presence and absence" (109). The attention the latter gives to the mother offsets the threat of female dissolution posed by the Oedipus plot within which Angie is submerged. Having no relationship with her stepmother, Angie lives within a drama centered on men. Hirsh argues that "the plot of mother-daughter reunification," inscribed through Angie's secret desire, "offsets the threat of marriage and appropriation" (113). This point is initially sustained by the narrative, which lures the spectator into a misogynist web.

Angie, signifying some of the free-spiritedness attributed to her mother, thereby sustaining a point of connection, decides even though she is pregnant with his child, to separate from Vinnie her boyfriend of thirteen years. Striking out on her own, she soon takes up with a successful Irish attorney; it seems that she will constitute her life on her own terms. Her life with Noel is everything her life with Vinnie was not. Noel introduces her to culture and allows for Angie's independence. It is her attempt at constituting what Hirsch refers to as the modernist "female family romance." It centers on "the fantasy of the man-who-would-understand." This concept introduced by Adrienne Rich suggests a man who would combine maternal nurturance with paternal power. The man-who-would-understand often appears as a 'brother' figure "who's fraternal stance protects the heroine from becoming a mother and can thereby help her, in spite of the closure of marriage, to remain a subject, and can help her not to disappear from the plot as the object of her child's fantasy" (p.58). The narrative soon reveals that escaping motherhood is Angie's inclination.

Angie gives birth to a son missing a bone in his left forearm. Her guilt seems reflected in her son's refusal to nurse. She recognizes that "he don't want me," but she is projecting her desire on to him. Angie, preoccupied by Noel's absence since going into labor, goes to his apartment during the baby's christening party. Her father, as she's leaving, calls attention to the fact that she hasn't selected a name, further signifying her resistance to maternity. Noel tells her that he can't be a father to her child; he has his childless marriage to contend with. He is some other woman's man-who-would-understand; not Angie's who recognizes that she is now on her own. Later that evening, when she eventually responds to her son's cries, Angie finds her stepmother in the nursery with the baby at her breast and she runs away. The scene signifies the movement from the modernist female family romance to the feminist one with its focus on a pre-Oedipal reunion with the mother. Angie's clothes are invisible under her coat; her shoes are oversized rubber boots that do not properly cover her ankles. Her footprints make a mark in the falling snow. Unlike her mother, she's not dancing; she is most certainly running. She tells her friend "my mother ran; now I'm running too" before boarding a bus to Texas. The urgency of her escape back to the pre-Oedipal moment and from the Freudian family romance is palpable. But as the woman spectator cannot help but notice, the narrative is critical of her choice. It has no interest in offering a positive pre-Oedipal experience. Angie's son has persistently rejected her breast; yet he grasps that of her stepmother, signifying that she is his chosen one. Why? The answer requires an inquiry into the nature of the representation of women in general. The spectator is forced to confront the reason why Angie is not living up to the standards of femininity. Her rejection of marriage and motherhood does not stem from her choice but rather from her flaw. She is the daughter born of an Italian mother; her Italian nature is the problem. The spectator's hope of finding a way out of the hegemonic script is dashed. The narrative intends to purge Angie of her Italian nature so that she can legitimately be rendered within the hegemonic. The trip to find her mother takes a bitter turn.

When Angie arrives, she finds her Aunt who tells her "you don't want to know about your Momma. I promised your Daddy." The message that women collude with the Father against other women enacting his will is clearly signified. Angie's mother sits in a dimly lit room contained within the silence of her mental illness; yet Angie is told to "talk with her, she's your Momma." Angie is being confronted with her own nature; the biological connection between the two women is raised to highlight Angie's own position within the family drama. She is unable to take her place because she is unworthy of it. Her mother has passed on her damage. Angie lights a cigarette that her mother has been holding and shows her the picture she has of the two of them. Angie then turns to look at the photos that chronicle her life hanging on the wall. In that moment of turning away, her mother burns herself out of the picture. This visual annihilation is intended to set Angie free by rendering her motherless thereby purging her of her Italian nature. There will be no return to the pre-Oedipal with this mother. She understands what is needed in order for her daughter to be firmly interpolated into the Freudian drama. At this moment, the spectator's resisting reading is resurrected. She knows that self annihilation is the price exacted of her. It is knowledge that can guide her own path despite the fact that the narrative propels Angie forward in her own Oedipal drama. Angie now acknowledges that her belief that her mother had left for something better and that she could follow in her path was "so wrong." She returns to her baby critically ill in the hospital. Recognizing that she's "finally caught up in something bigger than (herself)," she sits vigil until her son awakens. The narrative, having retreated from the possibility of the feminist pre-Oedipal family romance, now also retreats from the modernist female family romance that holds out the possibility of the woman retaining subjectivity. The Oedipus story is one told from the child's point of view. The mother is always already objectified. Angie's embracing of her object status is complete when she whispers to her son "think of me as a human fridge."

The film returns again and again to its hegemonic function of inscripting women into patriarchal culture. The woman spectator's only source of resistance is to stay committed to what Mary Daly (1978) has called "the journey of radical being" which ends in "boundary living," the "discovery and creation of a world other than patriarchy" (1). The first step on the journey requires that the traveler "... see/hear/feel how we have (she has) been tricked by their (patriarchal) texts" (6). She must learn to recognize these texts for what they do to her, for how they define her and keep her contained. She must come to recognize that they are "male mazes," myths, practices, social arrangements that keep her in "a state of anesthesia" (316) assuring a disconnection from her "wild woman" self, the be-ing that precedes patriarchal enclosure.

The Freudian maze through which *Angie* wanders reduces women to objects that do for men what they can not do for themselves. The woman's function is to give her father a baby and then provide the nurture and support they both need. This recognition requires that she reverse-the-reversal Freud so elaborated constructed coming to understand that his theory reflects male desire projected on to the woman as if it was hers instinctually. The film's narrative helps her do this. But it is helpful to first remind the reader of Freud's position. In his 1932 lecture *Femininity* he argued, "the wish with which the girl turns to the father is no doubt originally the wish for the penis. The feminine situation is only established, however, if the wish for the penis is replaced by one for a baby." He then goes on to note his clinical observation that girls play with dolls which leads to his conclusion that it is "not until the emergence of the wish for a penis does the doll-baby become a baby from the girl's father and thereafter the aim of the most powerful feminine wish" (Young-Bruehl, 356).

The film's narrative reveals that Angie's father had begun his relationship with his second wife while he was still married. He tells his daughter that "that woman saved my life when I was married to your mother." The spectator can only surmise that her mental illness, entwined with her Italian nature, prevented her from fulfilling the domestic responsibilities of a wife and mother. The stepmother is never rendered outside them. Her father is angry that Angie has never come to embrace this woman. From his point of view, she is the woman her wild mother could never be. He wants her to understand that "some things just die" meaning mothering by Italian women. He wants her to recognize that they "have a life here" meaning that he has been able to assume a legitimate place in the patriarchal order because he has a functioning, appropriate wife. Angie, by accepting the Irish woman as her mother can join in their family. This containment provides legitimacy for women. Her father's attachment to the non-Italian woman has provided him with hegemonic legitimacy. He wants this for his daughter as well. The stepmother does have one flaw; she's remained childless since the death of her infant son born during her first marriage. When Angie becomes pregnant, it is she who lectures her on the "miracle" of motherhood. Her act of placing the child at her breast signifies that she is more suited for the role. Angie leaves because she knows this is true. The baby is being left within the safety of the nuclear family her mother was not capable of achieving. Angie's return to her is an act of purging and self-purification.

After Angie is set free, she returns to find her critically ill baby has been named Sean by her stepmother after the son she had lost. The stepmother is perceived by the hospital staff as his mother. Angie's father reaffirms this when he chastises her for putting his wife in the position of losing another child. It is at this moment that the vigilant spectator comes to fully see what the male maze obfuscates. The objectified bodies of Angie and her mother serve as conduits for procreation between her father and his wife. Angie's mother, through her self obliteration gives them her daughter and Angie now gives them their son. The narrative insists that Italian daughters distance themselves from Italian mothers, women who invokes what anthropologists Sharon Tiffany and Kathleen Adams (1985) have called the Romance of the Wild Woman, "a constellation of images, metaphors, and meanings about women and their sexuality set against the contrast between civilization and the primitive" (1).

The Romance of the Wild Woman, as an ideological construct, establishes a "virgin/Amazon continuum" (80) distinguishing the good from the bad woman, the one under patriarchal control and the one not yet conquered. It has particular resonance in relation to the cinematic representation of Italian women who tend to be rendered within the framework established by the nonwhite, primitive other. As I have previously argued, the representation of race in the American cinema can be traced back to the 1915 film *Birth of a Nation* (Esposito, 1996). The attributes of people of color are defined in negative opposition to those of whites. People of color are signified through their failure to achieve the standards of civilized men who can control their women. A comparison of *Birth of a Nation* and films depicting Italian ethnicity reveals that the representational attributes of Italian women closely resemble those generally attributed to women of color. Italian women are defined through their bodies and marked by uncontrolled emotional and violent impulses. This quality is repeated in literary narratives about the uncivilized native as this example from a short story by Beatrice Grimshaw makes clear.

> Sophia, sometimes looked almost as white as you or I. On this day she had drawn down the blind of sulks that is always at the command of the creature cursed with dark blood; ... resembling the pictures of the Papuan head-hunters on the wall ... she might have passed for a girl of Palermo.... Today she was in all essentials black. (Tiffany and Adams, 32).

To include the notion of woman-as-man-eater within the Romance of the Wild Woman is to signify the danger she poses and to stress the urgency of taming her. The source of her wildness, the "principles of fertility and procreation" associated with the paradigm of the Primal Mother with its emphasis on woman-as-mother, was contained by the development of patriarchal institutions which elevated the "higher concerns of male intellect and creativity. Men forged civilized society by conquering the matriarch" and reforging her in their image (Tiffany and Adams, 9).

The Victorian "cult of domesticity" is an ideological field of containment that underpins contemporary western discourse and gender representation. The true woman was defined as the wife and mother who exercised moral control over the behavior of others. Never far from her biological nature and thus always at risk of becoming victim to her "archaic body," the woman was expected to turn from her sexual desire as well. The "true Victorian woman (was) ... a nervous, hysterical and sexless entity who submitted to her conjugal duties only out of desire for maternity." If she failed to control her body she became the whore. As Tiffany and Adams emphasize, "women as mothers, virgins and whores are evocative images in Western thought" (14-15). The "cult of domesticity" modeled on the white, middle-class, Victorian wife and mother who had Freudian theory to guide her, became the model for all women. Characteristics associated with the Wild Woman defining her as "perverted, immoral, irrational, dark, savage" (32) were "images of foreign (nonwhite) people" (7). These are the very features that exclude the Wild Woman from achieving the status of true womanhood. The Wild Woman image is persistently relied on as the framing device for the representation of Italian American women in contemporary cinema as the above analysis of *Angie* and the following of *Household Saints*, (1993) directed by Nancy Savoca, with a screenplay by Savoca and Richard Guay based on the novel by Francine Prose demonstrate.

Tiffany and Adams argue that "all women are wild but some are wilder than others. According to the Romance men have tamed some but not others" (23). *Household Saints* demonstrates strategies of containment and resistance, while at the same time delineating what is at stake for the woman who comes under male control. The movie revolves around the plot of a nuclear family that gets formed due to a pinochle game played one hot summer's night. Joseph

Santangelo wins his wife Catherine Falconetti. She is the bet her father offers in exchange for a bath of cold air from the freezer of his meat shop. Without any awareness, she is involved in what anthropologist Levi-Strauss (1969) through his study of primitive people has identified as the circulation of women between men in which women are reduced to commodities or objects who do not speak for themselves. The narrative may propel Catherine into her husband's bed but it is her positioning between her mother-in-law, Carmela and daughter that is most interesting. Carmela Santangelo is the quintessential Wild Woman; her black clothes and exceedingly slow hand gestures signify that she is from another land. Her spirituality, defined through its reliance on old wives tales, superstition, and the miraculous intervention of the Catholic saints, marks her. Catherine signifies different manifestations associated with the Wild Woman. "A victim of her biological destiny, the Wild Woman does not act, produce, or perform; she merely *is* - passive and unaware" (Tiffany and Adams, 19). Together, the two women reflect the duality of female nature: "spirituality and the womb" (Tiffany and Adams, 15). The connection between them is rendered quite early in the narrative. Catherine is shown lying on her bed when her father tells her that she must cook dinner the next night for the Santangelos. Her lack of attentiveness in the kitchen, a signification of her passive nature results in a dinner that sets off her future mother-in-law's worst fears about omens and bad luck. "Raw meat, dirty escarole, hair in tomatoes are bad omens." Marry that girl, she tells her son, and "the rest of your life will taste like that meal."

The rendering of Catherine on her wedding night, apparently shy but immediately fulfilled by sex, signifies her as a Wild Woman easily containable. She is the Wild Woman with "anabolic nature," passive, stored up energy necessary for reproductive functions that waits for its "katabolic", active male counterpart (Tiffany and Adams, 14). She'll present no problem to her husband since her nature suits her for her location in the cult of domesticity; the roles of wife and mother are fulfillment of this biological nature. Her mother-in-law's view of her as a uterus reveals that which the ideology obfuscates. Control of women's bodies through the ideology of romantic love and domestic bliss is what is at stake. Carmela's certainty that Catherine is going to give birth to a chicken is explained through the narrative by the old woman's superstitions. Catherine watched a turkey's neck cut open exposing her to "nothing but blood and dead meat," and by her ability to converse with her dead husband who told her "you're (Catherine) gonna give birth to a chicken." Catherine in her terror submits to the old woman's ways. Together they invoke the intervention of "Santa Anna, the mother of the Blessed Mother" asking her to "not let me give birth to a chicken." Their prayers fall on deaf ears. Catherine's dead baby has chicken wings. The old woman burns the religious image over the kitchen stove in response. It is her symbolic ending; the vigilant woman spectator is not surprised that she dies soon after.

Carmela, despite her years of cooking and cleaning, is the Wild Woman uncontained by the man-made cult of domesticity. Her death at the stove does not change this deeper awareness. The spectator remembers the tone of her voice standing over the counter making the sausage. The deep intonation of a mother tongue recalls more primitive rituals. It is the impending destruction of her wildness that is being signified by the stillbirth. The Freudian family romance has taken a hold that she can no longer resist. Catherine's turning away from this wildness within herself is the final affront. She has been lost to the patriarchy. The old woman's time is over. She dies the morning Catherine, awakened from her depression, conceives a child. The fact that these events occur on Easter Sunday is significant. The narrative of resurrection pertains to the Wild Woman. Shortly after Carmela's death, Catherine is depicted making the sausage but her incantation implies the voice of the other woman. Carmela's return in the guise of her granddaughter Teresa provides the occasion for the narrative to reveal another strategy of containment as well as an insight into resistance for the spectator who wants to retain her own wildness.

The old woman's death paves the way for Catherine's full inscription into domesticity. She embraces the part of modern wife and domestic homemaker. She gets a new haircut and clothes, packs away Carmela's black outfits and religious icons, paints the apartment in decorator colors and delivers her baby in the hospital. It's not long before Teresa brings her grandmother's presence back into the family space. She hangs the icons back on the walls and wears dark, Catholic school uniforms. The uniforms clue the spectator into what the grandmother's spirit is up against, patriarchal religion, man's image of himself raised up to the heavens that eliminates the woman as fertile mother and condemns her to the perpetual state of virgin bride. As Mary Daly has indicated, "... the Christian trinity legitimates male mating. This trio might be named "The Legitimates," united with their offspring (Incarnation), Christ, and with his corporation, The Mystical Body of Christ, attempt to incorporate the world. Christian myth, like refined sugar, has been "purified" of the cruder elements that were present before its processing" (74). Teresa dedicates her life to God following the path of the Little Flower, a saint quite committed to the labors of domesticity. She devotes herself to the "monotony of daily toil and chores, all the things that go unnoticed and unappreciated." She asks for nothing but love and the opportunity to be the bride of Christ in return.

Her father's refusal to let her join the Carmelites is the catalyst that sets Teresa on the path into sainthood. Her devotion leads her to her boyfriend's ironing board where Jesus comes to keep her company. He thanks her for "grooming one of his lambs." She's placed in a convent rest home and dreams of playing pinochle with God the Father, Jesus and the Little Flower. She dies the night after telling this dream. The garden flowers, dead weeds the day before, are in full bloom the day of her death. Her father is overwhelmed by the smell of roses emanating from her body, signs of a saint's death. The stigmata on her left hand is further evidence. Neighborhood people place requests for interventions in her coffin; they swear that she delivered results. Only her mother and the woman spectator know better.

Teresa went crazy. She had a psychotic break falling victim to what Freud would call moral masochism. "Moral masochists take their pleasure in being tormented by ideas ... God punishes moral masochists, and the humiliation they feel can come to substitute in their lives for sexual activity (as often happens, for example, with religious cult members)" (Young-Bruehl 32). Teresa fell victim to the planned destruction of the Wild Woman within her. She succumbed to what Mary Daly has called the "myths of (patriarchal) Processions ... a symbol system (in which) there is a circular pattern/model for muted existence: separation from and return to the same immutable source ... a reconciliation with the father" (36). The Processions of Freudian theory and the family romance, the cult of domesticity, hegemonic femininity and the Romance of the Wild Woman have directed women from our source and strength, the wildness within. The Procession of cinematic representation demands that the Italian woman be relegated to the location of the primitive other where she can await colonization of her mind, her body and her strength. But as Mary Daly reminds us we can resist. "Within a culture possessed by the myth of feminine evil, the naming, describing, and theorizing about good and evil has constituted a maze/haze of deception. The journey of women becoming is breaking through this maze" (2). Resisting the hail of the cinema is the beginning of recovery.

REFERENCES

Althusser, Louis. *For Marx*. Trans. Ben Brewster. London: New Left, 1977.

Bona, Mary Jo, *Claiming a Tradition: Italian American Women Writers*. Carbondale and Edwardsville: Southern Illinois U P, 1999.

Daly, Mary. *Gyn/Ecology: The Metaethics of Radical Feminism*. Boston: Beacon Press, 1978.

de Lauretis, Teresa. *Alice Doesn't:: Feminism, Semiotics, Cinema*. Bloomington: Indiana U P, 1987.

Esposito, Dawn. "Looking at Myself But Seeing the Other." *Italian American Review* 5 (1) Spring 1996. 126-35.

Grimshaw, Beatrice. *Eyes in the Corner and Other Stories*. London: Hurst and Blackett, 1927.

Hirsch, Marianne. *The Mother/Daughter Plot: Narrative, Psychoanalysis, Feminism* Bloomington and Indianapolis: Indiana U P, 1989.

Levi-Strauss, Claude. *The Elementary Structures of Kinship*. Trans. James Harle Bell, John Richard Von Strumer, and Rodney Needham. Boston: Beacon Press, 1969.

Rich, Adrienne. *On Lies, Secrets and Silence: Selected Prose, 1966-1978*. New York: Norton, 1979.

Tiffany, Sharon W. and Kathleen J. Adams. *The Wild Woman: An Inquiry into the Anthropology of an Idea*. Rochester,Vermont: Schenkman, 1985.

Young-Bruehl, Elisabeth, ed. *Freud on Women: A Reader.* New York and London: Norton, 1990.

FILMS CITED

Title	Year Released	Director
Angie	1994	Martha Coolidge
Birth of a Nation	1915	D. W. Griffith
Fatso	1988	Anne Bancroft
The Godfather I, II, III	1972, 74, 90	Francis F. Coppola
Household Saints	1993	Nancy Savoca
MAC	1992	John Turturro
Moonstruck	1987	Norman Jewison

A CLASS ACT
UNDERSTANDING THE ITALIAN/AMERICAN GANGSTER

Fred L. Gardaphè
STATE UNIVERSITY OF NEW YORK, STONY BROOK

> "If we want to go on believing in categories like so-
> cial class, then we are going to have to dig for them
> in the insubstantial bottomless realm of cultural
> and collective fantasy."
>
> Fredric Jameson
> "Reification and Utopia in Mass Culture"

> "Italian gangsters,
> all my life Italian gangsters;
> you too, Leonardo, and Galileo,
> and you too Pop."
>
> Felix Stefanile
> "A Review of the Film 'Godfather VII'"

Since the gangster's earliest appearance in American cinema, there has been regular association between the gangster figure and the Italian/American male. In Felix Stefanile's poem, the gangsters created by Hollywood eventually come to represent all Italian and Italian/American men past, present, and future. Perhaps no cinematic figure has had such a profound effect on the development of an ethnic stereotype than the American gangster. While formal protest of the image of Italians as gangsters goes back to Fiorello La Guardia's letter written to protest the very first gangster film, *Little Caesar* in which the New York City mayor writes: "Mr. Hays would not dare to produce such a picture with a Jew as that character – he would lose his job if he did" (Munby 105), there was little organized outcry by Italian/American organizations concerning portrayals of Italians in the media prior to the appearance of Mario Puzo's novel and then the Coppola film. Since then, for more than one-half a century, a great deal of energy and money has been expended by local and national Italian/American organizations in an effort to fight the seemingly incessant portrayal of Italian Americans as gangsters. And while a few victories can be counted, such as getting a Capone museum in Chicago to shut down and a restaurant chain to change its advertising pitches, the image of the Italian as gangster is as strong as ever in American culture. The gangster, especially the Italian one, has captured an important place in society by its proven ability to separate people from their money. Be it the latest film, a best-seller book, style of music, the promise of being near to, associated with, or watching a gangster in action continues to attract spenders big and small.

The frustration of Italian Americans surfaces in such publications as *Finalmente! The Truth About Organized Crime*, by Richard A. Capozzola. A retired New York State educator and administrator, who also served as police commissioner for Westchester County of New York from 1974-1978, Capozzola argues that the defamation and denigration of Italian Americans through the news media and Hollywood should be "equated to ethnic genocide." He finds the origins of the mafia mania in the Kefauver Senate Crime Committee hearings of 1950-1951. Based on the information provided by John Scarne, "the world's foremost authority on gambling," and author of *The Mafia Conspiracy*, Capozzola proposes that the mafia is a government fabrication designed to keep authorities' eyes on Italians, all the while overlooking the real sources of crime in America. Capozzola's point is that anti-Italian sentiment born out of the mafia myth, has kept the best of Italian/American culture out of sight and the worst of it in everyone's face.

His self-illustrated history covers a twenty year period and stops at the murder of Joseph Colombo, but not short of suggesting that the shooting of Colombo was orchestrated by a government agency interested in eliminating the Italian-American Civil Rights League. Capozzola's evidence comes from his own feelings and from a conversation Scarne had with gangster Frank Costello who said "no mob guy did the job." Capozzola wants us all to see what he calls the real Italian Americans, and to understand that the gangsters on the screen have been used to keep Italians down.

As outrageous as he might seem, Capozzolla does have a point. From its first appearance in the film, *Little Caesar*, the gangster has been associated with Italian culture. A study conducted by William Dal Cerro noted that there were one hundred "mob movies" made prior to the appearance of Coppola's *The Godfather*, and more than 300 made afterwards. While other American ethnic groups, such as the Jewish-, Irish-, African-, and Asian-Americans have been cast as gangsters, most often the immediate association with Italian Americans and the so-called mythic antecedents of American organized crime in Sicily's *mafia* and Naples' *camorra*. There are many reasons for this association.

First, there actually were Italian gangsters; secondly, they appeared in America at a time in which fear of immigrants, especially from southern Europe, was commonplace and strong enough to warrant public outcries that attached any crime to the Italian immigrant. Third, Italians were not quick to (re)present their own culture to the public. What David Richards refers to as, "the privatization of culture" (the idea of being Italian in the home and American outside the home) has enabled others to publicly present Italians any way they please. America learns about Italian Americans through organized crime. Italian Americans are portrayed as people who cling to their foreign tongue, their dark foreign ways, and their inability to organize effective campaigns to counter the media portrayals, articles in national papers, a flood of Hollywood gangster films, and later, live televised hearings of congressional investigations into organized crime. Italian Americans are still trying to find a way to keep the media from using their culture to fulfill America's addiction to the gangster figure, as evidenced by the swarm of protest surrounding the HBO television series *The Sopranos*.

While Italian Americans might find enough evidence to suggest an Anglo conspiracy to use their culture to make money, they'd have to still answer to the powerful representations created by their members of within their own culture. More than protesting what they can see, Italian Americans need to learn how to see, what most have not been able to see. Beginning with the late Mario Puzo's 1969 novel, *The Godfather*, and continuing to the latest novels of Don DeLillo and other Italian American writers, the gangster in literature, theater, and film, has been more often than not been the product of Italian America's own sons. And therein, I believe, is the key to the incredible impact the figure has had on the construction of the American man.

Beyond affecting American gender definitions, the gangster also figures in the development of a means of transgressing the social boundaries set up by definitions of class. Fredric Jameson sees the gangster as a key player in mafia movies that "project a 'solution' to social contradictions – incorruptibility, honesty, crime fighting, and finally law-and-order itself – which is evidently a very different proposition from the diagnosis of the American misery whose prescription would be social revolution" (32). While mafia movies may keep us from thinking about revolution, they are focusing our attention in other directions.

What does the gangster mean in American culture, how is that expressed in cinema, and how do Italian/American filmmakers use the figure differently are some of the questions I wish to raise in this article. Some of the earliest depictions of the Italian male in American cinema include Rudolph Valentino's exotic foreigner, the stupid immigrant, and the exploited worker. Even when Italian Americans began directing films, they were hesitant to do more than portray the Italian as a marginal, working man, as the Martini family in Frank Capra's *It's A Wonderful Life* (1946).

It would be in the 1960s, when slogans like "Power to the People" surfaced to shake up a working-class complacency, that Italian Americans would gain their share of power in a society that only a generation earlier had exploited them as workers. The gangster became the symbol of the transformation of the Italian/American male from worker to power broker. The gangster took power and became an accepted figure for that task. He became a parasite in the Michel Serres sense: a stable partner to the economic system that had kept him trapped until he took his future into his own hands, along with his gun. This was not a revolutionary, but reactionary act that few have paid attention to. As Michael Klein observed: "Hollywood films seldom foreground their ideology – more often it is encoded within the conventions of a popular genre: science-fiction, westerns, thrillers, gansgter films.... These films are often fantasies, in some cases fantasies of a special kind in that in restructuring the past, heightening/stylizing the present, or projecting a future, they may defamiliarize and thus clarify aspects of their audience's present situation, or provide a forum for the expression of contradictions, concerns and feelings that the dominant culture represses" (Klein 221).

In this essay, I will explore the gangster as embodying the traits that the dominant culture represses. I suggest that the gangster has become a necessary figure in U. S. culture and try to explain why Americans are so obsessed with it. I use the figure of the gangster to gain some insights into the past, present, and future of American culture. I see the gangster as a mode of being a man, a roadmap of sorts for masculinity in America. I see the gangster as a model for moving from poverty or working class to middle or upper class. I see the gangster as a trope for signifying the gain of cultural power that comes through class mobility.

I want to make it clear, that I am speaking of the gangster as an artistic device rather than as an actual thug who belongs to a group of organized criminals. The gangster I am most interested in is the one with the capital "G," the one around whom others form a feudal fraternity. Within this system, the Gangster is the leader who receives the efforts of everyone's work, and who then doles out a share he deems appropriate for each member. In return, the Gangster provides direction and protection. The Gangster is the man with the plan; the man of action who knows how to get things done and who has a strong sense of two worlds: the one inside and the other outside the gang. The first part of this essay searches for this Gangster's archetypal roots, and the second explores the figure of the Gangster in the films of Martin Scorsese, Francis Ford Coppola, and in *The Sopranos* television series created by David Chase. It is my contention that the Gangster, in the hands of Italian/American artists, becomes a telling figure in the tale of American race, gender, and ethnicity, a figure that reflects the autobiography of an immigrant group just as it reflects the fantasy of a native population.

The Gangster as we know him today is a strange mix of fact and fiction. More than an urban evolution of the western outlaw, the gangster came into American culture at a time when great change was occurring in American society. Al Capone's rise to Gangster god status came during America's "Roaring Twenties," a time of great excess and changing morality caused by a booming

economy. In reaction to this mixture, reactionary religious fc
created enough pressure to legally prohibit the production and sale
of alcohol. This created a ripe opportunity for smart street thugs to
thrive. A legend in his own time, Capone became a symbol of contemporary power and that legend became the basis for the many
gangster films that emerged in the 1930s. It is this transference of
fact into fiction that occupies my study because, as New York police detective Remo Franceschini witnessed during his surveillance
of John Gotti, the real gangsters started imitating the characters in
The Godfather films. After a generation one could hardly tell the
difference between the real and artificial gangster.

Now that Home Box Office has sold its television series, *The
Sopranos*, to markets throughout the world, the American gangster
may once be a prime model for imitation and again be the primary
association many make with the U.S.A. This show has generated a
great deal of national discussion and little of it goes beyond arguing
for or against it. My goal is to help us all better understand why
America keeps creating this figure and exporting it throughout the
world. We need to understand what is it about the gangster figure
that keeps Americans returning to the theaters for more, and why
are the gangsters usually Americans of Italian descent. These and
many other questions directed my search for the roots of this contemporary archetype that has become a strong model for male behavior in the United States. Before we look at the Italian/American
representation of the gangster, let's take a look at what might be the
origins for this archetype.

Hermes and the Emergence of Greek Democracy

The importance of retrieving ancient archetypes and using
them to help us understand contemporary human behavior has
been well established by psychologists such as Carl Jung. In this
section, we'll take a look at how the Greek god Hermes came to
represent a popular appropriation of the trappings of aristocratic
culture. There are two sides of Hermes that attracted me to him as
a possible source for understanding the behavior of the American
Gangster.

As the son of Zeus and Maia, Hermes has served many functions in the Greek pantheon and these have changed over time.

Stephan Hoeller, in his introduction to G. R. S. Mead's *The Hymns of Hermes*, tells us "Hermes was the Greek god of the higher Mind, and so may be called a god, or even the God of Wisdom. Any writings within a particular time and within a certain cultural milieu that were held to be inspired by true Divine Wisdom were attributed to the God of Wisdom, and were frequently said to be written by Hermes himself" (8).

Besides his role as a god of writing, Norman O. Brown tells us in *Hermes the Thief*, that the original core of the mythology of Hermes is represented by the infant Hermes' clever theft of the cattle of his elder brother Apollo, and that this story "reflects the primitive mores of Greek pastoral tribes" (3). It is this theft that tells us much about the rationale for thievery – Hermes wants to be considered an equal to Apollo. Hermes tells his mother that her scruples about his theft are childish, that he intends to put his own interests first, and follow the career with the most profit in it, that a life of affluence and luxury would be better than living in a dreary cave, and that he is determined to get equality with Apollo – by illegal means if he cannot get it by legal means (that is, by gift of Zeus) (76). Brown extends his discussion to identify Hermes as a trickster, whose "trickery is never represented as a rational device, but as a manifestation of magical power" (13). Hermes, like any kingpin Gangster, is the man with the plan.

Grecian society changed radically from 1500 to 500 BC evidenced by the decline of the self-sufficient family and tribe and the rise of monarchy, which forced a new organization onto the failing family. Over this time class divisions were created and the landowner aristocracy gained control over the state. Eventually the aristocracy was overthrown and the ancient democracy was founded. Brown points out that "In this vortex of social change were crystallized other phenomena which are themselves potent catalytic agents – the development of slavery, the codification of law, the invention of money" (47).

Brown notes a similar shift occurring in the gods. The Olympian pantheon reflects the change in society. "The component gods were given ranks and positions analogous to the component orders in society. Hermes, previously an independent and autonomous trickster, becomes the subordinate of Zeus the King, his messenger and servant-in-chief" (48). Hermes, becomes the patron of "a class of 'professional boundary-crossers' – skilled and unskilled workmen" subordinate to the king. Hermes thus came to represent "service obtained beyond the boundary, from outside the family" (50). But Hermes' image eventually becomes tarnished.

In the Age of Hesiod, around 800 BC, the figure of Hermes becomes associated with the sinister through a gift he gives to Pandora, a woman whom Zeus created to answer to Prometheus' theft of fire. That gift was "the mind of a cur and a stealthy disposition." Through this act, Hermes plays a role similar to that in the Christian myth of the serpent to Eve. Hermes' reputation begins to represent a power against familial collectivism and for acquisitive individualism. Hesiod reinterprets Hermes' trickery as trickery designed to gain profit. Wealth, up until this point came the old fashioned way, through the gods, and this became the ideal of success. But the new way to succeed would be through individualism. Hermes becomes the model for the self-made man who gains power through profit; this represents the very antithesis of the behavior championed by Hesiod, Solon, and Plato who, in Brown's words, "begin to use 'theft' and 'robbery' as interchangeable metaphors in their denunciations of acquisitive individualism, thus ignoring the earlier distinction between forcible and fraudulent appropriation" (81).

What we see here is a traditional battle between powerful and the helpless. "The theme of strife between Hermes and Apollo," writes Brown, "translates into mythical language the insurgence of the Greek lower classes and their demands for equality with the aristocracy" (85). Hermes goes on to become god of the lottery, the means by which Athenians elect public officials. The lottery, as Aristotle tells us in *Politics* and *Rhetoric*, reflects "the democratic principle of the absolute equality of all citizens" (101). In the Homeric *Hymn to Hermes*, we find the aspirations of the industrial and commercial classes are projected into the figure of Hermes; their conflict with the aristocracy is projected into the conflict with Hermes and Apollo. On a final note, Brown tells us that "Hermes' intrusion into the musical sphere [through his invention of the lyre, which he soon gave to Apollo] paralleled the initiation of the lower classes into the cultured pursuits previously monopolized by the aristocracy [...]. The termination of this monopoly of cultural pursuits and the establishment of institutions made literature, music, and athletics available to the lower classes" (123).

In sum, Hermes becomes a champion for equality through the acquisition of what the ruling class has. I see him as the archetype of the Gangster, especially if we see the fictional Gangster as a trickster figure used to represent deviant forms of behavior against which a society can form its ideas of proper behavior and to create a sense of shared cultural identity.

The Gangster as Trickster

Stanley Diamond tells us in his introduction to Paul Radin's *The Trickster*, that civilization, as we know it, changes the trickster into "a segregated and vicarious aspect of human experience" by suppressing the concrete image of the trickster and changing it into "the problem of injustice" (Diamond xiii). The "dual image of the deity as expressed in the trickster" which "are fused in the network of actions that define primitive society," becomes separated into two distinct, abstract notions of good and evil. And this, says Diamond is what enables the development of "moral fanaticism, based as it is on abstract notions of pure good, pure evil, and the exclusive moral possibility or fate of any particular individual – what may be called moral exceptionalism." (Diamond xxi).

I propose, that in the moral fanaticism of Anglo-American based culture, good and evil were separated. As American man strived toward his notion of pure good, he had to be able to measure his progress by personifying evil in others. As Paul Radin remarks, "Only if we view it as primarily [psychological], as an attempt by man to solve his problems inward and outward, does the figure of the Trickster become intelligible and meaningful" (Radin xxiv). This, as we will see, is one of the functions of the American Gangster; he figuratively embodies problems facing American society.

Noted mythographer Karl Kerenyi sees the trickster figure as the one who brings disorder to a system: "Disorder belongs to the totality of life, and the spirit of this disorder is the trickster. His function in an archaic society, or rather the function of his mythology, of the tales told about him, is to add disorder to order and so make a whole, to render possible, within the fixed bounds of what is permitted, an experience of what is not permitted" (Kerenyi 185).

The trickster also works to help us organize our sense of community. Carl Jung sees the trickster as: "A collective personification...the product of a totality of individuals and is welcomed by the individual as something known to him, which would not be the case if it were just an individual outgrowth" (Jung 201). The trickster, Jung writes, serves as a reminder of our shadow selves:

> The so-called civilized man has forgotten the trickster. He remembers him only figuratively and metaphorically, when irritated by his own ineptitude, he speaks of fate playing tricks on him or of things being bewitched. He never suspects that his own hidden and apparently harmless shadow has qualities whose dangerousness exceeds his wildest dreams. As soon as people get together in masses and submerge the individual, the shadow is mobilized, and, as history shows, may even be personified and incarnated. (Jung 207)

Jung sees trickster stories as having therapeutic value: "It holds the earlier low intellectual and moral level before the eyes of the more highly developed individual, so that he shall not forget how things looked yesterday" (Jung 207).

Only if we see the figure of the gangster as a trickster figure, can we begin to explain America's fascination with gangsters. What we have then is the need for a society to have a figure that can represent fringe behavior against which the center of society can formulate its values and identity. The mafia myth has thus served an important function in American society in both defining what is American and what is acceptable behavior in American society.

The Gangster in American Culture

In *The New Science*, 18th century Italian philosopher Giambattista Vico identified what he called the mythic stage of history as developing after families and social institutions were established. During this stage an aristocracy would develop against which the common people would revolt as they attempted to gain greater control of their lives. Out of this struggle would rise heroic figures who replace the divinities of the previous age, what Vico called the poetic age, as models for human behavior. Vico notes that this shift occurred when Man moved away from agrarian culture and into an urban culture, from a theology based on fear of the gods to one in which man would begin to struggle with the gods. Vico theorized that men rewrote the stories of gods as divine creatures in myths that gave the gods human qualities. The result would be that man could then "sin with authority;" after all, if a god could sin, well, then a man couldn't be expected to behave much better. Vico came to these conclusions from his studies of Greek and Roman culture, two cultures which have directly influenced Italian culture. Thus what he has to say can be beneficial to examining the myths of Italian/American culture.

The key to understanding this mythic mode lies in Vico's suggestion that "poets do not make ethnic myths; they simply record in allegorical poetic form, the histories of their people" (Bidney 274). Myths are histories that over the years become stories that change as the need for change arises in each generation. Thus, we can look at the history created around Italian Americans to determine how what once had happened has now become myth.

So what type of myths have been created from yesterday's recording of reality? Beginning with the late Mario Puzo's 1969 novel, *The Godfather*, the gangster in literature, theater, and film, has been more often than not been the product of Italian America's own sons. Puzo, Coppola, DeLillo, Martin Scorsese, Brian De Palma, Gay Talese, Frank Lentricchia, Tony Ardizzone, and Anthony Valerio, are just a few of the more established artists who have been drawn to the figure of the gangster. In their hands, the gangster has become a cultural figure of mythic proportions that can help us understand a number of features of American ethnic culture.

Critic Richard Gambino noted nearly thirty years ago that "the mafioso rivals the cowboy as the chief figure in American folklore, and the Mafia rivals the old American frontier as a resource for popular entertainment" (277). According to Gambino, this has caused a great obstacle for Italian Americans in their attempts to become accepted as good American people. But beyond pointing out the obvious, and screaming discrimination, Americans, especially Italian Americans, must understand why contemporary America needs the gangster, and more importantly why it needs to be an Italian/American gangster. The answers are many as they are complex.

Just as its Puritan ancestors needed the Native American Indians as a primitive "other" against which it would fashion its social mores and cultural identity, contemporary U.S. culture needs to have its "other" who can become an enemy to fight; this has been especially true since Communism has stopped being perceived as an internal threat to our democratic structure and socio-economic order. That Anglo-American culture of the U.S. founders, based on Christianity, looks for a separation of good and evil; this creates a worldview which posits Christians as good, and non-Christians, if not evil incarnate, then at least prime suspects for evil's presence. The fundamental structure of this country requires, in spite of the so-called separation of church and state, an embodiment of that evil.

Since the movement and extermination of the Native Americans, the United States has had to maintain an other against which the nation could build the social and cultural identity of the American. Key suspects were those self-sustaining groups or tribal cultures that are able to survive within their own cultural and often geographic boundaries. The Italian/American gangster makes for a perfect "other" by virtue of his connection to a tribal culture which does not play the game of capitalism according to the rules; they have not resigned themselves to working hard so that others can get rich. The Italian gangster often rises out of poverty or from America's working class through a world that depends not on his individuality, but his ability to contribute to the betterment of the entire community of criminals. When that fails, the gangster is usually killed or turned over to American authorities for imprisonment, and inevitably another leader arises. This is what gives America its endless supply of gangsters, of others upon whom blame can be lain for any number of social problems.

The Gangster figure emerges at the time when the nation is shifting from an agrarian to industrial based economy; this was also a time when immigration to the United States was at its highest and xenophobia was rampant. David Ruth, in *Inventing the Public Enemy: The Gangster in American Culture, 1918-1934*, argues that as America's urban centers grew, as the U. S. economy was becoming more corporatized, and as the government became more bureaucratized, the American was losing the traditional sense of individuality. Amidst this social upheaval, the gangster became "a central cultural figure because he helped Americans master this changing social world" (3).

Prior to the invention of the gangster, Ruth tells us, crime was presented through a deranged individual who performed his deeds single-handedly in dark and dreary urban ghettos. Based on the realities of 1920s and 1930s, crime scenes in films such as *Scarface*, *Little Caesar*, and *The Public Enemy*, moved from ethnic ghettos to downtown commercial centers. This enabled the criminal to more closely resemble those in the rising business class, and less so those dark, ethnic foreigners of earlier depictions. Thus the criminal is rising in class and assimilating to mainstream culture at the same time American urban white ghetto ethnics are trying to do the same. Easier access to stylish consumption, through fancy dress and cars, blurred the earlier lines that separated social class. As street criminals began associating with the upper echelons of society, it became harder to tell the gangster from the corporate elite.

The prototype for this gangster, says Ruth, is none other than Al Capone, what he calls an "attractive and repulsive" figure that "illuminated the lives of urban Americans." Capone's story, as a microcosm of how the individual could "escape from obscurity to wealth, power, and fame," also epitomized the gangster's adoption of corporate strategies through the need to "organize or perish." In 1931 the film *Little Caesar*, based on Capone's life, catapulted the gangster into American consciousness, and led the way for the creation of a new type of film. The great social impact of the film has been attributed to it being one of the earliest talkies, but the film did more than help us hear the gangster's voice and violence. Film scholar Jonathan Munby tells us that: "The gangster film is a genre like pornography and the horror film, held in contempt so-cially and intellectually not because it may corrupt and not because it is artistically inferior to other kinds of film but because it realizes our dreams, exposes our deepest psychic urges.... The genre speaks to not merely our fascination/repulsion with aspects of our socio-economic milieu that we prefer to shut our eyes to but also to our fascination/repulsion with the most haunting depths of ourselves"

(2). Munby sees the gangster as providing us with a view into our world from a different perspective: "If there is a problem the society is worried about or a fantasy it is ready to support, odds are it can be located in the gangster" (4).

As Jack Shadoian points out in his study of gangster films entitled *Dreams and Dead Ends*, the gangster film can make us "see things that would otherwise be hard to see. It locates an underworld, a world beneath the surface and shows it to us – a literal embodiment of those things that exist but are difficult to see in American life" (4). Shadoian finds the gangster embodying: "Two fundamental and opposing American ideologies – a contradiction in thought between America as a land of opportunity and the vision of a classless, democratic society" (5). The gangster functions as the scapegoat for the obsessive desire for self-advancement, and unrelieved class conflicts are played out in films. He becomes, for the United States, the only sanctioned soldier in the class war; and ultimately he teaches us that it is a losing battle. The gangster is also a guide to the underworld, taking us places that we might never go on our own. Other themes surrounding the gangster include the disintegration and destruction of the family, the substitution of a "false family" – the gang – for the real family, and a son in a New World rebelling against a father from an Old World.

The same forces that combined to create Prohibition pressured Hollywood to stop making gangster films, which were believed to corrupt the morals of society. This censorship would put the figure to sleep through World War II. And when the gangster returned he would have his greatest impact through the work of Italian/American artists. The truth is that the fiction of the gangster is stronger than the facts, and the facts of American history will never be as attractive as the fictional myths that have been created around the gangster. Prior to Puzo's *The Godfather*, the gangster was usually a singular individual whose gang dissolved when he was jailed, killed or reformed. Through filmmakers Francis Ford Coppola, Martin Scorsese, and Brian DePalma, and writers Mario Puzo, Gay Talese, Frank Lentricchia, Don DeLillo, and Anthony Valerio most of us have come to know the American gangster as a more rounded figure, a man who thinks before he acts, one who rarely pulls the trigger of a gun. From Mario Puzo's *The Godfather*, to *Lucchesi and the Whale*, the latest novel by Frank Lentricchia, Italian/American culture has taken hold of the figure of the gangster and elevated it from a common criminal to a god of sorts that can help us understand much about ourselves and our societies.

While some Italian Americans believe they have gathered enough evidence to suggest an Anglo-American conspiracy against them, some would say bordering on ethnic genocide, they'd still have to come up with a theory that would explain why the most powerful representations of Italians as gangsters have been created by their members of within their own culture. Here are two examples of the many that can be used: Mario Puzo's *The Godfather* and David Chase's *The Sopranos*.

The Gangsters of Mario Puzo and Francis Coppola

With the publication of *The Godfather* in 1969, Mario Puzo was instantly promoted to celebrity status. Not since the publication of Pietro di Donato's *Christ in Concrete* (1939) had an American author of Italian descent been thrust into the national spotlight on such a grand scale. The timing of *The Godfather*'s publication had much to do with its rapid climb to number one and its sixty-seven week stay on the *New York Times* best-seller list. The novel came off the press in the middle of the ethnic revival period of the 1960s. It also followed nationally televised Congressional hearings on organized crime and the publication of Peter Maas' non-fictional best seller, *The Valachi Papers*, through which mobster-turned-informer Joe Valachi described his activities inside organized crime.

The Godfather has done more to create a national consciousness of the Italian/American experience than any work of fiction or non-fiction prior to or since its publication. It certainly was the first novel that Italian Americans, as a group, reacted to either positively or negatively. It appeared during a time when Italian Americans were just beginning to emerge as an identifiable cultural and political entity. Even though this book was a work of fiction, more obviously so than any of the earlier, more autobiographical novels written by Italian Americans, the novel created an identity crisis for Italian Americans throughout the nation. Anti-defamation groups denounced Puzo for creating a bad image of Italians in America;

young Italian/American boys formed "Godfather" clubs; and real "mafiosi" claimed Puzo knew what he was writing about.

The effect of this one novel was tremendous. Since its publication, and especially since its film adaptations in the early 1970s, Italian/American novelists have been writing in its shadow and Puzo became a virtual recluse until his death last year. Though sociologists and literary scholars may forever debate the value of Puzo's work, most would agree that he is one writer who has left a permanent imprint on the American cultural scene through his representation of *Italianità* and his creation of a mythic filter through which Italian/American culture would be read.

In *The Godfather*, Mafia is seen as a natural force in the Sicilian world from which Vito Corleone comes, a world that he attempts to recreate in his new home in America. In this world, the Don and his family are portrayed as the "good guys" and the American establishment with which they struggle, i.e. the institutions of law and business, are set up as the "bad guys." Throughout the novel, the Don is referred to as a god or as a demi-god who can negotiate affairs between man and the supernatural. This is evidenced by the hospital scene in which the Don's original consiglieri, Genco Abbandando, lies on his deathbed crying out, "Godfather, Godfather...save me from death....Godfather, cure me, you have the power" (47). The Don replies saying that he does not have such powers but if he did, he should "be more merciful than God" (47). Genco then appeals to the Don to stay with him as he faces death, "Perhaps if He sees you near me He will be frightened and leave me in peace. Or perhaps you can say a word, pull a few strings, eh" (47)? When he is not referred to as a god, Don Corleone is portrayed as a heroic figure who is able to struggle with the gods. Puzo characterizes Don Corleone as a rarity, a man of will, a man among "...men who refused the dominion of other men. There was no force, no mortal man who could bend them to their will unless they wished it. They were men who guarded their free will with wiles and murder" (287).

In the Don's speech to the heads of the other crime families after the murder of his oldest son, he attempts to make peace through an appeal to the American dream, but the whole speech is designed to cloak his true plans to set up his son Michael as his replacement. He presents the illusion that he is willing to assimilate to the more American ways of doing business:

> Let me say that we must always look to our interests. We are all men who have refused to be fools, who have refused to be puppets dancing on a string pulled by the men on high. We have been fortunate here in this country. Already most of our children have found a better life. Some of you have sons who are professors, scientists, musicians, and you are fortunate. Perhaps your grandchildren will become the new *pezzonovanti*. None of us here want to see our children follow in our footsteps, it's too hard a life. (292)

The Don speaks of the hard life, which fostered the continuation of the traditional family collectives and proved to be a formidable enemy for the American state once the 50s obsession with internal communism fizzled out. By connecting the story of the development of American capitalism to the immigration saga of Italian Americans, Puzo, and through the film Coppola, have fashioned a convenient symbol towards which revolutionary rage can be deflected. They have also, inadvertently perhaps, set up the model for the media representations of gangsters as real human beings, as capable of showing affection to a kitten as they are of killing relatives who are perceived as having put the family in danger. A modern replication of Hermes, the original Don Corleone (Vito) enables the family to rise from poverty to riches, as the heir, Michael refines his father's tricks of the trade to help the family thrive in a post-immigration world in which the trickster gains acceptance as an American businessman, but loses his family.

David Chase's The Sopranos

Things begin to change in the hands of *The Sopranos* creator David Chase – whose family's name was changed from De Cesare. *The Sopranos* has become to America of the new millennium what *Dallas* was to the 1980s, and in this respect it reveals that the Italians have finally, after more than one-hundred years of living in this country, assimilated sufficiently to capture enough prestige to warrant a prime-time cable soap opera. But people are missing the mark when they try to limit interpretation of these characters to their Italian/American makeup and wardrobe. This hit series signals a major change in what the gangster represents.

The original American gangsters represented a traditional, patriarchal sense of manhood that came from an old European model. The key to portraying this sense of manhood was that violence could be used to bring and sustain honor, a notion that is being clung to all the tighter in the death grasp of a dying patriarchal mode of organizing our world. And for this type of gangster, the swarthy European looking Italians made for instant identity with the type.

The Sopranos, if it has anything to teach us, is about the emasculation of the traditional American male presented to us through even the most American of films such as those starring John Wayne. The American man is changing; this is what *The Sopranos* is telling us.

There is only one way I know by which a man can be made into a soprano; metaphorically this is what is happening to Tony Soprano who happens to be a gangster in a time in which manhood is changing. Like many male baby boomers in the throes of middle age, Tony is trying to figure out who he is and why he does what he does. He has come to realize that he is not the man his father was and that his son will not be able to carry on. Trapped between the past and the present with an unimaginable future, he begins to feel weak and after a couple of incidents in which he loses consciousness, he visits a doctor. When his doctor suggests he visits a psychologist to help him deal with stress, he stumbles upon a way of feeling better, but for Tony Soprano, it comes with a cost, and that cost is betraying the tribal code of keeping silent, especially to strangers. Tony Soprano begins to lose a traditional sense of manhood by first talking about his work, and secondly by talking about it with a woman. Hesitant at first, he finds that as he continues to talk, he begins to question the traditional order of things, and this lead him to question his role as a husband, a father, a son, and a gangster. After Tony Soprano there can be no mafia, in the traditional sense. When Tony breaks "omertà," he is no longer behaving the way a man should, as the Spanish source "ombredad" suggests. This behavior, coded and displayed by the Spaniard aristocracy who occupied Italy, says a man should be known through actions more than words: "Le parole sono femmine," goes an Italian saying. Words are feminine.

The reason *The Sopranos* is so popular is that it, on a superficial level, gives its audience an acceptable bad guy whose job it is to uphold an alternative system that lives off capitalism without contributing its "fair share" of dues to the power brokers; he comes from a tribe that had decided it won't work hard to make someone else rich. Unlike the operatic qualities of Coppola's films, *The Sopranos* features typical American family qualities radiated by the program's form and content. The Soprano family functions in the everyday world of middle-class America, but maintains an old-world sense of structure and obligation which separates them from their neighbors. And while the patriarchal mode of that world is weakening, its matriarchal foundation is surfacing. Whether its through Tony's wife, his mother, or his psychiatrist, the power of women to change the world is featured as never before. Whereas Coppola gives us the feminine power of Connie Corleone, who essentially mimics the violent ways of her brothers, Chase presents the strong women of the Soprano family who wield power and who shape reality through their hearts and minds. There is a trajectory started in the early episodes of this series that suggests a development of this Gangster that we haven't seen in any of the earlier representations. This suggests that the Italian American has created a gangster that can speak beyond the confines of an ethnic ghetto, about issues that concern not just cops and robbers.

Whether Tony Soprano represents a degeneration or a regeneration of the Gangster remains to be seen, and actually is not as important as the fact that he has come to signify the post-modern American who struggles to fashion an identity that reconciles an ethnic past with a multicultural present. Perhaps it is the Gangster that will lead the United States into a Post-Multicultural period in which Old World chauvinism will succumb to acceptance of New World diversity.

But then again, society has always needed its tricksters and scapegoats, and the gangster serves that purpose well. Gangsters are the guys who at least try to bypass the system's standard ways of living. When they're successful, they give us all a sense of how things could be if we were outlaws; when they fail, they give us a sense of relief that it wasn't one of us. This, I believe is why America is obsessed with the Gangster. We have quite simply run out of types to play the role of trickster. So, in the hands of American artists, and especially those of Italian descent, the Gangster represents victory in the class war and presents the last stand for patriarchy in America and a chance for Americans to relive a known past as they head into an unknown future.

Works Cited

Bidney, David. "Vico's New Science of Myth." *Giambattista Vico, An International Symposium*. Ed. Giorgio Tagliacozzo. Baltimore: Johns Hopkins Press, 1969. 259-67.

Brown, Norman O. *Hermes the Thief: The Evolution of a Myth*. Great Barrington, MA: Lindisfarned Press, 1990.

Capozzola Richard A. *Finalmente! The Truth About Organized Crime*. Altamonte Springs, FL: Five Centuries Books, 1992.

Dal Cerro, William. "Italian Culture on Film (1928-1999). Image Research Project." Floral Park, NY: Italic Studies Institute, 1999.

Diamond, Stanley. "Introductory Essay: Job and the Trickster." Radin xi-xxii.

Gambino, Richard. *Blood of My Blood*. 1973. New York: Anchor, 1975.

Hoeller, Stephan A. "Introduction." G.R.S. Mead. *The Hymns of Hermes*. Grand Rapids, MI: Phanes Press, 1991.

Jameson, Fredric. *Signatures of the Visible*. New York: Routledge, 1992.

Jung, C.G. "On the Psychology of the Trickster Figure." Radin 195-211.

Kerényi, Karl. *Hermes: Guide of Souls*. Woodstock, CT: Spring Publications, 1976.

_____. "The Trickster in Relation to Greek Mythology." Radin 173-91.

Klein, Michael. "Beyond the American Dream: Film and the Experience of a Defeat." *An American Half-century: Postwar Culture and Politics in the USA*. Ed. Michael Klein. London and Boulder, CO: Pluto Press, 1994. 206-31.

Lentricchia, Frank. *Lucchesi and the Whale*. Durham, N.C.: Duke UP, 2001.

Munby, Jonathan. *Public Enemies, Public Heroes*. Chicago: U of Chicago P, 1999.

Radin, Paul. *The Trickster: A Study in American Indian Mythology*. With commentaries by Karl Kerényi and C.G. Jung. New York: Schocken Books, 1956.

Ruth, David. *Inventing the Public Enemy: The Gangster in American Culture, 1918-1934*. Chicago: U of Chicago P, 1996.

Shadoian, Jack. *Dreams and Dead Ends: The American Gagnster/Crime Film*. Cambridge, MA: The Massachusetts Institute of Technology Press, 1977.

Stefanile, Felix. "A Review of the Film 'Godfather VII'." *The Black Bough.* (Spring 1985). 13.

Stephens, Michael L. *Gangster Films: A Comprehensive, Illustrated Reference to People, Films and Terms.* Jefferson, NC: McFarland, 1996.

THE MAFIA AND THE MOVIES
WHY IS ITALIAN AMERICAN SYNONYMOUS WITH ORGANIZED CRIME?

Ben Lawton
PURDUE UNIVERSITY

Americans are fascinated by the "Mafia" and its very different depictions in the media by, among others, "Italians," "Italian Americans,"[1] "Jewish Americans," and "Other" Americans. Any attempt to study this phenomenon risks running aground on the twin shoals of the intended meaning of the terms used to describe it and the preconceived understanding of those terms by one's audience. And yet, given that this is the topic at hand, one can't avoid using these expressions.

What do we mean when we speak of "Mafia," and of its depiction by "Italians," "Italian Americans," "Jewish Americans," and "Other" Americans? If I may repeat myself (Lawton 1995), it should be self-evident by now that many terms have broken entirely free from their etymological and semantic moorings and are, if not automatically under erasure, at least capable of "different" interpretations. As a result, they have come to mean whatever the speaker/writer and the reader/listener wish them to mean, however antipodally. In this first paragraph and whenever I felt it particularly necessary, I have, therefore, chosen to enclose in quotes such free-floating signifiers to indicate that, while I may presume to ascribe a particular meaning to them, I am fully aware that different readers may opt to understand them otherwise. This is certainly true of terms such as "Mafia" and "mafioso" (and its variants)

---

[1] As Pellegrino D'Acierno acknowledges in his "Introduction" to *The Italian Heritage: A Companion to Literature and Arts*, the "discussion [of how to write the expression "Italian American"] is greatly indebted [to] . . . Anthony Tamburri." I refer the reader to Tamburri's *To Hyphenate or Not To Hyphenate. The Italian/American Writer: An* Other *American*; to D'Acierno's "Introduction" cited above; and to Thomas Belmonte's defense of the hyphen in "The Contradictions of ItalianAmerican Identity: An Anthropologist's Personal View" (D'Acierno). As for me, while I am tempted to continue to use the orthographically questionable but, I hope, ethnically more optimistic neologism, *ItalianAmerican* which I first used in "What is 'ItalianAmerican' Cinema?" (Lawton 1995) in response to Tamburri's essay, I will return to orthodoxy given that I do not want to lose myself in a debate that deserves to be developed more fully elsewhere.

which are used so ubiquitously that they have become virtually meaningless. The same is obviously true of expressions such as "Italians," "Italian Americans," "Jewish Americans," and "Other" Americans. When does an "Italian" become an "Italian American," or an "American"? The media of the times considered Al Capone an "Italian"; he considered himself an "American" (Yaquinto 7). To the best of my knowledge, at that time, neither the media nor he ever used the expression "Italian American" to describe him. When does a "Negro" become a "Black," an "African American," or an "American"? Do we think of the "American" descendants of "white" South Africans as "African Americans"? Probably not. When does a "Jew" become "Jewish American," or an "American"? What do we think of when we speak of "Hispanics"? Very probably not someone who comes from Spain. And when we speak of "Latinos" we certainly don't think of the descendants of the ancient Latins.[2] The adoption of arbitrary labels by given self-defined "minority" "groups" which only the given "group" can use to speak of self is, essentially, a device intended to make it impossible for "others" to speak for and about the "group." "Minority" "groups" frequently reject any attempt to be categorized as "group" while laying claim to benefits which accrue only as a function of belonging to the given "group." To cite only one example, "race," we are told, is a "social construction" which is to be eschewed. And yet, many of those belonging to that presumably non-existent category accuse those who question the advisability of "affirmative action" of being "racist." At first blush this appears to be a paradox or a conundrum. "Race," ethnicity," and the "Mafia" are and are not at the same time. Like nation states, they are arbitrary constructs. They are "fictions," and yet the are very "real." Like nation states, they have borders which, however arbitrary, can be crossed only if one is in possession of the appropriate passport and, quite frequently, visa. Like nation states, the differences between those within are frequently far greater than those with "foreigners" residing just across the border. And yet, like nation states, those within, no matter how different, almost invariably speak a common

---

[2] Interestingly, my MS Word spellchecker offers me, inter alia, the following alternatives: Latino; Latinos; Latin. The plural of Latin is not contemplated.

language, one all too frequently incomprehensible to those without. Like nation states, they engage in internal political strife, foreign policy, and, not infrequently, wars to conquer other "lands" or defend their own "turf." While understanding and respecting the usefulness and perhaps even the necessity of such tactics from a "political" perspective, I shall plunge forward between Scylla and Charybdis, my ears deaf to the deadly appeal of their siren songs, my eyes on my objective – to attempt to understand why "Italian American" is synonymous with "organized crime."

Some films *seem* [emphasis mine] to glorify what is self-evidently unacceptable criminal behavior (*The Godfather, Goodfellas*). Others condemn the pernicious influence of this allegedly very dangerous "shadow" government (*Salvatore Giuliano, Seduction of Mimi, The Godfather 2, The Sicilian, Lucky Luciano*). Some would seem to depict the "Mafia" as metaphor for the U.S. government (*The Godfather; The Godfather 2*). A select few condemn this unacceptable behavior (*The Flight of the Innocent; Bronx Tale*); Far too many seem to suggest that certain kinds of behavior are intrinsically Italian-American (*Some Like it Hot, Mean Streets, Prizzi's Honor, Analyze This, Mickey Blue Eyes*). Finally, there are those that suggest that organized crime is simply one means of achieving the American dream, means that has been adopted to a greater or lesser degree by all immigrant groups (*The Godfather, Cotton Club, Scarface, Year of the Dragon*). The cumulative effect of all these films creates the impression that all Italian Americans are somehow connected to organized crime. A quick search of the Internet Movie Data Base for films that include the word "Mafia" in their title results in 67 movie titles, eleven television movies, one made for video movie, and three television series.[3] Carlo Cortes has observed that Hollywood produced "film after film involving the Mafia or other Italian-American criminal agglomeration referred to more generically as the mob or organized crime," and lists 21 titles.[4] The number of

---

[3] See Appendix 1: http://us.imdb.com/Tsearch?mafia.

[4] *The Don is Dead* (1973), *Crazy Joe* (1974), *Mr. Majestyk* (1974), *Capone* (1975), *Silver Bears* (1978), *Gloira* (1980), *Absence of Malice* (1981), *Sharky's Machine* (1981), *The Cotton Club* (1984), *The Pope of Greenwich Village* (1984), *Code of Honor* (1985), *The Naked Face* (1985*)*, *The Big Easy* (1987), *Heat* (1987), *Sweet Revenge* (1987), *The Untouchables* (1987), *The Dead Pool* (1988), *Last Rites* (1988), *Kill Me Again* (1989), *GoodfFellas* (1990), and *Mobsters* (1991).

films that deal with organized crime and that either state or imply that it is comprised of Italian Americans is virtually endless.

Other studies have considered and will no doubt continue to consider these depictions, their frequently questionable historical accuracy, their "intent," and reactions to them. They have and will also ask if the "Mafia" really exists as all-powerful criminal organization whose tentacles reach into all aspects of American life, or if it is the equivalent of the Wild West and the Pony Express, phenomena of relatively brief duration and of marginal importance even in their heyday, occurrences that were immortalized by the media. What I am concerned with here is why mainstream American movies and television always, seemingly, depict Italian Americans as members of organized crime. Why has "Mafioso" become a synonym for Sicilian, for Italian, for, in short, Italian American?

It should go without saying that this assumption is wildly inaccurate. This has been demonstrated repeatedly in study after study (Iorizzo, 1970, Homer 1974, Smith 1975, Potter and Jenkins in NIAF 1986, Hess 1998, Mangione and Morreale 1992, Morreale 1995, De Stefano, and Kappler et al. 2000). This point was made repeatedly by the distinguished participants in the NIAF-sponsored crime symposium held in November of 1986.[5] There is absolutely no reasonable correlation between the extremely limited involvement of Italian Americans in organized crime and the pandemic depiction of this alleged involvement in the media. The discrepancy between these figures is made particularly apparent by the statistics furnished by a recent publication of the Italic Studies Institute which reveals that, while the total number of Italian Americans was 14.7 million according to the 1990 U.S. Census, the total number of Italian criminals were less than 5,000, according to 1999 FBI Statistics. The study goes on to point out that historically, "Italian gang members never numbered more than 5,000, which amounts to less than .03% of the overall Italian-American community." Others reports seem to suggest that even these figures are inflated. Justin Dintino, citing figures taken from the President's Commission on Organized Crime, stated that in 1986 there were only "seventeen hundred members of the La Cosa Nostra in

[5] See Appendix I.

this country," out of a total of approximately "five hundred thousand" members of organized crime nationwide (NIAF 1986).[6] In other words, "when you look at the total number of L.C.N. members and you divide it into five hundred thousand, the L.C.N. is one-twenty-fifth of the organized crime members in this country." He concludes by arguing that, in fact, the members of L.C.N., "many of whom are not Italians," in fact constitute only .01% of Italian Americans.

Not only are Italian Americans not connected to crime in any statistically significant manner, historically, as a whole, they have always been extremely hard working, law abiding citizens. Turn of the century police reports describe them as the most law-abiding ethnic group in New York, to cite only one example (Giacosa 170). They have also been extremely successful economically. It should suffice to remember that until the advent of the Japanese megabanks, the largest bank in the world was the Bank of America, institution that was originally called the Bank of Italy of California, and that it was founded by Amedeo Peter Giannini (Schiavo 311; Mangione and Morreale 198-99 and 388-89). It should also be remembered that by 1974 the average family income of Italian Americans was above that of Baptists, British Protestants, and Episcopalians, among others. They were surpassed only by Irish Catholics and Jewish Americans (D'Acierno 700).

When one contrasts these facts with the depiction of Italian Americans in American movies as reported by the Italic Studies Institute, one can't but be astonished, to say the very least:

Total Italian related films since sound era (1928)		1057
Films which portray Italians in a positive light		287 (27%)
Films which portray Italians in a negative light		770 (73%)
Individual categories		1057
Mob characters	422(40%)	
(Real mob characters)	59 (14%)	
(Fake mob characters)	363 (86%)	
Boors, buffoons, bigots or bimbos	348 (33%)	
Positive or complex portrayals	287 (27%)	

---

[6] "Justin Dintino is currently the Chief of Organized Crime nd Intelligence for the New Jersey State Commission of [sic] Investigation; he served on the President's Commission of Organized Crime from July of 1983 to April of 1984." NIAF Panel on Organized Crime (1986).

Influence of *The Godfather* (1972)
Mob movies before *The Godfather*   108 (25%)
Mob movies after *The Godfather*   314 (75%)" (*Italic Studies* 2000)

These figures and these general conclusions are echoed in a study by William Dal Cerro published in *The Italic Way*. The author looked at some 450 films which feature images of Italians and Italian Americans, starting with *Little Caesar* in 1931, and found that 88% stereotyped and caricatured Italian Americans. He further breaks down the depiction of Italian Americans in film as follows: positive characters, 12%; mob characters, 52%; boors, buffoons, bigots, 36%.

Given that I am usually primarily interested in film as "art," I don't necessarily agree with either study's assessment of each and every film. To cite only one film explicitly mentioned by both studies, *The Godfather* is perceived by them as highly problematical. Dal Cerro, is quite explicit in stating that it is perhaps the worst of all films depicting Italian Americans because, before it's appearance in 1972, only 13% of films about Italian Americans were "Mob Movies," while after 1972, 87% were "Mob Movies." Dal Cerro also describes films such as *Beach Blanket Bingo* (1965) as positive because, even though, in his words, it is "cheesy commercial drivel [in which] nevertheless, leads Frankie Avalon and Annette Funicello are presented as wholesome and attractive."[7]

Still, these differences to the contrary notwithstanding, one can't help but be struck by the incredible number of films in which, as Dal Cerro and the Italic Studies statistics point out, Italian Americans are depicted as mob characters, as boors, buffoons, bigots, bimbos, or all of the above. And so I return to my question, to the question that haunts not just Italian Americans: Why is

---

[7] I do have one quibble with Dal Cerro's otherwise important study. His article is entitled, "Hollywood versus Italians: Them 400; Us-50." My problem is that in this rubric he includes not just movies made in Hollywood, but movies made by Italian Americans (from *The Godfather* to *Goodfellas*), by African Americans (*Harlem Nights, Hoodlum, Jungle Fever, Do the Right Thing*), movies that, to the best of my recollection, depict at very best very few Italian Americans (DePalma's *Scarface, Once Upon a Time in America*), movies about a time before the existence of Italy in which Romans are depicted in a negative light (*Jesus Christ Superstar, Spartacus,* and *The Robe*), movies that present the study of Latin as stultifying (*Dead Poets Society*), and even Italian movies made by Italians in Italy (*Stealing Beauty, Palermo Connection*).

this?[8] Why do we get the impression that all films about organized crime are about the Italian-American Mafia?

In order to explore the discrepancy between the realities of organized crime as they relate to various ethnic groups, as much as these realities can be determined, and their cultural construction in relation to and by various ethnic groups, a couple of years ago I began to teach a course entitled, "The Mafia in the Movies."[9] As a result of the courses, of varied readings, of conversations with friends and colleagues, and of lively debates with the members of the American Italian Historical Association internet-based discussion group, I have developed a theory which I will present here. However, before I present my theory, I must define what I mean when I speak of theories in a humanistic context. I will borrow my definition in large part from Francesco Casetti's *Theories of Cinema: 1945-1995*. He writes that theory "is a device that is not necessarily scientifically rational (as those who reserve the label *theory* for a highly formalized construct would like). . . . Rather, theory is a device that is used to acquire knowledge. Theory cannot be reduced to an abstract form of knowledge; it is more nuanced, just like metaphor, analogy, parallelism, which provide a basis for equally efficient explication.... The primary characteristic of a theory is its *cognitive* capacity in the broadest sense of the word. In particular, it is the ability to present itself as *institutionalized, social, and historical knowledge....* Theory is a device that focuses and at the same time charts thoughtful content, means of observation, attitudes toward the world at large ... it 'institutionalizes' knowledge; theory defines both its limits and its utility. Furthermore, a theory is knowledge that circulates among those working in a give field and through them reaches broader audiences, producing discussion, loyalties, and dissent. In this respect, it is a social device, something that is diffused and shared within a community. Finally, a theory is also a historical event: it is a discourse that comes on the scene at a given

---

[8] Suffice it to think of the many non-Italian-American scholars who have been engaged in research which has proven that Italian Americans are not involved in organized crime to any significant degree.

[9] In the context of this essay, I am using the term "ethnic" to signify any distinct group of people, whether they be such because of language, national origin, or race, or any specific subdivision within these groupings.

time, in a given place, and by its very presence it is capable of defining the ambiance in which it appears. In this sense, it is a historical reality, something that reflects the path (or even the error) of thought" (314-15).

What I am presenting is precisely this, the provisional result of an ongoing discourse. I do not presume to have definitive answers or that my path is without error. Furthermore, I certainly do not intend to imply that my theories are predictive, replicable, or falsifiable. Along with Casetti, I wish only to encourage further discussion, whether the result be consent or dissent. I should add that when I speak of "my" theory, it is "mine" only to the extent that I am articulating it here. I do not presume to suggest that is necessarily original with me. The sources, the inspirations, the participants in this discourse are far too numerous and diverse to be cited.[10]

Casetti has postulated that a theory can be a metaphor or an analogy. I will posit that the image of Italian Americans in mainstream media is much like a river that eventually empties into the sea of public opinion. Like the Po river, it has many tributaries, each of which contributes waters enriched, but more frequently contaminated, by specific, identifiable organic and inorganic materials. Like the Po river, it has many estuaries which pour into the Adriatic sea. Finally, like the Po river, its presence, resulting from the confluence and divergence of waters, can be detected for miles into the Adriatic. What I am suggesting is that the main course of the image of Italian Americans in mainstream American media might be called "iella," a peculiarly Italian form of bad luck.[11]

There are many tributaries to this main stream, not all of them negative. In fact, among the images of Italian Americans that flow

---

[10] This notwithstanding, in particular I want to thank John DeMatteo for furnishing transcipts of the NIAF Symposium on Organized Crime held on Novermber 16, 1986, and for a bibliography of works on this topic; Michael Bacarella for his invaluable research tool, *Italactors: 101 Years of ItalianAmericans in U.S. Entertainment.* Also Anthony J. Tamburri, Paolo Giordano, Fred Gardaphè, Joe Stornello, Vivian Cassandra, Richard Annotico, and Joseph Sciorra for their thoughtful suggestion, insights, and recommended readings. And, of course, the many students at Purdue University and Dartmouth College who challenged by assumptions and made me clarify my ideas.

[11] "Iella" refers to the effects of the "malocchio," the evil eye that has been cast upon a person and all the pertains to him or her, usually as a result of jealousy or envy. It is an evil fate of virtually epic proportions that can only be removed by a fattucchiera, a sorceress.

into this river are also "hard work," "honesty," "family values," "honor," "pride," "self-reliance," and "patriotism." Unfortunately, however, as they flow into "bad luck" they are joined all too soon by two major tributaries: "bad timing" and "bad marketing." As a result, by the time the river of Italian-American images reaches its delta, every estuary, no matter how positive its source waters, has been contaminated by the "iella" of the main stream. It is, obviously, incredibly difficult and frustrating to try to unravel these liquid threads. Whenever you begin to trace one strand, you have to consider the influences of one or more others and the way they reciprocally influence each another. Thus, inevitably, when I have seemingly finished with one thread and I have begun to trace another, I find myself once again dealing with the former. For all of this, I beg the readers' indulgence.

According to my "theory," Italians and Italian Americans, have become identified with organized crime because of bad timing, bad marketing, and, most importantly, "iella." "Iella" seems to pursue Italians and Italian Americans in the United States. Like a black cloud, it seems to hover over them so that any event, no matter how positive, somehow is transformed into a negative.

Iella and Timing

As I have stated repeatedly, there is no justification for the depiction of Italian Americans as particularly prone to becoming involved in organized crime or as having a preponderant role in organized crime in the United States (Dintino, Homer, Iorizzo, Kappler et al., Kelly, Lyman and Potter, Mangione and Morreale, Morreale, Morris, Potter 1986 and 1994, De Stefano). In fact, the use of "mafia" as synonymous with organized crime is, to a very large extent, an invention of "white" American media, of "white" American law enforcement, and, not surprisingly, of "white" American business interests (Hess, Homer, Morreale, Smith, NIAF).

The great migration of Southern Italians to the United States began in part because of intolerable conditions in Italy,[12] but also

---

[12] "Booker T. Washington, [. . .] remarked after visiting Italy: 'The Negro is not the man farthest down. The condition of the coloured farmer in the most backward parts of the

because good, reliable workers were needed, particularly in the Southern United States in the years immediately following the Civil War to replace the African Americans who had emigrated to the industrial North (Gambino 51, Mangione and Morreale 181). One might have expected the immigrants to be welcome and that their achievements be celebrated. Instead, as a result of the xenophobia of the time, their very successes became the source of their indictment. The term "Mafia" was first used from 1890 to 1913 primarily as a way of explaining the entrepreneurial successes of the new "nonvisibly black" immigrants (Richards, 12). Given the racism of the times, it was easy for individuals who wanted to eliminate the Sicilian competition on the New Orleans docks (Gambino 59, Mangione and Morreale 200-13) to explain their successes in terms of the "myth of an alien conspiracy" (Kappler et al 101). It also served as a "weapon of immigration restriction" (Smith in NIAF 90, Gambino 108, Mangione and Morreale 181-213). The most dramatic result of this attitude, but not the only one by any means, was the murder of 11 Sicilians in New Orleans in 1891, the largest mass lynching in American history (Gambino, Mangione and Morreale, 200-213). The feelings of hatred for Southern Europeans became so prevalent that several Southern states passed laws forbidding their immigration (Gambino 108, Mangione and Morreale 213).

The most interesting thing is that from 1913 to 1944 the "Mafia label virtually disappeared from the American scene" (Smith in NIAF, 90). And yet, like a bad penny, it continues to resurface.

Iella, bad timing, and bad marketing came together again with the rise of Italian Americans to visibility in organized crime during prohibition. While it is difficult to say precisely what was the order of arrival and ascendance of the ethnic criminal groups in the United States, it is clear that Italian Americans were not the first ethnic group to be involved in organized crime in the United States. They were obviously preceded by WASP, Irish American, and other Northern European criminals, and among their contem-

---

Southern States in America, even when he has the least education and the least encouragement, is incomparably better than the condition and opportunities of the agricultural population in Sicily.'" Mangione and Morreale, xv).

poraries at the very least we find, in addition to the former, Jewish American, African American, and Chinese American mobsters. Nor were Italian Americans the last ethnic group to become prominent in organized crime. They were followed, among others, by Hispanics, Eastern Europeans, other Asians (Japanese, Vietnamese, inter alii), and Africans (from the Caribbean and from Africa).[13]

Basically, all ethnic groups that have become involved in organized crime in a serious manner in the United States have one thing in common: in their country of origin they were outcasts of one kind or another (Homer, 67-73). The Irish were brutally oppressed by the British; the Jews were victims of endless pogroms in Russia; the Sicilians, Calabresi, and Campani, who not coincidentally came from that part of Magna Graecia and of the Kingdom of the Two Sicilies most exposed to the Mediterranean and thus to depredations of various kinds. They were oppressed for centuries by foreign and home-grown tyrants, starting with the Greeks, Carthaginians, Romans, Saracens, and Normans, and ending with the Bourbons (both French and Spanish) and the (Northern) Italians. (Bacarella H-NET List on Italian-American History and Culture)[14]

Regardless of who came first, or who was in power first, turn of the century America was packed with criminals of every immigrant ethnic group. The names of the gangsters who were to come to power over the next couple of decades reflect this fact: Edward Osterman (Jewish), Tom Lee (Chinese), Arnold Rothstein (Jewish), Frank Costello (born Francesco Castiglia, Italian), Meyer Lansky (Jewish), Dutch Schultz (né Arthur Flegenheimer, Jewish), Charles Dion O'Bannion (Irish), Charles "Lucky" Luciano (Salvatore Lucania, Italian), Ellesworth "Bumpy" Johnson (Black), and Mock Duck (Chinese). The titles of the earliest films, however, do not, as a rule, reflect any necessary connection between ethnicity and crime: *The Burglar* (1898), *The Kidnapper* (1903), *The Thieving Hand* (1904), *Burglar Bill* (1904), *The Moonshiners* (1904). However, by 1906 we begin to find titles such as *The Black Hand* (re-

---

[13] For an eye-opening account of what appears to be the dominant criminal organization worldwide, see Robert I. Friedman's *Red Mafiya: How the Russian Mob Has Invaded America.* While I had read and heard about Russian organized crime, I had not previously had any inkling that the so-called Red Mafyia is comprised overwhelmingly of Jewish emigrés.

[14] See Appendix II.

made in 1912 and 1913), and its sequel, *The Black Hand Conspiracy* (1914). Still, the identity of Italian Americans and crime in America had not been yet been established. D.W. Griffith made a number of films set in the tenements of New York City. He featured a Chinese white slaver in *The Fatal Hour* (1908), and showed Italians devoted to vengeance in *At the Altar* (1909), and in *The Cord of Life* (1909). However, in 1912, in *The Musketeers of Pig Alley*, the gangsters are Irish and the alleys are teeming with Russian Jews (Yaquinto 1-14). In short, there were plenty of choices. In addition to Italian Americans, the movies could have continued to depict the Irish Americans, Jews, Blacks, and Chinese as gangsters. Why did this not happen?

Italian Americans acquired greater visibility in organized crime around the time of Prohibition (1919). The Volstead Act was, to put it mildly, unpopular with the American public at large. As a result, many otherwise respectable, law-abiding citizens began to reject laws that they considered absurd and were ready to start glamorizing the picturesque characters who brought them the liquid solace they so devoutly desired.

At first, this chance to grab the American brass ring seemed to be proof that luck was smiling on Italian Americans. Italian-American criminals might well have made their fortunes and then merged with the American establishment, as did the WASPs, the Northern Europeans, the Irish, and the Jews before them. This might have happened had sound not come to movies in the same decade (1928). As a result, movie attendance exploded. Approximate weekly movie attendance skyrocketed from 57 million in 1927 to 90 million in 1929 (Yaquinto 26). In the search for subject matter for the new technology, it was inevitable that the existing gangster genre be included in the mix. The sound of shots, wailing sirens, and screeching tires seemed to be made to order to bring back to life a genre that was waning.

The first major gangster movies made in 1930 after the advent of sound were: *Little Caesar*, starring a young Edward G. Robinson as Rico Bandello, and modeled on Al Capone, and *Scarface*, also obviously based on Al Capone (starring Paul Muni as Tony Camonte). Even though the equally successful *The Public Enemy* (starring James Cagney as the Irish Tom Powers) was made in the same year, henceforth it will increasingly be Italian Americans who are depicted as criminals. Why? Why the Italian Americans and not the Irish Americans or the Jewish Americans? Why did the overwhelming majority of films about organized crime focus on Italian Americans from the 1930s through the 1970s? What happened to all the other ethnic groups, the Irish Americans, Jewish Americans, African Americans, and Chinese Americans that had been depicted as criminals of one kind or another during the first 30 years of American cinema?

Why were the other ethnic groups, which still continue to play a significant role in organized crime, no longer available as filmic images?

Although African Americans have always been real players in organized crime, they were essentially invisible to white America because of racism. Ironically, this was in part as a result of the depiction of "black bucks" and "black brutes" in the most racist film ever made in America. (Bogle 13) According to Donald Bogle, "one thing was certain after *The Birth of a Nation* [1915]: never again could the Negro be depicted in the guise of an out-and-out villain. This treatment was too touchy and too controversial.... Consequently, blacks in Hollywood films were cast almost exclusively in comic roles."[15] Bogle goes on to add that, "Not until more than half a century later, when Melvin Van Peebles' *Sweet Sweetback's Baadasss Song* (1971) appeared, did sexually assertive black males make their way back to the screen.... Afterward ... the screen was bombarded with buck heroes in such films as *Shaft* (1971), *Superfly* (1972), *Slaughter* (1972), and *Melinda* (1972)" (Bogle 16-17).[16] Before this time, white filmgoers were simply not ready to see physically and sexually threatening blacks. Interestingly, so far as I can tell, it wasn't until 1984 that an Italian-American director,

---

[15] In 1936, Black director Oscar Micheaux "took the typical Hollywood script and gave it a racial slant. *Underworld* was a gangster film with black gangsters and a black gun moll." (Bogle 115). There were other films by black directors in which black actors played heroes and heroines. "Certainly ghetto kids could look up to Herb Jeffries, the lead in *The Bronze Buckaroo*, just as their white counterparts admired Gene Autry" (Leab 193).

[16] In reality, as Bogle himself points out on page 220: Jim Brown "arrived in motion pictures at a time when the mass black audience was in a desperate need of him. Even though he was to be nothing more than the black buck of old, he answered – because of his unique charisma and astounding physical presence – the need for a viable black-power sex figure."

Francis Ford Coppola in *Cotton Club*, through the fictional char-
acter of Bumpy Rhodes, tells us about Bumpy Johnson, an African
American gangster who dealt as a virtual equal with the likes of
Lucky Luciano and Dutch Schultz.[17]

The presence of the Chinese in America for five generations
has also largely been obliterated from history, as Tracy Tzu (Ari-
ane) tells Stanley Fish (Michael O'Rourke) in Michael Cimino's
Year of the Dragon (1985). The same can be said by and large about
the Chinese as criminals in film for several decades after *The Fatal
Hour* (1908) in which a Chinese is depicted as a white slaver
(Yaquinto 14). Those that do appear are usually cut from the mold
established by serials such as *The Yellow Menace*, films such as *The
Red Lantern* (1919), and *The Mysterious Dr. Fu Manchu* (1929),
directed by Rowland V. Lee. They may be evil, but their physicality, be it related to sex or violence is concealed by long flowing
robes. It is only with the invasion of Kung Fu movies, that exploded on American screens thanks to the martial arts virtuosity of
Bruce Lee in the early 70s, that we once again see Chinese as physically and sexually attractive subjects who can be desirable to white
women and thrash white men.[18]

By the late 20s, the Irish Americans had become somewhat integrated; they no longer confronted the material poverty, political
oppression, and spiritual despair that drives some people to crime;
they had gone from being the dominant criminal group to being
policemen, judges, politicians, and businessmen. They had, in
other words, begun what has been called their transformation into
"white" people and thus, while individual Irish Americans would
occasionally be depicted as gangsters, they were no longer to be
depicted as a criminal "race" (Ignatiev). While the Irish may have
been despised and mistreated by the British, in the U.S. they were
perceived as English-speaking whites. Italian Americans, and in

---

[17] It should probably not be surprising that, while *Cotton Club* is a highly self-conscious
artistic film that in many ways is reminiscent of American musicals, it is also the most
historically accurate depiction of the multi-ethnic nature of (dis)organized crime during
Prohibition.

[18] Interestingly, in 1972, even though Bruce Lee had been very well received as Cato in *The
Green Hornet* television series, Warner Brothers, fearing that the public would not accept a
Chinese hero, rather than star Bruce Lee in the *Kung Fu* television series, which had been
conceived with him in mind, selected the rather torpid David Carradine.

particular Italian Americans of Southern extraction, instead, were perceived as both foreigners and as colored, or as Richards puts it, as "nonvisibly black" (186). This does not mean that the Irish Americans didn't continue to be involved in crime and, in particular in bootlegging. Among the many Irish American mobsters it should suffice to recall Owney "the Killer" Madden who at age 17 "had killed his first man, an Italian, for no other reason than to celebrate his election to leadership of the Gophers" (Sifakis 205), and Vincent "Mad Dog" Coll, who at different times was at war with Dutch Schultz, Owney Madden, Legs Diamond, Lucky Luciano, Vito Genovese, and Joe Adonis (Sifakis 78). Among the most socially prominent Irish Americans, Joseph Kennedy, a Harvard graduate, United States Ambassador to Great Britain, and the father of assassinated former president John Fitzgerald Kennedy, is reputed to have been actively involved in bootlegging (Gray, Sifakis). Still, in those days political, legal, and financial power offered great cover and concealment.

Jewish Americans, who had worked hand in hand with Italian Americans during prohibition, were still a long way from being considered "white." Given their prominent role in organized crime and the pandemic racism of the time, Jewish Americans would have seemed like a very desirable choice as movie mobsters. Interestingly, they are virtually non-existent as protagonists of the gangster films of the 30s and 40s. In part this is because, given past experiences of anti-Semitism in Europe, they understood the importance of participating actively in the public discourse (Richards 195). One can't help but wonder if, in part, this isn't also the case because Jewish Americans, by and large, controlled the movie studios.

Even a cursory glance at any history of American cinema reveals that the five "Major" studios (MGM, Paramount, Warner Bros., 20th Century-Fox, RKO) and two of the three "Minors" (Universal Pictures, Columbia Pictures) were run by Jewish Americans. Oddly, the fact that Jewish Americans essentially controlled the production, distribution, and screening of American movies for several decades seems to be completely transparent. I have found only one history of American cinema that confronts, however tangentially, the impact of the Jewish immigrant experience on the film industry. Gerald Mast writes that "The first Hollywood producers were not just businessmen; they were a very specific breed of businessmen. Most of them were either Jewish immigrants from Germany or Russia or Poland, or the sons of Jewish immigrants. They sold herring or furs or gloves or second-hand clothes. They jumped from these businesses into running amusement parks and penny arcades.... When movies left the peep-show box for the screen, these arcade owners converted their stores into nickelodeons" (Mast 125).

Given this rough and tumble immigrant heritage, it should come as no surprise that they had connections with organized crime. Jack Warner, whose father was a cobbler from Kraznashiltz, Poland, boasted of being a mobster and a member of the Westlake Crossing gang in Youngstown, OH, a gang led by John Dillinger. (Yaquinto 10) Thus perhaps it should not be surprising that Warner Brothers, which received the special Academy Award (1927-1928) for producing *The Jazz Singer,* "the pioneer talking picture, which has revolutionized the industry," was responsible for revitalizing the gangster genre with films such as *Little Caesar* (Melvyn LeRoy, 1930), *Public Enemy* (William Wellman, 1931). Other Jewish American individuals prominent in the film industry who were in some way involved in criminal activities or connected with organized crime include Harry "King" Cohn, of Columbia Pictures, who admitted to having been a thief in his youth and Adolph Zukor, of Paramount Pictures, who reported that the studio bosses hired gangsters to protect their operations. (Yaquinto 10). According to David A. Cook and other sources, "gangsters began loan-sharking to the studies following the Wall Street crash. Harry Cohn, e.g. wrested control of Columbia pictures from his brother Jack in 1932 with mob money borrowed through Johnny Roselli, and William Fox turned to similar sources in his unsuccessful bid to regain control of his own company in 1933. At the same time MPPDA [Motion Picture Producers and Distributors Association, more commonly known as the Hays Office] was hiring gangsters as strike breakers against Hollywood unions, and the Chicago mob was infiltrating the International Alliance of Theatrical Stage Employees and Moving Picture Operators (IATSE). By 1935, the racketeers George Brown and Willy Bioff had taken control of the IATSE and begun to extort protection money from the Big Five in the sum of $50,000 per studio per year. In *The Hollywood Studio System* (88), Douglas Gomery estimates that over $1 million changed hands this way before the racket was exposed by the decade's end" (Cook 293).

Other prominent Jewish leaders of the film industry include Samuel Goldwyn (né Goldfish), Louis B. Mayer, and Irving Thalberg of MGM, whose parent company was owned by Loew's Incorporated and "ruled from New York by Nicholas Schenck" (Cook 302); Carl Laemmle of Universal, Joseph M. Schenck (who as chairman of 20th Century-Fox was the Big Five's corporate bagman and went to jail, briefly, for tax evasion in the transfer of payoff funds to Browne and Bioff (Cook 293); Darryl F. Zanuck of 20th Century-Fox, Jesse Lasky, Marcus Loew, Lewis J. Selznick, Thomas Ince. I don't think it is anti-Semitic to suggest that, in the racist climate of the times, one should not be surprised that these Jewish American producers protected their own people. In fact, Cook points out that "Warner was also responsible (and rather courageously so) for the first American anti-Nazi film, Anatole Litvak's *Confessions of a Nazi Spy* (1939)." I am not suggesting here that there was a deliberate Jewish American anti-Italian conspiracy. Among other things, as James Monaco points out, "By 1936 it was possible to trace major holdings in all eight companies to the two powerful banking groups of Morgan and Rockefeller" (207). It was simply more bad luck. More "iella" for Italian Americans that one more group of eligible ethnic criminals was eliminated from the palette of possible film gangsters.

The "iella" of Italian Americans was compounded by the fact that, thanks to "movie magic," Italian Americans not only became de facto the only ethnic criminal organization in the United States, they also came to be perceived as beasts, boors, and buffoons deprived entirely of brains. While it was impossible to conceal completely the Jewish American involvement in organized crime, it was sanitized. Hollywood American films almost inevitably depicted Jewish American criminals as outsiders, as "consiglieri" for the Sicilian Mafia families. In essence, allegedly they were the brains of the operations, the non-violent mathematical geniuses thanks to whom those bumbling, violent clowns, the Italian Americans, reaped unjustified and unexplained fortunes.

What most Hollywood American movies conceal is that Jewish American gangsters took a back seat to no one when it came to participation in criminal endeavors. American style organized crime was invented by Meyer Lansky and Lucky Luciano. When Luciano was deported from the United States, the guests at his farewell banquet offer a excellent indication of the multicultural nature of organized crime: "Meyer Lansky, Joe Adonis, Willie Moretti, Bugsy Siegel, Longy Zwillman, Moses Polakoff, Joe Bonanno, Tommy Lucchese, and Owney Madden" (Mangione and Morreale 257). And yet, the public at large has bought the myth that organized crime is a Sicilian thing. Furthermore, Jewish American mobsters were easily as violent as the most violent Irish American and Italian American mobsters. Suffice it to remember that Dutch Schultz was Jewish American and that "not only was he the flakiest of the bosses, he was also the most cold-blooded" (Sifakis 296). And while his violence and his "matta bestialità," his insane rage are depicted convincingly in films such as *Cotton Club* (1984), *Billy Bathgate* (1991), and *Hoodlum* (1997), the fact that he is Jewish American is, to the best of my recollection, never an issue. At the peak of the power of organized crime, Jews, Irish, and Italians worked together. Murder Incorporated, the enforcement arm of the national crime syndicate, was comprised predominantly of Jewish Americans, a fact which becomes immediately apparent at a reading of the names of the principal operatives. The orders came from Louis Lepke and Joey Adonis and were carried out by, among others, Albert Anastasia, Louis Capone (no relation to Alphonse), Mendy Weiss, Abe Reles (who, along with Buggsy Goldstein "may have killed at least 60 men") (Sifakis 231), Phil Strauss ("who easily held the top score in kills . . . was named in 58 murder investigations and authorities agreed his total of kills was probably twice that number") (Sifakis 231), Vito Gurino, Happy Maione, Buggsy Goldstein, Blue Jaw Magoon, Frank Abbandando and Charlie Workman. Ironically, the most notorious Italian American gangster, Al Capone, the object of the greatest number of stories and films, was not born in Naples or Sicily. He used to say proudly: "I am no Italian. I was born in Brooklyn" (Yaquinto 7).[19] And his organiza-

---

[19] Ironically, Al Capone came from a law-abiding, lower middle class family. His early years

tion was for an American corporation of the time, very progressive: it was completely integrated.

The "iella" that was befalling Italian Americans on Hollywood screens was compounded by events in the halls of Washington. In 1950, Senator Estes Kefauver became "chairman of a special committee to look into organized crime in interstate commerce" (Homer 41). He made the mistake of confusing criminal societies with criminal matrices of activity (Homer 41). The McClellan Senate Permanent Subcommittee of Investigations, established in 1955, repeated his mistake, particularly after November 14, 1957, when several leaders of crime families were discovered at a meeting at the Apalachian home of Joseph Barbera. Further seeming confirmation of the existence of an Italian-American criminal organization was furnished by Joe Valachi in 1963 when he spoke of "la cosa nostra." The questionable accuracy and importance of Valachi's testimony is the object of other studies (Mangione and Morreale, 345-348; Homer, 30-45). The 1967 Task Force Report repeats and reinforces the definition of organized crime of the President's Commission on Law Enforcement and Administration of Justice according to which "organized crime is a society" (Homer 6-12). One result of these descriptions of organized crime is that in order to receive funding from the Federal government, law enforcement organizations felt they had to name as targets of their inquiries either the Mafia or La Cosa Nostra. Not coincidentally, it was at this time and for this reason that J. Edgar Hoover suddenly and belatedly discovered the existence of organized crime in the United States. Another result was that it became virtually impossible to publish articles in newspapers or in academic journals that did not at least mention these organizations and that did not include Italian-American names (Jenkins in NIAF 79).

---

gave no indication that he would, eventually, become a legendary criminal. Even more ironic is the fact that his older brother, James Vincenzo Capone, served honorably in World War I (he was promoted to the rank of lieutenant). Later he changed his name to Richard Hart and moved West. Thanks to his extraordinary skills with guns and his brace of pearl-handled revolvers and his heroic exploits in busting stills and arresting horse thieves and other criminals, he acquired the nickname of "Two Gun Hart." Over the years he served as a prohibition enforcement agent, a marshal, an U.S. Indian Service agent, and a bodyguard for President Calvin Coolidge.

The Italian-American image was struck by further *iella* when Joseph Colombo, the head of the Bonanno family, founded the Italian-American Civil Rights League in 1970. An organization which should have protected the image of Italian Americans became the source of further embarrassments. After a few successes – the June 29, 1970 rally attracted fifty-thousand people and many politicians, including then Governor Nelson Rockefeller, took honorary membership in the league – Colombo began to irritate the FBI by picketing its offices and, more fatally, Carlo Gambino. The latter, it seems, did not appreciate the loss of revenues caused by Colombo stunts. The result was that on June 28, 1971 Colombo was assassinated by Jerome A. Johnson who, in turn, was killed by Colombo's bodyguards.

Colombo did succeed in forcing the Justice Department and the FBI to drop all references to the Mafia and to La Cosa Nostra. He also forced "movie producer Al Ruddy to eliminate references to Mafia or Cosa Nostra from his adaptation of *The Godfather*" (Hammer 326). Unfortunately for the Italian-American image, the film, which is included among the best films ever made by virtually everyone, was so successful, and misunderstood, that it elicited hundreds of imitators, as both Dal Cerro and Italic Studies have shown. And while in *The Godfather* neither the Mafia nor La Cosa Nostra are ever mentioned, they will be, *ad nauseam*, in the plethora of films which follow in the newly reborn genre.

The most recent manifestation of *iella* has to be the Emmy-winning series, *The Sopranos*. Regardless of what one thinks of it, the result is that the presence of Italian Americans in organized crime, never dominant in the first place, has been foregrounded once again. Recent studies suggest that Americans overwhelmingly think that Italian Americans are, somehow, connected to crime – when nothing could be further from the truth (Response Analysis Corporation).

The oddities, in the depiction of Italian Americans as criminals, never seem to cease. One the one hand, the Mafia is supposed to be an all-powerful, secretive, terrifying, massively successful criminal conspiracy. On the other, while it is true that Italian Americans are depicted as beasts and boors in many Hollywood films, they are even more frequently portrayed as buffoons. How they can be both at the same time is beyond comprehension. How can the alleged masterminds behind this purportedly incredibly successful business, the "soldiers" who fought in this war for absolutely unfettered laissez faire capitalism, be depicted as retarded clowns, as inept, incompetent, bumbling idiots who can't speak English or shoot straight?[20]

The roots of this humiliating depiction of Italian Americans in the movies can already be seen in *Little Caesar*. While Rico himself is all beast for most of the film, many of his colleagues are depicted as boors and buffoons throughout. And by the end of the film Rico himself has become a pathetic drunken bum who is reduced to living in a flop house. By the time we get to *Some Like It Hot* (1956), which was inspired at least in part by both Al Capone's St. Valentine's Day massacre of Bugs Moran's gang on February 14, 1929, and by *Little Caesar*, the Italian-American mobster has been stereotyped as a violent, erratic, dangerous, incompetent, sentimental, opera-loving clown who couldn't hit the broad side of a barn with a machine gun. This is what Hollywood will give us time and time again, *ad nauseam*, in an endless series of absolutely deplorable films, from *The Gang That Couldn't Shoot Straight* (Goldstone 1971), to *Prizzi's Honor* (John Huston 1985), to *Married to The Mob* (Jonathan Demme 1988), *Jane Austen's Mafia* [sic!] (Jim Abrahams 1998), to, most recently, *Analyze This* (Harold Ramis 1999) and *Mickey Blue Eyes* (Kelly Mokin 1999).

Conclusion

For the past 28 years I have been speaking and writing both in praise and in defense of the films of Italian American filmmakers such Coppola, Scorsese, De Palma, and Cimino. By and large, my response to films about the Mafia has been that of a person raised in Northern Italy. It was something that did not touch me. The alleged criminals were the Other. However, after having lived in the United States off and on for the past 35 years, I have come to realize that I too am that Other. Even though my name does not finish in a vowel, by the mere fact that I teach Italian language,

---

[20] For an original, thought-provoking essay on the genesis of the Mafia in the United States, see Morreale 1995.

literature, culture, and film, I too am tarred by this scurrilous brush. As deplorable as I find knee-jerk ethnic tribalism, I am coming to the conclusion that Italians, Italian Americans, and, in fact, all people of good will must become actively engaged in public discourse on these issues.[21]

WORKS CITED

Arlacchi, Pino. *Mafia Business: The Mafia Ethic and the Spirit of Capitalism.* Trans. Martin Ryle. London and New York: Verso, 1987.

Bacarella, Michael. *Italactors: 101 Years of Italian Americans in U.S. Entertainment.* Washington: NIAF, 2000.

Bogle, David. *Toms, Coons, Mulattoes, Mammies, & Bucks: An Interpretive History of Blacks in American Films.* 3rd ed. New York: Continuum, 1997.

Casetti, Francesco. *Theories of Cinema: 1945-1995.* Trans. Francesca Chiostri and Elizabeth Bartolini-Salimbeni, with Thomas Kelso. Austin: UT Press, 1999.

Cook, David. *A History of Narrative Film.* 3rd ed. N.Y and London: Norton, 1981.

Cortes, Carlos E. "The Hollywood Curriculum on Italian Americans: Evolution of an Icon of Ethnicity." *The Columbus People: Perspectives in Italian Immigration to the Americas and Australia.* Ed. Lydio F. Tomasi, Piero Gastaldo and Thomas Row. New York: Center for Migration Studies and Gianni Agnelli Foundation, 1994. 89-108.

D'Acierno, Pellegrino. *The Italian Heritage: A Companion to Literature and Arts.* New York: Garland, 1999.

Dal Cerro, William. "Hollywood versus Italians: Them - 400; Us - 50". *The Italic Way* 27, 1997. 10-32.

De Stefano, George. *Ungood Fellas. The Nation* website at http://www.thenation. com.

Dintino, Justin. National Italian American Foundation. *Conference on Organized Crime & the Media: Exploring the "Mafia Mystique."* New York: NIAF, 1986. Tape transcripts 54-77.

Friedman, Robert I. *Red Mafiya: How the Russian Mob Has Invaded America.* Boston: Little, Brown and Co. 2000.

---

[21] Inevitably, involvement in public discourse is political and requires joining organizations that promote one's concerns. Among the organizations that are working intelligently to change the image of Italians and Italian Americans in this country are: NIAF, UNICO, FIERI, and SONS OF ITALY.

Gambino, Richard. *Vendetta: True Story of the Worst Lynching in America.* 2nd ed. Toronto: Guernica, 2000.

Giacosa, Giuseppe. *Impressioni d'America.* 2nd ed. Milano: Cogliati, 1902.

Gray, Edward, producer/director. *Mafia: The History of the Mob in America, 2: The Kennedys and the Mob.* A&E Home Video. 1993.

Hammer, Richard. *Playboy's Illustrated History of Organized Crime.* Chicago: Playboy Press, 1975.

Hess, Henner. *Mafia & Mafiosi: Origin, Power and Myth.* Trans. Ewald Osers. New York: New York UP, 1998.

Homer, Fredric D. *Guns and Garlic: Myths and Realisties of Organized Crime.* West Lafayette, IN: Purdue UP, 1974.

Ignatiev, Noel. *How the Irish Became White.* New York: Routledge, 1995.

Internet Movie Data Base: http://us.imdb.com/Tsearch?mafia.

Iorizzo, Luciano J. *An Inquiry Into Organized Crime: Proceedings of the American Italian Historical Association.* New York: AIHA, 1970.

Jenkins, Philip. National Italian American Foundation. *Conference on Organized Crime & the Media: Exploring the "Mafia Mystique."* New York: NIAF, 1986. Tape transcripts 76-82.

Jones, Thomas F. *Letter to John De Matteo.* Washington, D.C.: U.S. Department of Justice, Federal Bureau of Investigation. May 21, 1992.

Kappler, Victor R., Mark Blumberg, and Gary W. Potter. *The Mythology of Crime and Criminal Justice.* 3rd ed. Prospect Heights, IL: Waveland Press, 2000.

Kelly, Robert J. *Organized Crime: A Global Perspective.* Totowa, N.J.: Rowman & Littlefield, 1986.

Lawton, Ben. "What Is 'ItalianAmerican' Cinema?" *Voices in Italian Americana* 6.1 (1995): 27-51.

Leab, Daniel J. *From Sambo to Superspade: The Black Experience in Motion Pictures.* Boston: Houghton Mifflin, 1976.

Lyman, Michael D. and Gary W. Potter. *Organized Crime.* New York: Prentice Hall, 1999.

Mangione, Jerre and Ben Morreale. *La Storia: Five Centuries of the Italian American Experience.* New York: Harper, 1992.

Mast, Gerald. *A Short History of the Movies.* N.Y.: Pegasus, 1971.

Messick, Hank. *John Edgar Hoover.* New York: David McKay, 1972.

Meyer, Nicholas, director. *Vendetta.* HBO, 1999.

Monaco, James. *How to Read a Film: The Art, Technology, Language, History, and Theory of Film and Media.* Rev. ed. New York: Oxford UP, 1981.

Morreale, Ben. "Mafia in America from Alexander Hamilton to Richard Nixon." *Voices in Italian Americana* 6.1 (1995): 74-90.

Morris, Norval, and Gordon Hawkins. *The Honest Politician's Guide To Crime Control.* Chicago: The U of Chicago P, 1972.

National Italian American Foundation. *Conference on Organized Crime & the Media: Exploring the "Mafia Mystique."* New York: NIAF, 1986. Tape transcripts.

Order Sons of Italy. *Americans of Italian Descent: A Study of Public Images, Beliefs, and Misperceptions.* Princeton, NJ: Response Analysis Corporation, 1981.

Potter, Gary W. National Italian American Foundation. *Conference on Organized Crime & the Media: Exploring the "Mafia Mystique."* New York: NIAF, 1986. Tape transcripts 82-86.

———. *Criminal Organizations: Vice, Racketeering, and Politics in an American City.* Prospects Heights, Ill.: Waveland Press, 1994.

Response Analysis Corporation. *Americans of Italian Descent: A Study of Public Images, Beliefs, and Misperceptions.* Princeton, N.J.: 1981.

Richards, David J. *Italian American: The Racializing of an Ethnic Identity.* New York: New York UP, 1999.

Roediger, David R. *The Wages of Whiteness: Race and the Making of the American Working Class.* London: Verso, 1991.

Schiavo, Giovanni. *Four Centuries of Italian-American History.* New York: Center for Migration Studies, 1992.

Sifakis, Carl. *The Mafia Encyclopedia: from Accardo to Zwillman.* New York: Facts on File, 1987.

Smith, Dwight C. *The Mafia Mystique.* New York: U P of America, 1975.

Tamburri, Anthony Julian. *To Hyphenate or Not To Hyphenate. The Italian/American Writer: An Other American.* Montreal: Guernica. 1991.

Yaquinto, Marilyn. *Pump 'Em Full of Lead: A Look at Gansters on Film.* New York: Twayne, 1998.

APPENDIX I: PERSONAL CORRESPONDENCE FURNISHED BY DR. JOHN DE MATTEO

Drs. Potter and Jenkins

"Demolishing the Mafia Myth has laid the foundation for a minor academic industry, and it is appalling to see how few of these revisionists attacks have been incorporated into the views of the press, government, or law enforcement."

A. Bartlett Giammatti

"It is finally as foolish to deny existence of Italian-American gangsters and criminal combines of various kinds. It is as it is [sic] bigoted to believe that the Mafia (or Cosa Nostra or any other media-sanctified name) is all-pervasive or that in America only Italian-Americans are gangsters, worse that [sic] because one has an Italian surname one may be must be [sic], 'connected,' in some sinister way."

Drs. Morris and Hawkins

"a large proportion of what has been written [about organized crime] seems not to be dealing with an empirical matter at all. It is almost as though what is referred to as organized crime belongs to the realm of metaphysics or theology."

Dr. Robert J. Kelly

"Since the late 1960s, when the government began to show some interest, public hearings, prosecution, and the testimony of members of crime groups, have focused attention on Italian dominated criminal activities. For the public organized crime and Italian Mafia or La Cosa Nostra became essentially synonymous. This slanderous impression was and is more fiction than fact; other crime groups also were deeply involved in vice and rackets.

"As the apotheosis of organized crime, Cosa Nostra reflects not so much an obsession with the folklore of feudal bandits descending on Brooklyn and Little Italys as it betrays an ignorance of the facts. The fabrication have [sic] become glossed over so creatively and ingeniously, they have created an intrinsic fascination that not even the participants in the real thing, who ought to know better, are tempted to believe. Not unlike the debates about the existence of God, all that is known about the Mafia seems to be known by now except whether it really exists. Many scholars still find the evidence conflicting and unreliable – particularly the idea of a nationally coordinated conspiratorial brotherhood. Scholars demythologize the legend as quickly as popular writers and film makers re-mythologize the grandeur of Godfather."

Dr. Peter A. Lupsha

"Unfortunately, the attention to organized crime has often been myopic and monocular, focusing narrowly on Italian-American groups, referred to as Mafia or Cosa Nostra, when in fact organized crime is a process which can occur within any ethnic group or social system."

Potter and Jenkins

"... in the recent federal war on organized crime, the great majority of targets have been Italian."

Professor Messick
"... -the Mafia as such, was but a minor part of the whole [of organized crime]. Robert Kennedy focused on Italian criminals because the Italian community is politically impotent."

Drs. D. Smith and R.A. Alba
"The notoriety of Italian-American gangsters does not justify belief in the Mafia but merely reflects it, since that belief leads law enforcement agencies [and the press] to concentrate their energies on Italians with the result that much is known about them and little about others."

Dr. Hess
"As it did [and does] for Northern Italians, today these theories of Mafia conveniently serves Americans as an explanation of social problems by reducing them to purely criminal problems.... The Mafia conspiracy enables Americans to embrace self-satisfying illusion that their problems are not the manifestations of a deep-seated structural stresses within the polity itself."

U.S. Senator Sam Nunn
"Organized crime should no longer be − if it ever should have been − described as being dominated by individuals belonging to any one ethnic group. Nor is it limited to 'traditional' criminal activities such as gambling, loan sharking, prostitution, pornography, and the like." "Organized crime never has known any ethnic bounds, and its activities run the gamut from the gutter to the board rooms of legitimate business and labor unions in this country."

Rudolph Giuliani
"If you do a case involving 19 members of the Mafia − Pizza Connection of the Colombo case of the many cases we've done − it gets a tremendous amount of attention. Front page. If you do a similar case, say a black organized crime group or a Colombian or Israeli or motorcycle gang or Nigerian, all of which we have done cases on in the last year − they get moderate attention. The end result is that it creates a impression that the Mafia is the only significant crime group. It isn't

true. It's only one of 20 or 25. We should try to find a way to balance the attention given to these so we don't continue this impression."

FBI Letter to Dr. John De Matteo

In a letter I received from the FBI, dated May 21, 1992, we note welcome changes in the government's position regarding Mafia predominance. The FBI had the following to say about Italian-American criminality: "It would be not only inaccurate, but unfair, to suggest that organized crime today is made up exclusively of individuals of Italian origin. Organized crime is not monolithic and consists of individuals with a wide variety of backgrounds".

THE EYES OF THE OTHER

Bruno Roberti
ROME, ITALY

A line of American cinema I would consider *foundational,* at least since work on *mise en abîme* has assumed a formalistic value for the gaze, in which theory was implicit, is that of the connection to other cultures following immigration (whether related to economic or intellectual reasons). The contamination between visual cultures and styles, such as "Latin" and Middle-European (I have in mind Capra and Von Sternberg), has always translated into a particular imaginary attitude. In this sense, there would not seem to exist a specificity of cinema realized by Italian-American directors if not, paradoxically, in their shunning a specific identity; in the exaltation of the "Other"; in the construction of a space that jibes with a notion of difference contained in the very act of looking – a difference that is displacement, dislocation, contamination. Above all, Italian and American elements are present in the gaze of Italian-American directors who have characterized the cinematographic imaginary of the last thirty years, as a type of double, imaginary valence – a gaze shifted to the second power. Indeed, the actual "feeling," imagining, and thinking Italian are, in themselves, as Mario Perniola rightly points out, a site of blending which ignores the pure subject, the original identity: "The Italian mix is something profoundly different because in Italy these original identities are initially absent; from the beginning, we have dealt with copies, with repetitions, with simulacra that have taken the place of the originals."[1]

Thus the "difference" constituted by this blended Italian creativity paradoxically assumes a type of "altered" identity, an "impure purity" or "diversified specificity" that is very much in tune with and expresses itself in the *mise en abîme* and in the filmic space intended as the "dislocation" of the gaze, as the "impurity" of the aesthetic act. On the other hand, the American space contains an equally "original" contamination due to dislocation, the myth of

[1] Mario Perniola, *Transiti* (Bologna: Cappelli, 1985), 131.

the border, the fluidity of colonies, and a collective nomadism that, however paradoxically, takes its shape in the supremacy of the individual as an affirmation of solitude in relationship to the emptiness of space and territory. Opposing this is anarchism, and an Italian "agrico-sedentary" collectivism; a constitutive paganism of blending and "feeling," external to the "I" and overflowing onto the community landscape. This is characteristic of another Italian specular paradox: a community, an enlarged "family" that feels well beyond the subject, in the landscape, in a "land" that shuns borders, taking roots only in the imagination, in a type of "processionality" of vision and feeling that does not have any sense of ownership but rather of belonging to the external, to the outside alone, to feeling out of sight – not part of the "scene." In fact, Perniola writes:

> At the moment in which men become statues, mannequins, marionettes, their sensibility moves towards the external, to the environment, to the landscape of which they themselves are nevertheless an integral part. The Italian enigma consists in the fact that the human element is endowed with an external emotionality which does not belong to it in an intimate manner, but with which it nevertheless participates. Actors and spectators are part of the scene to the same degree as the curtain and backdrop: if the scene is imbued with emotionality, they too are infused with it. The adoption of a point of view in favor of blending and repetition implies the entry into a ritual rather than mythical mode of thought, whose fundamental traits only now have begun to spring forth. The specificity of feeling without subjectivity, of anonymous affectivity, of an impersonal emotionality, which makes up the nucleus of the Italian experience, still remains unthinkable.[2]

In this sense, feeling Italian becomes a collective "corpus;" the fellow citizen is blended with a communal form of the city, not at all fixed into an idea superimposed as rule, but rather into an autochthonous inter-subjectivity that excludes a divine or metaphysical identity, which concerns the movements of chance and custom constituted as "habitus," dress, clothes. And in this sense, the "short-circuit" of the two elements, Italian and American, in the imaginary construction and in the visual obsessions of the directors we shall examine (Brian De Palma, Martin Scorsese, and Michael Cimino), can be traced back to the critical reading of their films according to an aesthetic idea which brings us back to the concept

---

[2] Mario Perniola, *Enigmi* (Genova: Costa e Nolan, 1990), 162.

of "impure cinema," as intended by Andrè Bazin. This is cinema as representation to the second degree; the manifestation of technique and its transformation into style; the unification of art and technique as a blending of purity and contaminated movement; a merging of the immobile and mobile. This is the "broad" notion of *displacement* understood as contamination and "fusion" of glances in the filmic space, precisely as Sandro Bernardi describes it in a collection of essays dedicated specifically to the notion of the "displaced narration" of cinema.

Displacement is the enemy of every necrophilic purity and of every closure of borders. It is also a movement of escaping oneself. We could also say that cinema always proves to be different; it always has its own roots and models elsewhere; it continually transforms the movement of appropriation into a movement of expropriation; it makes acquisition a loss, and loss an acquisition. In this regard, one is reminded of John Ford's view of cinema as a great machine of hybridization and contamination. In a *New York Times* article from 1928, Ford speaks of the great cities – crossroads where race and culture are blended: Babylon, Samaria, Rome, Alexandria, Baghdad, Constantinople. We can have an idea of these city-crossroads, says Ford, by looking toward Hollywood: an intersection of worlds and cultures as much as cinema, slippage, and displacement of territories. He states: "It is, since I know it for what it is, a city of successes and failures, of hopes realized and not, of doubts and prostrations, from which I can deduce that the other great places of the universe have been, throughout history, neither greater or lesser than my city, which has less monuments erected in honor of the great accomplishments of man and more restless tribunals where one is in constant search of that which man will never find."[3]

In this sense, we find displacement configured in a construction of space which we will see is typical of the directors discussed here. This is attained by filming the "set," both the landscape and the bodies, beyond a prospective identification and "an ideology of the identity of the gaze, and instead intrinsic to the predilection for visual flux, for the sequence of shots, for the concentric, circular,

---

[3] S. Bernardi, ed., *Storie dislocate* (Pisa: Edizioni ETS, 1999), 16.

and orbital design of the camera, as well as to the design and action of the characters, and also to the way of thinking that organizes the story with visionary reach. In the imaginary of these directors, then, the displacement of vision and of knowledge is a rereading by another name, a projection of personal models and landscapes on other models and other distant landscapes, a finding oneself in the Other and vice versa, a discovering that each one of us finds him/ herself in communality with other unknown subjects whom s/he carries within him/herself. Displacement is not only reception, but also projection and interpretation; we could say, inverting a famous phrase of Proust, a "looking with one's own eyes after having seen with those of another." A fusion of two, or indeed many gazes: "It is therefore a blending overall, a hybridization of cultures, of points of view, of perspectives. Projection, super-impression: these words show us that dislocation is cinema by another name, that cinema is dislocation, an impure art," as Bazin says. Above all, because of this impure constitution, cinema is the privileged object of twentieth-century aesthetics and of the entire twentieth-century culture, which develops under the sign of impurity, contamination, and hybridization. Dislocation is primarily, I would say, contamination, in which one unites oneself with another, remaining nevertheless oneself; it is similar to the vital process in which, as Freud observed, all individuals, joining together, renew themselves.[4]

I. The Drifting of Identity

In De Palma, Scorsese, and Cimino, the theme of *drift* becomes, by means of a visual obsession, a *form* that reveals a thought – that of the dissolution and blending of identities, to the point of their disappearance or metamorphosis. With regard to what we have said above, it is not by chance that the fusion of the gaze in alterity, in a *drift* understood as much as *point of origin* from a land imagined and contaminated such as Italy, as well as an undecidability about one's own belonging or, better, one's mixed roots, produces a visionariness that inserts itself both into the themes and forms of the films of these directors. It is as if the *other from oneself*, seen as a restless double but also a necessary com-

---

[4] S.Bernardi, "Fusione di sguardi" in *Storie dislocate*, 12

pensation and interior conjoining, is, from the first works of these directors, assumed in the formal context of the work, obsessively permeating it.

Early on, these films venture into a *dangerous* territory, raising the *other from oneself* as an obscure figure, but also as a form of aesthetic pleasure, as a capacity for *passing* through forms, as a necessity of living the creative and aesthetic experience, the construction of the imaginary, the filmic forms as a space of desire which simultaneously circumscribes and liberates. It is a gaze that, *crossing over* the point of "passage," the point of vision where it turns itself over into the "other gaze," is capable of redeeming the *original guilt* of the images, that is, of freeing itself, in a process of crossing over, of the metaphysics of an original and "judging" image. We will see how this creative and visual gesture is also a gesture of overturning, of insurrection, of an assault to the heavens; of a challenge to the "God" of vision, to an inimical father or brother in as much as they are figures of the struggle or interdiction, but also figures of the origin. With regard to the stimulation of the aesthetic experience of characters and the process of *passing* beyond forms and identities, Anna Camaiti Hostert states:

> The transitional element is indeed essential in so far as it is not a means but a different end, an end in itself. *Passing* in fact is a mode of conceptualizing the psycho-political dynamics that structure experience in all of us and constitutes a phase of continuous crossing over, which opens spaces to the expression of fluidity and the plurality of desire. It is running through the self again, mining at its foundations the authenticity of the "I." It is not *passing* "through" or "by way of" someone else, but entering into a foreign terrain for which one does not know the self that everyone has always interpreted as one's own.[5]

The obsession of filming from a window the *other from oneself,* the foreign, the stranger (but also filming as a coercion to repeat the variants of one's own desire), is possessed by the character of Rubin/De Niro in the early films of De Palma – *Greetings* and *Hi Mom.* Furthermore, the insistence on voyeurism and on the double, on the variants of looking without being seen, on the obsessions of the gaze and of guilt in later films such as *Carrie, Two Sisters, Home Movies,* and *Dressed to Kill,* confirm in De Palma's

---

[5] A. Camaiti Hostert, *Passing* (Castelvecchi: Roma, 1996), 26.

cinema how the *other from oneself* is incorporated so as to alter not only the identity of the characters but also the very process of vision.

It would seem that De Palma values highly a strategy that is characteristic of what Perniola consistently describes as the Italian cultural process, which is actually related to confrontation and the attitude toward other cultural identities – toward the *foreign,* seen as something that invades a territory. Thus it is not by chance that an Italian American would obsessively adopt this strategic module, precisely at a time in which he uses the machine of vision, the mechanical eye of cinema in order to *spy* on the American *modus vivendi.* Perniola, in fact, writes:

> Conquering the adversary without coming into contact with him, assuming his look, appropriating his reasons, taking his place. There is a way to conquer one's own enemy, much less dangerous and uncertain in its unfolding and much more effective and radical in its results [. . .]. It consists of stripping him of his identity, transforming oneself into an indiscernible copy of him [. . .]. Whoever puts himself in his enemy's place, vanishes, cancels, and abolishes his identity; he opens a space of indetermination and indiscernible differences. In fact, the absence of origin, of identity, of autochthony, tied to the multiplicity of relationships, bonds, and influences, not only allows for approaches, couplings, and other varied combinations, but more profoundly it attributes to blending a prominence and an essential function, an autonomous dimension where the difference of mere disorder is will.[6]

It is in *Raising Cain* where De Palma constructs a sort of insistent and perfect visual theorem of that "dark brother" (Cain, indeed) whom everyone carries within as a "double" personality, but also as the "other eye" that spies on you from within. De Palma implacably proceeds to an abolition of identity and the overturning of false and true, a slipping away of the real and an inversion of dream. The spectator becomes captured in this design; he falls into a trap precisely because he feels implicated in the game of entering and leaving the protagonist's gaze, of never being sure of who is watching what or if that which one is watching is reality or fantasy, present or past. With regard to the spectator's implicated gaze, De Palma states:

---

[6] Mario Perniola, *Transiti* (Cappelli: Bologna, 1985), 125ff.

> The film is based on a non-linear idea of time. Even when I play with
> the dream within the dream – within yet another dream, – I wish to
> transmit to the spectator the idea or the doubt that whatever he sees
> could be true or not. Therefore, what a person sees in a multiple per-
> sonality can be true or merely imaginary. With film, one immediately
> enters the perception of a character who has a multiple personality.
> Therefore, the task of the spectator is surely that of trying to understand
> what is or is not reality. When one works on form – and I refer here not
> only to film but also literature, music, and painting, – it thus happens
> that we must accept and assume the risk of a clash with the spectator.[7]

It is no coincidence that this continual and deadly overturning of
vision is a sign of an *upset* identity, yet it is also a sign of "growth,"
of "raising" the "dark" son/brother because of an obsession with
"family origins," with a "paternal line," with a generation as
displacement and regeneration, and with a blood-line that implies a
displaced identity. This double personality is also the dual meaning
of the title: "to raise," to make grow, but also upset, displace
identity; to allow the other to grow within oneself as much as
allowing another gaze to penetrate the spectator's gaze, but also an
other gaze, which does not belong.

Raising Cain enables the gaze "to raise hell," to create bedlam,
confusion; to introduce a "devil's eye" into the process of constructing the real. The "original" father splits into the father/psy-
chiatrist that substitutes him in Doctor Nix, who "raises" multiple
personalities, and then studies and analyzes them.

The "construction" of an unconscious image, the creative process as a continual search/divergence of paternal omnipotence, the
crucial rapport of this process with temporality, with time seen as
an abolition of space and a process of reversion, of continual creation, and of an opening into infinity of spaces of appearance – this
is the secret meaning of that "constructing" or "raising" Cain, the
other from oneself or the dark brother: *Raising Cain*. De Palma, as he
tells us in the title, "displaces" continually the stature of imagistic
identity, engaging with the spectator in a game of "clearing" and
"constructing" both the image and the perception, confusing (this
is the idiomatic meaning of *Raising Cain*) both who sees and what
is seen.

---

[7] "Conversazione con Brian De Palma," Bruno Roberti e Stefano Paba, eds. *Filmcritica* 429
(November 1992), 484ff.

The temporality of this film becomes a type of abstraction, a depository of every possible identity, of every possible level of reality, of every possible image. Clocks, like transcendental objects *à la Dalì*, become liquid and render into liquid form the film, "dipping" it in its very own imagistic virtuality. The lake where bodies sink and reemerge is a mirror/lake of time, a transcendental depository of images, an infinite bubble of "virtual" reality. Equally "virtual" and conceptual is the delirious and lucid construction of the set in *Raising Cain*: the park-games, the bedroom, the elevator, and the lake are all sets closed in on themselves and opened continually onto other universes of identity.

This "bringing up" and "raising" within oneself an Other, or rather, the same "alterity" as opposition, or even destructive impulse, with respect to the calm, smiling, and mystifying "identity" of society, we also find in the process of crossing over, of sliding into the night of Travis's own mind in a film such as Martin Scorsese's *Taxi Driver*. When De Niro/Travis tries to pull out his gun in front of the mirror and turns to his own image, questioning it, or even when his eye is constantly shifted and displaced in the rear-view mirror of his taxi, we see an ecstasy of lost identity, to the point that this progressive drifting of identity, this "ritual" transformation (Travis cuts his hair as a sign of his radically different tribal membership) presents itself in the end as a realistically documented pathology in the eyes of the spectator. Reality and fiction, in this sense, short-circuit in hand-book fashion. A key to Scorsese's cinema could readily be the mixing of fiction with simulations of a documentary-like reality. One need only think of the opening sequence of *Who's That Knocking at My Door*, where Scorsese's mother is preparing a meet loaf, anticipating the culinary scenes in *Italianamerican*, or even *The Last Waltz*, or *Made in Milan*, where the function of the staging lies in the reconnaissance of the surrounding reality. In *Taxi Driver*, Steven Prince is a Mephistopheles figure who, with his arms, allows Travis Bickle to overstep definitively the threshold of sanity. Following this film, Scorsese shoots *American Boy*, a sort of portrait in which Steven Prince hyperbolically narrates his past as drug-user and murderer, from which we deduce that he was always on the other side. The story of his life is as much a self-destructive calvary as that of Travis. Like the latter,

Steven isn't surprised by anything, and seems to have reached the very same apathy that the protagonist of *Taxi Driver* attains only at the end. In this regard, Alberto Pezzotta states:

> Already in *Italianamerican*, the documentary of his parents and of the Sicilian origins of his family, Scorsese's own presence in the images is the source of a particular ambiguity. The director's presence has always functioned as a seal; it guarantees that the image is signed, and indeed Scorsese's appearances in *Taxi Driver* and *After Hours* also function at this level. Scorsese's presence in his documentaries, instead, renders uncertain the property of the image. If Scorsese is in front of the camera, he is obviously not behind it to control what happens. In *Italianamerican*, his parents never address their son, who is on the margins of the frame. He is not a character, but he is neither the eye that watches. He is a witness, most likely, who with his presence on the side guarantees the veracity of the images. In *American Boy*, Scorsese's presence is more oscillating (at times he is there, at others he is not) and has a different function. Looking into the camera soon after the opening of the film, Scorsese complains that there is not enough film to shoot the scene of Steven's entry into Mamoli's house. The scene, however, with its macho fight between both characters, is shown in its entirety, without any breaks, which proves Scorsese has lied. Later on, he addresses the camera man to tell him to stop shooting, and that anyhow the material he is shooting is too weak to be kept in the editing. We, however, see the scene. Scorsese thus introduces a certain displacement between the film (the camera-cinema) and the reality he shoots; he wants to instill doubt in the spectator, before (and after) having subjected him to a disturbing experience, such as that of the story Steven Prince tells of his own life.[8]

In the chronologically last film, *Bringing Out the Dead*, Scorsese shoots the crossing-over and mental displacements of *Taxi Driver* and, with the same ambiguity of vision of *American Boy*, he positions the eye of the camera in the frenzied design of the character's perception and memory. Here, Nicholas Cage is the nurse who works the night-shift in an ambulance in order to save those on the verge of death, and it is his mind, his interior gaze, that transports us visually into the streets of the living and dead, ghosts and real passers-by. His gaze/thought, which slips progressively into the gaze of the camera and into Scorsese's own thought, is obsessed by guilt: that of not having saved a woman from death in time – and this guilt materializes into a vision and almost

---

[8] Alberto Pezzotta, "American boy, una storia vera," *Filmcritica* 428 (September-October 1992), 438ff.

identifies itself with the delirious and mysterious capacity of the protagonist to see the dead mixed with the living. The spaces of *Bringing Out the Dead* are suspended between crude realism and intense mental hallucination, between a state of wakefulness and dream, between life and death, between closed and opened eyes. These are like the "stations" of a Medieval drama that stages the levels of sin and salvation: the hospital, the van, the "oasis" of the opium den, those living underground where an *other* virgin gives birth, the "romantic" sewers, the sidewalks, muddy or snow-covered or fading, if not rolling like tomb stones, the streets of blinding light, all sped up in their nocturnal fugue. This "double" coming to light and immersing oneself immediately into the dark, this double consisting and prolonging of visions of pain and death, of piety and violence, of nostalgia and rage, is the existential condition between the two "states" of consciousness: a "double view" and a double feeling, in pleasure and in guilt as well as in pain and redemption, which in Scorsese concretizes yet again in bodies that "feel" and "see" at the same time. This represents a sensoriality that unites the two levels of seeing, or the infinite levels of a vision frantically polymorphic, simultaneously present, trans-fixed and driven in the cutting razor of a doubled and multiplied temporality, becoming speed but also a breaking through of the visual trajectory. The form of a mobile and altered eye, as if popping out of one's head – like the eye in the painting "The Scream" by Munch, an eye fleeing from itself, – is shot here as a symbolic image of a condition between "heaven and earth," as it was in *After Hours* and *The Last Temptation of Christ.* This is an eye that has taken on the guilt of seeing, namely that of the connection between the gaze and the consummation of self, between the temptations of time and the promises of eternity.

In Scorsese's film about Christ, the temptations symbolize pre-cisely a trip of the eye that sees too much and becomes a fiery cir-cle; but it also transforms itself into a psychedelic gaze, which con-tains in itself the "becoming" between spirituality and animality, and throws vision back into time – in a false eternity, a game of simulacra and ghosts of guilt and desire. Even in *Bringing Out the Dead,* there's a psychedelic Christ, the guardian of the artificial paradise offered by drugs and the suspended space that is then sud-

denly lit up with visions – the opium den. This Christ is destined
to a crucifixion in mid-air, neither in heaven nor on earth, pierced
by a stiletto in the absurd breast of existence. His bloody body
hanging mid-air in one of the strongest sequences in the film is
indeed like the condition of suspension between life and death, day
and night, between the blinding light and the fireworks that punc-
tuate the background, and the profound dark of the nocturnal sky
against which the body is agonizing, crucified and tormented, like
Prometheus, by a devouring pain. In this film, the shifting of identity also becomes a means of escape from oneself; the sign of a wandering that presents itself as destiny, as a sinful brand on the one
hand, but also like a line of substraction of vision and the body
with respect to every possible subjection. Michel Maffesoli speaks
of this line of escape, of this wandering as a tension between mobile
and immobile, between open and closed, inside and out, stable and
unstable, typical of a tendency toward nomadism and a blending of
cultures and lifestyles. This constitutes an integration of two
spatialities that become, in the films of these directors, as we shall
see, the characteristic sign of a creative mode that explicates a
"contaminated" condition which is also aesthetic. Maffesoli states:

> Here is the problem that wandering poses: the flight is necessary, it
> expresses a nostalgia, it recalls a foundation. But for this flight to make
> sense, it is necessary that it have a stable point of departure. To go be-
> yond the limits, this limit must indeed exist. At the same time, rather
> than distinguishing separately one of the terms of the dialectic, it is
> indispensable to recognize them in their globality. It is a description of
> that which I have proposed to discuss as a "dynamic taking of roots." It
> is a question of a bipolarity which specifies as best I could the para-
> doxical antagonism of existence in its entirety. There is a place, and lines
> of flight are generated as a point of departure from this place; but so
> that this process acquires meaning, it is necessary that these lines be, in
> reality or phantasmagorically, denied, dissolved, exceeded, transgressed.
> This has to do with the sign of a tragic sense of existence: nothing is re-
> solved in a synthetic going beyond, but everything lives in a tension, in
> a permanent incompleteness. Thus the static needs errancy or, to refer
> to particular emblematic figures, Prometheus needs Dionysus, and vice
> versa.[9]

There is a film by Cimino, *Desperate Hours* – the remake of a
claustrophobic *film noir* by William Wyler – in which compene-

[9] Michel Maffesoli, *Du Nomadisme* (Paris: Le Livre de Poche, 1997), 54.

tration from within (the house where the criminal holds hostage the family) and from the outside (the mountainous landscape that becomes a tragic scenario and the destiny of the flight toward self-destruction) becomes indeed the tightest connection between belonging and its refusal. The theatrical setting that gave Wyler an almost geometrical spectrum, in order to penetrate into the psychology of the two characters – of gangster and head of household, to the extent of placing them squarely face to face, in an equal and reciprocal relation in which both are determined to kill in order to defend their reasons, – gives Cimino the means of creating a series of points of view, and of playing with the contemporary vision of obtuse narration, which relies on a game of tensions. With regard to this film, Massimo Causo writes:

> The "inside" and "outside" reverse themselves and generate a flight-of-vision speed, a sort of crazed perspective. Michael's flight is an impossible one, similar to that which ends *The Sicilian*. It is a flight considered a sanctification of the abstraction of freedom (by itself) and blocked by a betrayal, a deception, which is projected by its own mind. Michael is a god who constructs himself from within and from without, internally and externally, looking and being looked at – a game that has fiction as its rule and emptiness as its space. Between him and reality, there is nothingness; that is, there is cinema, a place of gods deceived by images.[10]

This is the speed of a flight from one's own image projected "from an outside" (the set) into an "inside" (the house-trap, the prison, the trial chambers, but also cinema itself as a mental place in which bodies become phantasms). It is the speed of a flight toward imaginary spaces in which becoming "natural" and "animal" implies the openness of vision toward an alterity that both attracts and frightens, in the exchange of the gaze which contaminates the escape from oneself and the instinct of conservation of one's own image (such as the deer that comes directly out of *Deer Hunter* and the lake in the mountains that prefigures *Sunchaser*). This constitutes the pushing of the body, the deformation of destinies and the connection with the Other as "passage" (or "transference") through instruments – prosthesis of something that has "taken refuge within ourselves" and makes us assume, in flight, an animal-like existence,

[10] Massimo Causo, "Le illusioni di un dio," *Filmcritica* 411-412 (February 1992), 36ff.

revealed indeed by "signs or bits of animality," of corporeal deformation, all of which comprises in Cimino an imaginary of contamination and blending of identities in a majestic slippage of landscapes. In Cimino (see the animal totems – the deer, the buffaloes,
the bears, the greyhound, the dragon, and the eagle – that appear in
each of his films), man becomes animal not without the animal
becoming at the same time spirit, human spirit, the physical spirit
of man present in the mirror. Causo continues:

> A barren spatiality opens *Desperate Hours*, the exhibition of a limpid and
> serene limitless horizon, described by a gaze free of prospective
> coordinates, open and capable of losing itself in the visual space. It
> almost seems that Cimino amplifies his gaze in front of the rounding of
> space; he breaks it into a thousand decentered and peripheral visions,
> which are in some ways perimetric. Without granting time to the organ-
> ization of vision, the camera seems to take on an autonomous rhythm
> with respect to the priority of the gaze, pretending to ignore the
> necessity of polarizing vision. Following a kind of schizophrenic geome-
> try, Cimino organizes the entire sequence of the escape from court
> according to a masterly perspectival disarticulation. It stuns the gaze,
> upsets the order of vision; it mutes the angular incidence, displacing
> itself in the field of the eye with unexpected swervings and perspectival
> inversions. And the instability of vision becomes a slave of the instability
> of meaning: we are led by the hand by a fluctuating eye, brought into a
> flight that is an illusion, a "coming into play" or, better still, the coming
> into a play made of fiction and dispersions in the space of the mind.[11]

Even in a film like *The Sicilian*, Cimino constructs a false visual perspective and, in an almost baroque manner, presents to us not
the dry chronicle of the parable of Giuliano the bandit (as in Francesco Rosi's film), but an imaginary game that takes on the figure
of the bandit and of Sicily like a great mythological topos. This
enacts the continuous irruption of dreams, of the images and fantasies on/of the bandit, in the visual framework of a majestic and
blinding landscape, filmed from reality and felt with both one's
own and the "altered" eye of one who, like Cimino, has developed
as a director in an equally adhering and impassioned way, loving
Ford and American spaces, but also Visconti and Italian landscapes.

In *The Sicilian,* death frames the Dream. When the film begins, after an ascending spiral and a circular panorama that emphasizes the baroque and the empty sky of Palermo, it is the cadaver

---

[11] Massimo Causo, "Le illusioni di un dio," 36ff.

thrown in front of a church and devoured – under fire – by the eyes/flash of the photographers that, like an image offered up to consumption, meets us head-on, multiplied by photography and the blinding light. Death and the earth, like shadow and light, the dark of the casket where the stolen grain is hidden and the gold from the grain fields where the peasants work, wrapped by a fiery light, as well as by the very spikes of corn that stick out like a mythological trace, are all a concrete and eternal metaphor of the destiny of images. It is as if those images stuck out in the eternity of a myth or cycle, and were stolen by the "foreign" eye of the lord of death, just as the beautiful, young, and illusory image of Persephone was stolen in the fields of Sicily by the shadowy figure of Hades. This duality of blinding light and shadow is recurrent in Cimino, and functions as a sign of inside and outside; an exchange of gazes between the stranger and the friend, between one's own woman and the woman of the Other. It is the archetypal image of the "couple," the individual who reflects himself and dissolves in his own Other, in a companion (male or female) as a collective sign of a community's destiny (that same "originary couple" signaled by destiny that we saw disintegrate and then come back together in the *Deer Hunter;* duplicate itself and then each member cross roads into an ultimate, unforgettable duel in *The Year of the Dragon;* the couple multiplied and violated by the history of collective destiny in *Heaven's Gate*). This characteristically Ciminian image between solitude and the need to see oneself reflected in the Other gives rise, in *The Sicilian,* to an imaginary schism, to an irrealism that breaks up continually in images. Character and Set, the individual destiny of Salvatore Giuliano and the collective space of the imaginary Island, hide themselves at the time when they should be even more visible. Andrea Pastor thus writes:

> Giuliano is a simulation, a hyperbole, a Rhetorical Image that presents itself as such and aspires only to a presence in the visionary space on the screen. The imperturbable gaze of Christopher Lambert is similar to that of a blind man: his struggle is, in fact, that of someone who, not wanting to see an unacceptable and frustrating reality, blinds himself and adopts a second vision, another gaze, the propeller and motor of a subversive action only partially destined to failure ("I shall remain with you" is one of his last evangelical affirmations). While Prince Borsa is captured in a frame that constitutes the circuit of the seer and the seen,

of the subject and the object of the gaze in the act of spying with a telescope on the peasants' revolt, and while Don Masino claims to be both-
ered by the Sicilian dust which at times blocks his vision, Giuliano, on
the other hand, does not worry about looking at reality according to the
coordinates of a gaze both omnipotent and sure of its own detached
identity. But he upsets reality from a specular point of view by day-
dreaming, with anarchic omnipotence, of a timeless gaze, forever returning in a subversive imagination that no longer has fathers or sons.[12]

Cimino's cinema continually sets up a multiplicity that is becoming, a dislocation in real geography as well as in the imaginary
one on the screen, not only of cultures and ethnicities, of territo-
riality and of grand temporal and spatial areas, but also of tales and
stories that carry with themselves characters, as a wind that blows
not from official History but from distant legends. These are new
lands and new models of "peoples" that dislocate themselves, as a
community, in a becoming that is constituted by their surroundings, by a set of events that naturally reclaim an intense
geography rich in cultural events, different from history's linearity
in a static conception of culture.

II. The Eye from the Sky

A stretched-out eye, the oblong form characteristic of the Asian
eye, seems to obsess Martin Scorsese in *Kundun*, the film dedicated
to the childhood of the Dalai Lama and set to music by Phillip
Glass. The images, and their generation, are from the beginning set
up against those almond-shaped eyes that the Dalai Lama "closes"
in front of reality, opening them on a "dream scene." The eye of
Kundun is literally the eye of the film *Kundun*, the eye of a "man,"
who in the religious community is a manifestation of the god – it is
the eye of the film itself. Man/god coincides with the film, and
therefore with the eye of the man/director Scorsese. It is the process
of "hubris," of a gesture of challenge to the heavens, that we know
well in Scorsese (Paul's upward cry in *After Hours*, or the call that
plummets down from above, like a voracious bird that "elects" the
Christ of *The Last Temptation*) – a gesture always connected to the
guilt of looking. Looking too much and too insistently signifies (as
in *Life Lesson*, a Scorsese episode in *New York Stories* where the eye

---

[12] Andrea Pastor, "Mitogrammi," *Filmcritica* 380 (December 1987), 668ff.

of the painter is obsessed by his lover's foot) hallucinating the real, rendering it delirious, absorbing it in a process of vision that carries with itself the process of creation and that of the destruction of this creation when it is seen. The process of *impermanence* of images in Scorsese seems to concern the very destiny of cinema, or the setback of the filmmaker who, although stopping time and space in an image, destines those same images to a process of deterioration closely connected with its opposite: conservation (the images that disappear and deteriorate and the attempt to safeguard their challenge to eternity, a theme that is also the *ragion d'essere* of Scorsese's continued project of restaurating classic films).

Thus we understand how Scorsese's *religious* tension is inseparable from a *secular*, almost materialistic, if not nihilistic, immanence; and how a certain Buddhism (one close to the hermeneutics of "vanity" and to the moral-didactic use of the concept of "illusion" innate in a baroque and Jesuit Catholicism) has always been present in his films. The power of the Dalai Lama *to see with his eyes closed* on the border between dreaming and being half-awake, the *direction* of time that materializes in a *real* form and configuration, is the same power that both elevates and condemns Christ in *The Last Temptation*, and is namely the power to be destined to vision *in every direction*, to an *impossible* vision, always in motion, of time and space, which is the same power of the "mechanism" of cinema. Thus the figure of Kundun in flight, who closes his eyes in both directions of time, the coming and going, in order to see the skies and mountains "from a bird's eye view," as well as his own eyes which, in the end, after having seen the "return" signaled by the blood of the mortal wounds which will pierce his acolytes and horses, hesitate to contemplate a simple and majestic landscape similar to a Zen painting. In this manner, Scorsese tells his tale through an eye that seems not to belong to the individual as much as to a transcendental universe of vision.

In *Kundun*, it is a matter of shock, "wonder," and an opium-like vision of one who is both trapped and saved by images, an alternation between the prison of the gaze and the liberation from it. On the one hand, a hallucinated reality: the holy city, the walls, the veils, the drapes, the darkness of the rooms and temples (so similar to the "prohibited city" of the last emperor of Bernardo

Bertolucci's film); under the "tutelage" of priests and regents, the *innocent* eyes of a baby become burdened with an original guilt, with the "choice" of sacrifice, as well as of a totally different vision of the world. On the other hand, there are Kundun's dreams, a place where not by chance does reality seem to be more accessible; and in this sense, the film seems to be the story of an "education" and "vocation" for cinema, for the recounting of the real through a dream, the vision, a type of autobiographical novel of education and apprenticeship of Scorsese himself, a "man of dreams" like Kundun, and like him, despite his imagination, immersed in the violence of the world. The telescope, the magic lantern, the light in the dark, the golden watch dissembled and reassembled, the "mandalas" drawn and erased, the pictures cut from the newspapers – these are all "figures" in the film that result in a sort of *transposition* of that very obsession of the *superimposed eye* that had already marked Scorsese's other films. Visual obsessions are metaphorical of the process of composition and decomposition of the staging of the film, of the guilt as well as the innate grace in the act of generation and creation, which brings, through its reversal, the ever-returning destiny of destruction and dissolution. We think of the same eye superimposed and yet contained in the circle of Kundun's telescope, which refers to that other fluctuating and glowing-red eye in the night waters of *Cape Fear*, or the eye "out of sink," composed and "broken up" in the metaphor of the *gaze of the others* that crucifies the unknowing victim in *The Age of Innocence*.

Similarly, in Cimino's *Sunchaser*, a transcendental eye seems to attach itself to the moving camera, generating a visual nomadism that becomes increasingly pressing and adherent to the materiality and visionariness of the imaginary landscape associated with the animistic traditions of the Navahos. The film deals with the desperate journey of a terminally-ill man and a doctor kidnapped by him, who is forced into the search for a totem-image, a visual sign that, while reclaiming the kidnapper to his origins, will dissolve him in an aerial place cut off from time. The predominant image is of Sacred Mountain, which is simultaneously the image of an esoteric book that depicts it wound up in the clouds, like a talisman; the Mountain is thus both an abstract reality and a concrete representation. In this respect, Edoardo Bruno speaks of

> [an] image that imposes itself like a specter, like a myth of the indefinite. Cimino, with the camera glued to the two protagonists, follows the adventure along the long paths of an initiatory journey; he confirms his own visionary choice and traces the map of a "philosophical story," traversing step by step the principles of a reason that destroys rationality, in order to immerse itself fully into the native legend. The film rediscovers the wing of the legend as the landscape nears a dreaming state, the phantom of the Mountain where what is perceived is recreated in the imaginary space of a set four thousand meters high above the Utah mountains. To follow this initiation is an experience of the hermeneutic link that unites two different cultures.[13]

Once again, the split of the gaze in Cimino, the displacement of identities, the irruption of diversity in the mythical territories, all this has to do with a kind of fusion of the eye of the one who sees in the different visual planes (filmmaker, character, spectator) with a flux, a becoming, a dissolving of the visions themselves, as if led by an animal instinct. This is the theme of the "mobile" connection, the open link between the "animal" (and that multiplicity which "stirs" man, as [Elias] Canetti says) and the environment which, as Ubaldo Fadini writes,

> sends us further back to a pre-individual intensity, to the fluxes of energy which are difficult to codify, which delineate on different planes and in various forms the becoming-animal, the becoming-other, and this becoming as *expression* of the mutant whole. With regard to this optics, it is pertinent to consider Deleuze and Guattari's notion of metamorphosis as a becoming human of the animal and a becoming animal of the human in a single circuit. This represents a displacement or dislocation of the territory, which is a kind of "immobile and static journey," lived or understood intensely: the becoming animal is a "card of intensity" that shifts and escapes identity, giving rise to multiplying processes of subjectivity.[14]

Sunchaser deals with an animistic transformation, a becoming that is seen or imagined, a moving with the magic eagle that will signal the way from above, in the sun above the Mountain towards which the gaze will turn, as in the case of a different "hunter" – the *Deer Hunter*. The "hunter" of Cimino's most romantic and desperate film, with its "analogous" mount, takes place on the summit of an *altered state of consciousness*; it *maintains* the animal gaze, that of

---

[13] Edoardo Bruno, "Una linea filosofica," *Filmcritica* 465 (May-June 1996), 212ff.
[14] Ubaldo Fadini, *Principio Metamorfosi* (Milan: Mimesis, 1999), 70-71.

a stag, thereby becoming the animal itself. A shamanic film, *Sunchaser* attains its climax when the vision becomes unsustainable – a point of view beyond (good) conscience. It is more a *fusion of gazes* than an exchange, a contamination, a *crossing* of points of view: what the doctor sees (as a sign of the need to alter his eyes, to transform the gaze), he evidently *sees* by moving into the gaze of Blue (a name that is not only a color, but also the cypher of a vision that indicates the sky as much as the screen, the physical body as much as the spirit, the totem or protecting deity). By moving into his eyes, the doctor is penetrating the animal and spiritual eye of the eagle that "sees from the sky," and he participates in the chain of images associated with it: the canyon, the majestic clouds, the witch doctor's mysterious daughter and his own stone face, the disneyesque peak covered with fog, the Ford-like skies, the Spielberg-like flights. But the spectator is also able to move in those altered gazes, to inhabit Blue himself, who is at the same time a body, a man, and a mental state. Just as his body is both seer and dislocated eye, so the spectator sees by "becoming" Blue, taking his point of view, which is that of desire.

It is therefore a sacrificial ethics, the "sacred" sense of death as rebirth, which Cimino places at the center of the film. As in his *Thunderbolt and Lightfoot, Deer Hunter,* and *Heaven's Gate,* the victims are sacrificed in the name of a communal ethics or secret link that confounds mercy and guilt, relying on a "secret" anthropological belonging (emphasizing the ethnic element typical of a "tribal society," such as the Mafia of *The Sicilian,* the Polish emigrants of *Heaven's Gate,* the secret Chinese society in *The Year of the Dragon,* the Navaho ritualism and legend in *Sunchaser).* The entire final sequence is admirably done in a precipitous montage: a race towards the motionless waters of the sacred lake, a flight of three figures that are also three bodies in transition between human, animal, and spiritual, which become the vision of the Other in a vertiginous and abysmal exchange of subjectivities. This final sequence becomes therefore an *opening* of spaces, in which the waters of the lake and the abyss where the bodies disappear and dissolve in air are overturned by a ray of lightning that pierces the sky, generating a symphony of primal elements: earth/mountain, water/lake, air/eagle, fire/light of a sun in which the filmic image finds its own dissolution. It is an image that is ultimately concretized in the desert: seen, imagined, dreamed, faded, still with the eyes and the senses of the soul, transposed from the page of the design to the monumental but always intimate cinemascopic space of the wide screen. Pastor has noted how this empathetic process of the gaze is also connected to an "excessive" appropriation of visions, which constitutes a guilt as much as a choice, a sickness as much as a cure. He writes:

> One is liberated, dies, cries, feels closer and more solidary, is reborn, mutates identity because of too much seeing and its excess of visions: of monumental valleys and of hell's angels. Through this film [Sunchaser], one realizes an initiatory apprenticeship. We have learned to love and respect our gaze, our *pietas*. through a cinema both epic and intimate, which does not want to dissolve itself and which, by placing itself beyond codified genres, partially and tangentially pierces them in order to transcend them, thereby taking refuge, at the end of the game, within the solar and dazzling bosom of melodrama, the only act capable of containing and undoing such a disrupting act of force.[15]

This generates a reabsorption of the landscape, a swirl of images toward an elsewhere that does not have dimensions, where high and low coincide: an "apocalyptic" transfiguration of the landscape, which we re-encounter in Martin Scorsese's *Casino*. The filmmaker says it himself: "It is a chain reaction. Above all, I love movement and expansion in every sense. From a certain point, I almost expect that they lose control of what they do, that they become dragged by the movement of the film. All this is actually not very classical, but it is my method."[16] The form that the film gives to the psychological and narrative space contained in its very title is a baroque vision of the universal judgment, an expansion of the images carried into the spiral of their own composing and decomposing: the Casino, Las Vegas, the cathedral of game in the middle of the desert, the city of vice and of the chain of guilt, the new Gomorra, where the circuit of money moves every impulse and visionary signal. This is the concentric spiral of the Casino and the desert of "apparitions," of obsessive sublimation and the desert of temptation, of the guilt of seeing as well as of negated risk – the

[15] Andrea Pastor, "Rubando bellezza," *Filmcritica* 465 (May-June 1996), 219ff.
[16] Martin Scorsese in *Ecran* (Paris, 1975), 89.

fall into nihilism. One associates "The Passion of St. Matthew" with the film's initial trajectory of a body that is propelled into the air after a car explosion – its deflagration in a crucifixion of fire. It represents a vortical circle of visions that are ignited, punctuating a story of deceit and treason, of illusion and malediction. In *Goodfellas*, the Irish Henry Hill betrays the "family" that has accepted him, while in *Casino*, the Jewish Sam "Ace" Rothstein tries not to be excluded from the "family" that tolerates him, and is ultimately betrayed by those in whom he had put his trust.

Once again, we are witness to Scorsese's emphasis on the fallaciousness of appearances and their multiplication of the levels of fiction; to their tracing of a *fantastical* topography: the desert surrounding the city is an immense cemetery of potential graves. Moreover, as exemplified in a splendid sequence of shots of the Casino, there is always one who watches another without being seen; and above all, there is the eye of the camera or microphone of the FBI, which nevertheless does not provide closure, since those behind the camera are also being watched. The moral question of vision is either adhesion to or divergence from the point of view, never the mystifying acceptance of a presupposed judgment; guilt is inscribed in the gaze itself like a "vicious circle" in which interpretation is not exhausted in the (camera's) movement, but implies and complicates it. *Casino* starts from a gesture that is "given" as accomplished, one which will happen in the course of the film; and this twisting of the diegetic time establishes itself as a stylistic factor, a crossing of the baroque and the classical. Referring to the baroque design of the film, Bruno writes:

> It is nostalgia, as a given fact, as cold lament for not having been able to interrupt the flow of events, that expresses this sense of the baroque in which one finds that apparent contradiction defined by [Walter] Benjamin as "the destructive character" of the individual who does not see anything as lasting: "Where others clash against walls and mountains, he sees a street. He destroys that which subsists, not because of his love of ruins, but because of his love of the street that runs through them." [17]

The red dice turned in "Ace's" fingers is the eye of chance, the occult side hidden in the creases of the hand, the eye inscribed and

[17] Edoardo Bruno, "Ragione e nostalgia," *Filmcritica* 464 (April 1996), 117.

designed in its palm, the eye dug out, cupped and turned in the hand. "Ace" is a symbolic nickname that represents the ace of the "hand," the trick, the absolute cypher inscribed in the name, the absolute risk, the bet. In this universe where everyone spies everyone, where control becomes obsessive, Ace's love for Ginger and his subsequent marriage constitute an act of absolute faith. This embodies risk itself, the impossible bet, the Mallarmean throw of the dice (a "throw of the dice will never abolish chance," says the French poet), the "hand" and the "the shooting glance," in which one either wins or loses all, and yet chance itself can never be conquered.

The body propelled into the air in the film's opening scene is the one telling the story, and his voice would seem to come from the dead. In the end, however, the one who appeared dead resuscitates, and the one who seemed to survive is eliminated. Therefore, the burial of the dead in the desert holes becomes an unearthing that is accompanied by the "destruction" of the temples of game and the resurfacing of *other* pyramids. The figure of resurrection – the return of the dead out of the tombs excavated in the desert, the "day of judgment," the apocalyptic "Dies Irae" – unites almost in a single point of vision the various symbolic-religious forms: the Hebraism of the divine ire, the Protestantism of the act of faith as bet, and the Catholicism of the resurrection of the flesh. Alessandro Cappabianca writes about this "eschatological" aspect of the film:

> We thought we were seeing a gangster movie, and instead we are confronted with the Apocalypse. But by now it becomes clearer that for Scorsese there is not a big difference between the Apocalypse and a gangster story: it cannot be anything other than the "Dies Irae," the deferred apocalyptic gaze, the characters implicated in the keeping watch of each other, and everyone under the inscrutable surveillance of the great (electronic) meta-Eye, the Ur-camera hidden in the highest point of the Casino, the closest to heaven, where the "children of Paradise" do not enter.[18]

Casino is about a stairway to heaven, but also about a chain of transformations: the cycle of money – its almost alchemical quality – and the vortex that constitutes its design, make up the apoca-

---

[18] Alessandro Cappabianca, "La città e il deserto," *Filmcritica* 464 (April 1996), 179ff.

lyptic structure of the film. Among Scorsese's most religious films, set to the tune of Bach's "Passion," this film seems to come out of the bursting of colors of that space where the Christ of *The Last Temptation* earned a psychedelic heaven. In a way, Sam's story is a "long epilogue" to it (Scorsese says instead that it is the long epilogue, rather than the sequel, to *Goodfellas*). Scorsese's cinema seems to have attained in this film that which Michel Serres insightfully formulates as the "multiple," the "fluctuation of multiplicity," the "thermodynamic inclination."[19] This generates a system of writing that makes text and form endlessly coincide. The mark of the initial explosion makes this "a film that burns;" the more it rises into the sky, by waves and thrusts that break the "story" and the bifurcation of voices, the more incandescent it becomes.

It would appear to be a voice from beyond, the one that gives rise to the story, but only apparently, since the fall reveals a deviation; the explosion is nothing but the form of the film itself, and therefore Sam's body lights but does not burn. Sam is a dead *undead*, or the glorious sign of a necessary resurrection, a Dionysian "passion," Nietzschean and nullifying; he is the "vicious" sign of a circle, and his voice generates the light of an "eternal noon," the vibration of the flames that becomes glitter, dazzle, and a sandy color. His irresistible ascent is configured as a voice and gaze that, although divergent, do not cease to inscribe themselves in the chain of exchanges and gazes. The crowd in the Casino is punctuated by the gaze that sees its game: the control of the circuit ends with the *eye from the sky*. Scorsese's camera shifts with this incessant chain reaction, leading the trajectory of money to a vortex, until it is raised to the level of the vision from above. It is not by chance that the filming design continually makes a *sign of the cross,* a perpendicular oscillation, a rapid movement from one place to the other according to a horizontal axis, followed by unexpected vertical capsizings in a vertiginous sequence of shots from above. In this way, the chain of value is transmitted without continuity within the chain of gazes, and this is an entry into the chain of bodies which *cannot die*. Money becomes bodies, the word becomes flesh, that is, the "god" that exercises total control from above cannot avoid re-

---

[19] Michel Serres, *Genesi* (Genova: Il Melangolo, 1985), 155ff.

flecting itself inversely in the abyss, in those holes excavated in the desert around Las Vegas, which look like the blazing graves of an apocalyptic scenery. In this sense, Scorsese's camera seems to tear apart from above, like a drill or an excavator, the multiple abysses of the earth, thereby apocalyptically envisioning the *last days.*

The figure of the eye's alternating elevation and fall is also present in other Scorsese images. This is a camera that, with rapacious speed, is precipitated into the crushed body that we know from the opening of *The Last Temptation,* or from the biblical "invective" towards heaven in *After Hours,* or the swirl of the camera's eye in the emptiness and blackness out of which, in the first film, Lazzaro comes out. It is this movement of the eye *from* the sky and *towards* the sky that signals the beginning of *Casino,* in which the camera flies in an indefinite and incandescent atmosphere in order to discover the abstract territory of light over Las Vegas, and then dive headlong only to regain flight over a desert very similar to that of Christ's "temptations." This movement provides throughout the film an impulse to other impossible points of view, which go through many other overturnings of visions. This is what happens in the refraction of a prism, or through the cocaine straw, or in the long sequences of shots that follow the trajectory of money and become sucked in by the black of the safes, or in the unexpected brusque shifts of the camera in a zig-zagging, vertical way, from one place to another in space, up to a point of release – a position of the gaze that invariably coincides with that from above, with somebody who watches from that position; with an impersonal *eye from the sky,* an incandescent eye often coinciding with the dazzling lights.

The point of vision of this *eye from the sky* returns us to the location of Scorsese himself, ironically proposed as a "hidden god," reminding us of a sequence of shots in *After Hours,* in which Scorsese himself directs the beams of light from the top of the dance-hall, or watches from above, a shadow on the window in the New York night. In the words of Serres: "The small pyramid grows, the average one grows even more, the large one makes it seem possible to construct a larger one, and soon the space of the world will be contained in the tomb of an immense, transparent, and boiling pyramid."[20] This is confirmed by Scorsese's visual and theoretical assertion that "I love pyramidal constructions. First of all, you establish a base, and then little by little all the elements take their place."[21]

Serres further explains how serial progression brings with itself the movement of violence, almost like a fatal design: "The law of the series is repeated in every ring, the place grows step by step. There is reason here, but there is also violence; there is order, but also growth and invasion."[22] This constitutes a visual labor that implacably gives shape to a story and to its meaning; it is a way of treating the time- and space-coordinates which we find in analogous form in the films of Brian De Palma. In them, space and its course throughout the slipping of the visions in the sequence of shots asks us to "work" *its* time, going as far as the excessive 10-12 minutes of opening of such films as *Carlito's Way*, *Snake Eyes*, and *Mission to Mars*. As Causo explains:

> De Palma also deals with a time in which space is not his, which does not belong to him, but is recovered in the sensory capacity of memory, in an elsewhere that uncovers itself in the slips of reality. This is the reason for the sounds of *Blow Out*, the mnemonic superimpositions of *Victims of War*, and all the rifts of past/present/absent/perennial that pervade the Depalmian frames – all extremely sensual, terribly sweet and distressing in their muffled dynamic, suspended on the fright of the assaulted present by the regurgitations of a recovered conscience. De Palma always allows the languid course of the present, understood as an act of being of his characters, who are disbanded in the territory of times relived with the open eyes of memory, recovered inside themselves in the anfractuosities of conscience that open unexpectedly to actuality, or to their potential for being an act of the present – a concrete vision of times and spaces uprooted from their elsewhere.[23]

This constitutes Greek tragedy revived by the inoculations of psychoanalytical discoveries. *Scarface* registered the dissolution of reason in the face of this discovery. *Carlito's Way* represents a reaction: the will to potency that resists fate. The predominance of a fall and the subsequent ascents, the overturning of visions, a ground upturned, a taking account of vision as slippage between

---

[20] Michel Serres, *Genesi*, 155ff
[21] Martin Scorsese in *Ecran* (Paris, 1975), 89.
[22] Michel Serres, *Genesi*, 155ff
[23] Massimo Causo, "Le illusioni di un dio," *Filmcritica* 411-412 (February 1992), 36ff.

life and death, and between dream and reality – these are the trajectories that are specified in the film and that become metaphor, like the sequence of shots of the insect trapped in a glass. Even if the outcome does not change, it remains the design of an inversion, the unmaking/making of an identity, the *other face* of a destiny.

The circle and the vortex are the visual sign of a story that, for Carlito, is about leaving or entering into/out of the circle of crime, the surrender of a design that both traps and liberates. It is a design that renders exactly the collision of desire and reality, the effort to resist and the inversion of the images – the imagery that resists up to the point in which it is inverted and becomes reversible. The flow of consciousness, its fluidity, is a trap; it is the confirmation of Carlito as prisoner in his labyrinth, the uncertain wandering of the coils of life. The camera rises, descends, drags, throttles – a detached, prehensile eye. It turns vitreous the gaze of its victims (the window of the camera and the drinking glass; the foggy glass of the dance school windows, through which Carlito sees the loved body of the girl); the camera moves the gazes inside and outside of the screen. As Carlo Scarrone has noted, the influence of Fritz Lang in this film is increasingly evident: "not to be able to see why one is enclosed in a maze of subterranean tunnels, the expectation of an ascent, the triumph of lowness, the characters as prisoners of the unconscious. For example, in the detail of the barrel of the gun that is about to shoot Carlito, the camera becomes the target of the bullet, which maintains throughout the film this extraordinary ballistic speed. Also evocative of Lang is the use of spaces that determine and trap (the station, the sequence of shots, and the stairs, the detail…)."[24]

In *Carlito's Way*, the *slowed-down*, suspended, frozen visions in the atemporal fixity of the white and black that vanish against color, soon cease to be a hypothesis about our field of perception: they *capsize*, physically and sensorially, by the action of a metonymical montage, within the single experience of the subject/actor/spectator who distances them as visual objects. De Palma's film, as described by Walter Mazzotta, becomes "the (visual) x-ray of an ontological schema: the figurality of a vision, the orbital form of

---

[24] Carlo Scarrone, "Flusso di memoria," *Filmcritica* 443 (March 1994), 113.

the eye – the out-of-orbit. As Levinas says in *Time and the Other*, "the present is the time of the existent and the act of its beginning, something that realizes the 'from-itself;' as such, it is pure evanescence, the form of an event closed in itself."[25] Carlito's desire, his approach to desire, is based on *seeing*, on detachment and on the *perception* that all visions imply. Detachment is in the projection itself, in the need for the object of desire to stand out like a shadow behind the glass, in a *fascinating* distance – a nearness/distance of the projection, an integrating dissolution of identities.

In De Palma, the sequence of shots is the unexplored territory of a cinema that is reborn in the movement of dislocation, in the oneiric but real displacement of a pleasure principle that superimposes itself over a reality principle; of a gaze of the Other that becomes a gaze of the *alteration of the real*. It becomes, as Lorenzo Esposito asserts, "the filmic space in which, in Welles-like manner, the fusion of the past in the present unfolds, where the depth of field evokes the part as well as the extension of a recovered memory, a wide mental space that exacerbates the generation of meaning. And cinema becomes, with De Palma, a visionary trajectory (the sequence of shots), a space-time continually contracted and expanded (the deconstruction of the sequence of shots), which renews the eternal search around the image, underscoring the uncertain but fascinating future."[26]

This is what happens in *Snake Eyes*, in the true/false reconstruction of a murder perpetrated in front of millions of gazes, and dissected into infinity by the protagonists and the TV cameras located around the ring, where "sliding" doors, ceilings, and walls, simultaneously open and closed, form the impossible dimensions of the world-arena in which almost the entire film takes place. This gives rise to transcendental dimensions that are re-engaged through a kind of opening/shutting from above, a mechanical prosthesis, a mechanical eye, a gigantic eye that flies over the arena and moves again the vision and the live "shooting," aligning itself, in the same "shot," with the movement of the murder.

---

[25] Walter Mazzotta, "Gli occhi di Carlito," *Filmcritica* 443 (March 1994), 117.

[26] Lorenzo Esposito, "I Milleocchi del serpente," *Filmcritica* 491-492 (January-February 1999), 19.

These are the "thousand eyes" of the crowd that attends the boxing encounter, of the serpentine coils that are stretched and flattened from above in the form of electronic eyes, composing a serpent-like, rotating, impersonal gaze. The eyes continuously *altered* by their own "*action*" ("*presa*") constitute the *crushed* space of a vision that incessantly disassembles, reinvents, and differentiates the frame of the events. These are the "thousand eyes" of Lang's films, which design, as Esposito writes, "a uninterrupted line of mental reconstructions, a procedure of geometrically overflowing contours, which simultaneously specify and disarrange the lived and represented universe, removing and adding fragments, shifting details, seeing each time from a different point of view."[27]

They are "flying eyes," balloons with a camera, gigantic spheres, like a world eye attached to a gigantic body that is out of orbit. The only implacable eyes are those of the "flying" cameras – of the *eyes from the sky,* – and the only way of *seeing* the crime, although taking place *live* and *under everyone's eyes,* is by *passing* through the electronic recordings that permeate, engulf, and are positioned in a Kubrick-like labyrinth, which redesigns the perceptive and optic coils of the mind. Although fractured, the spaces are always offered to the indiscretion of the implacable eye, which flies over them from ceilings, or climbs over the separations as in a split.

In contrast to the temporal use of traditional flashbacks, Cappabianca remarks that, in *Snake Eyes,*

> we often see actors who do not re-evoke, but see again in replay, recorded pieces of what has just happened to them; together with us, they watch themselves on a small screen, and we see them, seeing and being seen – agents in different temporal sessions made contemporaneous. De Palma's dream is that of a space/time entirely actualizable and transitable, and an ubiquitous eye for which nothing can become an obstacle. It is from concrete matter that the revelation bursts out: the ray of light is inserted in the red eye of the ruby set in cement (on the credits) that would signal a crime (a body buried) if someone (including the hurried eye of a spectator who is not impeded by the time of dislocation) made the effort to pay attention to us, to see *beyond the maximum time* and therefore prolong in time the space of the vision, concretizing and also making it shine in the light.[28]

---

[27] Lorenzo Esposito, "I Milleocchi del serpente," 19.
[28] Alessandro Cappabianca, "Replay/Flash-Back," *Filmcritica* 491-492 (January-February 1999), 22.

After all, also in Abel Ferrara, whether in his homonymous film *Snake Eyes*, or in *Black Out* or *New Rose Hotel*, it is always and only about the process of vision that short-circuits in the mind. Although accomplished differently in these films, it is also about a coincidence between *actuality* and *virtuality*, between temporal *memory* and *spatial* coincidence, between screen phantoms and bodies that encompass those same phantoms.

In De Palma, one traces continually the capacity to compress the space of action and to expand into infinity the trajectories of the eye. *Snake Eyes* shows itself in this sense, as Simone Emiliani notes, as an "authentic work of visual engineering, precisely because it is capable of elevating itself beyond the multiform points of view; it is able to surpass the numerous epiphanies of the typical gazes of Di Palma's cinema."[29] The breaking up of the real which is seen once and again, filmed, lived and relived, produces, *in the fiction* itself, a reality that is beyond the gaze of appearance, like the mechanical eyes behind the human eyes, and vice versa. This contradicts a first reading, and shifts the imaginary and the actual, thereby achieving the disassembling and tearing apart of the cinematographic edifice – the camera as well as the set, – making them into a trace, a map, a trajectory of the visionary movement of the mind.

The form that subverts the psychophysical dimensions in *Mission to Mars* also capsizes the spatio-temporal coordinates, turning the "earth" and its orbit literally inside out, as well as the *evolutionary* vortex of the *human* space within a spatiality that is *too human*. As Esposito notes, it is about an "upheaval"

> that makes us become "them" (the aliens) and "them" become us (the "humans"), which is the philosophical sense of De Palma's film, constantly strained to tell us that "I is the Other." This is the constitutive metaphor of the cinematic realm, an experience of oneself through the other of oneself (and in fact *Mission to Mars* is a film of connections, of solid friendships, of melodramatic losses, of a *common* adventure) – in an endowing of *other* images (barely alien and very human) the waiting and desire for a full life."[30]

---

[29] Simone Emiliani, "Sguardi infiniti in spazi finiti," *Filmcritica* 494 (April 1999), 207.

[30] Lorenzo Esposito, "Cronache marziane," *Filmcritica* 506-507 (June-July 2000), 301.

We are thus witness to a process of exploration of alterity, which is very cinematographic in that it presupposes a gaze, a consciousness, an existential state contaminated and altered, but precisely therefore made more intense, *foreign* but also *present* to itself, at once static and Dionysian.

THE ITALIAN AMERICAN IMAGINARY:
THE IMAGINARY ITALIAN AMERICAN
GENRES, GENDERS, AND GENERATIONS

Vito Zagarrio
UNIVERSITY OF ROME, III

Lee and Scorsese: Genres, Ethnicities, and Models

"Only niggers and Puerto Ricans live on welfare," says one of the Italian American characters of Spike Lee's *Summer of Sam*. This remark underscores Spike Lee's important *mise en abîme* of racial relations: the reciprocal prejudice of Italian Americans and the still more ghettoized African Americans and Puerto Ricans.

A strange parenthesis in the work of Spike Lee consists in the fact that despite his well-developed sense of irony, he persists in stereotyping Italian Americans. Caricatures, cartoons, masks of *commedia dell'arte*, the "Italians" of *Summer of Sam* (the "S.O.S." of the title is emblematic) have no sociological or philological value. Moreover, the very choice of a story from 1977 (which adds to it the quality of a "costume drama") can bestow upon the film a mythic flavor and, thus, quasi dehistoricize it.

In *Summer of Sam*, Lee plays on the rich lexicon of Italian American cinematographic stereotypes. This interesting metalinguistic game invites comparison with Martin Scorsese's Italian Americans: from the characters of the early, self-referential films (*Italianamerican* and *American Boy)* to those of the early "New Hollywood"[1] (*Mean Streets* and *Raging Bull)*, and especially to the characters more recent *Goodfellas* and *Casino*. Indeed, no discussion of Italian Americans can ignore the "Americanitaliano"[2] Scorsese. Spike Lee knows this very well. The cinematically refined self-reflexive exercise and mixing of genres (ethnic comedy, horror, and serial killer thriller) of *Summer of Sam* – a direct

---

[1] See Michael Pye and Lynda Myles, *The Movie Brats: How the Film Generation Took Over Hollywoo* (London and Boston: Faber & Faber, 1979); Diane Jacobs, *Hollywood Renaissance* (New York: Delta, 1977); Franco La Polla *Il nuovo cinema americano 1967-1975* (Venezia: Marsilio, 1978); Jim Hiller *The New Hollywood* (New York: Continuum, 1992).

[2] Gian Carlo Bertolina. *Martin Scorsese* (Firenze: La Nuova Italia, 1981).

challenge to Scorsese – demonstrates Lee's talent as a director.

The first shot of the film after the prologue (the scene of the killer's apartment and the journalist who tells the story) is a striking example. This long, elaborate shot begins from up high. A mixed crane and a pan movement of the camera from right to left follows Vinny's red sports car. The camera, hidden behind a crowd of people, trails the car (in the more complicated movement of a steady cam operator descending from a crane) and the two protagonists, as they get out in front of the discotheque. It stays with them as they move, between two crowds of people, into the dance club (with obvious problems of illumination in the passage from the interior to the exterior). The shot concludes with a long dance sequence that recalls the mythic film of New Hollywood – John Badham's *Saturday Night Fever* – and its Italian American stereotype, John Travolta.

But Lee's stylistic exercise does not end there. Later in the film, Lee shoots another shot sequence inside the discotheque (again a steady cam follows Vinny from the outside to the inside); and another elaborate long take in the sequence inside the restaurant where Dionna works.

These shot sequences strongly remind us of Scorsese's famous steadycam shot in *Goodfellas*. In an almost maniacal single shot, the camera follows Ray Liotta as he enters through the emergency exit of the restaurant where he and his mafia cronies usually hang out. Scorsese underscores the acrobatics of the camera with the occasional shoulder of a waiter and doors that open with punctual timing. This shot, one of the most famous single-shots of the so-called "New New Hollywood" (that of the Eighties forward),[3] has become a model for contemporary cinema and has given way to infinite repetitions.

Spike Lee's references to this technique announce a play on citations all his own.[4] But for the Lee of another ethnicity, another race, another generation, this play on cinematographic citations justifies his stereotyping of Italian Americans. Lee views Italian

---

[3] See Jon Lewis. *Whom God Wishes to Destroy. Francis Coppola and the New Hollywood* (Durham and London: Duke University Press, 1995).
[4] See for instance the detail of the "Dead End" sign that explicitly recalls Wyler's film on another generation of youth gangs (See William Wyler, *Dead End* [1937]).

Americans through the filter of the "Mafia" film (such as those of Scorsese, Coppola's *Godfather* saga, and Abel Ferrara's *The Funeral*, and more recently – this time, since Spike Lee could not possibly have seen it, he actually anticipates a similar rhetorical strategy – the mafia family of Jim Jarmusch's *Ghost Dog*). Lee's clever cinephiliac exercise absolves him of his approximate reconstruction of the setting, lack of philological rigor, abuse of folklore, and even his negative representation of white women. Indeed, this film offers no shortage of scenes for gender analysis. Take for instance the scene in which Vinny, the protagonist, cheats on his wife with her Italian cousin. With the excuse of giving her a ride home, he parks on a dark street and violently penetrates her from behind. His wife, after all, has to be more "chaste"; later in the film in fact Vinny attacks her violently for having enjoyed herself at the "Plato Retreat" he had forced her to attend. This scene, though violent not only from a strictly feminist point of view, is particularly violent for its representation of Italian Americans as vulgar erotomaniacs, insensitive and immature, violent and dirty men. Vinny is a sick sex maniac, and Lee enjoys making fun of him. In one of the first scenes of the film, he shoots him nude in front of the mirror inside of the beauty shop where he works and has sex with the boss. A triangular Italian flag stuck to the mirror covers his pubis.

Dionna's cousin is an especially interesting character. She speaks Italian and comes from the "motherland," as if the Italian American inflection of the characters in the film were not already enough. In a curious cultural twist, in the dubbed Italian language version, she speaks "only dialect," a laughable strict Sicilian that verges on hilarity in the sex scene when she expresses her pleasure by screaming in Sicilian dialect. By way of contrast, in turn, and with a bit of nostalgia, the use of Sicilian dialect in *The Godfather* (gone in the Italian language version) we hear in a few tender phrases of Mamma Corleone and Al Pacino.

Certainly more accurate is Lee's representation of Italian Americans in *Do the Right Thing*. In this film, one of Lee's first, Italians and Blacks, who have the same desperate spleen in common, confront each other in the same social "laboratory": the Italian pizzeria located in the middle of the black neighborhood in

Brooklyn. But, as victims of the same common social violence, they are both absolved.

Nonetheless, in *Do the Right Thing* we also find a schematic and somewhat dated representation of the Italian American environment: "It's like I'm coming to work at *Planet of the Apes*. I don't like being around them animals," says John Turturro, "my friends, they laugh at me. They say, go on, go to Bed-Stuy. Go feed the Mulies." And he insists, "No Mulanyan can be trusted, the first time you turn your back, ahh, a spear right here man in the back ... I know, I read ... Read your history. It's historical." Danny Aiello in turn plasters his "Wall of Fame" only with photos of Italians and Italian Americans (Sofia Loren, Frank Sinatra, Al Pacino, John Travolta, and so forth) and kicks the "fucking nigger" out of the restaurant. But Lee views the blacks critically and expresses sympathy for the Italian American who sees his life's work (the pizzeria that he constructed) overrun by black violence. And the poor Korean shopkeeper, in the face of the anger of the blacks, repeats insistently, "I no white."

After the fights and the violence at the end of the film, blacks and whites – Danny Aiello and Spike Lee (in the part of the black delivery boy of the white pizzeria) – face each other in front of the smoking ruins of the pizzeria. They both realize they are in the same boat, victims, in Brooklyn, a symbolic microcosm of the world.

As we see, the films on the Italian Americans are always in the middle field between stereotypes and folklore. The party scenes in Francis Ford Coppola's *Godfather* saga are rife with folklore: to name a few examples, Don Vito Corleone's waltz with his newly married daughter Connie at her wedding reception in *The Godfather* (clear homage to Visconti's *The Leopard*); the Sicilian song, "C'e' la luce in mezzo o' mare," faithfully reconstructed with the appropriate obscene gesturing; the entire very beautiful Sicilian episode in *The Godfather*, with the love and death of Apollonia, (a small homage to Pier Paolo Pasolini with the cameo of Franco Citti, leading actor of *Accattone*); and the delicate song, "Avia nu sciccareddu" sung by the young Vito Corleone in the *Godfather II*.

Coppola, however, employs folklore with philological precision and poetical overtones we do not find in the post-modern Lee. And it is just this poetics of folklore that I would like to compare to that of another great Italian-American director: Frank Capra.

Capra and Coppola:
Myths, Generations and Authorship in Comparison

Lee Lourdeaux has proposed this comparison in his interesting *Italian and Irish Filmmakers in America.*[5] But Lourdeaux complicates his analysis of Italian Americanness in Capra, Coppola, and Scorsese by mixing the Irish and Italian immigrant cultural traditions together. He unites Ford and Capra – correct perhaps in absolute terms, in their common role as American mythmakers[6] – with the questionable bond of Roman Catholicism. If viewed in isolation, Capra's very complicated relationship to religion, not only Catholicism,[7] would obscure a correct historical and philological analysis of his films. It is necessary instead to compare problems of staging, recurrent elements of style and screenwriting, use and transgression of models, traditions, and roots.

I shall therefore, by means of Capra and Coppola, compare two generations of Italian American directors: one at the beginning of the history of cinema, when it was making its first steps, when all of its solutions and inventions were still open; the other at the end of the journey, when cinema recycles itself in a more vast and complex iconic universe – from silent film to television and the media. The theme of Italian American roots – or more exactly, the relationship between American and Mediterranean myth, between integration and return to origins – connects the several generations situated between the point of departure and the point of arrival.

Born in 1897 in Bisacquino, Sicily, Frank Capra emigrated to Los Angeles in 1903. He became the war-horse of Italian cinematographic nationalism: In the thirties, the Fascist regime exalted the "Sicilian" and the "Italian" *Franco* Capra as of one of the great *Italian* successes. He confirmed "Italian superiority" in a

[5] Lee Lourdeaux, *Italian and Irish Filmmakers in America. Ford, Capra, Coppola and Scorsese* (Philadelphia: Temple UP, 1990).
[6] See Robert Sklar, *Movie-Made America. A Cultural History of American Movies* (New York: Vintage Books, 1975).
[7] See Charles Maland, *Frank Capra* (Boston: Twayne, 1980).

cinema that was trying to manifest itself at all technical and poetical levels. In 1934, film journals dedicated specials issues to the
inauguration of the General Direction for Cinematography – and
the first year of the era of Freddi, grand manager of Italian Cinema under the Fascist regime – with articles on Frank Capra, the
"most representative Italian director in the world." The journal
Quadrivio (edited by Luigi Chiarini, one of the fathers of the
Italian film critique) points to Capra in the moment in which the
cinema of the Fascist regime was founding its own public structures on the economic model of the New Deal and on the myth of
Hollywood productivity. Moreover, the Regime exalted Capra
when "Cinecittà" was founded: *Cinema* dedicates a large part of
its special issue "For the Inauguration of the City of Cinema" (25
April 1937 [XV])[8] to the great Italian American director. It was
natural that an issue – on the occasion of the birth of the city of
cinematography – dedicated principally to the past, present and
future of Italian cinema – concluded with an attentive and comprehensive study of the most important filmmaker in the world:
the Sicilian Frank Capra. The critical essay of Emilio Cecchi and
the biographical essay of Gramantieri intended to represent *Cinema*'s necessary homage to the luminous and charming figure of
the Italian artist, defined "one of the most worthy representatives
of our art abroad." As Mussolini boasted that New York was the
"Greatest Italian City" (it had over a million Italian inhabitants),
so Capra – in spite of the indigenous Blasetti and Camerini –
rightly became the greatest Italian filmmaker.

What role does Capra play in this ritual exchange of American myth and Italian pride? No role that may justify Italian provincial chauvinism. Capra – as Gian Piero Brunetta has also
noted[9] – in some way "removes" his Italian roots; he rebuffs Italy,
the Great Mother. His new great mother is the Statue of Liberty
that met him majestically in 1903; it is the land of America that
his relatives kissed when they disembarked. Italy means poverty,
closed mindedness, death. America means new horizons, unlimited
possibilities, chances for everyone, physical and psychological mo-

---

[8] *Cinema*. 25 April 1937 (15th year of the "Fascist Era").
[9] Gian Piero Brunetta and Gianfranco Mingozzi. *Storie di emigranti* (documentary
produced by RAI, 1982).

bility. "I hated being poor. Hated being a peasant. Hated being a scrounging news-kid trapped in the sleazy Sicilian ghetto of Los Angeles. My family couldn't read or write. I wanted out. A quick out. I looked for a device, a handle, a pole to catapult myself across the tracks from my scurvy habitat of nobodies to the affluent world of somebodies." These are the first words of the preface of Capra's autobiography, *The Name Above the Title.*[10] They are bitter words. A backdrop of tragedy and misery.

The first chapter of his autobiography looks like the only Capra "script" on Sicily or Italy. It is the script of a film – on the environment of the Italian-Americans and on Sicilian roots, full of episodes, narrative sequences, small film plots, rather than recollections or memory – never realized, or better, "realized" by Coppola only several generations later.

The first pages of the autobiography are a little jewel of popular literature. Take for example a few episodes: the arrival, in the small Sicilian town, Ben's (the son believed lost) letter, the fearful expectation that the letter provokes among the illiterate people of Bisacquino. The adventures of Ben from Palermo to Los Angeles (described in flashback), by way of New Orleans, San Francisco and even the Japanese Islands, among various flights, fights and kidnapping, have the elements of a novel: the voyage towards America on the stormy ocean where only mamma Saridda has the courage to challenge the wind, the arrival, after a thousand misadventures, in Los Angeles, and even the first years of little Frankie, described with moving realism and in a language often mixed with rich dialectal hints, a wonderful fairy tale. In this vein it is worth citing the episode in which the young Frank returns home upset and cries on his mother's lap, who says to him in Italian, "Coraggio, figlio, corraggio. . . ." (be brave, my son, be brave). Or that in which Frank, to make ends meet, teaches music to a rich, but stupid, young man: "The rich have it all; but accomplish little; and, had Baldwin been born a poor boy in New Orleans or Memphis, he might have become one of our great jazz musicians." This is the typical Capresque populist moral. And, to

---

[10] Frank Capra. *The Name Above the Title. An Autobiography* (New York: MacMillan, 1971).

finish, the episode, important for understanding Capra's approach to "Italianess," in which a Mafia boss offers him work and "dirty" money.[11] The very cinematographic Italian-American stereotype – the 'chico' in whose face Frankie throws the money – is called "Tuffy."

What about his cinema? In the many films of Capra's long career, Italy and Italians do not exist. They are rejected, removed, and forgotten in his attempt to emerge, to liberate himself and to become one of them, more than them, to become "American." While Capra often potrays situations that recall the humble origins of his family, he always masks and integrates the references into the American model. For example, the protagonist of *The Younger Generation* – Capra's important transitional film between silent films and "talkies" – is a poor Jewish family of Manhattan's lower east side, even though the mother resembles Coppola's Sicilian women.

The only "Italians" we find in all of Capra's films are in *It's a Wonderful Life*: Martini (and his large family), the Italian immigrant whom James Stewart helps to purchase a house, and Nick, the second-generation Italian American bartender. And in the same film, the only Italian environment is Martini's bar, where the juke box plays the Neopolitan song "Santa Lucia." But it is only a fragment of the soundtrack. It will be overturned in the nightmare scenario (in which, interestingly enough, the bar is no longer managed by the first-generation Martini, but by the second-generation Nick) where the bar is a horrid site of perdition and corruption.

Why this "removal" of roots? I had a chance to ask Capra himself in an interview in 1981. "I never made," responded Capra, "films that didn't have an American background, even when they took place in China or Tibet. I have often thought of making a film in Europe, in France or Italy. But then I said to myself: I don't know the French, I don't know what they think, how they talk when they talk among themselves, what words they use in real life. As for Italy, I was only six years old. What roots could I have had? I don't remember anything before, because when we left

---

[11] *Ibid.*

Palermo and got out into the open ocean, it was such a marvelous thing that all preceding memory was wiped out. That is the originary moment. From there my memory begins. It begins on the ship. Before the big ship I don't remember anything. And to say that I returned to Bisacquino three years ago. I didn't feel any emotion. I didn't recognize anything."[12] The "rejection" of Italy is confirmed by the autobiography: Ben, the older brother, immigrated to the States some years earlier, writes a letter to the Capra family, trough Mr. Orsatti, the Italian-American who helps the young man to write the message: "And, Orsatti added, if the Capra family wished to see Ben again they would all have to come to Los Angeles, because Ben says he is never coming back to Sicily."[13] So no one is returning to Sicily. The true fatherland is America: "Los Angeles – America, America!" the Capras yell, like a character from Joseph Roth's *Hotel Savoy*. But here there is no catastrophe of MittelEuropa, no purifying fire. They leave only miserable and desperate Sicily behind them.

Many generations and many films later, Francis Ford Coppola returns to the very same desperate and beautiful Sicily, charged with originary myths. Though many of the prejudices against "Italians" were gone when Coppola studied at UCLA, he too aspires to have the "name above the title." He forcefully represents, to cite the title of a book by Gelmis,[14] "the director as superstar," no longer an anonymous artisan, but an author. Like Capra, Coppola is motivated by familial "revenge": Capra had his motive in his father – Salvatore – an illiterate peasant. His revenge against the world was to study, to become somebody. Coppola's father, Carmine, never broke through; he remained an anonymous and grey figure, a flautist in Toscanini's orchestra. Coppola's "revenge" is therefore familial, against his father's frustrations, and generation, against taboos and anti-Italian racial prejudices. Coppola wages his oedipal battle against Capra's inferiority complexes, against Italian shame, violence, death. It is also an entirely American fight for survival. And, like in Capra, it is the genuine "American Dream" – the desire to attack and to

[12] The interview is in Vito Zagarrio. *Frank Capra* (Milano: Il Castoro, 1995).
[13] *Ibid*.
[14] Joseph Gelmis, *The Film Director as Superstar* (London, Secker & Warburg, 1971).

emerge (the so called "pull and push theory"). Coppola, following a generational trend, goes in search of "roots": the first datum is in the family archive, in the image and the name of the father and the mother: Carmine and Italia (Coppola's sister is also called "Italia": Talia Shire).

Cinema mediates the more mature Coppola's appreciation for Italian culture (he is a great admirer of Bertolucci and the great Italian masters). Italians become recurrent characters in the narratives, cast and in the troupe of his films. Coppola portrays Italians, on the one hand, with the usual folkloristic deformations (the Sicilian *mafioso*, the paternal and virile man of honor of *The Godfather*, but also the spaghetti that are shipped to Coppola in the Philippines during the making of *Apocalypse Now*) and, on the other, with admiration for their "humanistic" qualities, their combination of poetics and technique. So he chooses the Bertoluccian Vittorio Storaro as cinematographer for *Apocalypse Now* and, before that, the Fellinian Nino Rota for the music of *The Godfather*. Rota and Storaro represent – like a brand name – *Europe*. Coppola's attitude towards his own, towards "Italians" – the image of emargination and the minority – wavers between absolution and condemnation. In *The Godfather II* he puts the Mafia on trial and absolves them. But he levels the more general accusation against the ways, the presumption, the showy suits of the Italian American *mafioso*. Senator Geary says it at the beginning of *The Godfather II* when he challenges Michael Corleone. Coppola, like Mario Puzo, doesn't reject the popular stereotypes of the "Italians," he exalts them: the Italian Americans in *The Godfather* are tender fathers and at the same time brutal assassins, respectful supporters of the morality of the clan and vigorous stallions. But the stereotype becomes myth: so the lawyer Tom Hagen (Robert Duvall), the adopted brother of Michael Corleone, meets the boss Pentangeli (who betrayed the Corleone Family) in jail, and suggests that he commit suicide. He doesn't do it explicitly, but rhetorically by reminding him of the ways of the ancient Romans, whose honor would remain intact after a failed revolt if they took their own lives.

The image of the "Italian" in Coppola becomes the condensed form of human myths and rituals. So much so that this image is often associated with the feast: we see this in the *Godfather* saga, but also in an almost subliminal piece of *The Rain People*, an extraordinary little film of the early "New Hollywood." In a very brief flashback, the protagonist Natalie thinks back for a moment to her wedding; and it is a "tarantella," the dance of the newlyweds, who are called (an Italian name, though the last name is also Jewish) Ravenna.

Coppola's relationship to Italy parallels his oedipal relationship to his real father, Carmine, and a symbolic Father (the Super Ego, Power and the other possible metaphors including Cinema) that the filmmaker tries, ritually but uselessly, to kill. Captain Willard (Martin Sheen) kills, as in some sort of sacrificial ritual, the paternal figure of Kurtz (Marlon Brando) in *Apocalypse Now*. But, at least in one of the versions of the film, he substitutes him (there are in fact three versions: in the first, Willard remains village chief; in the second, he leaves the village; in the third, the most common one, he does not only leave the village, but he has it bombed). In the *Godfather*, the more cynical, though more cultured, Michael (Al Pacino) substitutes the paternal figure of Vito Corleone (again Marlon Brando). Finally, Coppola realizes this oedipal dynamic in the anti-family vindication of *You're a Big Boy Now* and *Peggy Sue Got Married*, and in the paternal metaphors of Vietnam in *Gardens of Stone*. This oedipal structure embodies the typical dynamic of the Sixties, a product of campus revolts, (which were also revolts against the family, through the reading of R.D. Laing and Cooper), and the attempt to upset a system of political and social values.

But in order to continue our comparison, in Capra too there are moments in which the generations are put against each other. In *The Younger Generation* (1929), for example, the relationship between father and son explodes. The father, Papa Goldfish, is an old Jew of the Lower East Side, attached to the Family and to the old Values; his son Morris, however, rejects the old Values, and tries cynically to scale the social ladder (represented by his arrival to the Upper East Side). But in the end he remains alone. Capra sides with the Father, Coppola is, or tries to be, on the side of the Son.

There is a moment in which the two filmmakers (and the two

generations of Italian Americans that embrace almost the entire history of cinema) meet directly. In the film *Tucker,* Coppola draws directly on the great themes of Frank Capra, and identifies with him and the great heroes of his films. But Coppola enriches Capra's narrative and utopian universe with a stylistic charge, a touch that the old, rediscovered master never had. It is as if Coppola wanted to rehabilitate Capra's universe, valorizing the *aurea mediocritas* of the character-symbol, but instead of the "middle" style of Capra's films, Coppola chooses a highly stylized cinematic language. Coppola rereads Capra through Welles: he rethinks the "middle" style of the older artisan in a higher form and with a touch of authorship. Coppola's debt to Capra is obvious: Preston Tucker revokes the epics of the Jefferson Smiths and George Baileys, of the small heroes battling against the corrupt world in the name of the American Dream (the word "dream" appears in the title of the film: *Tucker the Man and his Dream*). But if Coppola's dream is the same as Capra's utopian vision, from the point of view of production or aesthetics, it is quite another cinematic project. Coppola's dream to re-found cinematic reality began with *One from the Heart* (whose Italian version was not by chance entitled *Un sogno lungo un giorno* [a day-long dream]), continued with *Rumble Fish* and *Cotton Club* necessarily became one of refounding the productive models of the Studio system. And here, in this second challenge, it is destined to fail.

Like Tucker, who is beaten by the big companies of the automobile industry, even Coppola has been reevaluated by the major studios in Hollywood. He has tried to set an autonomous and creative mode of production against the serialized and standardized American cinematographic system. He has tried to respond to that system with a return to a democratic and original studio system: the great ambitious project of his own production company, Zoetrope. The result was an economic failure, and Coppola was forced to return to the Major studios of Hollywood.

Coppola has to take stock of his life without Zoetrope, as he declares melancholically, with a play on words, in one of his films (co-directed with Scorsese and Woody Allen): *Life without Zoe* – Life without Zoe (trope)? But notwithstanding all of this, he has survived and picked himself up again like a Capresque hero, like the entrepreneuer George Bailey in *It's a Wonderful Life*, coming to grips with the Building and Loan Co. and Bedford Falls. He survives public and private tragedy (the failure of Zoetrope and the death of his son Gio), and persists in following his dream. So the Don Quixote of the Seventies and Eighties stretches out his hand towards the Rooseveltian champions of the Thirties by way of the Forties of *It's a Wonderful Life* and *Tucker*.

In *Tucker*, Coppola pulls the cords of the American dream, from the New Deal to the Reagan era, and binds together the hopes and the frustrations of two generations of Italian Americans: the one which left the homeland and removed its roots (Capra), and the one which re-appropriated its ancestral places and motives (Coppola).

The fable of Tucker, orchestrated by the Italians Carmine (Coppola) and Vittorio (Storaro), has more and less obvious Capresque themes. In the first place, it is the fresco of a story mediated by the prominence of the individual. From the opening credits, fictive reality and historical reality, document and imagination, offer the viewer a voyage across the borderline that the film constitutes: oscillating between biography (the story of Tucker), autobiography (the story of Coppola) and social parable (the car as a metaphor of industrialized society and mature capitalism). The film is enclosed between two parenthesis of reality: the chaotic reality of the opening credits (a remarkable and intriguing puzzle) and that of the closing credits (cold and embalmed, where the photos of the real Tucker give the spectator the sensation of running through, in a more mediated and distant way, the events already seen in the film).

Tucker begins with a sequence that corresponds exactly to Capra's *It's a Wonderful Life*: the montage sequences that describe, with ample chronological synthesis, George Bailey's adolescence and war years. Capra describes with quick cuts the years from Mary Bailey's first pregnancy to the news of Harry Bailey's military decoration, a rapid montage combines news footage with scenes of fiction, and constructs back projections in which documentary reality and history reflect each other. Capra self-satisfactorily cites himself when he describes the Second World War, as if it were an advertisement for *Why We Fight*. This is an important sequence in the narrative structure of the film since it precedes the dramatic climax of the sub-final sequence (the loss of the money, the risk of failure and his attempted suicide). Coppola recalls and draws from this less maudlin Capra, in which signs of a less reassuring reality emerge, signs that recall also the famous newsreel sequence of *Citizen Kane*. Even the opening credits show us the route that he wants to take: to join craft and art, (reproducible) reality and (cinematic) fiction.

Like Capra, Coppola presents himself as a story-teller of a half-lived and half-imagined America. In the first scene of *Tucker*, Preston Tucker (Jeff Bridges) comes home holding a large piece of paper (in the style of the local ballad-singers) with which he shows and explains to the public (that is, his family) the project of his automobile.

We see the first apparent citation, the first intentionally disseminated sign, of Capra in the very first sequences of the film: Preston Tucker takes the wheel of the science-fictionesque armored truck he constructed during the war and his wife Vera pretends to hitchhike by putting up her thumb and lifting up her skirt – synthesizing the gestures of Clark Gable and Claudette Colbert in *It Happened One Night*.

Another Capraesque *topos* – one that Coppola has always projected in his films – is the family: the close Family (also in the mafia sense of the term) of *The Godfather*, the nervous couple of *One from the Heart*, the exploded family of Rusty in *Rumble Fish*, the anxious family of *Jack*, or even the absent family in *The Rain People*. His father Carmine, composer of many of his soundtracks, his brother Augusto (to whom he dedicated *Rumble Fish*) his son Gio (to whom he dedicated *Tucker*) and his sister Talia (who appears in the Godfather films), populate Coppola's world, with indirect homages and affectionate citations (like the cameo of his parents Italia and Carmine in *One from the Heart*).

The more direct presence of the family – it is the bearing structure of the entire story – positions *Tucker* closer to the Capra model. The family is the nucleus, the core: Vera, capable of being a loving wife but also of transforming herself into an aggressive business woman; Tucker's son who chooses to work with his father instead of going to college; the designer Alex and the Japanese engineer who are "adopted"; the entire staff of Tucker's bizarre company who builds a homemade car, that is to say, in a loving, amateur, and independent way, are free from industrial corruption.

The corrupt ones are, as it is obsessively the case in Capra's films, journalists and politicians. As in *Mr.Smith Goes to Washington*, the phone call of a journalist "uncovers" the naive deception of the false prototype, and later informs the senator in the service of the major carmakers of the progress of Tucker's car. Ferguson, the dishonest politician ("Now that's something I thought I'd never see: a politician with his hands in his own pockets," jokes Tucker) takes us to another typically Capresque place – in a scenographic and spatial sense: the courtroom.

"This is Washington, a Punch a Judy show," Abe says to Tucker after their first meeting in Washington, recalling Mr. Smith and the political "court" where James Stewart holds his moving appeal to the country.

"A Christmas present that Detroit gave itself," whispers Tucker and his lawyer in the real courtroom shortly before the trial; in so saying they cite Capra doubly: in the many "trials" of his films, the many speeches inside and outside public arenas (judiciary halls, banks and stadiums) and Christmas, narrative *topos* and recurrent cathartic element of Capra's stories.

At this point the Capresque remake is perhaps even too explicit: Tucker's self-defense is a child of the rhetoric of Mr. Smith, Mr. Deeds, and John Doe. So, also the character actors of the sequence of the trial are direct descendents: the judge, captured in the first shot on the background of the statue of justice and the American flag, distracts himself by swatting flies during the prosecution's opening statement; he smiles, a sly accomplice, when the jury declares Tucker innocent. He's a copy of the judge of Mr. Deeds, but above all of the Speaker of the House in *Mr. Smith Goes to Washington*.

Even the jury foreman, with his first motion of defense towards Tucker ("Let the man speak. . ."), with his fair and honest face, is a typical example of the common people who were so close to Capra's heart. The heart of the trial is classic: Tucker, in a close-up, asks the jury for the "Plain old common sense of the

American people." Coppola does not hesitate to reproduce this re-
gurgitated Capraesque populism and demagogy.

In *Tucker*, the director can afford the tears of Abe at the
trial when the prosecution asks if he expects one person in the
courtroom to believe him. Moved, Abe responds, looking at
Tucker, "one." It's the so called "capracorn," the rhetoric of the
good neighbor, of the friend who does not abandon you, of trust in
your fellow man and the American dream. Abe speaks of not
"catching" other peoples dreams in an important scene in front of
the factory warehouse. "What's the difference, fifty or fifty million," – affirms a confident Tucker, after the trial, referring to
the number of cars produced – "it's the idea that counts." This is
all Capra, not only the Capra of *It's a Wonderful Life*, but also
the earlier Capra, as in the silent *That Certain Thing*. In this
early film of 1928 it was the "idea," that certain thing invented
by the protagonist Molly, that mattered, a winning idea, for familial and social redemption, but above all for the ethics of Capitalism (as in the story of Tucker, the "idea" was relative to an industrial enterprise; Molly had invented lunch boxes, food, Tucker
dreams of making refrigerators and makes utopian cars) .

Christian symbolism, the acme of Capraesque ideology, lurks
behind all of his rhetorical figures and it forms the base – oscillating between heroism and martyrdom – of his protagonists. Take
one example for them all, in *Meet John Doe*, the Christ John Doe
is crucified on a secular Golgotha – the stadium where the meeting of the masses takes place – by the crowd that had praised him.

Christian symbolism, in the form of parody, returns punctu-
ally in *Tucker*. In the scene before the launching of the prototype
(that takes the form of a show), Tucker, ironic but worried, says
"Do you know what's even more cheerful? Having ringside seats at
your own crucifixion." A quick, and intentional, cut to the following shot shows us a "cross" being raised up high, as if in preparation of Tucker's martyrdom on the sacrificial mountain. The
cross in reality is the "T" of Tucker, part of the sign of the factory
under construction, but that letter (and that name) subtend
expiation.

We can speak of a sense of "expiation" common to the heroes
of Capra and Coppola: Lulu of Capra's *Forbidden* (who sacrifices

her life for the man she loves) or the protagonist of *Meet John Doe* (clear Christological symbol), but also Kurtz in Coppola's *Apocalypse Now*, or Motorcycle Boy of *Rumble Fish* (who, like Christ, "reigns" over his little violent world and is immolated for it).

Frank Capra and Francis Ford Coppola occupy opposite points of a historical journey from one end of the Twentieth Century to the other. But their positions are not opposed. If anything, they are complementary, part of a generational, epochal development. Capra embodies the need for integration of the first generation of immigrants, without apparent nostalgia, with anger, with aggressiveness dictated by generations of suffering. Coppola, on the other hand, represents the more detached retrieval, the rediscovery of roots of a third or fourth generation of young intellectuals. But Italy and Europe are nothing but a necessary stop on the way to new horizons, electronic supertechnology or the all-American worlds of the novels of Susan Hinton (*The Outsiders* and *Rumble Fish*). There is no longer a place for the Italians Storaro or Bertolucci.

Both filmmakers (and both generations) have an "Italian" complex of inferiority and superiority mixed together. A common symptomatology in the years and in the generations: that of the persecuted, taken advantage of, unlucky character. But not for this reason less egocentric, presumptuous and ambitious.

The world on its own measure. The name above the title, citing again Capra's autobiography, anyway and always, that is perhaps typical of the "egocentrism" of Italian Americans. Or at least of those imaginary Italian Americans (in the triple sense of Imaginary Italianamericans, imaginative Italianamericans, but also of Italianamerican imaginary systems) that I have tried to represent.

The "Bad Boys"
of Italian/American Cinema

MEN IN (G)LOVE(S)
MARTIN SCORSESE'S *RAGING BULL* IN LIGHT OF LUCHINO VISCONTI'S *ROCCO AND HIS BROTHERS*

Dorothée Bonnigal
PARIS, FRANCE

That the cinema of Martin Scorsese should bear the marks of a rich and often fore-grounded debt to the Italian auteuristic tradition[1] is no groundbreaking news to speak of. Surprisingly enough, however, the salient intertextual links that Scorsese's films have consistently woven, over the years, with the cinema of Fellini, Pasolini or Visconti – to name the most obvious influences – have not been given much critical attention. Scorsese's inscription of the Italian filmic heritage has somewhat been taken for granted, leaving out a complexity and an ambivalence which vitally contribute to the originality of Scorsese's cinema.[2]

Scorsese's use and incorporation of the legacy of the 'Italian Fathers' can thus not be reduced to a simple identification which would, incidentally, cast Scorsese as an Italian *auteur* and *Master* wanna-be, instead of accounting for the fertile hybridity of his cinema. If anything, Scorsese is avowedly a 'wanna-be wanna-be,' a filmmaker keen on championing his Italian-American identity and on celebrating the doubleness of his cinematic heritage. This is especially true of Scorsese's handling of the legacy of Luchino Visconti, which, perhaps in light of *The Age of Innocence*'s obvious tribute to *Senso*, has often been dismissed, sometimes with a hint of

---

[1] My use of the term "Italian auteuristic tradition" refers here to a corpus of films produced in Italy in the 1960s and 1970s and whose open intention is an attempt at authorial signature or mark through the fore-grounding of distinctive styles. For a theorization of such a cinematic practice, see Pier Paolo Pasolini's "The Cinema of Poetry" in *Heretical Empiricism*, pp. 167-86 (translated by Ben Lawton and Louise K. Barnett [Bloomington: Indiana UP, 1988]). All further references to the notions of *auteurism* and *auteur* will thus simply imply that, in the structure of cinematic production and critical reception, an "author-effect" is recognized and privileged, without leading to psychologizing or essentialist reductions.

[2] Scorsese's use of the Italian legacy presents much more interesting characteristics than Woody Allen's blatant plagiarism of the cinema of Federico Fellini, for example. Only as a graduate student in the 1960s did Scorsese indulge in such a simplistic practice of expropriation when dealing with his Italian heritage, as seen in the ending of his second short film, *It's Not Just You, Murray!* (1964), which awkwardly replicates the end of Fellini's *8 1/2*.

condescension, as Scorsese 'trying to be Visconti.' What I would argue, thanks to a joint reading of Visconti's *Rocco and his Brothers* (1960) and Scorsese's *Raging Bull* (1980), is that it is less an issue of Scorsese trying to 'be' Visconti as one of Scorsese trying to 'do' Visconti – aesthetically that is, but not without a salient inscription of the transgressive impurity of such a cinematic desire. This impurity is, in fact, the very premise of Scorsese's cinema and a key to an understanding of how this cinema negotiates its debt to Italian *auteurism* in general, and to Visconti's cinema, in particular.

Rocco and his Brothers and *Raging Bull* present striking diegetic similarities. In both films, one finds working-class Southern Italian brothers who have moved "North" (add a generation and an ocean for Jake and Joey La Motta) and are attempting material and personal success in a corrupt world ruled by perverted fathers; one also finds a narrative of redemption and expiation framed by a *ménage à trois* that lethally binds two brothers and a female character coded as 'fallen.' Finally, both films feature boxing, a practice that grants success and failure at once and simultaneously signifies salvation and corruption. A dream, a triangle and a ring: all three doomed to destruction and dissolution as they recount the tragedy of defiled purity and lost innocence. As Jake La Motta would say, "that's entertainment!"

For us it is, I hope, as I offer to focus on three of the aforementioned narratives:

- The archetypal *ménage à trois*, first of all.
- The myth of the fallen woman and its redemption corollary, secondly.
- And the boxing paradigm, thirdly.

My selection of those three specific paradigms is not only a result of their significant convergence in both films. It also stems from the fact that all three involve and address three sets of oppositions that will prove to be central to the respective aesthetics and politics of *Rocco and his Brothers* and *Raging Bull.*

- The opposition between masculinity and femininity.
- The opposition between purity and corruption.
- The opposition between plenitude or wholeness and lack or castration.

While *Rocco and his Brothers* offers a dialectical resolution of those dichotomies through a reliance on a formula which, quite traditionally, equates femininity with corruption and lack, *Raging Bull* radically revises this formula by collapsing the oppositions and inscribing each paradigm in its unresolved form, so as to denounce them as fraudulent fantasies. As such, *Raging Bull* unravels the metacinematic scenario which presides over Scorsese's aesthetic and political relation to the Visconti heritage specifically, and to the Italian filmic tradition, more generally. In order to gauge Scorsese's departure from Visconti's aesthetics and politics, each of these paradigms needs, as a preliminary, to be investigated and discussed in general terms to then be applied to the films specifically.

Though linguistically coded as a French specialty, the *ménage à trois* has haunted cinema on a much more international scale. The endemic recurrence of this trope, especially in its 'older male/younger male/woman in the middle' configuration, in fact reflects how film syntax commonly relies on a few dominant psychoanalytic scenarios – dominant in the sense that they prevail in the ideology which produces the film – in order to set off, diachronically, the unconscious mechanisms of film spectatorship, be it narcissistic identification or scopophilia. Among those scenarios strategically 'acted out' on the screen from crisis to resolution, the Oedipus complex, featuring a familiar triangle, remains a privileged conflict. Generally featuring a woman as a token of exchange between two men, one coded as father, one coded as son, the *ménage à trois* thus commonly reenacts the Oedipus in keeping with the original myth of "Oedipus Rex," recounting the 'death' of the fatherly rival and eliciting an otherwise thwarted access to the motherly love-object. That a woman should be caught in an oedipal triangle more often than a man, statistically, is due to an easily diagnosed phallocentric bias which is more dedicated to comforting patriarchy than to addressing the devouring conundrum of female desire. For privileging such a male fantasy (incestuous fusion with the mother) presents a double advantage. Its resolution usually consists in a reinstatement of the taboo of incest through the eradication of the woman in the middle. Once 'consumed' by the transgressive 'son,' the woman coded as 'mother' can indeed no longer exist as such. She is killed off in turn, one way or another, through actual death or defilement, so as to contain the transgression and the threat of castration she simultaneously embodies. She ultimately comes to bear the castration which temporarily threatened the male hero, redistributing lack and wholeness according to hegemonic gender categories and underscoring the Law of the Fathers. In short, Woman bears the burden of male lack and her disrupting desire is discounted.[3] Yet, such a convenient eradication further elicits a more repressed transgression and sheds an interesting light on one of the most dominant expressions of male desire in popular culture. Indeed, since the woman in the middle only exists in order to be obliterated, the fantasy also expressed in this recurrent scenario consists in an unmediated codification of an otherwise forbidden homosexual relation between father and son.

The myth of the fallen woman as a prerequisite for male redemption, on the other hand, can be read as an opportune resolution of the previous brain-teaser. In the biblical myth[4] and even more in Milton's account of the episode,[5] the possibility of redemption is tied to a recognition, on Adam's part, of Eve's essentially corrupt nature. Verbally defiled by Adam, Eve repents, admitting baseness as a constitutive trait. Only then can the first steps to redemption be taken. The construction of woman as fallen is thus a requirement on the path to redemption that is therefore and by definition a male prerogative. To quote one of Freud's most controversial statements, just as there is only one libido, there is only one redemption and it is male, pointing to yet another phallocentric bias. In fact, one could find an interesting convergence between the biblical myth of the fallen woman and the Oedipus myth. The fall of woman indeed spares man the burden of an

---

[3] This phallocentric bias however attempts to comfort patriarchy merely because it needs to deny female desire as the actual object of most of its inquiries. The phallus is originally attached to the mother, not the father, and one of the main impulses of the Oedipus complex is precisely to castrate the mother and phallicize the father so as to reinstate heterosexual orthodoxy. Strikingly enough then, in *ménages à trois* featuring two women and a man, it is usually the phallic mother who defeats the castrated daughter in the end, especially through scenarios of sacrifice which ultimately reinscribe the phallic mother as redeemed saint, however complicit she has been in betraying her daughter. Pedro Almodovar's *High Heels* (1991) comes to mind as an interesting take on this scenario.

[4] See *Genesis*, Book 3.

[5] See John Milton, *Paradise Lost*, Book 10, lines 834-946 especially.

original sin that would otherwise mark him with lack and transgression in a triangle involving Adam, Eve and God the Father. The original sin is, in this light, reminiscent of Oedipus's sin and Eve's repentance is equivalent to the eradication of the mediating woman in the previous scenario. By repenting, she acknowledges her status as official bearer of male lack but she also guarantees that she is *not* the idealized female figure that, precisely, cannot and must not be desired in the oedipal conflict. Having fallen off her pedestal of desexualized innocence and perfection, she can be desired with the blessing (or the curse, rather) of God the Father. And since the fall has plagued man with a cumbersome package of sexuality, desire, and mortality, it is convenient that, through her accepted defilement, woman should thus paradoxically become a 'legitimate' object of desire, however marked by abjection. Thank God the Virgin Mary was later created to re-erect the lost pedestal and reconcile the feminine with modes of sublimation, thus locking woman in the radical dichotomy that makes her either Madonna or whore.

As for boxing, which I propose to decipher here as a paradigm, let us say that it is a rare example of culturally-sanctioned acknowledgments of the structural coincidence, in the male psyche, between compensation and castration, or, less phallocentrically, exposure, i.e. the process of encountering constitutive lack. By acting out the most repressed material of the Oedipus complex narrative – an unmediated intercourse between two men on the official grounds of a contest in masculinity – boxing spells out the doubleness of male desire as it encounters its castration: to deny and to embrace, to be phallicized and castrated at once, in a staged dance with and against the phallus in which the "beating" and the "being beaten" coincide[6] in a literality as brutal as the violence of the modalities of convergence. In keeping with its claim that it is the "manly art of self-defense," as encyclopedias com-

---

[6] See Freud's essay "'A Child is Being Beaten': A Contribution to the Study of the Origin of Sexual Perversions" (1919) which has been an indispensable companion in my reading of the boxing paradigm as a literal instance of the convergence of masochist and sadist impulses and their link to the mechanisms of repression of sexual difference and to auto-eroticism (in *On Psychopathology, Inhibitions, Symptoms and Anxiety and Other works,* The Pelican Freud Library, Volume 10, ed. by Angela Richards, trans. by James Strachey, Pelican Books, 1979, 159-93).

monly refer to it, boxing reflects the radical instability and relativity of gender categories and divisions in the male defense mechanisms mobilized in response to lack. As the premise of boxing implies, when man is to prove his adequacy with the masculine as it is constructed by and in dominant ideology, an adequacy which fraudulently guarantees the possession of the phallus, he paradoxically demonstrates the inadequacy and the failure of the construct of masculinity. Combining masochism and sadism in a positioning at once active and phallic (the hitting fist) and passive and vaginalized (the wounded, bleeding face), boxing not only strikes us as a displaced form of auto-eroticism, it further reveals how male strategies of over-compensation (i.e. attempts to deny castration and sexual difference) include and foreground the coded-as-feminine formula officially targeted by those strategies in the process of repression.[7] In order to be man, one must also be defiled as woman and marked by the bleeding wound of castration. In order to beat, one must be beaten, in order to possess, one must be possessed. The boxing ring collapses the opposition between the masculine and the feminine; it offers a resolution to the double desire of *having* the phallus and *being* the phallus; it reduces the contradiction that tethers the phallus to its constitutive absence, in the *jouissance* of condensing transgression and expiation. Ultimately however, since masculinity is here to be reinstated, the denied formula must be projected onto the absent woman in the middle who, as *Raging Bull* and *Rocco and his Brothers* both illustrate, appears as a convenient bearer of lack and an indispensable agent of redemption.

In both films, the lethal triangle that launches the redemption narrative (a narrative conveniently supplemented by the boxing paradigm) thus gathers two brothers and a sexualized and fetishized female character. In *Rocco and his Brothers*, Rocco and

[7] Throughout I am implicitly referring here to Jacques Lacan's authoritative essay, "La signification du phallus" (in *Ecrits*, Paris: Editions du Seuil, 1966, pp. 685-695). As Lacan explains, at the end of his essay, after having posited that femininity functions as a mask in the phallocentric order, as a masquerade aimed at making woman *be* the phallus in response to male desire ("it is for that which she is not that she wishes to be desired as well as loved"): "the fact that femininity finds its refuge in this mask [i.e. this simulation of the phallus through fetishization], by virtue of the fact of the *Verdrängung* [repression] inherent in the phallic mark, has the curious consequence of making virile display in the human being itself seem feminine" (p. 280 in Alan Sheridan's English translation, *Ecrits: A Selection*, London: Tavistock, 1977).

Simone are both in love with Nadia the prostitute. Having left the 'bad' brother Simone, Nadia sees a chance of redemption in the 'pure' love that Rocco is willing to offer her. As we can see, in this *ménage à trois*, Nadia thus functions as Simone's abject double, on the one hand, just as Rocco functions as Nadia's sublimated surrogate, on the other hand. The woman in the middle, she merely embodies the strategies of abjection and sublimation that at once link and oppose the two brothers in the film. As such, she is an indispensable token in the mechanisms of denial and projection that preside over the brothers' interdependent constructions of self and other. While Simone projects his abjection onto her in an attempt to deny it, Rocco sublimates her in response, so that she becomes instrumental in his own denial of Simone's corruption and may thus be the recipient of Rocco's idealizing projections. As the shared object of Rocco's sublimation and Simone's abjection, Nadia is at once a symbol of purity and corruption. Her mediation epitomizes the radical contradiction between the two brothers and her eradication offers a dialectical resolution of the film's structural discordance: the phallus in the middle, she must be castrated so that lack may be redistributed "properly" among the brothers and according to their respective pathologies. Her castration – quite literal in the film as she is successively raped and stabbed to death by Simone – not only marks Rocco with lack by symbolically defiling the purity he embodies, it also elicits the fusion between Rocco's projected yet defiled purity and Simone's projected and denied corruption. The woman at the heart of Visconti's Oedipal triangle is therefore inscribed in a double bind: the traditionally-sanctioned recipient of imaginary castration, she is also the metaphorical locus of an otherwise forbidden embrace between the two brothers. Boxing merely replicates this metaphorical locus while providing the means of its expiation.

In its inscription of the three aforementioned paradigms, *Rocco and his Brothers* largely relies on a binary organization, despite the film's tendency to stress the relativity of the dichotomies involved and despite its attempts at dialectical resolution. Indeed, even if Rocco's excessive goodness is explicitly denounced as equally bad as Simone's depravity, the two brothers are diametrically opposed on the spectrum of good and evil. Simone, loyal to his abjec-

tion only, lies, steals, betrays, rapes, sleeps with the perverted father[8] and kills. Rocco, on the other hand, is consistently sublime in
his nostalgia for the lost motherland and his sacrifice in the name
of the dead father. As such, he embodies a persistent ideal of non-
urban and pre-capitalist purity, just as he is a marker of lost plenitude, of the denied fall of the idealized maternal body. Only boxing, and that is another key function of the paradigm in the film,
will confront him with his own rage and impurity. Echoing the
castration narrative in which Nadia is sacrificed, the boxing ring
is where Rocco's purity is defiled[9] in order to meet the brutal demands of the capitalist world and expiate the inevitable corruption that this world entails. The political message is clear enough,
leaving the opposition between corruption and purity ultimately
untouched.

Same thing with the Madonna-whore dichotomy epitomized
by the promiscuous and fallen Nadia whose role is to propose a
radical alternative to the saintly and desexualized matriarch and
thus enter the brotherly triangle. Granted, a character like Gi-
netta, the wife of the elderly brother, interestingly blurs the dominant female dichotomy by presenting a less manichean but nonetheless marginal combination of both archetypes. But the structure
of the film fully depends on Nadia's devastating sacrifice, a sacrifice which allows for the film's final redistribution of wholeness
and castration and of purity and corruption, through a tragic and
costly reinscription of a pre-Oedipal status quo.

As evidenced by the faultless implementation of the film's
strategies of sublimation and abjection and by its politics of castration and compensation, we see that, despite *Rocco and his Brothers*'s dialectical impulses and its many subversive traits (which,
among others, include devastating realism), the film consistently
salvages one essential chiasmus: the X of Nadia's crucifixion[10]

---

[8] In *Rocco and his Brothers*, Simone indeed sleeps with the mob boss Morini as a form of
payment for a debt he cannot afford to settle.
[9] As Sam Rohdie insightfully remarks in his study of *Rocco and his Brothers*, the technique
of cross-cutting is significantly used to foreground the parallel between Nadia's brutal murder by Simone and Rocco's victory in a boxing match: "Simone's blows at Nadia are echoed
in the blows by Rocco in the ring. (...) As Rocco tries to save Simone, Simone is destroying
himself by the murder of Nadia in a symmetrically opposite and simultaneous action"
(*Rocco and his Brothers (Rocco e I suoi fratelli)*, London: BFI, 1992, p.38.
[10] The murder of Nadia is indeed explicitly represented as a crucifixion. Before receiving

which binds wholeness to purity and lack to corruption, thanks to a familiar scenario of female castration. As such, *Rocco and his Brothers* offers a rather classical configuration which makes the castration of the fetishized woman the condition for resolution. As has been amply discussed and demonstrated in recent feminist film criticism, such a scenario of castration has indeed been the stepping-stone of the Hollywood tradition. Over the years, Hollywood has developed true mastery when it comes to turning the threatening over-fetishized jezebel into a corpse or, at best, into a dull and subservient wife – a possibility which is included in *Rocco and his Brothers* but ultimately thwarted, perhaps because the film would otherwise be just another Hollywood movie climaxing in the triumph of petit-bourgeois and heterosexual orthodoxy. Granted, the resolution of *Rocco and his Brothers* is not aligned with Hollywood's pro-capitalist and bourgeois conclusions. It is quite the opposite actually and the commodified portrait of glamorous 'boxing whore' Rocco at the end of the film is a clear, however ambivalent, statement on capitalist corruption. Yet, in the fixed perfection of Rocco's face left miraculously unspoiled by years of professional boxing, we may read Visconti's refusal to let go of a crucial ideal of plenitude and innocence that guarantees the 'purity' of his own political statement and position – a purity also disturbingly guaranteed by an uncontained reliance on an all but too familiar narrative. Not that *Rocco and his Brothers*'s Marxist conclusions are problematic in themselves, what is more questionable, nonetheless, is that they should require the mediation of a somewhat reactionary paradigm, to serve a pre-capitalist, if not aristocratic, ideal of purity.

Though *Raging Bull* presents the same sequence of paradigms (*ménage à trois*, myth of the fallen woman and boxing paradigm), their treatment throughout the film inherently differs from Visconti's approach. What Scorsese's film proposes instead is a collapse of *Rocco and his Brothers*'s structural dichotomies which culminates in a radical blurring of the vital opposition between corruption and purity. The La Motta brothers, first of all, cannot be divided into the good and the bad. While Jake may beat up his wife

---

Simone's first blow, Nadia stretches out her arms as if lying on a cross.

and act like a raging pig most of the time, he also has integrity and refuses to sell his soul to the perverted 'father' (once again in the form of a mob boss) who offers him "protection." Joey, on the other hand, is a small-time wise guy and is far from being a model of moral virtue. The dynamics of the brothers' relation thus do not rely on strategies of sublimation and abjection, as they do in *Rocco and his Brothers*.

The woman in the middle is the recipient of such strategies but in a context which is strictly limited to and framed by Jake's paranoid and pathological constructions. First sublimated and fetishized, Jake's wife Vickie starts out as Madonna in the hero's disturbed psyche. Being in love with such a symbol of purity and innocence naturally dooms Jake to be constantly confronted with the impurity of his sexual desire. The only way to counter the prohibition and the guilt therefore consists in reconstructing the Madonna as whore, the source of his pathological jealousy which, in fact, expresses his most urgent desire. Jake demands that his wife be a whore, otherwise he is guilty of having desired a forbidden love-object. Her sole function is to mark the impurity of male desire as it is experienced by the character and entail the collapse of the Virgin-Whore opposition.

We see how *Raging Bull* reverses Visconti's inscription of the Madonna-Puttana dichotomy and rearticulates both purity and corruption as destructive fantasies. Unlike Nadia in *Rocco and his Brothers*, Vickie's status as official recipient of castration functions only as an internalization on the part of Jake, an internalization consistently foregrounded throughout the film as we follow Jake's gradual alienation from the symbolic order (family, career, the law) and are led to measure his progressive break with the reality principle. Unlike *Taxi Driver*, in which the spectator fully shares Travis Bickle's psychotic perspective on the world's constitutive impurity, *Raging Bull* stresses Jake La Motta's pathological estrangement from what is coded as 'reality' in the film, by inscribing alternative viewpoints (Vickie's and Joey's, centrally) and sustaining a narrative omniscience which positions the audience as radically external to Jake's psychosis.

The fact that Jake is systematically alienated by his pathology actually points to the most salient difference between Visconti's and Scorsese's films, for it marks the crucial internalization of lack carried out in the film. Jake would want his wife Vickie and his little brother Joey to bear his lack and exorcise the mortifying and defiling femininity he experiences within himself but he is given no break by his two privileged targets – whom he significantly fantasizes as one in the anthologized "you fuck my wife" sequence, revealing that the climax of his paranoia not only coincides with his repressed homosexual desire (leading Joey to call him "a sick fuck" with unwitting accuracy), but also with a desire to annul the sexual difference which marks him with lack. The early sequence in which Jake explains to Joey what his "problem" is, i.e. the fact that he has "woman's hands," leading him to request a beating from his brother's bare fist, is a perfect illustration of the mechanisms of Jake's pathology and a rare example of its 'success' outside of the boxing ring. By forcing his brother to adopt a phallic and sadistic position to counter his sense of lack, Jake literally becomes the masochistic woman that defiles him within, in the fantasy of an unmediated intercourse (as the insistence on the bare fist suggests) with a reluctantly phallicized Joey who fails to see the point of castrating his brother. Jake's pathology is based on his irreconcilable desire to at once be and have the phallus, a desire which places him in a double bind. The condition for *having* the phallus is castration in terms of *being* the phallus. And that is what he is explaining to Joey in this sequence: Jake's "problem" is that he *is* the phallus (his "woman's hands," an easily identifiable fetish, [11] rely on the masquerade of femininity to construct him as phallus, the way woman simulates 'being what she is not' in order to be desired) and as such, he must be castrated to be reinscribed as *having* the phallus. As he triumphantly pinches Joey's cheek at the end of the sequence, re-coding Joey as "castrated little brother/son," Jake experiences the *jouissance* of having gone full circle, from having to

---

[11] In this regard, Leslie Stern, in her book *The Scorsese Connection*, has an interesting reading of Jake's boxing gloves, which she deciphers as totemic objects which ritualize and act out the character's self-destructiveness. She also points out the mutual contamination of the masculine and the feminine in the film, thus addressing *Raging Bull*'s exploration of "masculinity as fantasy," masculinity defined as "a game that can never be mastered but must be played out, a game in which each manoeuvre is provoked by the force of a bad-object, the annihilation of which would amount to an annihilation of self" (*The Scorsese Connection* [London: British Film Institute and Bloomington: Indiana University Press, 1995].27).

being to having the phallus. Yet, Joey, like Vickie, is rarely complicit with Jake's vicious circle. The boxing ring remains the only context in which Jake gets to act out and embrace his fantasies of castration, expiation, and redemption, by reconciling the defiled woman and the defiling man he simultaneously embodies. The boxing ring in *Raging Bull* is not a place of corruption and defiled purity, as it is in *Rocco and his Brothers*, it is the most successful theater of Jake's hysteria in a world where all possibilities of redemption are otherwise thwarted.

Unlike Simone in *Rocco and his Brothers* (who actually shares many pathological traits with Jake), Jake thus cannot rely on anybody to bear his lack and that is his tragedy. A parallel between the famous sequence in which Jake "takes the punishment for what he feels he's done wrong," as Scorsese himself describes it,[12] and the brutal murder of Nadia in *Rocco and his Brothers*, is interesting in this regard. By letting 'Sugar' Ray Robinson beat him savagely for fifteen rounds while insisting that he is "never going down," Jake triumphantly asserts the turgidity of his phallic position while subjecting it to ruthless castration. Embracing his lack as *Homo Erectus*, Jake leads the woman inside to expiate by taking the punishment of her reinscribed castration so as to redeem his manhood from the burden of lack. In *Raging Bull*, as this sequence powerful conveys, the process is fully internalized. In *Rocco and his Brothers* conversely, Nadia is the external recipient of the same process, as she is repeatedly stabbed by Simone, poignantly asserting that she does not want to die, interestingly echoing Jake and his "I never went down" in the boxing ring. Conveniently for Simone, she does die however, so that he may be led to have the phallus and to lose it at once. Jake does not have that 'luck' and his fantasies of brotherly betrayal actually make him sound as if he wishes he were in *Rocco and his Brothers*. For the world of *Rocco and his Brothers* salvages room for plenitude, ideals and sublimation. In it, at least, or so Jake would think, the scenario of female castration is not thwarted and boxing whores pick up the tab.

But in the world of *Raging Bull*, the woman inside must be

[12] *Scorsese on Scorsese*, ed. by David Thompson and Ian Christie, London: Faber and Faber, 1989, p.80.

killed off *inside* because the opposition between purity and corruption has collapsed; except in the sick mind of the eponymous hero, it is no longer distributed according to hegemonic gender categories, as it ultimately is in *Rocco and his Brothers*. Jake La Motta is doomed to the impossible task of embodying the two categories at once, in order to salvage the purity of his impurity (and the impurity of his purity). In order to be "the boss," as – in a pathetic display of virile animality ("I'm the boss, I'm the boss, I'm the boss") – he reminds himself that he *is* before entering the stage of his hysteria (be it a ring or a shabby New York music hall), he must *not* be "that guy," *not* "that animal," as he laments in the devastating prison sequence. Instead, he must be 'that woman' whom he punishes and defiles by beating his head against the wall of his prison cell.[13]

There is thus no possibility of redemption, or only perhaps in the impure internalization of a scenario of female castration and of an idealism denounced, not without a hint of nostalgia, as irrelevant and obsolete. Why? Because as Visconti's film has poignantly revealed, the persistence of such an idealism, especially when mediated by the fantasy of female castration, may in fact be radically at odds with the aesthetic and gender politics of Scorsese's cinema. There remains the internalization – crucial, as I hope to have shown, to an understanding of *Raging Bull*. This internalization is Scorsese's, of course, as he negotiates his cinematic desire for and debt to an otherwise sublimated father and tradition in the American context of his productions. What Scorsese is bound to let go of, as he makes films in the 1980s, is a certain faith in one's ability to change the world, thus bearing the lack of a cinematic heritage that insisted on believing in such a possibility and yet killing it off in a devastating deconstruction of the mirage of purity and innocence. Like Jake's "woman within," idealization is the element inherent in the Italian filmic heritage which must be at once included and killed off, just as the scenario of female castration which, conversely, is a recognizable marker of alignment with

---

[13] Interestingly enough, Paul Schrader's original script featured Jake's failure to masturbate as a substitute for the self-beating which Scorsese preferred in the final version. This revision only confirms the link posited earlier between auto-eroticism and the conflation of 'beating' and 'being beaten,' as Freud argues in "A Child is Beaten" (cf. note 6).

Hollywood orthodoxy must be both salvaged and jettisoned, in order to maintain the vital doubleness of Scorsese's cinematic identity. For let us not forget one thing: in the Italian-American world of Scorsese's cinema, there is no "age of innocence."

BIBLIOGRAPHY

Brunette, Peter, ed. *Martin Scorsese: Interviews.* Jackson: UP of Mississippi, 1999.

Freud, Sigmund. *On Psychopathology, Inhibitions, Symptoms and Anxiety, and Other works.* The Pelican Freud Library. Vol. 10. Ed. Angela Richards. Trans. James Strachey. Pelican Books, 1979.

Gay, Peter, ed. *The Freud Reader.* London: Vintage, 1995.

Kelly, Mary Pat. *Martin Scorsese: A Journey.* New York: Thunder's Mouth Press, 1991.

Lacan, Jacques. *Écrits.* Paris: Seuil, 1966.

_____. *Le Séminaire, Livre III: Les psychoses (1955-1956).* Paris: Seuil, 1981.

Metz, Christian. *The Imaginary Signifier: Psychoanalysis and The Cinema.* Transl. by Celia Britton, Annwyl Williams, Ben Brewster and Alfred Guzzetti. Bloomington: Indiana UP, 1982.

Milton, John. *Paradise Lost and Other Poems.* New York: The New American Library, 1981.

Mulvey, Laura. "Visual Pleasure and Narrative Cinema" (1975). *Movies and Methods, Volume II,* ed. Bill Nichols. Berkeley: U of California P, 1985. 305-15.

Pasolini, Pier Paolo. *Heretical Empiricism.* Trans. by Ben Lawton and Louise K. Barnett. Bloomington: Indiana UP, 1988.

Rohdi, Sam. *Rocco and his Brothers [Rocco e i suoi fratelli].* London: BFI, 1992.

Silverman, Kaja. *The Acoustic Mirror: The Female Voice in Psychoanalysis and Cinema.* Bloomington: Indiana UP, 1988.

Stern, Lesley. *The Scorsese Connection.* London: BFI, 1995.

Thompson, David and Ian Christie, ed. *Scorsese on Scorsese.* London: Faber and Faber, 1989.

PARIAHS OF A PARIAH INDUSTRY
MARTIN SCORSESE'S *CASINO*

Robert Casillo

UNIVERSITY OF MIAMI

I Although legalized gambling became a big business in Nevada in the 1950s and '60s, financial institutions shunned it because of the stigma of gambling and fear of embezzlement by organized crime. The state preferred, mainly for moral reasons, to approve individual licensees rather than deal with corporate shareholders, and thus forbade corporate investment in and ownership of casinos. As the dominant power in the Teamsters locals, the mob determined the election of Teamsters pension fund trustees, who invested in casinos and controlled their management to permit kickbacks and embezzlement of casino revenues. Known as the "skim," these stolen profits were deposited with crime families. With the Corporate Licensing Act in 1969, corporations began their rise to dominance over the mob in the gambling industry, and yet for over a decade the mob continued to exert a powerful covert presence in Las Vegas. In 1974, Allen R. Glick received from the Teamsters pension fund a loan of nearly 63 million dollars, which Midwestern crime families gave to him for the purchase of the Stardust and other hotels; he later claimed that he made this deal without realizing that the loan entailed submission to the mob. On May 18 1976, a raid on the Stardust and other hotels uncovered the biggest slot machine skim in Las Vegas history. Next came the accidental discovery in 1979 by FBI wire-tappers in Kansas City of the truth about the skim. The conviction of many major mob bosses in 1983 terminated the mob's power in Las Vegas even as the corporations continued to prosper.[1]

---

[1] Nicholas Pileggi, *Casino* (New York: Pocket Books, 1995), 120-40, 176, 183-86, 209-22, 248-49, 256-58, 264-68, 319, 336-40; page numbers are given parenthetically in the text if possible. See also Jerome H. Skolnick, *House of Cards: The Legitimation and Control of Casino Gambling* (Boston: Little Brown, 1978), 4, 13, 108, 141-42, 144, 209-11, 298-99, 301, 310-18; Ronald A. Farrell and Carole Case, *The Black Book and the Mob: The Untold Story of the Control of Nevada's Casinos* (Madison: Univ. of Wisconsin Press, 1995), 13, 15, 22, 28, 53-56, 57-60, 91-93, 103; Roger Munting, *An Economic and Social History of Gambling in Britain and the U.S.A.* (Manchester: Manchester Univ. Press, 1996), 146-47, 152; John M. Findlay, *People of Chance: Gambling in American Society from Jamestown to Las Vegas* (New

Frank "Lefty" Rosenthal began his career as a gambler and bookmaker in Chicago, where he had close ties to the mob. He was arrested on bookmaking charges in 1959, and in 1963 was charged with conspiracy to fix a basketball game, but escaped conviction. By 1968 Rosenthal was living in Las Vegas, where he married Geri McGee, a former call-girl, with whom he had two children. After Glick's purchase of the Stardust, the mob forced him to yield control to Rosenthal, whose job was to supervise the skim. However, on January 15 1976, the Nevada Gaming Board denied Rosenthal a license because of his gambling record. Upon the discovery of the skim, he was suspected of having masterminded it.[2]

Rosenthal's licensing problems resulted partly from the arrival in Las Vegas in 1971 of Tony Spilotro, his boyhood friend. Although Steven Brill views Spilotro as a major underworld figure, Nicholas Pileggi and other commentators regard him as a minor gangster of merely local significance. Doubts have also been raised concerning the seriousness of Spilotro's criminal activity. According to Pileggi, he had been "arrested many times" for "infractions considerably more minor than the ones he had actually committed." Besides leading a band of thieves known as the Hole-in-the-Wall Gang, Spilotro is believed to have taken control of bookmaking, loan-sharking, and prostitution throughout Las Vegas. Yet citing the limited evidence against him and the fact that he was never convicted of major crimes, Ronald A. Farrell and Carole Case believe that his bad reputation reflected media exaggeration and anti-Italian prejudice. In any event, the publicity-hungry Spilotro's constant appearances on television and in newspapers hurt Rosenthal, whose friendship with him was played up by the media at the time he sought licensing.[3]

After his licensing denial, Rosenthal returned to the Stardust as

York: Oxford U P, 1986), 123; Steven Brill, *The Teamsters* (New York: Simon and Schuster, 1978), 4, 13-14, 189-249.

[2] Pileggi, *Casino*, 13, 17-18, 29-31, 42-44, 58-69, 70-77, 176, 194-99; Skolnick, *House of Cards*, 206-21; Farrell and Case, *The Black Book and the Mob*, 78-79, 80-83, 84, 86, 115, 116; Brill, *The Teamsters*, 226, 227, 229.

[3] Brill, *The Teamsters*, 205-6, 210; Pileggi, *Casino*, 103-16, 141-55, 163, 241; Farrell and Case, *The Black Book and the Mob*, 67-74.

its food and beverage director. Having decided to appeal the decision, he used his own television show, broadcast from the Stardust, to impugn the gaming authorities, but this only angered the state and the mob bosses.[4] In 1978 Spilotro was barred from Nevada's casinos. While Rosenthal was offended that Spilotro's reputation jeopardized his appeal, Spilotro resented Rosenthal's higher status within the mob and retaliated by having an affair with his wife; divorce came in 1980. Around the time Spilotro and his gang were caught during a heist, the Midwestern mob bosses were under indictment for having engineered the skim and thus all the more incensed at the bad publicity fueled by their underlings. To prevent incriminating testimony, the bosses eliminated likely witnesses. This was a possible motive for the 1982 car-bombing in which Rosenthal nearly died – although some blame Spilotro. Rosenthal left Las Vegas in 1983 and retired to Boca Raton, Florida. Three years later Spilotro and his brother Dominic were beaten and buried alive in an Indiana cornfield. Some lawmen say that Spilotro was killed because he had failed to maintain the mob's position in Las Vegas.[5]

In Scorsese's *Casino*, Rosenthal, Spilotro, and Geri McGee become Sam "Ace" Rothstein (Robert de Niro), Nicky Santoro (Joe Pesci), and Ginger McKenna (Sharon Stone).[6] The Stardust Hotel becomes the Tangiers. In reality the Stardust skim preceded the wiretaps that led to the bosses' indictments, but the film treats these events nearly simultaneously, so as to intensify the climax. Whereas Rosenthal's marriage seems to have been marked by his infidelities and physical abuse of Geri, Rothstein's marriage fails because of his coldness and Ginger's addictions.[7] And whereas Spi-

---

[4] Pileggi, *Casino*, 198-99, 206-07, 224-26, 229-31, 233-36.

[5] Pileggi, *Casino*, 198-99, 203-08, 224-25, 237-38, 269-93, 300-07, 311-17, 340, 344-46; Farrell and Case, *The Black Book and the Mob*, 8, 86, 99, 100, 101, 102, 113, 114, 116-17, 141.

[6] Scripted by Nicholas Pileggi and Martin Scorsese, Scorsese's film was not inspired by Pileggi's book of the same title, since the script was written before the book. Based on research and interviews, the book is a largely factual account of the decline of the mob in Las Vegas. A fictionalized treatment of the same period, the film alters characters' names, omits or adds details, transforms and transposes events. But in essentials there is a close congruity between the book and the film. The following discussion of the film relies on Nicholas Pileggi and Martin Scorsese, *Casino* (London: Faber and Faber, 1996). Page numbers are given parenthetically in the text if possible.

[7] Pileggi, *Casino*, 165-66, 275, 279-80.

lotro was barred from Las Vegas casinos after his entry in the Nevada Gaming Board's Black Book in 1978, two years after Rosenthal's licensing denial, Nicky is in the Black Book when Ace is denied. This change serves to stress that Nicky had hurt Ace's chances for a license.

II. Like many of Scorsese's films, *Casino* depicts a closed society, characterized by its own rituals and codes, which must defend itself against the hostile mainstream. Besides reflecting his fascination with those pariah figures who exist on the social margins, the film typifies Scorsese's analogical and therefore essentially Catholic sensibility, which seeks and finds traces of the sacred in the secular world.[8] Strange as it may seem, *Casino* finds a modern vestige of the sacred in gambling.

Best known for *Man and the Sacred* (Eng. trans. 1959) and *Man, Play, and Games* (Eng. trans. 1961), Roger Caillois accepts Johan Huizinga's conception of play as a free activity performed within a special "sacred" area. But unlike Huizinga, he attempts to define the cultural function of games of chance, which is harder to explain than games of competition. No less important, Caillois rejects Huizinga's conflation of play with the sacred, for he insists that, by contrast with the purely formal character of play, ritual is saturated with meaning.

Standing outside the ordinary, profane world, and attaching to certain objects, beings, places, and times, the sacred manifests a mysterious and capricious duality. Caillois observes that it conjoins the beneficence of life-enhancement and rejuvenation with a terrifying, death-dealing power of destruction, chaos, and panic. To derive its benefits while avoiding its bad effects, humanity must surround it with taboos, the violation of which causes the offending person to become the pariah whose expulsion purifies society. Yet society must also draw upon the sacred's life-giving power through controlled contact with it – the task of ritual and the priest. Another desirable means of contact is the festival, for though its topsy-

---

[8] On analogism as a characteristic feature of Catholic thought and sensibility, see Paul Giles, *American Catholic Arts and Fictions: Culture, Ideology, Aesthetics* (Cambridge: Cambridge Univ. Press, 1992), 8, 26-29, 38, 39, 57, 69, 85, 106-07, 119, 392-93. For Scorsese, see 336, 347-49.

turvy world is only temporary, it allows for revivifying invasions by the sacred in the form of violations of the social order. Games of chance figure typically amid such misrule, as signs of the gods' power to deal out good and bad unpredictably.[9]

Arguing that play and culture originate in ritual, Rene Girard holds that ritual has been society's chief means of controlling violence, which is the essence of the sacred. The bad or profane form of violence stems from mimetic rivalries which, as they develop into open, escalating hostility, cause the antagonists to become locked in imitative cycles of vengeance and thus to become each other's unacknowledged doubles. At the same time, more and more people are swept up, by mimetic contagion, into a seemingly uncontrollable vortex of retaliatory violence. If left unchecked, general hostility must level all cultural distinctions and differences, including those rituals, taboos, and laws whereby order is maintained. As violence becomes increasingly random, everyone is at risk, yet each antagonist hopes to strike that ultimate divine blow that ends the chaos. Girard terms this state of undifferentiation the sacrificial crisis.[10]

At the height of the crisis, an individual is singled out arbitrarily, heaped with false accusations, and thus transformed into the monstrous embodiment of the crisis in all its undifferentiation. The unacknowledged double of his accusers, such an individual is chosen from among those on the social margins, who not only fit the pariah role but recall the indistinction and confusion of the crisis. This individual is the scapegoat, whose seemingly miraculous elimination is followed by a return to order. But this murder is concealed through mythical distortions. The scapegoat becomes a god-savior; the gods, identified with "good" violence, are held responsible for ending the crisis; and ritual is established with animal victims substituting for the foundational human victim. Mediated by priests, ritual is the controlled mimesis, in disguised form, of the crisis that led to the restoration of order. Thus is defined the difference between sacred and profane violence.

---

[9] Caillois, *Man and the Sacred,* trans. Meyer Barash (New York: Free Press of Glencoe, 1959), 19-26, 32, 35-38, 42, 55-56, 60, 96, 97-99, 100-01, 103, 106, 108, 112-14, 117, 120-22, 125-26, 131, 135, 137-38, 158, 160; Caillois, *Man, Play, and Games,* trans. Meyer Barash (New York: Free Press of Glencoe, 1961), 126.

[10] The following discussion of Girard is based on his *Violence and the Sacred,* trans. Patrick Gregory (Baltimore: Johns Hopkins U P, 1978), *passim.*

For Girard, ritual distinctions give rise to the differential system of culture. Ritual is thus the origin of play, whose relation to the sacrificial crisis is evident in the arbitrary nature of prizes. Likewise, games of chance first appear in ritualistic form, and only later lose their sanctity. The link between ritual and chance is that the sacrificial crisis had been characterized by a leveling of distinctions through random violence, by arbitrary victimization, and by the community's miraculous recovery, interpreted as divine. The function of games of chance in ritual is to commemorate and imitate the crisis — the vertiginous atmosphere of hope and panic, and the unpredictable potential of violence for destruction or salvation. Themes of chance also appear in myths and festivals, which simulate the disorder of the crisis in order to rejuvenate society.

That games bear traces of their sacrificial and ritual origin is evident in games of chance. A quasi-ritualized environment beyond the ordinary world, the casino forms a consecrated space within which all actions must conform to ritualized rules. Another essential part of the atmosphere of gambling is the crowd, which figures in the sacrificial crisis as in ritual. The crisis also resembles the two types of games defined by Caillois: *agon* or competitive rivalry, in which victory depends mainly on will, effort, and skill; and *alea*, in which each player abdicates his will to pure chance, whose decision he awaits on a "democratic" level with other players. Although some forms of gambling combine chance and skill, the home of the *agon* is the sporting arena, while that of *alea* is the racetrack, lottery, pari-mutuel, and casino.[11]

The relation between gambling and the sacred is recognized by Pileggi and Scorsese. In Las Vegas, says Pileggi, the "average guy had a shot at a miracle" and a thousand dollar bill buys "canonization" (13, 80). Scorsese observes that people come to Las Vegas thinking that "with one throw of the dice their whole life will be changed."[12] In the film, Ace says that the city "washes away your sins" and offers "what Lourdes does for hunchbacks and cripples"

---

[11] Caillois, *Man, Play, and Games*, 12, 14, 17, 18, 40-41, 73, 74-75, 77, 114, 115, 118. See also Vicki Abt, James F. Smith, and Eugene Martin Christiansen, *The Business of Risk: Commercial Gambling in Mainstream America* (Lawrence, Kansas: U of Kansas P, 1985), 22-23, 60.

[12] Ian Christie, "Introduction: Stardust in Vegas," in Pileggi and Scorsese, *Casino*, xii.

(8). The casino count room is for him the "most sacred room in the casino" (9).

Yet unlike the sacrificial crisis and ritual games of chance, where pure luck predominates, the casino is a business with a slight edge over its customers.[13] Ace says: "It's all been arranged just for us to get *your* money . . . . In the end, we get it all" (9, 29). The prevalence of cheating in casinos suggests that they cannot rely on the power of the sacred to control behavior. And whereas rituals and festivals occur leisurely, Caillois finds modern gambling to have been contaminated by the grim earnestness of work. He further contends that, in contrast with the revivification of traditional societies through festival, the modern world treats the festival and its gambling elements as a meaningless "parenthesis" in routine.[14]

In analysing the vestigial sanctity of gambling, one must recall its identification with disorder, randomness, and the collapse of social boundaries. Hence many communities continue to denounce it as immoral and taboo; and even legalized commercial gambling has been what Jerome H. Skolnick terms a "pariah industry."[15] Gambling owes its immoral reputation largely to the fact that it violates the Protestant concept of success as exclusively the result of hard work, productivity, punctuality, prudence, self-discipline, self-sacrifice, thrift, and sobriety. For even if modern gambling is contaminated by work, Caillois acknowledges that the casino provides a partial escape from industrial discipline. It offers unrelenting hedonism for twenty-four hours a day in a hermetic, windowless setting where no clocks are allowed and unchanging illumination suggests a special place out of time. Its delights include endless banqueting, abundant alcohol, drugs, and prostitutes.[16] Another reason for gambling's stigma is that it has attracted pariahs, especially Italians and Jews of the underworld.

As a pariah, gambling has been banished until recently to the

---

[13] On the casino's advantage, see Bill Friedman, *Casino Management* (Secaucus, N.J.: Lyle Stuart, 1974), 18.
[14] Caillois, *Man and the Sacred*, 11-12, 123, 126-27, 131-32, 163-65; Caillois, *Man, Play, and Games*, 44, 45, 117, 157, 158.
[15] Skolnick, *House of Cards*, 13, 102, 117.
[16] Caillois, *Man, Play, and Games*, 5, 66, 115, 157, 158; Findlay, *People of Chance*, 88, 147; Munting, *An Economic and Social History of Gambling in Britain and the U.S.A.*, 29; Abt, Smith, and Christiansen, *The Business of Risk*, 2, 79, 194-95, 203; Skolnick, *House of Cards*, 20, 35, 36.

frontier or what remains of it – a borderland where sudden riches, violence, and immoral excess are normal. Just as America's gambling culture arose on the frontier, so in modern America gambling's chief home has been Nevada, a former frontier state. Accordingly, Las Vegas has sought to recreate a frontier atmosphere – the mood if not the reality of misrule.[17] In *Casino*, consistent with Nicky's notion of Las Vegas as the "fuckin' Wild West" (82), his Gold Rush jewelry store has wooden-planked sidewalks and hitching posts (77). This is the headquarters of his Hole-in-the-Wall Gang, named after the band of Western outlaws.

Like other states Nevada has had deep reservations towards casinos. The puritanical ethos of the Mormons who make up a large part of the population and exert a major influence on the state government is very much at odds with the unbridled hedonism of gambling culture.[18] Yet Nevada has accepted legalized gambling not only because a gambling culture persists in the state but because its ongoing "fiscal crisis" has required it to rely on casinos as a source of tax revenues. Although banned in Nevada in 1910, gambling was legalized in 1931, and since then many Mormons have been major financial backers of the industry. By the late 1970s it had long proved its fiscal indispensability to the state, with taxes on gambling and gambling-related entertainment providing roughly one half of Nevada's revenue.[19]

The legalization of gambling implies that a vice has been purified and decriminalized, divested of its pariah status and rendered indistinguishable from ordinary businesses. But because old anxieties over gambling have not been dispelled in Nevada, the state has chosen not simply to legalize but to regulate and control it. As a result, the state became a partner of private business in all gaming enterprises. Such a situation could only be fraught with moral ambiguities. Whereas upon legalization the barrier between gambling and the community seemed to have vanished, regulation implies that traditional moral distinctions still need to be protected. Thus a

[17] Findlay, *People of Chance*, 3, 4, 8, 80, 110, 116, 117, 127, 128, 131, 143, 170.
[18] Farrell and Case, *The Black Book and the Mob*, 19-20; Findlay, *People of Chance*, 120-21.
[19] Skolnick, *House of Cards*, 9-10; Farrell and Case, *The Black Book and the Mob*, 21, 22; Abt, Smith, and Christiansen, *The Business of Risk*, 82; Findlay, *People of Chance*, 172; Caillois, *Man, Play, and Games*, 117; Munting, *An Economic and Social History of Gambling in Britain and the U.S.A.*, 146.

pariah industry does not necessarily lose its stigma through legalization. The basic problem for the state regulators has been to maintain moral boundaries between "normal" society and an economy built upon vice – one that attracts and even requires disreputable people.[20]

The state's attempt to regulate the gambling industry has been compromised by the fact that the pariahs have remained very much part of the industry. Despite public fears of organized crime, the state has needed it to support and operate the casinos so as to insure tax revenue. A pariah industry also attracts pariah lenders, especially the mob. Organized crime has found ways of concealing its ownership of Las Vegas casinos, while those who operate, manage, and work in them often include gamblers, mobsters, and others with criminal records. As Skolnick observes, when the state took over the casinos, the illegal gamblers were allowed to remain, for people trained to such work are gamblers who "gained their experience in illegal settings." The legal gambling industry reconciles expertise with illegality "by imputing standards of morality to illegal conduct."[21]

If the mob is indirectly a business partner with the state, which side is it on, its own or the state's?[22] Not only has the mob customarily used casinos to launder money, it has bribed officials into relaxing regulations and conferring special favors and licensing. It has also been able to embezzle state tax revenues through control of casino management. The skim is accomplished by the rigging of machines and especially by mob infiltration of the casino's countroom, from which owners are barred because of their cheating.[23] Nicky's comment that the mob's purpose was to "skim the joint dry" is accompanied by a shot of Nance leaving the Tangiers countroom with a suitcase packed with money, which he brings to the bosses in Kansas City (10-11).

This is not the only cheating to occur in a casino. Even as the

[20] Skolnick, *House of Cards*, 8, 10-11, 31-32, 98, 115; Abt, Smith, and Christiansen, *The Business of Risk*, 81.

[21] Skolnick, *House of Cards*, 13, 31-32, 117, 176, 211, 217, 298; Findlay, *People of Chance*, 122-23; Farrell and Case, *The Black Book and the Mob*, 32-35.

[22] The question is Skolnick's. See *House of Cards*, 9.

[23] Pileggi, *Casino*, 16; Skolnick, *House of Cards*, 47-49, 75-76, 127; Munting, *An Economic and Social History of Gambling in Britain and the U.S.A.*, 146.

mob's hired cheats in the countroom steal money without the mob's permission, cheating is endemic on the gaming floor among players, dealers, and other employees. Former cheats are often placed in management (and lower) positions because they can best detect cheating on the floor. Dealers are subjected to careful controls, while pit-bosses and floormen observe their moves. The best known example of casino surveillance is the "eye-in-the-sky," a large overhead room permitting a view of each table through one-way mirrors.[24]

Despite legalization, the casino remains a scene of general vice, where money is stolen, drinks are free, and prostitution is built-in. Since the chief function of prostitution in the casino is to lure premium customers to the gaming tables, management encourages prostitutes to frequent casino bars by giving them complimentary drinks.[25] In Ace's description, Ginger "brought in high rollers and helped them spread around a lot of money" (35). Well aware that Las Vegas is "Kickback City" (36), she, like other prostitutes, gives money to floor managers, dealers, pit-bosses, and especially car valets (36, 38). Nicky has tipsters all over town, who give him and his gang information on possible victims among hotel guests (79-80).

Nor are law enforcement agencies outside the moral ambiguity of Las Vegas. Nicky notes that there are "a lot of holes in the desert, and a lot of problems are buried in those holes" (7). But while this is how the mob disposes of victims, the police do the same thing. Ace warns the newly arrived Nicky that "even the coppers aren't afraid to bury people out in the desert here" (43).

The public has long charged that legalized gambling gives undesirables a cloak of respectability. Thus, observes Skolnick, the problem has been to maintain gangster-generated revenue, "while dissociating the state from their disrepute."[26] The bulwark of the system of control is licensing, which is under the jurisdiction of the Nevada Gaming Commission and the Nevada State Gaming Control Board. Applicants must prove themselves untainted by con-

---

[24] Friedman, *Casino Management*, 36-45; Skolnick, *House of Cards*, 68-71; Pileggi, *Casino*, 15, 92-93; Christie, "Introduction: Stardust in Vegas," xv.
[25] Friedman, *Casino Management*, 129; Skolnick, *House of Cards*, 37-39; Farrell and Case, *The Black Book and the Mob*, 221.
[26] Skolnick, *House of Cards*, 118; Farrell and Case, *The Black Book and the Mob*, 11.

nections with mobsters and other stigmatized persons. A licensee may neither cater to criminals nor associate with them, and licenses may be revoked if these and other conditions are not met.[27]

The more dramatic method of control is the Black Book, which originated not in the days of Al Capone, as Ace and Nicky imply, but in 1960 (71, 76). The book lists persons whom the state excludes from casinos because their "notorious or unsavory reputation" threatens the public image of gambling. Nicky repeats this description indignantly (substituting "and" for "or") upon his nomination (76). Casino licensees must banish such persons from their premises, lest their licenses be revoked. Inclusion in the Black Book follows upon an individual's failure to clear his name before the State Gaming Commission in a public, show-cause hearing. A nominee faces criminal prosecution upon entering a casino.[28]

The criteria of selection are inconsistent in both methods of control, which fail to protect casinos from disreputables. Noting that most applicants for licensing have criminal histories, Farrell and Case comment that the fine distinctions made in the licensing process lack objectivity.[29] According to Findlay, licenses are given to former gamblers and even people with criminal records, if these are "not too shadowy."[30] Inclusion in the Black Book seems no less arbitrary, being tainted by flagrant ethnic prejudice. That the regulators are native Nevadans of primarily Anglo-Saxon Protestant and Mormon background explains why the Book contains very few people of this type. Since the regulators falsely assume that the moral threat emanates from alien forces, a pattern of exclusion has developed whereby certain outgroups are consistently singled out on the basis of social stereotypes of evil. The overwhelming number of nominees to the Black Book have always been Italian Americans, targeted prejudicially because their group is identified with organized crime. Jews have had a preferential advantage over Italians in gaining legitimacy in the gambling industry because they are associated with business acumen and probity. Yet Farrell and Case re-

[27] Farrell and Case, *The Black Book and the Mob*, 5, 80; Skolnick, *House of Cards*, 173-85; Friedman, *Casino Management*, 326-28, 337, 340.

[28] Farrell and Case, *The Black Book and the Mob*, xi, 3, 5-7, 9, 31, 76; Skolnick, *House of Cards*, 121; Friedman, *Casino Management*, 340-41.

[29] Farrell and Case, *The Black Book and the Mob*, 221.

[30] Findlay, *People of Chance*, 153.

mark that if all those who pose a serious threat to gambling were nominated to the book, the industry would have to shut down.[31]

What function do licensing and the Black Book really serve? When fears of criminal infiltration threaten public confidence in the gambling industry, regulators must show that they can not only control but purify it, and this requires resort to theatrical, ritualistic, and symbolic means. Based on the assumption that more drama means more control, hearings over licensing and entry into the Black Book are highly dramatic events widely reported in the media. Their chief aim is to enact symbolically the industry's purification by denouncing and expelling the supposedly contaminating individual. Thus is supposedly retraced what the public feared to have become blurred, namely the boundary between good and evil. But since such acts fail to fix or protect moral boundaries, the public is guilty of *méconnaissance*. Indistinguishable from many whom society tolerates, the banished individual is an arbitrary victim of exclusionary violence – in short, a scapegoat.[32]

But should the gambling industry still be considered a pariah? Over the last four decades the public, business, and the state have been increasingly willing to accept legalized gambling. This change results from the decline of the Protestant ethic amid a new culture of consumption and leisure. In 1984, voters' support of every lottery initiative demonstrated a general acceptance of the principle of funding government expenditures through state-operated lotteries. Pari-mutuel betting has also won wide popularity. Because gambling is increasingly under the control of publicly-owned corporations, whose credentials are indistinguishable from those of many businesses, it is less identified with organized crime. Besides owning and operating lotteries and off-track betting, the state blesses the corporations' gambling operations and even cooperates with them in the lottery business. Since gambling is now an enormous leisure industry, integrated with mainstream America, it cannot be characterized as a pariah or deviant. Nor is it a "parenthesis" outside

---

[31] Farrell and Case, *The Black Book and the Mob*, xi-xii, 4, 11-12, 13, 14, 19-20, 24, 32, 37, 51-52, 91-92, 107, 109, 111, 112, 113, 117, 142-44, 146-51, 157, 163-64, 167, 171, 173, 208-12, 218, 219, 222, 223, 224n, 228-29; Skolnick, *House of Cards*, 121-23.

[32] Farrell and Case, *The Black Book and the Mob*, xi, 3, 4, 9-10, 11, 67, 69, 172, 194, 217, 227, 218.

work. Just as gambling is now conventional behavior, so commercial gambling is a legitimate business, the institutionalization of what had formerly been a vice.[33]

To be sure, Vicki Abt and her colleagues acknowledged as late as 1985 that commercial gambling was still seen by many as a pariah, but they attributed this to the fact that social norms and ideals often fail to reflect behavior. The authors also conceded that public approval did not yet extend to casinos, which still had trouble obtaining long-term financing. Despite the triumph of gambling in Atlantic City since 1976, Abt and her colleagues saw the failure of many casino initiatives over the next decade as proof that historic questions about casino gambling, including the role of organized crime, still troubled Americans.[34] But more recently casinos have become more and more acceptable to the American public. This has resulted partly from corporate investment and sponsorship as well as from constant media coverage of sweepstakes, which has legitimated gambling while fueling interest in it. The public has thus come to view the criminal element as being less influential in casino gambling than in the past. Having lost what remains of their stigma, casinos no longer suffer the pariah label they bore in the 1970s, when Las Vegas shook with the *agon* between Lefty Rosenthal and Tony Spilotro.

III. Situated between the mob and state, Ace Rothstein embodies the moral ambiguity of the gambling industry. Belonging to neither of these powers, yet required to satisfy both, he is left unprotected against them. His interstitial position is in this way crucial to his transformation into a scapegoat.

As both a Jew and a gambler with a record of arrests, Ace bears two stigmas. Yet a stigmatized person is often seen as possessing special desirable skills and qualities.[35] This description fits Ace, who

[33] Abt, Smith, and Christiansen, *The Business of Risk*, ix, x, xii, xiii, 2, 4-6, 14-16, 99, 143, 144, 148, 152, 153, 174, 192-93, 203-04, 213, 217; Munting, *An Economic and Social History of Gambling in Britain and the U.S.A.*, 214-15; Findlay, *People of Chance*, 201-03, 205.

[34] Abt, Smith, and Christiansen, *The Business of Risk*, 14, 148, 212; Munting, *An Economic and Social History of Gambling in Britain and the United States*, 150.

[35] Erving Goffman, *Stigma: Notes on the Management of Spoiled Identity* (New York: Simon and Schuster, 1986), 1-2, 3, 4, 5, 10.

describes himself as a "hell of a handicapper . . . . I could change the odds for every bookmaker in the country" (3). Suffering from two social handicaps, Ace has learned how to calculate and compensate for defects, so as to make the game equal for all participants.

Though stigmatized by normal society, Ace enjoys privileged status in the pariah world of the mob – a world which, as the object of awe, fear and reprobation, partakes of the sacred. Mobsters are associated with violence, unapproachable remoteness and secrecy, and indifference to suffering. The criminal's "very impurity" renders him sacred, says Caillois.[36] Mobsters are also identified with that personal autonomy and power which is often seen as divine. The script for *Casino* calls for a vignette of the bosses "surrounded by food and wine like the gods of Olympus" (6). In their unflappable self-confidence and tranquil enjoyment of their self-created plenitude, they ignore the violence they inflict elsewhere. Girard writes of that "fascination of superior violence" that confers a "semidivine prestige" upon the "man who strikes the hardest" and who exhibits the "triumphant majesty" of the gods.[37]

Having gained admittance into the world of those he himself calls "the gods" (53), Ace owes this success to his gambling skills, which win the bosses money. The very Jewishness which in mainstream society is for Ace a second stigma gives him an advantage in the underworld, for unlike most Italian American mobsters he may consort with the bosses without asking permission (21). He is, to quote Nicky, the mob's "Golden Jew" (22). All this is explained by the logic of the sacred, for though the scapegoat is usually reviled, it is sometimes revered and sanctified.

Because the bosses need someone they can trust, they ask Ace to manage the Tangiers covertly (16-17). His job is to supervise the skim as well as to convince regulators that the casino conforms to gambling commission rules and thus provides its share of state tax revenues. Ace is the ideal person to bring regularity and discipline to gambling precisely because his values are mainly those of the non-gambling "profane" society. Whereas most gamblers reject

---

[36] Caillois, *Man and the Sacred*, 50.
[37] Girard, *Violence and the Sacred*, 152.

patience and calculation, submitting to chance, Ace approaches gambling rationally so as to counter it. Thus Nicky says that Ace "had to know everything," betting only on games he knew thoroughly; he was the "only guaranteed winner I ever knew" (18-21).

Imposing on the Tangiers a work ethic of managerial, bureaucratic discipline, Ace exemplifies Caillois' point that work contaminates modern play.[38] It is understandable that Ace suffers from the limitations of a workaholic. He is a naysaying, anhedonic type whose compulsive punctilio and attention to job details give him ulcers (107). The sign behind his office desk displays an enormous "No" beneath a very small "yes" (104, 106). Nicky seems right to say that Ace was "so serious about it all that I don't think that he ever enjoyed himself" (19). Admittedly he indulges in luxuries, but mainly for social status and self-advertisement.

Hard work brings Ace not just wealth but prestige. At the Vegas Valley Country Club, Philip Green (a double of Allen Glick) praises Ace as "indispensable" to the "gaming community," and then, after welcoming him as a member of the club, hands him a citation from the Charitable Foundations of Greater Las Vegas: Ace is now part of the city's "power elite" (72). "For guys like me," he says, "Las Vegas washes away your sins. It's like a morality car wash" (8). This legitimation means acceptance by what Scorsese terms the "American WASP community."[39] Indeed, it means becoming something of an upper-class WASP himself, partly by marrying a beautiful blonde Northern European woman (albeit a former high-class call-girl). Ace's old friend Nicky calls attention to his most ludicrous fantasy of ethnic metamorphosis, noting that he is "fuckin' walkin' around [his house] like John Barrymore" (121), with a pink smoking jacket and cigarette-holder – a disdainful aristocratic WASP pose.

One sees why Ace believes he has been given "paradise on earth" (3). What he most enjoys is participating in the bosses' power of wealth and violence, part of which he receives with the Tangiers. Ace has insisted that he be allowed to run the casino without interference, since he wants total control of it. To show the

---

[38] Caillois, *Man, Play, and Games,* 44, 45.
[39] See Christie, "Introduction: Stardust in Vegas," xiii.

extent of his control, Scorsese portrays his annoyance at the lack of blueberries in the hotel's breakfast muffins, followed by his order that each muffin must contain a sufficient amount. But Ace's dream of total control focuses on the gaming floor, where he aims to insure that the rituals of play are scrupulously observed and all infractions punished. Just as the priest, through knowledge of ritual, transforms profane violence into beneficent, so Ace's knowledge of the rules of gambling will make it socially acceptable.[40]

Ace's managerial methods confirm Skolnick's description of a casino as a "totalitarian state" organized to maximize surveillance and achieve complete control. Such control depends on creating conditions of "regularity and visibility" through "ritualization of the action." This includes programmed movement by dealers, color coding of chips, and other requirements. The floorman's main job is to observe deviations from normality, which requires a highly developed grasp of gambling. The ultimate measure is the eye-in-the-sky, providing the godlike prerogative of observing everything invisibly.[41]

For Ace, cheating is the greatest affront not only to his power but to the bosses and the state. As sacred beings, the bosses may cheat the state as they please, but cheating against them must be prevented, lest their sanctity drain away. But contrastingly, Ace must also prevent non-mob cheaters from stealing the state's tax earnings. As he and his colleagues search the floor for cheats, the atmosphere is heavy with suspicion (18). In one scene, Ace watches approvingly as Nicky bullies two cheaters into permanently leaving the Tangiers (46-47). The most appalling example of Ace's total control comes when he personally detects two cheaters at cards. After one of them is brought to a private room, Ace orders his dealing hand to be broken, warning that a power saw will be used next time. The cheaters are then thrown into the street, too terrified ever to return (48-53). Ironically Ace claims this extralegal right of judgment to protect the state's interests; the state probably knows this, but will hardly admit it.

The film's opening scenes show Ace looking out like a king

[40] Caillois, *Man and the Sacred*, 45.
[41] Skolnick, *House of Cards*, 71-73.

over his casino. Confident of his mastery of chance, of the protection given him by the bosses, and of the violence he is permitted to exert, Ace conveys disdain of others and remoteness from normal emotions. He cultivates an image of ontological plenitude, the autonomy and self-possession of either being a god or one favored by the gods. He seems not so much of the casino world as unapproachably above it. Ace thus embodies the arrogance that overtakes many of Scorsese's characters in their quest for godlike superiority – Jake La Motta, Travis Bickel, the gangsters in *Goodfellas*, Max Cady. Yet Ace's pose of self-autonomy like that of these characters masks an ontological lack, manifested in his obsessive concern for the gaze and opinion of other people; as Scorsese says of Ace, he is always "on display."[42] In *Casino*, as in Scorsese's other films, the quest for divinity is self-destructive.

Yet Ace knows that, unless he overcomes the stigma of his gambling past, in no small part by avoiding disreputable activities and associations, he will never be granted the gaming license required of all casino operators. Above all, his conduct must not call attention to what the public and the state have long ignored, that legalized gambling is a form of immorality in which they participate. Ace must therefore avoid becoming a *scandal* in the sense of a public object of simultaneous repulsion and attraction, since the person identified with scandal affronts society as a reminder of the moral ambiguities it normally conceals. Such a person risks being sacrificed as the community's dishonest means of convincing itself that its moral boundaries remain intact.

The most serious danger for Ace is Nicky Santoro, whose resentment of him was already being sown in Chicago. While Ace's money-making and Jewishness had enabled him to move freely among the bosses, Nicky was not only bound by mob protocols but ordered by the bosses to watch closely their "Golden Jew," a mocking phrase suggesting Nicky's jealous resentment of his privileged non-Italian friend. Nicky's humiliation is manifest when top boss Remo Gaggi kisses Ace in the Italian manner and then tells him to keep up the "good job, my boy." After ordering Nicky to "*vien aca* [come here]," Gaggi tells him that he must keep a "good

---

[42] Christie, "Introduction: Stardust in Vegas," xxi.

eye" on Ace, whom he contrasts with Nicky's "fuckin' friends . . . without brains" (21-22).

Subsequently Nicky is sent to Las Vegas to watch the skim and "to make sure that nobody fucked with Ace" (42, 46). But though Ace urges him to keep a low profile, his methods are the antithesis of Ace's measured calculation. Nicky imposes a street tax on numbers, narcotics, and prostitution, and is soon ransacking the city with his gang (44-45, 46-47, 77-79, 81-83). Not only do most of his earnings derive from activities the bosses had forbidden, but he lets his tribute to them dwindle to a trickle (89, 178). A publicity hound, Nicky appears constantly in the media. His nomination to the Black Book he dismisses as a "bunch of bullshit" (71).

But though Ace regards Nicky as his opposite, unacknowledged resemblances unite them. Ace too has an enormous ego, overweening pride, extreme ambition, and a desire for prepotency. Both men cultivate a pose of autonomy and self-sufficiency, and each enjoys the power of intimidation conferred on them through the bosses. So too, their common craving for publicity reflects a desire to be admired. Each would embody something of that fascination and terror which is the sacred.

That egotism propels Ace beyond reasonable limits is evident in his frequent changes of clothes and attention to their quality, tailoring, and cleanliness. He views sartorial perfection as essential to the unruffled demeanor of a "god" such as himself. Noting Ace's extreme touchiness, Nicky attributes his inflated ego partly to his having hired "Jonathan and David and their tigers," a popular show, away from the Palace Hotel by "buildin' them a new stage and then givin' them a silver Rolls-Royce" (69). Just as the proverbial love and loyalty of the Old Testament friends counterpoints ironically the antagonism between Ace and Nicky, so the entertainers' mastery of wild animals contrasts with the protagonists' failure to tame their own bestial forces of violence. Another sign of Ace's egotism is that, just before his licensing hearing, he announces that he is the "real boss" at the Tangiers, thus jeopardizing his chances (116).

As Ace's hearing approaches, and the media chatter about how his "boyhood friendship" may cost him a license, Nicky slips into Ace's house through the back door. Their confrontation is marked by classic features of the sacrificial crisis as a state of undifferentiation. Being close friends, Ace and Nickly resemble those feuding brothers whose mimetic rivalry makes them symbols *par excellence* of the crisis. This is because their similar desires and mutual antagonisms have so erased their differences that they have become unacknowledged doubles of each other.[43] According to Girard, Greek tragedy represents this situation through *stichomythia*, in which two antagonists exchange angry accusations and counteraccusations. Although each persists in opposition to the other, they fail to realize that their reciprocal violence and the identity of their accusations make it impossible to distinguish between them in moral terms. Although the demands of cinematic realism prevent Pileggi and Scorsese from employing *stichomythia* in the rigidly symmetrical form characteristic of Greek tragedy, and whose purpose is to emphasize the unrecognized identity between the feuding characters, Ace's and Nicky's exchange contains unmistakeably stichomythic features.[44]

To Ace's statement that he must have a license, Nicky says that he has no need for one, since Nicky plants his "flag" in Nevada. Interpreting this to mean that Nicky would take over the mob, Ace will not join his conspiracy. "I just want my license. I want everything nice and quiet," says Ace (118-21). Up to this point Ace has seemed the sober, retiring businessman threatened by the loud, exhibitionistic egotist. But Nicky reminds Ace of the recent magazine article which had revealed his role as manager of the Tangiers:

> Nicky: You mean, quiet like this: "I'm the boss." That's quiet? . . . .
> Ace: Everytime you're on television, I get mentioned. *That* looks bad. That looks bad.
> Nicky: What the fuck happened to you? Will you tell me?
> Ace: What happened to me? What happened to you?
> Nicky: Yeah.
> Ace: You lost your control.
> Nicky: I lost control?
> Ace: Yes, you lost your control.
> Nicky: Look at you. You're fuckin' walkin' around like John Barrymore [he refers to Ace's pink robe and cigarette holder] . . . . *I* lost control? (121)

---

[43] Girard, *Violence and the Sacred*, 63.
[44] Girard, *Violence and the Sacred*, 44-45.

Nicky then mentions the assault Ace had ordered on Lester Diamond (James Woods), his wife's old boyfriend. For Nicky, this mauling typifies the "disrespect" Ace had shown to many people, including Ginger. It makes no difference to Nicky that Ginger and Lester had shown disrespect to Ace, nor is he troubled by Ace's annoyance over the bad publicity of having to vouch for his friend whenever he gets into trouble with the law. As Nicky leaves he tells Ace that "Your fuckin head is gettin' bigger than your casino . . . . You better check yourself" (122).

Girard finds the essence of a tragic situation in those stichomythic moments when two characters' exchange of mutual recriminations leave the spectator with little or nothing to choose between them.[45] Notwithstanding Nicky's anger, fantasies of revolt, and threat to Ace's career, he justifiably rejects Ace's claim that he wants only quiet, and that Nicky is his sole problem. Not only has Ace attracted bad publicity by revealing his role at the Tangiers, he has used strong-arm methods on Lester just as Nicky would do. It is likewise true that Ace has used illegal violence at the Tangiers, and that, for all his pose of a law-abiding businessman, he is morally complicit with the mob, indeed a member of it. Nicky also notes signs of Ace's hubris – pink robe, cigarette holder, and aristocratic pose (121). In short, Ace and Nicky see only each other's flaws, not their mutual resemblance. Thus Nicky tells Ace that he has a "big head"; and though he helped to beat up Lester, he rebukes Ace for having ordered it. The characters' symmetry is evident in their parallel accusations: "What happened to you?"; "What happened to you?"; "You lost your control"; "*I* lost control?"

Ace's marriage to Ginger testifies to his seduction by the excess and self-intoxication of Las Vegas. Whereas Ace loves order and calculation and attempts to live by certain rules, she believes in astrology and betrays him with her adulteries. At the same time, Ginger represents two closely related kinds of play. One is *alea* or chance, typified by the throw of the dice. With *alea*, observes Caillois, the individual "lets himself drift and becomes intoxicated through feeling [. . .], possessed by strange powers." A "special kind of vertigo seizes both lucky and unlucky players," who are "scarcely

[45] Girard, *Violence and the Sacred,* 46-47.

conscious of what is going on around them." *Alea* shares these features with what Caillois terms *ilinx,* the most primitive form of play. Meaning "whirlpool" and implying vertigo, *ilinx* is a whirling movement which produces a sense of "falling, or being projected into space, rapid rotation, sliding, speeding, and acceleration of vertilinear movement, separately or in combination with gyrating movement." But *ilinx* is also a "vertigo" or "intoxication" of the "moral order." Like Ginger, a person captured by *ilinx* wants to adapt vertigo to daily life, and thus experiences a permanent need for intoxication through drugs or alchohol. Such a person disregards all rules and lives in a topsy-turvy panic-driven state where whirling vertical movement at ever-increasing speed promises total triumph but leads to self-destructive collapse.[46]

Why does Ace marry Ginger? A possible answer is suggested in the scene in which he falls love with her. Being a chip-hustler, that is, a prostitute who steals clients' chips, Ginger is rolling dice and winning big for a high roller while slipping his chips into her purse. Skolnick observes that casino management expects prostitutes to make sure that clients keep on playing, since the odds are with the house. Chip-hustling is regarded as a "sin."[47] When the high roller denies Ginger a generous tip, she plunges the whole casino into chaos by tossing racks of chips into the air. Meanwhile, Ace stands amid the general scramble with his eyes fixed on the ecstatic Ginger. However, the film introduces a detail showing that Ace allows her to violate his professional code. Whereas in Pileggi's account this scene occurred at the Dunes, the film transfers it to the Tangiers. When Ace observes Ginger incite anarchy, he is with two Tangiers executives whom he would normally want to impress with his managerial discipline. Yet Ace neither punishes nor rebukes Ginger for stealing chips and disrupting the floor (31-34). All he says is, "What a move . . . . I fell in love with her right there" (34).

Ginger has made a chaos of the ritualized world of the gaming table. The chips flying upward evoke *ilinx* in its reckless thrill-seeking and unruly intoxication. Why does Ace fall in love with her at that moment? Amid total confusion, nearly everyone scrambles

---

[46] Caillois, *Man, Play, and Games,* 17, 18, 24, 51, 73, 74-75, 77, 78, 97.
[47] Skolnick, *House of Cards,* 38-39; Pileggi, *Casino,* 76.

for chips – an undignified display of desire reducing all participants to the same level of commonness. Yet two people seem lifted above it like unmoved deities: Ginger, who walks away exempt from rules and punishment; and Ace, who finds in her a narcissistic reflection of his own haughty soul. She further carries the fascination of possible indifference, since she flouts the order he lives by.

Another explanation for Ace's marriage suggests itself if one realizes that his proud indifference and seeming self-sufficiency conceal an obsessive concern with the desires as well as the approval of others. Ace has his closest analogue among Scorsese's characters in the boxer Jake La Motta, who similarly pretends cold indifference and godlike self-sufficiency but really feels ontological emptiness, which he tries to fill by imitating other people's desires. Just as Jake's attraction to his future wife is kindled by the presence of her mob admirers, so the only woman who awakens Ace's passion is she who has attracted many men yet yielded them only her body. For Ace, the most attractive woman must be the one who does not love, since he would make her love him. In this masochistic enterprise Ace again resembles La Motta, but in the sphere of eroticism.

Being a "guy who likes sure things," Ace realizes that in marrying Ginger he is betting "the rest of . . . [his] life on a real longshot" (53), since she admits that she does not love him. Ultimately she plots Ace's murder and runs off with his money and jewels. Yet does Ace, whose behavior towards Ginger seems stiff and withdrawn, love her? Scorsese says that he is "responsible for [Ginger's] . . . emotional alienation."[48] This is suggested when Ginger and Nicky's wife enter a restaurant, whereupon Ginger tells the host that she is Mrs. Sam Rothstein, and Nicky's wife adds, "Well, you might as well get somethin' out of it" (76). As for what Ace gets out of it, he is able to parade his wife as a trophy before country club society. Ace and Ginger are "on display all the time," says Scorsese in an interview, since for them "appearance *is* everything."[49]

---

[48] Christie, "Introduction: Stardust in Vegas," xvi.
[49] Christie, "Introduction: Stardust in Vegas," xxi.

IV. A major instance of Ace's hubris occurs just before his licensing hearing, when he fires Tangiers casino employee Don Ward for incompetence or suspected cheating (92-94). The danger of firing Ward is that he is the son-in-law of County Commissioner Pat Webb, who has influence with the licensing board. In rejecting Webb's request for Ward's reinstatement, Ace has the pleasure of punishing the Mormons who despise him and whom he despises (104-07). To quote Ace, without the privilege of casino employment, Ward and his "cowboy" friends would still be "shovellin' mule shit" (25). However, in reminding Ace that he and his friends are only "guests" of the state, Webb hints at their possible exclusion (107). He soon tells gaming officials that "We may have to kick a kike's ass out of town" (116). Ace is becoming the Jewish outsider whom Gentile society will not tolerate.

At Ace's hearing the gaming commission is headed by the Senator whom Ace had honored with lavish gifts at the Tangiers. But though the Senator had reassured Ace regarding his licensing prospects, he now rushes through a vote to deny him his license (133-35). According to Skolnick, it was not primarily Spilotro's bad reputation that sank Rosenthal's chances for a license, but allegations that he had tried to fix games.[50] In the film, the chief cause of Ace's denial is Nicky's scandalous behavior. In one scene, federal agents who are tracking Nicky from a plane run out of gas and land on Ace's lawn at the moment he is explaining his case to gaming board representatives (128).

Both Rosenthal's hearing and its cinematic recreation show that the state conducts such events as dramatic, symbolic, and ritualized acts of exclusion; moreover, that they single out certain individuals arbitrarily, so as to "purge" the gambling industry of its bad elements, although the typical excluded individual is indistinguishable from many others whom the state accepts. After his hearing, Rosenthal accused the commissioners of hypocrisy and a disgraceful lack of jurisprudence, noting that some people in the industry "made him look like a choirboy."[51] Ace's response at his hearing is likewise to challenge the decision. Aware that Nevada is rejecting

---

[50] Skolnick, *House of Cards*, 216-17.
[51] Farrell and Case, *The Black Book and the Mob*, 87-88, 90.

him as its guest, he reminds the Senator that he had often been a "guest" at the Tangiers, and thus ties him to the moral corruption he pretends to condemn. Unfortunately, Ace's behavior receives a highly unfavorable slant on the next day's news: "What should have been a routine licensing hearing turned into bedlam yesterday when the flamboyant [Rothstein] [. . .] accused the state's top gaming officials of corruption and hypocrisy." The newscaster's report of Ace's "wild and unprecedented outburst" overlaps a shot of him crying "Bullshit" to reporters. Next, he is addressing the commissioners: "If you look at your own lives you'd be in jail." Ace's charges of hypocrisy are ignored because television is interested only in scandal, preferring a seeming freak show to serious consideration of the morality of legalized gambling.

Ace returns to the Tangiers as its entertainment director and is soon hosting his own television show, "Aces High," whose real purpose is to attack the gaming authorities. Suggesting an endless supply of Aces, as if his ontological plenitude is so great that he can summon a host of selves, the title also implies that Ace has succumbed to *ilinx*. In describing him as a "man who will take you inside the real Las Vegas as no one has ever done before" (138), the show's announcer implies that Ace, as the ultimate insider, is impossible to exclude from the gambling industry.[52] A master handicapper, Ace would transform his unequal judicial relation to the commissioners into a purely agonistic one, with the public as judge. But he has not anticipated that such actions would outrage the bosses, who fear publicity. Having been ordered to keep Ace quiet, the mobster Andy Stone confronts him only to be told that the U.S. Supreme Court will hear his appeal. Stone explodes, telling Ace that Gaggi's order is like a "papal bull" (140-41). Ace's once advantageous place between the state and mob is becoming one of unprotected isolation – that of the scapegoat.

Meanwhile the conflict between Ace and Nicky intensifies through their rivalry for the bosses' favor. Although Ace sees the scandal Nicky makes for him, he is blind to the one he is creating for himself and others. As for Nicky, now under constant surveil-

---

[52] Ian Christie links Ace with Rupert Pupkin, who is obsessed with becoming a television entertainer in Scorsese's *King of Comedy*. See Christie, "Introduction: Stardust in Vegas," xv.

lance, he resents Ace for having communicated with the bosses behind his back, and is sure that he wants to drive him out of town. They meet outside Las Vegas in a desert landscape fit only for pariahs and scapegoats.

Nicky rightly denies total responsibility for Ace's licensing difficulties. Nor can he accept Ace's claim that he went on television solely to be able to "hang around" the casino. Nicky insists that he had wanted to be on television, for he could have kept his casino job without doing so (147). But though Nicky recognizes Ace's reckless egoism, he continues to ignore his own. Earlier, responding to the bosses' disturbance at the disorder in Las Vegas, Nicky had announced his readiness for a "fuckin' war." These dreams of power had contrasted ironically with the humble bus stop bench where he and Marino had been sitting (125-26). In the desert, when Ace errs in suggesting that Nicky had asked his permission to come to Las Vegas, Nicky tells him that he is "what counts out here," for Ace exists only because of him (147-48). In another prideful fantasy, he warns Ace to "get your own fuckin' army" (146). Having insulted Ace as a "Jew motherfucker," Nicky tells him that without Nicky's protection every "wiseguy skell around'll take a piece of your fuckin' Jew ass. Then where you gonna go?" (148). A skell is the "lowest form of wiseguy [Italian American gangster] – a drunken bum" (148n). In Nicky's fantasy, Ace is the victim of collective, expulsive violence administered by the dregs of the mob. His Jewishness is now his victimary sign.

What feeds Nicky's hatred of Ace is that he enjoys the publicity Nicky craves, and that his hubris has reached new heights. At the ironically named Jubilation Nightclub, Ace and his fawning entourage ignore Nicky and his friends, who look on resentfully (148-49). The scene typifies the Girardian theme of the holiday gone wrong, spoiled by boredom, malaise, and bad blood.[53] Among the symptoms of impending violence, Nicky is having an affair with Ginger, who tells Ace publicly that she is "fuckin'" her "new sponsor" (195). He realizes that her adultery is dangerous, since the bosses prohibit sexual rivalry among mobsters as a potential cause of faction (176-77). Another ominous sign of violence is that Ace's

---

[53] Girard, *Violence and the Sacred*, 125.

Jewishness is now held increasingly against him. Nicky informs Marino that when he wants Ace killed he will tell Marino to "Go see the Jew" (184). Even Ginger demands that Nicky kill that "Jew bastard" (190).

All this turmoil coincides with an unforseen threat to the bosses. Formerly masters of chance, they become its victims when FBI wiretaps unexpectedly uncover the skim. Soon the bosses are under indictment, and must protect themselves against informants.

The climax of *Casino* depicts a miniature version of the sacrificial crisis, in which violence proliferates unpredictably as society descends to those promordial antagonisms from which, according to Girard, ritual, like gambling, derives. In one scene Nicky plays blackjack at the Tangiers, thus jeopardizing its legal standing. Angered by a losing streak, he demands new cards and ample credit. Ace gives Nicky less credit than he had wanted and then prudently leaves, but not before Nicky has referred to his colleague Billy Sherbert as a "Jew motherfucker." Then Nicky beats up Billy, whom he calls a "bald-headed Jew prick" (149-53). The sacrificial component in this unexpected act of violence lies in the fact that Billy substitutes for Ace, whom he, as a Jew, resembles. In an earlier scene, Ace had tolerated Nicky's cheating at the Tangiers, but a cheat at least honors rules while breaking them (63-65).[54] In this scene, Nicky is a spoilsport, altogether rejecting gaming rules, which no longer check violence. To quote Ace, Nicky and his gang had hit "rock bottom." With its alcohol, drugs, and women, Las Vegas had made them "stupid," "sloppy," and careless – a prey, like Ginger, to *ilinx* (179-80). One of the members of Nicky's gang is killed by a policeman who mistakes the aluminum wrapper of his sandwich for a gun (180-81). In an earlier scene in a restaurant kitchen, Nicky's brother had spit into a sandwich subsequently served to local policemen. The killing suggests a symbolic if not conscious retaliation (84-85).

Of the rash of murders resulting from the bosses' decision to eliminate incriminating witnesses, the most chilling are those in which chance is the decisive factor. Nance, the mob's errand run-

---

[54] Johan Huizinga, *Homo Ludens: A Study in the Play-Element in Culture*, trans. R.F.C. Hull (New York: Roy, 1950), 11.

ner, might have survived except for his son's recent arrest. The bosses decided to kill Nance lest he trade his freedom for testimony. But the more memorable assassination is that of Andy Stone, a Jewish gangster. At a recess in their trial the bosses sit around a table and ponder Stone's fate. Each boss offers his opinion, and only one negative vote seals a man's doom. Stone receives solid testimonials from three bosses, but then Gaggi asks: "Why take a chance?" (209). For Stone, the bosses' final effort to dominate chance is a cause of ill-chance; their round-table has become his fatal wheel of fortune.

The decision to kill Stone contains an element of calculation, however. Its rationale lies in Stone's marginality as a Jew in relation to the Italian in-group. Ironically, this position must have given him preferential advantage over most Italian mobsters in dealing with the bosses. But now, assuming that Italians are more loyal to fellow ethnics than Jews could ever be toward Italians, they sacrifice Stone as an outsider.

The same anti-Semitism helps to explain the attempt to blow up Ace in his car – a plot engineered by Nicky or the bosses. The climactic fire-bombing is anticipated at the film's opening, in which Ace is thrown high in the air. Ironically, his television show had been called "Aces High." To quote the script, "His body twists and turns . . . like a soul about to tumble into the flames of damnation" (3). This imagery represents Ace's submission to chance. His tumbling resembles the random fall of a dice cube, while his vertical propulsion into the air, like his twisting and turning, evokes *ilinx*. Ace too has been swept up by the "high" of Las Vegas and pitched seemingly to self-destruction. Yet the bombers could not have known that "that model car was made with a metal plate under the driver's seat," says Ace. "It's the only thing that saved my life" (213). The ambulance driver tells him, "You sure are lucky, mister" (218). He who sought mastery over chance owes his life to pure luck.

But not all Italians are exempt from sacrifice by the mob, for Nicky and his brother Dominic are beaten and buried alive in an Indiana cornfield. In accentuating the plenitude of this agricultural landscape, Scorsese hints at a pagan theme of violence, death, and rejuvenation – a Frazierian sacrifice to insure the crops' fertility.

Such symbolism would also apply to the coda, summarizing the demolition of the old Las Vegas of the mob and its replacement by the grander city of the corporations – as if it were a Phoenix "rising out of [. . .] [its] ashes."[55]

This transformation began in 1969 with the Corporate Licensing Act. By 1977 corporations had gained predominance in the Las Vegas gambling industry, and since then their power and prosperity has only increased while that of the mob has dwindled.[56] Not only did the indictment of the bosses deal the mob a severe blow in 1983, but according to Pileggi, that year marked the end of its "main muscle" in Las Vegas casinos, as the Teamsters pension fund yielded to junk bonds as their primary means of financing.[57] Casinos had become just another service provided by publicly-owned leisure conglomerates.[58] At the same time, new and vaster sources of financing enabled Las Vegas casinos to expand enormously while acquiring a new character and clientele. Already by 1983, notes Pileggi, slot machines had become the largest revenue producers, showing that casinos now had wide appeal (340). When in 1993 MGM opened the biggest hotel in the city, with over 5,000 rooms, it included both a casino and an immense theme park. The Luxor Hotel-Casino, shaped like a gigantic pyramid, contained an entertainment center with simulated Nile cruises. Unlike the old hotels, which emphasized casinos with a few added attractions, the new ones were complexes for the whole family, where children's amusements were highlighted, and casinos were only one attraction, although economically the most important.[59] But as Findlay observes, the new corporated Las Vegas "seemed faceless" after the hoodlum era.[60] For Pileggi, Las Vegas is now an "adult theme park," where dealers no longer know your name, and checking into a hotel is "more like checking into an airport" (347).

Scorsese depicts the transformation of Las Vegas by juxtapos-

---

[55] Scorsese observes: "A whole new city comes rising out of the ashes." See Christie, "Introduction: Stardust in Vegas," xiv.

[56] Abt, Smith, and Christiansen, *The Business of Risk*, xii, 99; Findlay, *People of Chance*, 201.

[57] Pileggi, *Casino*, 340, 348.

[58] Abt, Smith, and Christiansen, *The Business of Risk*, 99.

[59] Munting, *An Economic and Social History of Gambling in Britain and the U.S.A.*, 151; Pileggi, *Casino*, 347.

[60] Findlay, *People of Chance*, 201.

ing actual footage of the destruction of the Dunes Hotel and casino with shots of the MGM Grand. "The town will never be the same," says Ace, for after the collapse of the Tangiers the corporations "took it all over," and today it "looks like Disneyland" (218-19). His statement accompanies a slow-motion shot of tourists as they enter a vast casino, stupefied by the spectacle. These are what the shooting script of *Casino* terms the "living dead," whose regimented pleasures lack the vital though destructive energies of the old mobsters (219). Another crowd gathers to watch a mock pirate ship in a tank, a typical children's attraction in the new family-style Las Vegas, where, as Ace observes, "Mommy and Daddy" squander the "house payments." A shot of the Excalibur, another 5,000 room hotel shaped like an Arthurian castle, accompanies Ace's complaint of the corporate impersonality of the new Las Vegas: "If you order room service, you're lucky if you get it by Thursday" (219). He adds that, after the Teamsters faded, the corporations tore down most of the old casinos, using junk bonds to "rebuild the pyramids." By night the Luxor appears, a glass pyramid thirty stories high with a huge sphinx outside (220). The sacred symbol of the Sphinx has been reduced to a cartoonish gimmick – but not by Scorsese, who, as we shall see, is using it to invoke and comment upon the sacred.

Girard notes of gambling that it originates in ritual and is then divested of sanctity until it is almost entirely secularized. The question thus arises whether gambling can retain its sacred character if it is transformed from a vice into just another business routine and family diversion. Even as the taboos surrounding gambling have been dismantled, so with the end of its pariah status its violent criminal overlords and servants have largely disappeared from the scene. All this can only drain gambling of its former fascination and even terror. It is now probably less sacred than ever in having become one more neutral practice of the technicized and bureaucratized world – one more casualty of modernity's assault on the intimidating yet provocative system of prohibitions which is the sacred. Under such circumstances it seems doubtful that gambling can ever recover even the residually sacred resonance it had possessed. There is only the mechanization, dullness, and impersonality of which Pileggi, like Ace, complains.

But that the gambling industry is still not altogether removed from the sacred is evident in the fact that, even amid its modernization and success, it relies on those means by which societies have traditionally concealed, distorted, commemorated, and sanctified the violent origins to which they owe their order and prosperity. Besides portraying the elimination of Nicky, pariah of the bosses and the state, the final scenes of *Casino* depict the state's expulsion of the bosses from Las Vegas and the near murder of another outcast, Ace, who leaves the city. These scenes correspond thematically to images of the old Las Vegas, the pariah city, being demolished to make way for the "purified," still more prosperous city of the corporations. It is as if, just as the state has expelled the underworld, so the corporations have removed every tainted reminder of that earlier gambling era. In doing so, the corporations conceal the disturbing fact that the pariahs and scapegoats had made the "new" Las Vegas possible by laying its foundations.

Mob investors and illegal gamblers provided not only the skills and muscle but the necessary financial support for the plant and infrastructure of the Las Vegas gambling industry. They did this, moreover, with the tacit approval of a state which professed hypocritically to condemn them. Without the immensely productive contribution of these despised and hounded criminals, the wealthy oasis would never have existed.[61] They are its foundation victims. But though neither the corporations nor the public can acknowledge that their present prosperity and enjoyments owe a major debt to the now-expelled pariahs, they nonetheless commemorate in disguised, mimetic form the violence in which Las Vegas originated. Thus the make-believe depredations of pirates fighting in a tank at a hotel are a dim reminder of those real pirates, Tony Spilotro and his Hole-in-the-Wall Gang. The pyramid shape of the Luxor evokes albeit in highly distorted fashion those countless victims still buried in the surrounding desert. And the Sphinx at the Luxor calls to mind the riddle that haunted that other scapegoat Oedipus, of the inextricable connection between social health and social violence.

---

[61] Findlay, *People of Chance*, 123, 172.

THE SURNAME TARANTINO
CINEMA AND THE SHORT TIME THAT SUBMERSES IT

Alberto Abruzzese & Lorenzo Esposito

UNIVERSITY OF ROME, "LA SAPIENZA"

1. *Italy and America, Surname and First Name*

Aperson's surname tells us about the long time of his geographical and cultural origins. His first name tells us about his life, the short time from the moment of his birth. A first name can speak in a language different from its surname. A German surname, for instance, subtracts the absolute generality and, at the same time, the absolute particularity from an Italian first name; or, as in the case we will examine here, an Italian surname unmasks an Americanized Italian first name. The surname hosts the first name and, in turn, the first name – a sign of discontinuity – progressively adapts itself to the surname, lives with it, and shares in its history even when its history is forgotten, unconscious, and consumed. A person goes through life with the first name and the surname that have befallen him. Nevertheless, the first name and the surname that identify him have a life of their own; they automatically establish – for the person and the people he meets – cultural references and connections; they evoke sensations and memories which in turn solicit contact and reflection. The first name's short time searches the long lost time of the surname, often pushing itself well beyond the very agents of this temporal and spatial division of the self. This is the complex web of relations within whose boundaries an identity constructs itself, is constructed, and perceives itself by means of the perceptions of the Other. How much does the surname matter to the first name? In the case we are about to examine, how much does the surname of a filmmaker matter when it, and not the first name, exhibits itself in a language foreign to the nation and therefore the culture, the tools of production, the market and system of imagery that hosts it?

These questions pertain to a more basic theme: the personal identity of a film director and the identities (the text and its protagonists) that filmmaking puts on screen. The singularity of the director presides over this multifaceted and interdisciplinary task; the spectator consumes it in his name, as he is the narrator of the story and the story of the narrator. The most sound justification therefore for a critical approach that searches for an interpretive key in the surname of a director resides in the mute mirroring between narrator and narratee, a reciprocal mirroring on which filmmaking, the event of its consumption, and therefore the real cinematographic text depends.

We intend to analyze here the identity *Tarantino* within the context of a collection of filmmakers whose common identity trait is *Italianness* of origin, not of birth. They are inhabitants of a temporal, not a geographical dimension; they are figures of a typically modern uprooting of ethnic origins. As hybridized forms, these origins are doomed to the oblivion of the past and of the elsewhere.

This theme therefore obligates us to observe a filmmaker digging under his identity as a film director in order to verify how much the identity components reported by his surname – his nationality, country, and family – matter. These original, genetic elements concern, in the historical dimension of national foundations, not only the public sphere, but also the local, parental, and private sphere of a single birth-registry entry. In the past, this type of observation might have had a different meaning, perhaps even the richness of a biographical portrait. Today, instead, it means to search for the *remote* traces of substances and beliefs (fatherland, land, family) de/ceased in the in/difference of the post-modern, or, in any case, cast in the depths of the new conflicts between globalism and localism.

The fact that we are talking about Italian-American film directors brings up, as we shall see in analyzing Tarantino, the problem of the nexus between two distinct relations: on the one side, the general frame that is the relationship between the United States of America and Europe; on the other side, the particular instance that is the specific relationship between the USA and Italy. In turn, Italy has its own particular relationship with Europe: it inherits – and, more than that, symbolizes – on the one hand the Mediterranean roots of the West, Athens, and Rome and, on the other, the Catholic Church and the Renaissance. Moreover, Italy is the emblematic expression of a pre-national and European (insofar as it is pre-European) culture.

Italy, in fact, anticipates, and at the same time, denies the Europe of which it is a part. An amphibious nation, divided into North and South, it is the cradle of the European Mediterranean and, at the same time, edge of the Asian and African civilizations. The *Italian Regions* come well before the birth of modern European nations (they come, that is, from the break-up of the Western Roman Empire), while the *Italian Nation* comes much after them (that is, after 1860).

Italy adjoins another, equally significant factor to its characteristic duplicity: it is at the center of the Mediterranean sea, an *enclosed sea*, but one that has in any case to do with the *open sea*. Italianness accesses the *Ocean Sea* twice: in the dawning of modernity, by discovering America; and in the full-fledged modernity of the twentieth century, by populating it with emigrants.

All of this belongs implicitly to the Italian-American duality that, with regard to the more global relation between America and Europe, has its own absolutely original character. That is to say, a stateless Italian in America represents a complex separation of National Identity and European Identity. This separation is also expressed in Italian traditions, already very different among themselves: high and low, open and closed, ordered and dis-ordered: the culture of the Princes and the culture of the People; the culture of the peasant world and of underdevelopment; the cultures of urban and non-urban forms; of industrial and post-industrial chaos; the dearth of market standards and the successes of small industry; rhythms that still move with difficulty towards the advanced models of consumption and rhythms that still resist or oppose their values. It is not by accident that the most interesting Italian cinema – or the most historically compatible with American cinema – is the cinema that either has radically refused a mediation between these radical distances (such as a few ingenious pieces of neo-realism) or that which has been able to realize this difficult mediation in the serial form of the comic genre (as for instance in the *commedia all'italiana*).

Before beginning our brief analysis of Tarantino, the principle theme of the European nature of an Italian American in reference to the America-Europe duality warrants further analysis: it is in the dialectic between these two worlds that modernity was born and within which Tarantino can be called *post-modern*. To study the historicity of this relationship means to touch the heart of the international relations that founded industrial development, the destiny of the West, and thus also Hollywood (by which we mean the form and the ideology of cinema, the modernization of lived experience and the *metanational* strategy of dominance over the collective imagination).

America is the product of a precocious unification of diverse European national cultures: a unification realized in the free space of a new frontier, of a land *discovered* beyond, and therefore outside of, the Old World, which, at that time, was merely a simple geographic contiguity of national destinies in conflict among themselves. It is in this *naturally innovative* context that – as a European observer such as Tocqueville could see – the true constitutive difference between the New and the Old World could be formed: a social and expressive system characterized by democracy of the masses and of the market, or more precisely, by the substantial interdependence of these two dimensions. In the difference between these worlds, the qualitative root – the *new* technology – of cinema also has a place. It is precisely in that epoch turn, already quite evident in nineteenth-century America, that one can see the Twentieth century mystery of a European culture that produced a radically non-European Hollywood style cinema.

The directors of the historically Great American cinema have German, Irish, English and even Italian (for example, Frank Capra) surnames. Yet precisely insofar as they are European (diverse and foreign, therefore participants *par excellence* in the American dream) they are above all not only directors but American citizens, authors of Hollywood. It was only later that in this rather clamorous multinationality Italian surnames began to stand out from the rest of American film artists. This occurred, in one way, at the point of crisis of American cinema, cinema *par excellence*, precisely insofar as it is a planetary language, a model no longer adequate to function as a form of the ancient imperialistic vocation of the European nations. And it happened, in another way, at the point of crisis of the very same European nations, due as much to their process of economic and political unification as, reflexively, to their centrifugal and dispersive attempt towards localism and its processes of progressive destructurization of collective identities and their great narratives.

In sociology, the literature on Identity is immense indeed. To analyze the concept of identity through the *screen* of symbolic, artistic, and image-rich constructions – in this specific instance cinema – is a richer and more advanced way of grasping not so much the social reality of Identity (attainable by other instruments and indicators) but rather its deeper, hidden meaning. The *lightness* of cinema offers Identity the protection of one mask among the many available in the many permutations of real life. Besides, the history of cinema coincides with the age of ethnic migrations – that is, with the history of America.

The route that we have taken in this essay begins with the modern nature – innovative and non-traditional – of the metropolitan subject, that is, of the figure of the *foreigner*. This figure crosses the classic borders of the *city*, of the *community* as a native spring, a homogenous geographical and social *body*, in order to repropose the problem of socialization in an open and contested space. This open territorial dimension, from New York to Los Angeles, is the result of enormous processes of abstraction and commodification of social relations. Here Italian surnames solicit a very definite sense of conflict. They are the trace of a rustic, pre-metropolitan origin, of a traumatic, though perfectly assimilated, fascination for the New World and all of its phantasmagoria.

What we have here are decidedly ancestral, primitive and *dialectical* factors of local conflict. They are pushed inside *American*, that is, global, contexts which themselves are already strongly, though of a different register, conflict-ridden. These contexts speak and act in *another* language, insofar as they are dramaturgically compatible precisely as contrast or integration of the social distance between development and underdevelopment. They are a representation of the point of *delirium*, of the zone of extreme condensation of models of socialization that should be irreconcilable but instead are forced to con-found themselves in one emotive space.

This situation – this narrative – can be seen at a glance from the gangsters of classic film noir to the Mafia family of the films of Coppola and Scorsese: characters and events in which the strongest human trait is captured perfectly by the concept of *amoral familism*. Not by chance, this term is the product of those students of Italian society who think and write in English.

This line of study offers us a few clues for analyzing American films about Italians or Italian characters. It helps us much less, however, in adding something to the knowledge and the valorization of those Italian-American authors for whom the long time of the surname has been fully assimilated by the time of American cinema. For them, the short time of the name – Quentin in this case – expresses the desire for a *difference*, of an urgency for something else that passes over the surname just as it overcomes cinema. And perhaps it is just in this disparity of identity between the self and the self that the filmmaker finds himself – with a few traces inscribed in the non-sense of his own surname – coinciding with, consisting in the substance and matter that the surname evokes.

We are dealing however with surnames of directors that in themselves determine a specific moment of American cinema: to rediscover itself and its strategies of surviving its own death, or to give way to the neo-primitivism of the cinema of special effects? To be able yet to tell stories or only to surprise? These are the stakes. And we are tempted to say that, with regard to American directors – that is, those who are completely integrated and therefore native – Italian-American directors are more clearly in favor of narrativity.

The Italian *aura* – as authors or characters – that we are talking about (explicit or implicit, programmatic or unconscious) stands to mean something that has more to do with the medium of art than with its underlying social composition. Are the directors of Italian origin who work as Americans rediscovering America? Or are they merely rediscovering themselves? From this point of view, we have to distinguish different levels. Martin Scorsese, for example, in claiming to have studied Italian cinema and to owe it very much, bears witness to the not unique but exemplary case of a director who, perhaps in making his countryless nature coincide with the cultural leap of a post-classical American author, has begun to rethink cinema as a critic, pushing himself beyond classical American cinema (though another surname – Cassavetes – had already done this).

The very same Scorsese, in using characters that have to do with his Italian origins, attests, as a director, to something much less meaningful. A great author after all is great precisely insofar as he succeeds in interpreting worlds and not in reproducing them. That these worlds belong to him or not biographically may have a philological meaning or certain formal effects, but nothing more. For us, we would like to repeat, Italian-American directors are *condemned* to be completely American. Therefore, if they deal with the Italianness of their surname cinematographically, only two questions matter: Why? What are its expressive results? We do not now have convincing evidence to sustain that they do so in order to discover or reveal their immigrant characteristics. We can only suppose that there is some relation between their postmodern practices and their countryless nature (no longer Italians and not completely Americans).

We have instead many more reasons – and they are textual – for sustaining that these directors exhibit (or are exhibited by) traits of Italianness not in recovering their own surnames, but rather in carrying, to its most extreme consequences, the short time of their first name into the terminal time of cinema. But at this point a new question comes up: does their Italianness consist in them referring themselves or being referred to by an effective Italian root, or is it something that is inscribed perfectly in their American nature?

Just when it seems that we have understood the marginality or the unimportance of the surname *Tarantino* for the quality or the meaning of his films, another possible route emerges. In order to trace its origin we have to go back to the first manuals of Hollywood screenwriting, in which Italian characters (or those of color) – as fictional devices, and therefore still more as characters than effective identities of the actors – were considered particularly well-suited to represent the passions. The Mediterranean character exhibits the instinctive presence of the body and the possibilities of a dramaturgically efficacious sense of language precisely because it is liberated from the strong linguistic traits of Anglo-Saxon civilization and socialization. The language of development literally had to fill itself out by means of the language of underdevelopment. The screen had to absorb the earth and its passionate, preliterate regimes; the commodity had to absorb the dimensions of gift and sacrifice; and in the end, entertainment had to inscribe in itself the attraction between bodies. The ceremonies of conversation had to reach towards their sexual origin, collect and reverberate the pulses of desire, make clear a profound sense of conflict of which the body of the actor would be the vehicle.

The Italianness to which Hollywood was referring is not therefore geographical but technical. As living flesh that opposes the controlled character of the American social structure, it was one of the fundamental ingredients of cinema, of the emotive machine American cinema was readying to dominate the world: an apparatus in which the mind of the cultural industry of the masses made itself a body to be consumed and the corporeity of consumption; an apparatus so perfect as to erase its original ingredients in its uniqueness as an American product.

Now that this very efficacious machine of the emotions has begun to erode, directors and screenwriters like Quentin Tarantino return to it and deconstruct its components, making the progressive disintegration of that which was synthesized in classical cinema – the body and the mind, the land and the screen, desire and its representation – material of their dramaturgy. Tarantino works on the vacuums that have been opened between passions and intelligence, between the body and the brain's apparatuses of control, and therefore between order and dis-order, between real life and the life of the forms, between desire and its representation.

Here is a sub-culture that emerges and attributes the trait *too human* to its origins. But, at the same time, it also emerges with the trait *too intellectual* which it, as is always the case, superimposes as a system of rules on those origins. The loss of the system of rules is confused with the expectation of a new regeneration of their corporeal origin. Here is the creative task that the film writing of this confusion practices. The cinematographic set has become the backstage of a form of textual production that, in the obsessive attempt to find the lost set, works entirely by means of this uprooting of points of view.

Here the distance between the body and the mind is consumed; the separation of cinema and Italianity becomes an object of narration, and the technique of which it is the emblem is no longer able to count on the intelligence of Americans (forced not by chance always to return to the pulses of the serial killer and therefore to be tempted by the new libidinal economy of special effects) who are obligated instead to surrender themselves to the popular opacity (*Pulp Fiction*) that was once the material of their intelligence, an instrument of seduction, a body to render transparent.[1]

---

[1] One might think, and we will return to this later, of how Tarantino plays on the disparity between the body of Travolta the star and no-longer star, a dancing body that from the musical, by means of the post-modern discothque, ends up dying in the bathroom.

In this vacuum between intelligence and the senses another vacuum, that is, the distance between the instinctive interiority of the passions and the inevitable exteriority, the necessary theatrical staging and verbalization, of the order of seeing is located as its obscure desire to come into the light. Here we see the modern need, which the body in itself still conserves, of giving a cultural form to that which makes it different from culture and civil society, a need therefore of giving a classical form even to that which denies the roots of modernity, a cinematographic form even to that which denies cinema.

Now we can finally reread Quentin Tarantino. His work belongs fully to cinematographic milieu of Italian-American cinema. This is a milieu large enough not to be considered in a strict sense a minority one, and varied enough in content and form to evade monolithic attempts to give it coordinates valid for one and all. If Italian-American cinema, or better, an Italian American way of seeing exists, it reaches out towards practices of homogenization and centrifugal fluxes. Quentin Tarantino, in particular (like De Palma, and more than Scorsese, Cimino, or Ferrara), embodies this complex notion of identity in his constant repositioning of himself in a zone marked by multiplicity of contributions and fascinations. Scorsese and Coppola (and more generally the so-called *New Hollywood*) were able to import narrative *localisms* of their childhood and youth, attaching them to new visual structures – *nouvelle vague* and underground – as well as to the classical structures (above all, those of gangster films and melodrama) of American cinema. They ended up redefining the productive and authorial universe of Hollywood itself (Cimino and Ferrara, instead of such a revolution, are still the marginal and marginalized version). Today Tarantino represents an uprooting due in a certain sense to the failure of American multicultural politics (in the direction of an unattainable as much as longed for stability of the melting pot). His work, acting on the late modernity of an expressive logic, seduced by different levels of impurity and by the *art* of recycling, subtracts its own hypothesis of vision, its own reading of the real, from both the nightmare of assimilation and the anger of separatism or of marginalization.

2. *From Samuel Beckett to Ringo Lam* (Reservoir Dogs)

If, on the one hand, the system of conventions from which the gangster-movie has always drawn – action novels, police stories, or crime reporting – has defined identity in terms of a phenomenology of almost abstract languages, internal to the genre, then, on the other hand, it has constituted a privileged field for that type of deconstruction, generated by the meeting of authorial forms and codes of consumption. This theme will be clearer with *Pulp Fiction*. For now it is enough to recall that the route from the classics of William Wellman (*Public Enemy* [1931]), Howard Hawks (*Scarface* [1932]), Robert Siodmak (*The Killers* [1946]), John Huston (*The Asphalt Jungle* [1950]), or Fritz Lang (*The Big Heat* [1953]), will lead the genre to the eruption of psychoanalysis in the Forties and Fifties (e.g., *White Heat* [1949] by Raoul Walsh), to the metaphysical film noir of Welles (especially *Touch of Evil* [1958]), to the post-metropolitan neuroses of Henry Hathaway (*Kiss of Death* [1947]), of Roger Corman (*Machine Gun Kelly* [1958]), or of Budd Boetticher (*The Rise and Fall of Legs Diamond* [1960]). That which in the beginning was the *narrative mode* most clearly contrasted with the Western – that substituted urban and industrial expansion for the story of mythic origins, and narrow and dirty spaces of the city for the endless horizons of the plains – immediately finds its own innate heterogeneity, its continual inharmonic mixing, in this more definitely *social* symbol [2]

Here is why Scorsese and Coppola initially turned towards this cinema of blood and violence, translating the ideal of the self-made man into the petty crime of Little Italy (*Mean Streets* [1972]), or into the epic story of a family (*The Godfather* [1972]). In this kind of cinema, they found an already contaminated area within whose boundaries they were able to create a new style.

Not even Tarantino, in his first film, *Reservoir Dogs* (1992), escapes this line of reasoning. Nevertheless something has changed. From the initial sequence, intensely filmed on the circular trajec-

[2] But this kind of centrifugal paroxysm, which will be found again in Tarantino, of the *gangster-movie* format, will have an even more uneven path from the experimental improvisations: from the psychedelic infiltrations of the late Sixties, or from the extreme rages of Aldrich, it will reach all the way to the splatter film – one can even see the rivers of blood flowing in *Reservoir Dogs* – and to the Hong Kong school of the Eighties.

tories of an attentive hand-held camera, the close-ups of this *band apart* sitting around a table in a diner do not reveal any type recognizable identity traits. There is no great *paterfamilias*, only a boss and his son who have recruited various experts, all Caucasian, who are capable of moving from a discussion of the meaning of Madonna's *Like a Virgin* (perhaps the only exterior and symbolic sign of Italian Americanness), to the sound of the so-called *Bubble-gum music* of the Sixties, which, by the way, constitutes the film's sound architecture.

In another sense, however, this prologue stands alone. The unstoppable Tarantino begins just where codes and redundancies would suggest he should end: the meeting after the robbery. Besides, there is a natural tendency to overturn the forms of the already seen, which, in Tarantino's films, by virtue of extreme rigor in scene framing and camera movements, becomes a geometrical abstraction, a long line of temporal vacuums. (Nevertheless this is far from the mathematical exactitude of Kubrick in *The Killing* (1956) – inappropriately taken by too many as a comparison – and it is much less seduced by the Kubrikian obsession of absolute control).

But it is just such rigidity (including the almost total compression of present and past events in interior shots – respecting thus one of the fundamental rules of the gangster film), that indicates a kind of Italian-American optics and a typical tendency to follow to the times and the ways of European cinema (and in fact Tarantino has more than once cited the cinema of Jean-Pierre Melville). But not only that. The theatrical construction of the set, the enclosure of the characters in a single environment, their suffering in an eternal monologue without meaning, the lack of action and communication, make for a sort of movement in a void that urgently recalls the Samuel Beckett of *Fin de partie* (In a similar vein, watching Tim Roth struggle on the ground so as not to bleed to death, how can one not think of *How much blood!* of Shakespeare?).

Yet, with regard to these references the gaze of Tarantino evades any type of linearity. Many have accused him of having copied the plot and some of the iconographic solutions (most of all the ending with the three gangsters who point pistols at each other) from the film *City on Fire* (1987) by the Hong Kong director Ringo Lam. Obviously, were this true it would be wholly consistent with Tarantino's poetics of extreme contamination of the classical and the modern: that is, if he is drawing from the hyperrealistic violence with which Lam is able to condense physicality and visionary nature of the thriller. But Tarantino goes deeper. The undifferentiated fusion of Beckett and Lam is resolved in an eminently cinematographic movement: a trap door brings the spectator inside the action, betraying its own theatrical appearance by knocking down that sort of *fourth wall* that circumscribes it. The sequence of torture is emblematic: one cannot get out of it, no scene cutting will save us, cinema will not help us. In front of the close-up of the ear cutting, the only way out is to close one's eyes (but in this case the music would remain, with an insistent rhythm, in contrast to the agony of the policeman, that one cannot but listen to . . .). Moreover, the screenwriting, continually divided between long master shots and extreme close-ups, coincides with the oscillation between theatrical vocation (unity of time and place, preeminence of acting) and of the subversion of always more vertiginous flash-backs that seem to want to emancipate themselves from the principle story.

The multiple ramifications of the work and culture of Tarantino flow together in this ethics of the *constrained to see* and of not being able to live without being able to see, lost in the spirals of a terminal vision without end (and Tarantino, in the small part that he gave himself, blinded by the blood that flows down his face, dies yelling: *my eyes, I can't see anymore!*).

3. *Screens of Time on Porous Paper* (Pulp Fiction)

While *Reservoir Dogs* has an imploded structure that realizes itself *in depth*, *Pulp Fiction* invests its narrativity in a decentering movement that it develops *in extension*. Moreover, and it is opportune to clarify this immediately, *Pulp Fiction* is in no way a film of different episodes more or less daringly sewn together (in the style of Altman), but it is instead a potentially unitary story that is deconstructed by a precise and intentional stylistic choice.

On the other hand, the references to the era of the pulp magazine, to that *cheap style* of the popular culture, which in redefining and specializing the genres and their mechanisms of production and consumption from the end of the eighteenth century until the first half of the nineteenth had underlined the first technological maturation of the cultural industry, immediately clarify Tarantino's expressive intention to reproduce a useful rhythm, rather than to show off great narrative expertise (Tarantino is also a very capable screenwriter). The intuition is to represent visually the dizziness of those stories, printed on the cheapest kind of paper, and so not meant to be materially conserved; or rather it is to recreate that bewilderment of the senses of progressively serialized and spectacularized mass production, which had gone on to rewrite in one great sedimentation urban and collective imaginary architectures.

It is not by chance then that *Pulp Fiction* asks whether a re-semanticization of lived time is possible. The bodies of Uma Thurman, John Travolta, Samuel L. Jackson, Bruce Willis, Tim Roth, Rosanna Arquette, Harvey Keitel, Maria De Medeiros are literally full of time that splashes out like blood and decomposes the form of the story. Immersed in the form of *pulp* they lose their identity as actors and are squeezed and smashed just like those cheap magazines that people used to carry in their pocket and read on the subway. The pages fall out and fly away at the speed of a car, a train, of the subway. In such a way film writing can no longer contradict its own fictional continuity, since it provokes a reading of *disordered pages*, where the characters are interchangeable vectors and the circle is continually recomposed and superimposed.

Yet again the Italian-Americanness of Tarantino seems to affirm itself in this dichotomy between immediate adhesion to the hypercodified culture of American cinema, and the complex formal re-elaboration (not by chance based on time) of European – and cinematographic – origin. Think for instance of the sadomasochistic sequence with the characters Marsellus and Butch. The real masochist is the gimp who, like a spectator at the cinema, can only see and hear. But, not by chance, in reality he doesn't see anything: first the closed door blocks his view, and then, when it opens, he lies fainted on his leash. This is the rationale itself of cinematographic representation: the deferment of the event by means of its image-laden control and development. In this sense, *Pulp Fiction* tends to become *organic*, its substitutes itself for vision, it plays the role of the one watching. This is why Tarantino chooses to submit the spectator to a hypnotic immobility of action. Why speak endlessly of foot massages in front of a door before committing a double homicide? At the beginning of the second episode, after the shower, Butch falls back to sleep while his girlfriend is brushing her teeth. Fade out. The next image is brusque reawakening from a nightmare; his girlfriend is still in front of him brushing her teeth. *Yet or again*? Who can say how long he slept? Or yet: why speak about hamburgers with the person one is about to kill? We all know, for the hypercodification of genre, that the two kids who ripped off Marsellus have to die. Yet their death is deferred to such an extent that we can act *as if* we had already seen it. Even if the first episode closes with the shots, we don't see for another two hours the reverse angle in which the kid is riddled with bullets.

Serial production lives on this infinite repetition in which the event (the death) is exorcized until it can come back as many times as it wants. The icon of repetition in *Pulp Fiction* is evidently the diner of simulacra where Hollywood re-lives and in which Travolta dances, a copy of himself, just like *Grease* or *Saturday Night Fever*.

Tarantino works on Paradoxes: to make repetition into a form to the point of deriding variation; to deconstruct the modern by showing that the illusory light of its intelligence has gone out. In the sentiment of its repetitions – the flesh that returns, always unsatisfied, on itself – there is a concrete negation, no longer abstract or ideolo- gical, of modernity, and together, a step backwards, that finds the roots of the world, a speaking the meaning of things by checking historical languages and their ability, as residuals, remainders, to signify (on this the work of screenwriting is concentrated). This is the mortification of the visible (everything has already happened and the work of screenwriting is in fact merely putting it into form) by means of the visibility of the modes in which the West has exorcized death (here is the originality of the set, to believe that not everything has happened and that something new can still happen).

Therefore, immobility, event, deferment of the event, repetition. The *pulp fiction* is this swamp of banality, pieces of happenstance and futile conversations that reawake the attention of he who watches them. And the perfect narrative joke advances mirror-like to the receptive modalities of the film itself. As we were forced to see in *Reservoir Dogs*, here we are forced to *suffer*, ensnared in the tem- poral vacuums of a narration slowed down to the limits of the intolerable, waiting for an act of violence that in the end, since it is given as a residual, can even not take place.

That which is striking about Tarantino is the radicalism with which he is able to make personal obsessions, Hollywood traditions, *high and low* (Italian American) revision coincide: illustrations of mass culture worked on its audio-visual pieces, sequences that don't belong to the writing of the set but to the game of combining of editing. Tarantino digs in the mud. He plays at remodeling genres precisely insofar as they are worn out narrative materials, remixed as a necessary praxis. He finds nevertheless a new purity, a new possibility of meaning if not the non-meaning of everything.

4. *The Fiction of Time* (Jackie Brown)

Jackie Brown is completely different. Tarantino does not forgo his kaleidoscopic gaze. But he has it forge an already contaminated memory, rewriting it as a nexus of diversified experiences and constructions. *Jackie Brown* is an intense proteiform rehashing of disparate contributions: happiness of unhappiness. In the first place, the protagonists are Pam Grier (already relaunched a year earlier by Carpenter in *Escape from L.A.*), cult heroine and too long forgotten star of numerous blaxsploitation films of the Seventies (Mostly directed by Jack Hill, who is thanked in the credits), and Robert Forster (it is not by chance that in the film the two form an indissoluble romantic couple), an authentic star missed too much after that memorable beginning next to Marlon Brando in John Huston's *Reflections in a Golden Eye* (1967). And of course there is the awkward, alienated and alienating acting of an unplaceable Robert De Niro (he smokes as he did in Sergio Leone, explodes in sudden violence as in Scorsese or De Palma, he immerses himself in silent timidity as in John McNaughton), or the exuberant acting of Samuel L. Jackson and Bridget Fonda (ever more divine and unpredictable after her experience with Paul Schrader – *Touch* (1996) – and Sam Raimi – *A Simple Plan* (1999) – and Tarantino kindly has her die in an inaccessible flash off screen. . .).

Yet *Jackie Brown* is different. Constructed on the models of classical cinema, it proceeds like a theorem, a perfect puzzle, an entrance into a mental labyrinth solidified by a linked series of plans. By means of these, a digression on the human condition is developed: on melancholy, on solitude and violence given as enigmatic, ambiguous and contradictory forms of existence. The Beckettian rigor and cruelty of *Reservoir Dogs*, the stratification of meaning and vision's parallel slipping inside of it of *Pulp Fiction*, find an abstract fixity here. The unarticulated procession of multiple temporal levels translates into a ritual circularity that becomes dense in an insistent and assorted poetics of faces. This time the usual geometry of writing requires an equal and contrary dimension, measured on the *volume* of the word that, as always with Tarantino, broadens the sonic interlocking with the image.

Italian-American directors are strangers to themselves. If by *Italian-American cinema* we mean the capacity of certain film-makers to reread American cinema itself, making evident its irre-pressible historical and aesthetic merit of having founded cinema's *classical form* (including the great quality of always being popular, to the point of molding the collective imagination of ancient cul-tures), then Tarantino is an Italian-American filmmaker, and *Jackie Brown* is the heart of his cinema. It is a cinema essentially of bodies, a gaze classically magnetized by bodies immersed in time. Pam Grier and Robert Forster, moving icons and *living* precisely because they are melancholic, assume the profound substance of Myth, and achieve a purity that only a fluid, dynamic and multiform culture can produce. Paradoxically, then, Tarantino is perhaps one of the *least contaminated* contemporary film directors. He is certainly one of the few who is able to unite base behavior and complex language, traces of genre, film, books, television and a rich assortment of cine-matographic syntax: the slow fade-outs, the superimposing of points of view, the gazes into the camera (such as the last and melancholic one in which Pam Grier whispers an old song), or even out of focus images that haven't been seen in years (see, for example, the one in which Robert Forster slowly goes away).

That which in the temporal hypnosis of *Pulp Fiction* was an ironic perplexity set up as a parallel to the reiterated recycling of consumed and already seen materials, in *Jackie Brown* becomes a sort of daily epic of intrigues, violence, and homicide that manage a reality *at its limits* where death arrives like an abstraction and in which even though the moral is to survive, friendship is nonetheless still possible (remember the reference we made above to *amoral familism*). In such a way, in the case of Tarantino, it is not a question of defining or indicating a specific cultural heritage, but above all of forming one's proper vision, of constituting it in a semantic structure that observes and, in so doing, dramatizes the Great Scene of the world from on high. And in order to govern such crazy fluctuation of visions and readings of modernity, Tarantino chooses to *give them a place* in a mosaic in which everything seems to have its own precise and luminous place. Think of the killing of the small-time crook Beaumont: an obsessive and meticulous movement of the camera circles him. Tarantino observes implacably, without resorting to special effects, but only slowing down the rhythms of the filming so as to transport the visible inside of the unstable boundaries of a hallucination.

Tarantino demonstrates a classical nervature. If on the one hand (as for much of Italian-American cinematographic culture, think for example not only of a Cimino but also the latest *small* films of a Coppola) it is far from the pre-packaged text of the blockbusters, on the other, it tends to rewrite the times themselves of Hollywood (and today to rethink the times of vision, means immediately to dent and modify the integrated times of writing, production and distribution). To found one's own cinema on an ample reflection on the concept of time is not a small thing, especially in a century like the twentieth in which the planetary multiplication and instantaneity of lived time is ever more bound to the constrictions the subject meets. The experience of alienated time is the element that most clearly characterizes contemporaneity (see literature that goes from Bergson to Benjamin, from Heidegger to Ricoeur). The relationship itself of temporality is constituted as one of the fundamental nodes of existence: Tarantino's cinema is one of stories and of characters, since to work on fiction is to work on a concept of time *for us*, not on a concept of objectified time. And therefore, in the same way as John Ford or Jean-Luc Godard (here also the primitive contamination of Italian-American directors), Tarantino returns to ask himself the age-old question: When to begin and when to end a frame? From what point of reality should I begin to film? Is there such a thing as the *right* frame?

For this reason, in *Jackie Brown* the identity of the actor assumes a double character: on the one hand, he is a symbolic body, image, and representation; on the other, a mortal body, subjected to the transformations that time carries along with it (the close-ups of Robert Forster show the furrows and the wrinkles of his face; those of Pam Grier are shaken by the uncertain and deviant moving of her lips; both, and also De Niro – when, trying to smoke, he coughs – complain of impending old-age). It is as if the character waiters of *Jackrabbit Slim* where Vincent and Mia dance in *Pulp Fiction* took on life and became in their own way characters of a film. From the museum to the theater: this is the movement that *Jackie Brown* completes, so much so that if the characters become *mortal,* they make it present on the screen. Their death as characters of fiction – as it has been seen – is no longer that important, it arrives suddenly, rapidly and the more banal the more cinematically effective. The melancholy of fiction opens, paradoxically, to the physicality of the character, to his decadence, to his death. It is at least unique that their last sacrifice, the extreme attempt to remain alive, is consumed in the symbolic fulcrum of a mall – one of the metropolitan non-places (for Romero territories of zombies) that modernity has accustomed us to read as signs of spatial and temporal ruin – a place full and empty at the same time, apparently full and apparently empty of people who live not with the communication of themselves but with that of their needs. There, where the community falls to pieces, Tarantino tries the last fiction, the last search for a lost identity.

BIBLIOGRAPHY

[AA.VV.] *American Movies 90.* Milano: Ubulibri,1994.

Abruzzese, Alberto. *Forme estetiche e società di massa.* Venezia: Marsilio, 1992 (1973).

_____. *La Grande Scimmia.* Roma: Napoleone, 1979.

Augé, Marc. *Nonluoghi.* Milano: Elèuthera, 1993.

Baudrillard, Jean. *Amerique.* Paris: Grasset, 1986.

Bazin, André. *Che cosa è il cinema?* Milano: Garzanti, 1973.

Benjamin, Walter. *Angelus Novus.* Torino: Einaudi, 1962.

_____. *Il concetto di storia.* Torino: Einaudi, 1998.

Brancato, Sergio. *Sociologie dell' immaginario.* Roma: Carocci, 2000.

Campbell, Colin. *L'etica romantica e lo spirito del consumismo moderno.* Roma: Lavoro, 1992.

Canevacci, Massimo. *Antropologia della comunicazione visuale.* Genova: Costa&Nolan, 1995.

Davis, Michael. *La città di quarzo: Indagine sul futuro a Los Angeles*. Roma: Manifestolibri, 1993.

Deleuze, Gilles. *L'immagine-tempo*. Milano: Ubulibri, 1989.

Frezza, Gino. *Cinematografo e cinema: dinamiche di un preocesso culturale*. Roma: Cosmopoli, 1996.

Harvey, David. *La crisi della modernità*. Milano: Il Saggiatore, 1993.

Hebdige, Dick. *Subculture: The Meaning of Style*. New York: Routledge, 1988.

Hobsbawm, Eric. *Nations and Nationalism since 1780.* Cambridge: Cambridge UP, 1990.

Horowitz, Donald L. *Ethnic Groups in Conflict*. Berkeley: U of California P, 1985.

Hostert, Anna Camaiti. *Passing: dissolvere le identità, superare le differenze*. Roma: Castelvecchi, 1996.

Kaminski, Stuart M. *American Film Genres*. Dayton: Pfaum, 1974.

Kellas, James G. *The Politics of Nationalism and Ethnicity*. London: Macmillan, 1991.

Kern, Stephen. *Il tempo e lo spazio: La percezione del mondo tra Otto e Novecento*. Bologna: Il Mulino, 1988.

Lippi, Giuseppe. "Weird Tales & Company." *Robot* II (10) 1977.

Lyotard, Jean François. *La condizione postmoderna*. Milano: Feltrinelli, 1981.

Perniola, Mario. *Del sentire*. Torino: Einaudi, 1994.

Young, Crawford. *The Politics of Cultural Pluralism*. Madison: U of Wisconsin P, 1976.

BIBLIOGRAPHY ON TARANTINO

Books

[AA.VV.] *Cinema autori visioni: Quentin Tarantino*. Scriptorium, 1996.

Barbes, Alan and Marcus Hearn. *Tarantino A to Z: The Films of Quentin Tarantino*. London: Basford, 2000.

Bouzereau, Laurent. *Ultraviolent Movies: From Sam Peckinpah to Quentin Tarantino*. Woodstock, N.Y.: Overlook Press, 1995.

Clarkson, Wensley. *Quentin Tarantino: Shooting from the Hip*. Woodstock, NY: Overlook Press, 1995.

Dawson, Jeff. *Quentin Tarantino: The Cinema of Cool*. New York: Applause, 1995.

Gandini, Leonardo. *Quentin Tarantino: regista pulp*. Roma: Fanucci, 1996.

Terribili, Daniela. *Quentin Tarantino: Il cinema degenere* Roma: Bulzoni, 1999.

Woods, Paul A. *King Pulp: The Wild World of Quentin Tarantino*. Medford, NJ: Plexus, 1998.

FILMOGRAPHY

DIRECTOR

1992 *Reservoir Dogs*

1994 *Pulp Fiction*

1995: *Motherhood* (episode of *ER* -TV series)

The Man from Hollywood (segment 4 of *Four Rooms*)

1997 *Jackie Brown*

SCRIPTWRITER

1992 *Reservoir Dogs*

1993 *True Romance*

1994: *Natural Born Killers* (uncredited)

1995: *Crimson Tide* (uncredited)

The Man from Hollywood

1996: *The Rock* (uncredited)

From Dusk Till Dawn

1997 *Jackie Brown*

PRODUCER

1992 *Past Midnight* (film TV, associate)

1994 *Killing Zoe* (executive)

1995 *Four Rooms* (executive)

1996: *Curdled* (executive)

From Dusk Till Dawn (executive)

1998 *God Said 'Ha!'* (executive)

1999 *From Dusk Till Dawn 2: Texas Blood Money* (executive)

ACTOR

1992 *Reservoir Dogs*

1993 *Eddie Presley*

1994: *Sleep with Me*

The Coriolis Effect

American Cinema (TV series)

Somebody to Love

Pulp Fiction

1995: *Destiny Turns on the Radio*

Desperado

The Man from Hollywood

1996: *The Typewriter, The Rifle & the Movie Camera*

From Dusk Till Dawn

Girl 6

Curdled
Steven Spielberg's Director's Chair
1997 *Full Tilt Boogie*
1998 *God Said 'Ha!*
1999 *Forever Hollywood*
2000 *Little Nicky*

QUENTIN TARANTINO: AN ETHNIC ENIGMA

Joshua Fausty
NEW JERSEY CITY UNIVERSITY

Edvige Giunta
NEW JERSEY CITY UNIVERSITY

Pulp Fiction is a film ... that leaves you with the distinct impression that Tarantino has thrown everything but the proverbial kitchen sink into the celluloid melting pot. (*Empire*)

PLAYBOY: What's the difference between Los Angeles Italians and New York Italians?

TARANTINO: There really is no such thing as a Los Angeles Italian. In New York there are Italian neighborhoods. In Los Angeles there aren't. There is no ethnicity here. You just are who you are. Of course, most of that Italian stuff is learned from movies like *Mean Streets* anyway. . . . But can I tell the genuine-article Italian from the poseur Italian? No. [laughs] To me they all seem like poseurs. (*Playboy*)

Truthfulness – verism – is an adolescent affectation. No one presents himself directly, even among friends. Everyone is more or less fictional, made up, constructed. (James Monaco, quoted in Gamson 10)

When we first started working on this essay on Quentin Tarantino, it seemed convenient to think of Tarantino as the latest in a list of contemporary Italian American directors that includes Francis Ford Coppola, Martin Scorsese, Brian De Palma, Michael Cimino, Nancy Savoca, John Turturro, and Robert De Niro. Film is one area in which Italian Americans have flourished, both commercially and artistically, on the American pop-culture scene. So we decided to trust the name. After all, with a name like Tarantino, he's gotta' be Italian. Soon, though, we had to face the real question of Tarantino's origins.

We turned for help to a friend who works on the David Letterman show, where Tarantino appeared as a guest when *Pulp Fiction* hit the screens. We tried to find legitimacy for this not-too-traditional research method in the fact that Toni, despite her non-Italian last name, is Italian American. She was also at one point offered a position as Martin Scorsese's personal assistant, and since Scorsese is one of Tarantino's idols and models, we felt the "stars" were with us. While she could not shed light on the ethnic enigma, she sent us a file, full of articles, reviews, interviews, and reports collected and prepared by Letterman's research team – none of which represent the type of source regularly consulted in serious scholarly research. All of the material – much of which reproduces almost verbatim information found in just about every source – testifies to the quick notoriety reached by Tarantino in the mid-1990s – one achieved through a carefully orchestrated publicity that Tarantino himself was heavily involved in creating.

Following the release of *Pulp Fiction* and its huge popularity, Tarantino engaged in the construction of an image of himself not only by appearing in each of his movies – including one he wrote but did not direct – but also by appearing in commercial introductions to videotapes of his movies on such popular TV shows as *Late Night with David Letterman*, and by allowing himself to be photographed in the company of other celebrities – not to mention the wide gallery of Tarantino portraits in the glossy pages of magazines like *Empire, Sky*, and *Premiere*. His movies quickly became cult movies, and the scripts of *Pulp Fiction, True Romance* and *Reservoir Dogs* were published, and placed in prominent view in large-selling bookstores as well as advertised with the soundtracks of his movies on Blockbuster video tapes. Tarantino's quick success seems rooted in his self-fascination and self-promotion, and in his love affair with the movies and celebrity – matched in intensity only by Hollywood's, and the public's, fascination with his movies, and with him. If in the Hollywood star system Tarantino represents the young, off-beat, unconventional director who can pride himself on having made blockbusters *and* won the Palme d'Or at the Cannes Film Festival, he has also achieved the kind of fame sanctioned by a number of biographies.

Tarantino's supposed quick rise from rags to riches makes him even more endearing to the American public. Every journalist will tell the story of how, in order to support himself while studying acting, Tarantino worked for several years in a video store, an occupation that allowed him to indulge his fascination with film. A high-school drop-out, Tarantino did not actually come to success all-of-a-sudden. His long-time involvement in show business ranged from writing scripts to playing an Elvis impersonator on *The Golden Girls*, an appropriate role for Tarantino since he is originally from Tennessee. (Elvis in fact makes a few cameo appearances in *True Romance.*)

But what about Tarantino's *ethnic* origins? Although Tarantino has repeatedly been compared to Coppola and Scorsese, none of his movies advertise themselves as "ethnic," nor do they reveal a specific concern with Italian American culture. Tarantino's mysterious ethnic origins and the little emphasis he places on his ethnicity raise questions about identity politics and subjectivity, not to mention the legitimacy of Tarantino himself as a subject matter for Italian American studies.

By 1996, Tarantino's four movie scripts (only two of which he directed as feature films) seemed to typify the evolution of a certain kind of ethnic cycle. *True Romance*, his first script to become a feature film, contains the most explicit references to Italians, that is, Sicilians. Scagnetti, the name of the detective who hunts down Mickey and Mallory in *Natural Born Killers*, is unmistakably Italian. And Scagnetti is a name Tarantino uses for Mr. Blonde's parole officer in *Reservoir Dogs*, which opens with a long conversation about the meaning of the Madonna song "Like a Virgin," the video of which was notably filmed in Venice, where Tarantino finished drafting *True Romance*. *Pulp Fiction* treats the question of ethnic identity in a distinctly postmodern fashion. In the tortured world of this film, racial, ethnic, sexual, linguistic, and narrative borders are continuously crossed, creating a story in which multiple sub-plots intersect in unpredictable ways. This is a strategy that derails the narrative even as it gathers its scattered threads. The multifaceted story of *Pulp Fiction* is brimming with allusions to myriad films, TV shows, and other artifacts of American popular culture.

There is a certain coherence established by the fragmented

and multilayered plots, the plethora of incongruous and disparate allusions, the rootlessness of the characters themselves, and the absurd or gratuitous explosions of violence. Quoting Sergio Leone, in an interview with Dennis Hopper, Tarantino contrasted the American public's response to his movies with the response of Italian spectators to violence: "Italians tend to laugh at violence. They don't take violence seriously. . . . The only people in America that take that attitude are Black people" (Hopper 140). The stereotyping of Tarantino's off-handed comment establishes a cultural connection between Italians and Blacks, one that is emphasized and magnified in *True Romance*. The Sicilian interlude in *True Romance*, directed by Tony Scott, captures feelings of racial discrimination and self-hatred, and problematizes questions of origins and identity, which are crucial to a discussion of Tarantino as an Italian American auteur.

Tarantino has a special attachment to this scene: "as far as I am concerned," he told Dennis Hopper, "[it] . . . should go into a time capsule for future generations to look at" (Hopper 21). While Tarantino does not quite explain why this scene is so important, his emphasis on future generations underscores the role of origins and heritage. The scene also raises issues of paternity and racial and cultural crossings. Don Vincenzo Coccotti (played by Christopher Walken), during his interrogation of Clarence's father Cliff (played by Dennis Hopper), claims the authority and power of the lie: "Sicilians are great liars. The best in the world. I'm a Sicilian. And my old man was the world heavyweight champion of Sicilian liars" (147-148). Coccotti believes that by demonstrating his "inherited" ability to tell when someone is lying or telling the truth, he will be able to extract Clarence's whereabouts from Cliff: "What we got here is a little game of show and tell. You don't wanna show me nothing'. But you're tellin' me everything. Now I know you know where they are. So tell me, before I do some damage you won't walk away from" (148). If Coccotti claims the authority of the lie, Cliff instead claims the authority of "history" – an overtly white history that figures Sicilians as Blacks.

Accepting his own death as the only alternative to betraying his son's location, and having given up all hope of survival – he knows by now that lying will get him nowhere but dead – Cliff makes the decision to strike an unexpected blow while he still has the chance. Cliff: "So you're a Sicilian, huh?" Coccotti answers, intensely, "Uh-huh." Cliff continues:

> You know I read a lot. Especially about things that have to do with history. I find that shit fascinating. In fact, I don't know if you know this or not, Sicilians were spawned by niggers. (148)

At this point in the script, "All the men stop what they are doing and look at Cliff, except for Tooth-Pick Vic, who doesn't speak English and isn't insulted. Coccotti can't believe what he is hearing" (148). Cliff goes on:

> It's a fact. Sicilians have nigger blood pumpin' through their hearts. If you don't believe me, look it up. You see, hundreds and hundreds of years ago the Moors conquered Sicily. And Moors are niggers. Way back then, Sicilians were like the wops in northern Italy. Blond hair, blue eyes. But, once the Moors moved in there, they changed the whole country. They did so much fuckin' with the Sicilian women, they changed the blood-line for ever, from blonde hair and blue eyes to black hair and dark skin. I find it absolutely amazing to think that to this day, hundreds of years later, Sicilians still carry that nigger gene. I'm just quotin' history. It's a fact. It's written. Your ancestors were niggers. Your great, great, great, great, great-grandmother fucked a nigger, and she had a half-nigger kid. That is a fact. Now tell me, am I lyin'? (149)

Cliff's history lesson leads Coccotti to kill Cliff – to kill with his own hands for the first time in years. The gravity of the insult is taken for granted by all present: the characters' laughter as Cliff recounts the story of their people is chilling, yet humorous, as it becomes increasingly out of place given the unfolding of the scene. Everyone knows – including Cliff – that his death is imminent, and this increases the seriousness of the situation – the story and its ultimately grave reception. It is through this story of historical "truth" that cannot be denied – after all, it is "written" – that Cliff is able to reassert his own authority, even during this confrontation to the death. It is the historical "truth" of Cliff's lesson that makes it so troubling for the self-proclaimed connoisseur of liars, who is implicitly forced to admit that he has been given what he has asked for – he has been told the "truth," but at his own expense. Coccotti's only response is to shoot Cliff in the head: he has been beaten at his own game of "show and tell"; there is nothing left to be said.

But what is the status of Cliff's and Don Vincenzo's prejudice? The racism of Tarantino's characters works in complex ways. Cliff's offensive use of the word "nigger" and his bigoted account of the "contamination" of Sicilian blood problematizes any sympathy or compassion the spectator feels for this character. But it is precisely his use of this bit of "history" in the face of certain death that makes him most admirable. A helpless victim, he finds the strength to spit in the face – so to speak – of the bad guy. The explicitly racial hatred of his otherwise noble performance (while enduring torture, we should add) does little to weaken his character. Don Vincenzo's reaction, on the other hand, provides the outlet for whatever judgement and tension we may have been building up. His inevitable, brutal response to Cliff's insult is to inflict injury – the kind of "damage" you don't "walk away from."

Tarantino's treatment of racism is self-consciously executed yet at the same time, totally unself-critical.[1] Cliff is likeable, unmistakably the good guy, in contrast to his gangster foe Don Vincenzo. But unless we go out of our way to read his frequent and comfortable use of the word "nigger" as completely strategic – it is intended to humiliate Don Vincenzo when all is lost – Cliff is also unmistakably racist. The juxtaposition of the Sicilians as "great liars" and victims of the Moor conquest and rape intensifies the conflict between torturer and tortured: for a moment it even reverses the dynamics of power. Interestingly, the example is one that performs another sort of reversal, in which Africans colonize Europeans.

Although Tarantino does not know Italian, he indicated in the script for *True Romance* that the characters should speak Italian, and Tony Scott remained faithful to the script in this case. Far from conveying a realistic portrayal, though, the use of Sicilian dialect in this scene articulates the twilight – better, the disintegration – of Italian American ethnicity. These gangsters, for

---

[1] This is not true of his treatment of homosexuality, in *Pulp Fiction* or in the other three films, which is not only unself-conscious but homophobic: every mention, or instance, of anal sex between men takes the form of, as one reviewer of *Pulp Fiction* uncritically put it, "a fate worse than death" [Corliss 73]).

example, are not modeled on the Al Capones of American history. They are distilled from the mafia characters of Coppola's and Scorsese's cinema. If ethnicity is never a tangible entity, but rather a kind of posture, performance, or self-representation, in Tarantino's cinema, ethnicity is an even more highly mediated form of representation – it is the representation of representation. These gangsters, who seem to come from another era and another world, shed light on the problematic narrative of origins and identity that haunts Tarantino.

Tarantino walks the line between an overt and persistent bigotry and an implicit critique of prejudice. Yet while his cinema brings to the forefront a racism pervasive in American society, Tarantino does not declare a social commitment of any kind. He problematizes essentialized notions of identity – racial, ethnic, gender, and sexual – without ever aligning himself with a specific political position. If it is difficult to identify a clear ethical stance anywhere in his films, this is because Tarantino assumes an ambiguous moral posture akin to what Linda Hutcheon characterizes as the postmodern "complicitous critique": "Postmodernism," she argues, "ultimately manages to install and reinforce as much as undermine and subvert the conventions and presuppositions it appears to challenge" (1-2). Tarantino's motivation is rather dictated by considerations of film-making and the conventions of cinema, which he both draws upon and undermines. In the interview with Dennis Hopper, Tarantino said:

> [A]s far as I'm concerned, if you're going to make a revenge movie, you've got to let the hero get revenge. There's a purity in that. You can moralize after the fact all you want, but people paid seven dollars to see it. So you set it up and the lead guy gets screwed over. And then, you want to see him kill the bad guys – with his bare hands, if possible. They've got to pay for their sins. (19)

The language in the passage is telling: not only is there a "purity" in letting the "hero get revenge," but the "bad guys" have to "pay for their sins" by getting killed with the "bare hands" of the "lead guy." Cinema becomes a sort of religion for this director, who couches his ethics of revenge film-making in religious terms of "purity" and "sin," but assigns "moralizing" a low priority compared to giving his audience "what [it] paid for." Hutcheon argues that "complicitous critique . . . situates the postmodern squarely within both economic capitalism and cultural humanism, two of the major dominants of much of the western world" (13). Tarantino's "ethic" takes shape through the language of capitalist exchange. His morality is derived from Hollywood economics.

Tarantino's fascination is with film itself, and with representation. According to Graham Fuller, Tarantino is interested in what has already "been mediated or pre-digested" (9), for example, in the opening scene of *Reservoir Dogs*, he is not so much concerned with Madonna "but [with] what Madonna has come to represent" (Graham Fuller ix). What interests Tarantino is not Italian American ethnicity as such, but what Italian American ethnicity has come to represent in American culture and, more specifically, in Hollywood cinema – hence the Sicilian interlude. There is no doubt that in Hollywood cinema, Coppola and Scorsese have produced – and, with De Niro, have become themselves – the most impressive icons of Italian American ethnicity. Of his pals in acting school, Tarantino says: "They all wanted to work with Robert De Niro or Al Pacino – and I would have loved to work with them too – but what I really wanted was to work with the directors. I wanted to work with Francis Ford Coppola. I wanted to work with Brian De Palma, and I would have learned Italian to work with Argento" (Hopper 50).

Although here, Tarantino does not identify himself as an Italian American auteur, he conveys the sense of a certain longing for Italian identity, aligning himself with Italian American actors, and Italian American and Italian directors. Talking about his notorious fascination with board games, Tarantino said: "I'm in a position now, as a kind of celeb, that I could look up the people that were in these shows and these movies, and play these games with them. I played the *Welcome Back Kotter* game and the *Grease* game with John Travolta. I had him sign the game and who won and what the date was and everything. . . . I've got a *Batman Returns* game that I can play with Danny De Vito, and I can play the Laverne and Shirley game with Penny Marshall, because I know Penny" (*Premiere* 1994). Need we add that all of these players have one thing in common besides the honor of having "played" their own characters in board games with Tarantino? Every one of them is Italian American.

While a director like Martin Scorsese, whom Tarantino often alludes to, grew up during the twilight of both cinema and ethnicity, and infuses a sense of loss and nostalgia for both in his films, Tarantino belongs to a different generation. In Tarantino's work, the mystification of the commodity value of cinema is replaced by a self-conscious flaunting of the power of the ultimate commodity created by the film industry: the videotape. The rewinding and fast-forwarding afforded by this postmodern form emerges in *Pulp Fiction* through complex editing that disrupts the conventions of linear and chronological development. As Tarantino himself put it, *Pulp Fiction* is three films for the price of one.

The kind of violent brutality Tarantino frequently depicts in his films often becomes funny – and not only when it's an accident. In the Hopper interview, Tarantino says, "I think it's humorous, but it's not all one big joke. I want the work to have complexity. So it's hah-hah-hah . . . until I don't want you to laugh at all. . . . And then you might even have to think about why you were laughing. And then I want to try to get you to start laughing again" (17). Scorsese's fascination with violence represents one of the most important allusive layers of Tarantino's cinema. In many ways, *Pulp Fiction* pays tribute to its Scorsesian antecedent, *Goodfellas*, and Jules is a parodic descendant of Max Cady in *Cape Fear*, with whom he shares a concern with biblical exegesis and revenge, or vengeance. If, as Robert Casillo argues, in the world of Scorsese violence is linked to the sacred in a Girardian sense, in Tarantino's world, violence is utterly decontextualized and deprived of any ritualistic function (although Jules's recital of the bible passage is ritualistic). The exception is perhaps *Natural Born Killers*. The film carries the unmistakable signature of its director, Oliver Stone (Tarantino was so disconcerted with what Stone had done with his script that he expressed his desire to have the credits changed from "script by" to "original story by Tarantino"). Even though most of the violence in *Natural Born Killers* is senseless and gratuitous (by most standards), the film is infused with a heavy moral vision completely absent in the Tarantino scripts and films. Mickey's accidental shooting of the innocent Indian, who embodies a connection with the past, with a mythologically rooted history, causes Mallory's vehement reaction: "Bad, bad, bad, bad, bad." But in Tarantino's films, things are different: the accidental murder of Marvin in the unforgettable *Pulp Fiction* car scene causes roaring laughter. In contrast to Stone's treatment, here there is no serious consideration of the reality of death, the loss of life. Even Joe Pesci's absurd violence in Scorsese's *Goodfellas* seems less senseless, and elicits at least a semblance of moral indignation in his not-so-moral partners in crime. But in Tarantino's world of quick consumption, lives become interchangeable, disposable.

While Tarantino seems to place himself in this multi-generational community of Italian Americans, and while Cliff does his best to protect his son Clarence from the mob, there is no nostalgia in this world for the comfort of either the ethnic neighborhood or the extended family: they have both disintegrated beyond traditional recognition. As ethnic and cultural assimilation and other social and political consequences of late capitalism and globalization, lead to the continued breakdown of multiple barriers and borders, and hasten the arrival of diverse, multi-ethnic, transnational identities and cultural hybridity, certain questions come up for scholars of ethnic studies. The emergence of an author/director such as Tarantino, whose ethnic identification is somewhat problematic, forces us to ask questions concerning the inclusion of such authors as subject matter for Italian American studies. It also becomes imperative to interrogate the validity of current methodologies in ethnic studies in general. If Italian American and other ethnic studies are to remain viable fields in a rapidly changing cultural milieu, what changes will these fields need to register, and how will the acknowledgment of the necessity for change be implemented in actual scholarly practices?

*

Before concluding, we feel the obligation to revisit our initial question: Is Quentin Tarantino Italian American? This is what we found out: "He was born on March 27, 1963 in Knoxville, Tennessee. His mother, Connie Zastoupil, is . . . a native of that state but was raised in Cleveland, Ohio before going to high school in Los Angeles, the town she has always considered home" (Dawson 96). Tarantino's mother turns out to be "half Cherokee," though

she says "you wouldn't know it" (Dawson 96).[2] She became pregnant when she was sixteen, but by the time she found out about
her pregnancy, she had already separated from her husband,
Tony Tarantino – and "never even contacted him" (98). Quentin
was named after the character "Quint Asper" in the TV series
Gunsmoke (played by Burt Reynolds), but he was also named after
Quentin in *The Sound and the Fury*. When he was two years old,
mother and son moved to Los Angeles, where he was adopted by
Kurt Zastoupil, his mother's second husband. Quentin took his
surname, but after quitting school he again began using the name
Tarantino, that of his biological father, with whom he had had no
contact. When asked about his father, Tarantino answered
"flatly": "I have his name." According to one of his friends,
Tarantino "took back his biological father's name . . . because he
couldn't stand being called Zastoupil – 'In school they had called
him disaster peel'" (Bernard 102). Tarantino's onomastic
narrative effectively captures the very themes that are played out
in his movies: reflexivity, gender and sexual ambiguity, ethnic and
racial crossings, name play, and multiple identities.[3] If, as Rosie
Braidotti argues, the "nomadic subject" is someone with "no
mother tongue, only a succession of translations, of displacements,
of adaptations to changing conditions" (Braidotti 1), then
Tarantino's films – and perhaps his life – represent a sort of parodic rendition of intellectual and cultural (artistic?) nomadism. The
epistemological crisis often associated with postmodernism is indeed
reflected in the crisis of identity in Tarantino's cinema – a crisis
that was, perhaps, first played out in his own life.

  We began writing an article about Tarantino's cinema, but

---

[2] Tarantino's mother is Catholic (*Premiere*, November 1994, 102), but since her maiden
name does not appear anywhere in the press, her ethnic identity remains enigmatic – even
more so than her son's.

[3] Other aspects of Tarantino's films serve similar ends: hero-characters like Marcellus
(another powerful crime boss) and Jules (who undergoes the radical transformation from
assassin to devout, and ethically oriented, biblical scholar); inter-racial marriages like those
of Marcellus and Mia, and the one between Tarantino's character and his African
American wife, and even that between Butch (Bruce Willis) and his Bora-Boran girlfriend
Fabian, serve, as notable additions to the racially liberal though critically problematic
dimension of many of Tarantino's characterizations.

our primary concern turns out to be the question of whether or not – and how – to write about Tarantino himself. As Tarantino demonstrates, writing about Italian American ethnicity, and ethnicity in general, can no longer be done unproblematically: What is a real Italian American? How do we decide who belongs? What is the object – or the subject – of Italian American studies? If Tarantino never met his father, and, for whatever reason, only adopted the name as a teenager, then what else – other than "blood" – is Italian American about Quentin Tarantino?

Works Cited

Bernard, Jaime. "Quentin Tarantino: The Man and His Movies." *Sky Magazine* (September 1995): 101-08.

Braidotti, Rosi. *Nomadic Subjects: Embodiment and Sexual Difference in Contemporary Feminist Theory*. New York: Columbia UP, 1994.

Casillo, Robert. "Scorsese and Girard at Cape Fear." *Italian Americana* 12 (Summer 1994): 201-25.

Dawson, Jeff. "Revenge of the Nerd." *Empire* (October 1995): 96-100.

Fuller, Graham. "An Interview with Quentin Tarantino." *Quentin Tarantino: Reservoir Dogs and True Romance*. New York: Grove Press, 1994. ix-xviii.

Gamson, Joshua. *Claims to Fame: Celebrity in Contemporary America*. Berkeley: U of California P, 1984.

Hopper, Dennis. "Interview with Quentin Tarantino." *Grand Street Magazine* *13.1 (Summer 1994)*: 10-22.

Natural Born Killers. Dir. Oliver Stone. Story by Quentin Tarantino. Screenplay by David Veloz and Richard Rutowski. Warner Bros., 1994.

Pulp Fiction. Dir. Quentin Tarantino. Writing Credits, Quentin Tarantino (stories), Roger Avary. Warner Bros., 1994.

Reservoir Dogs. Dir. Quentin Tarantino. Writing Credits, Roger Avary, Quentin Tarantino. Warner Bros., 1994.

Tarantino, Quentin. *Pulp Fiction*. New York: Hyperion, 1994.

_____. *Reservoir Dogs and True Romance*. New York: Grove Press, 1994.

True Romance. Dir. Tony Scott. Writing Credits, Quentin Tarantino. Warner Bros., 1994.

THE LAND OF NOD
BODY AND SOUL IN ABEL FERRARA'S CINEMA OF TRANSGRESSION

Rebecca West
THE UNIVERSITY OF CHICAGO

> And the Lord said unto Cain, Where is Abel thy
> brother? And he said, I know not: Am I my
> brother's keeper?

Coincidence, no doubt, that Abel Ferrara bears the name of the slain brother whose murder is recorded in *Genesis* as the first such violent act in the history of the created universe. Yet Ferrara's films have insistently investigated and put before our eyes the "Cains" of our contemporary world: those people, like his namesake's brother, who refuse to be a "keeper" of others, pushed by their needs and desires to act on their darkest impulses in paroxysms of destruction – and often, ultimately, self-destruction. The cinematic visions of Ferrara are for the most part driven by a street-wise acknowledgement of the negative charge of transgressive desire: for love, for power, for relief from the human condition. If Biblical citation seems an odd opening for a study of film work typically set in the "mean streets" of contemporary New York, populated by characters who are murderers, addicts, whores, *Mafiosi*, corrupt cops, and ravaged nuns, it might end up being less odd if, as I wish to do, we view Ferrara's body of work as religiously conditioned, ethically driven, socially relevant, and even prophetic, rather than merely in-your-face filmmaking with requisite guns, sleaze, and mayhem. Harvey Keitel, an actor who has worked with Ferrara, most famously in *Bad Lieutenant*, commented, on the program "Inside the Actor's Studio" that was filmed with host James Lipton on November 16, 1997: "Abel Ferrara is a man with a religious soul." Critics have called his films "moral fables." It is as if the ghost of the biblical Abel were haunting the natural habitats of the contemporary offspring of Cain, looking, searching, trying to understand the dark desires that caused and go on causing the "mark" whereby these lost souls are themselves spared vengeful murder but are branded by God as "fugitive," "vagabond," and "cursed from the earth" (*Genesis*, Chapter 4, verses 11-12). That *bodily* "mark of Cain" is incarnated in Ferrara's screen images, and those powerful images in turn point to the invisible *soul* of transgression and redemption toward which these films reach.

Abel Ferrara was born in the Bronx, New York City in 1951; the director has said that his paternal grandfather emigrated to the United States from Naples and changed his "too-Southern" last name "Esposito" to "Ferrara."[1] Known as a maverick, Ferrara has for over twenty years made both big-budget films and low-rent ones, although all of them are unmistakably "Indie" in sensibility. Among his most obvious Italian American cinematic "fathers" are Scorsese and Coppola, but, like these other filmmakers, he does not always make movies that are identifiable with specific ethnic concerns. The Catholic dogma of sin, free will, grace, and redemption does, however, condition his portrayals of souls in pain; the teachings of the Church, more than any other element of Italian and Italian American tradition, provide a running sub-text to his cinematic stories no matter how diverse their explicit subject matter. Ferrara himself has stated that he, along with his friend and screenwriter Nicholas St. John, would not make the movies they do if they were not Catholic: "We wouldn't be concerned with the battle between Good and Evil" (in Cremonini; my translation from the original Italian). In the discussion to follow, I shall describe and analyze selected films by Ferrara, concentrating on the religious, ethical, social, and prophetic elements in them. My goal is to show how Ferrara endows various film genres – the crime story; the horror story; the science fiction story – with more ethical weight than is often inscribed into them; a weight that is due, at least in part, to the director's (Catholic) penchant for probing the dangers of free will when untouched by grace, and the effects on self and others of the unquiet desires that motivate human actions now as in the time of the biblical Cain and Abel. That Ferrara was born and raised –

---

[1] Ferrara discusses his mixed parentage (Italian and Irish) in Casella, 367. It is interesting that he calls the Irish side "demenziale" (crazy) in light of the character played by David Caruso in *King of New York*, a young Irish American cop whose uncontrollable temper and impetuous behavior end up getting him and others killed. Perhaps the character is based on Ferrara's memories of members of his family! In the film *China Girl*, Ferrara "signs" both of his Italian last names, by shooting a bakery in Little Italy called "Ferrara's" and then by panning to a building inscribed in stone letters with the name "Esposito."

and continues to live – in New York City, and has made extensive use of its Inferno-like settings and its "sin-city" stories, is also not irrelevant to his identity as a director; it may well be that, in the final analysis, his city of origin and his Catholic upbringing are the two most significant factors (as they are also for Scorsese) in under-standing the look, feel, and messages of his diverse films.

I shall begin my consideration of Ferrara by briefly describing his films to date; then, I shall move to close analyses of some se-lected films in which the religious, ethical, and social concerns of the director are particularly apparent. Ferrara's first feature-length film, *Driller Killer*, made in 1979, was an extremely low-budget venture. Ferrara himself, under the assumed actor's name of Jimmy Laine, played the lead, an unsuccessful and alienated painter who, like Scorsese's taxi driver, is driven to distraction by the violence and sordidness of New York City street life. He begins to enact his purifying ritual by killing street bums with a hand drill, and he eventually kills his lover's husband in the same gruesome manner, then waits in her bed presumably to dispatch her as gruesomely as he has her lawful mate. Unavailable on video, this film caused such an uproar in England that a film censorship code, which had never existed there before, was enacted. The following film, *Ms. 45*, made in 1980, is also clearly low-budget, shot on the streets of New York City. It stars Zoe Lund, who co-wrote the script (and who also wrote and appears later in *Bad Lieutenant* as Harvey Keitel's part-ner in drug addiction), and who portrays a young mute girl who is raped twice in one day and decides she is going to take her revenge on all men. After killing the second rapist, she dismembers him, stores his body parts in her refrigerator, and proceeds to shoot down a number of other presumably "innocent" men with the rap-ist's 45. In the final scenes, which take place at a costume party, the girl, dressed as a nun, continues her violent vendetta against men until she is herself knifed to death by one of her ex-colleagues. The film has been read as a "feminist statement," but Ferrara himself said that it was women *tout court* who inspired him, not feminists.[2]

---

[2] When told by interviewer Gavin Smith that the film "almost implicates all men in the oppression of women," Ferrara responds: "That's a very simplistic way of looking at the movie. The dog deserved to die because it barked?" See also Lehman in Cohan and Hark for a useful analysis of rape-revenge films.

Moreover, it is an exercise in reversing action-film clichés as well as gender roles (Woman as Rambo or Dirty Harry, so to speak), and is more witty than politely politically correct. In 1984 Ferrara made a psycho-on-the-loose thriller, *Fear City*, and in the next couple of years he also shot two episodes for television's "Miami Vice," the pilot for "Crime Story" with actor Dennis Farina, and another pilot called "The Gladiator" for an unrealized television series.

From these films, all basically within the crime/action film genre, in 1987 Ferrara expanded his repertoire into the love story (albeit with plenty of violence) with *China Girl*, which is a sort of Romeo and Juliet, *West Side Story* remake.[3] A young Chinese American girl and Italian American boy fall in love, but cannot escape the deep hatred and violence that separate New York's Chinatown and Little Italy more than merely spatially. The girl's brother is an aspiring gang leader who abhors her involvement with a boy who represents the rival Italian American gang world; and both young lovers die violently as they are caught in the crossfire between the two worlds. In 1989 Ferrara had the unhappy experience of *Cat Chaser*, which was re-cut by the producers and never commercially released, but in 1990 *King of New York* appeared, a film starring the famous and respected actor Christopher Walken, and which brought Ferrara to the attention of the mainstream. Walken plays a New York gangster, Frank White (a name perhaps echoed in Quentin Tarantino's *Reservoir Dogs* in which all the gang members have colors as fake names, including Harvey Keitel's Mr. White), who has recently been released from prison after serving a long jail term, and is determined to reconstitute his illegal empire. There are several twists to this well-known plot, however. Frank White's gang is almost exclusively black (including a then much less famous "Larry" Fishburne, as he is listed in the cast credits), thus making him the target of jibes from rival gang leaders who disdain his association with blacks. More importantly, White is

---

[3] Ferrara emphasizes Shakespeare much more than *West Side Story* as his inspiration; he comments on the fable-like but also documentaristic quality of the "feudal world" of the two young lovers, adding: "It sounds like a joke to say that we were trying to stay close to the original material, but that aspect was in the original material too. Romeo and Juliet are having an affair, and meanwhile Genoa ia being torn apart by the local hooligans" (in Smith, 22). Ferrara calls *China Girl* his favorite movie.

intent on acquiring a fortune in order to consolidate his power in New York, but he also wants to save a hospital in the ghetto that cares for poor black children, and he even suggests that he would be a good mayor of the city. I shall be considering this film in more detail below.

The infamous 1992 *Bad Lieutenant*, a very intense story of a contemporary lost soul that helped greatly to propel Harvey Keitel to superstardom and that solidified Ferrara's reputation, has been characterized as a film in the "hardboiled tradition of personal/artistic/spiritual statement" (Smith 21).[4] (I have analyzed it at some length in another article [see West, 1998] and I shall therefore not deal with it again here.) It was followed by the director's remake of the classic sci-fi horror film, *Invasion of the Body Snatchers*, which came out under the title *Body Snatchers* in 1993. Ferrara reworked the scenario of the original film, relocating the story to an Army base in the American South, and infusing it with racial, generational, and ecological resonance. More on this film also will follow. There then came *Dangerous Game*, originally entitled *Snake Eyes* , again with Keitel, who plays the part of a kind of alter ego filmmaker, and with Madonna and James Russo as his enthralled actors; the film was a big hit at the 1993 Venice Film Festival where Keitel garnered the Best Actor Award, but it did not do well in the States.[5] *The Addiction*, with Lili Taylor and Christopher Walken, came out in 1995; superficially it can be seen as a

---

[4] In Marshall Fine's unauthorized biography of Harvey Keitel, entitled *The Art of Darkness*, Keitel is quoted (although where and when is not indicated) as saying: "Abel is in a place that is somewhere betwixt heaven and hell. He's a man who's dealing with the chaos of existence in, I think, a profound and divine way" (Fine, 201). The actor says specifically of the film *Bad Lieutenant:* "I was very proud when someone said it was the best anti-drug film they (sic) had ever seen because there was no moralizing in it. I believe that it is a religious film, because hell is here now and so is the opportunity to know heaven" (Fine, 208). Speaking of unauthorized biographies, there is one on Ferrara, entitled, with a conspicuous lack of originality, *King of New York*. It is by Nick Johnstone, and includes discussions of the films, and a bibliography.

[5] Ferrara tells an amusing story to Liza Bear regarding the discarded title of *Dangerous Game*: "The original title was *Snake Eyes*. But there's a porno film called *Snake Eyes* so we couldn't use it as a title. MGM was afraid of getting sued. . . It's funny, because whenever we are between films and people say, what are you going to say next. . . I used to say 'Snake eyes.'" Bear comments, "Oh, I see, like rolling the dice," to which the director responds: "Yeah, that's what it means. Snake eyes is a losing hand. If you roll two ones, that's a losing throw. . . . there's something about it that sounds official, but meanwhile there never was a movie that went with it. All we had was this title to shut people up" (Bear, 41).

vampire movie, but vampirism is used as a metaphor for addiction, with fascinating results that I shall discuss below. *The Funeral* came out in 1996, again with Walken as well as Chris Penn, Vincent Gallo, Benicio del Toro, Isabella Rossellini, and Annabella Sciorra, followed by one of the episodes of the multi-directed 1997 HBO production, *Subway Stories*, and the list is completed with the 1999 *New Rose Hotel* with Walken, Willem Dafoe, and Asia Argento, the daughter of Italian horror film director Dario Argento of *Suspiria* fame. The film is based on a story by William Gibson, and in it Walken and Dafoe play gangsters who use an Italian prostitute (Argento) to seduce secrets from a Japanese geneticist (Ryuichi Sakamoto).

The most openly "Italian American" of all these films are the Scorsese-like *Bad Lieutenant* and the Coppola-like *The Funeral*, in both of which the ethnicity of the characters and ambience is clear. The latter is "Godfather-like" in its concentration on the Mafia, its dark tones, its mix of domestic, familial relations and extreme violence. Walken, Penn, and Gallo play brothers who have inherited a legacy of violence and gangsterism from their father, and pay heavily for it. Cesarino (Penn) is literally driven mad by the memory of his father's suicide and the guilt he feels regarding his idealistic younger brother's death, and he shoots himself at his brother's (Gallo's) funeral before the horrified eyes of his wife and other family members. Ray (Walken), the eldest brother, tries to hold the family together, but he too is marked by the family legacy of violence and criminal behavior, and shoots down the very young killer of his brother before himself being shot to death by Cesarino. Ray's wife (Sciorra) speaks the main message of the film when she says that the men are not "rugged individualists," as they would like to consider themselves, but rather simply "criminals"; she insists that "there is nothing romantic about it," a declaration that seems to be an implicit critique of those Mafia films (by Coppola, Scorsese, and others) in which an air of ravaged nobility or a sense of honor, no matter how perverse, colors the gangsters' lives. Perhaps the most interesting aspect of the film is Walken's portrayal of Ray, who is searching for God's grace in order to do what is right, but who (unlike Keitel's bad lieutenant) is left only with his free choice or will, unaided by grace, and thus he is doomed to continue the legacy of evildoing. *China Girl*, one of Ferrara's favorite pictures, also concentrates on a portrayal of Italian American experience, which now seeks, in the figure of the young "Romeo," some connection with other ethnicities, in the figure of the young Chinese American Juliet. The hermetic quality of both ethnic spaces is highlighted in the film spatially (there is an invisible line that separates Chinatown from Little Italy, and woe to those who cross it), and in terms of the bitter rivalry of the gangs, much as Spike Lee has underscored the profound difficulties in crossing borders (in the case of his films, those between African Americans and Italian Americans) in *Do The Right Thing* and *Jungle Fever*. The view of the United States as a "melting-pot" is shown to be a myth, for racial and ethnic tensions run so deep as to result in death for those who try to mix with others outside of their given group identities. Turf issues, jealousies, and rivalries continue to plague humankind on the contemporary streets of New York much as they did in the times of the biblical brothers Cain and Abel.

If Ferrara's films add up to a relatively unified, *auteur*-like body of work, this is due in no small part to his fairly constant collaboration with screenwriter Nicholas St. John (a close friend since early childhood), musical director Joe Delia, and a stable of known actors who by now have appeared intermittently in several of his movies (Keitel, Walken, Sciorra). His *auteurism* is also, and more importantly, describable in terms of recurrent themes, preoccupations, and emphases, the most salient of which are the tensions between free will and grace; transgression and redemption; and body and soul. These could all be called "religious" concerns, and it could therefore fairly be said that Ferrara is a director of "religious" films, although, like many of Scorsese's Italian American characters, religion is deeply intertwined with the profane. *Mean Streets'* Charlie, played by Keitel, asserts, for example, that one expiates one's sins on the street, not in church; Keitel has commented: "[Scorsese] is Catholic, I'm Jewish but we both belong to the Church of Struggling to Do What's Right. It's a personal moral code rather than a formal religion" (in Fine 62). Like Scorsese, Ferrara upsets our expectations of what a religious film should be or is. There is no mere patina of religiosity – the "local color" we often find in some films that evoke the Italian American world – nor is there a saccharine tone of ponderous seriousness such as we see in overtly "religious" films (especially in films made in past decades) such as *The Ten Commandments* or *Ben Hur.* Instead, Ferrara crafts contemporary parables or allegories about sin and redemption, concentrating on the confusion, pain, and very profane struggles of people living in today's world. As I turn to analyses of specific films, I seek to show how Ferrara shapes diverse film genres into visual tales about deeply moral issues, all the while avoiding overt didacticism in favor of captivating, entertaining, in-your-face filmic techniques that have audience appeal; that, in other words, make religious and social topics come alive in vivid images of striking contemporaneity and understandable relevance for urban, particularly young, racially diverse viewers, and, in general, for audiences attuned to the modes of mainstream cinema. Audiences today may not easily respond to Biblical references or overt tales of redemption, but they do respond to well-crafted entertainment, in which are sometimes embedded—parable-like—religious, ethical, or social concerns. Like a priest who walks among the homeless, speaking their language, Ferrara brings it to the streets.

King of New York: *Gangster Soul*

Frank White (Christopher Walken), a gangster recently released from a long jail term, is hell-bent on reconstituting, consolidating, and expanding his once powerful kingdom. It could be said that he has delusions of grandeur, for he wants to control all of the drug trade in New York, he thinks he would make a great mayor of the city, and he is committed to doing good for the poor black ghetto population, all the while that he exploits their dependency on drugs and slaughters his rivals with no remorse. Ferrara has commented that the character is driven by "Blind ambition. One person's going to take over the drug trade in New York. How stupid is that?" Interviewer Gavin Smith responds: "Yet Frank White is a genuinely radical, contradictory figure – he forges a direct link between crime and social consciousness." Ferrara's answer is: "I wouldn't go that far. He's a homicidal maniac. But the Robin Hood theme is an age-old story" (in Smith 22-23). The film, artfully shot by cinematographer Bojan Bazelli, creates a New York of darkness interspersed with the brilliant lights of the skyscrapers (very evocative of film noir), of extreme contrasts between the lush interiors of the wealthy and the rotting buildings of the forgotten poor, and of apocalyptic rain. Ferrara commented to Smith that Bazelli had a particular take on how he wanted to shoot New York, which for him is a foreign place, and that the cinematographer has a classical approach to cutting and coverage as contrasted to "letting it happen." This classical approach is evident in the film's tight economy, which is narratively driven, moving from scene to scene with little material that is extraneous to the dynamism of the story being told. Musical director Joe Delia also adds much to the contrastive style of the film, using lyrical classical music (Vivaldi) as well as driving rap music. In all, the film's look and sound are very stylish if not stylized, and Walken's flat, white face – kabuki-like at times – and sudden shifts from smiling charm to sullen rage add much to the stylized quality of the overall film.

Frank White moves between two worlds, as we see in the opening scenes of the film. The first scene is in prison where we see White as he is being prepared for release; the din of constant voices, music, and the crash of barred metal doors immediately evoke the hellish nature of this enclosed criminal world. A big black limousine is waiting for Frank outside the prison gates, and he thus enters into his other world, which is equally imbued with criminality (the drug empire and the violence associated with it have paid for this fancy car), but is also luxurious, filled with the "perks" of all wealthy people. The scene cuts to a whorehouse where an obviously criminal type is taking his leave, after having enjoyed a session with a prostitute. He exits the building and goes to a phone booth nearby where he is shot to death by three men lying in wait. Another cut back to Frank, whose expressionless, eerily white face is lit by intermittent lights as he is driven through the back streets where drug addicts are hanging out, listening to rap music. The sparkling beautiful skyline of New York appears before Frank's eyes as the car slides by, suggesting a city of wealth and unlimited opportunities, in obvious contrast to the crummy alleys haunted by hopeless addicts. The hybrid nature of Frank's existence is emphasized in a variety of additional ways throughout the film: his gang of black thugs, led by the lowlife, maniacal killer Jimmy (Fishburne) likes the showy gold jewelry and sex and drug parties typical of most drug kings' tastes (and which Frank attends with his white and black prostitute girlfriends), yet Frank stays at the Plaza Hotel with his stable of high-class assistants, including his "straight" girlfriend, who is also his lawyer, goes to the Lunt and Fontanne theater to see Eugene O'Neill's *The Emperor Jones*, eats in the fanciest restaurants, and hobnobs with politicians and other highly placed people. The material contrast between these external worlds (rich versus poor; privileged versus abject) is matched by the inner or spiritual contrast between Frank's cold-heartedness in slaughtering his competition in the drug trade and his altruistic desire to do good by aiding the poor ghetto children, keeping their hospital open with the wealth he has accumulated through selling drugs.

Early on in the film, after Jimmy (Fishburne) and other gang members have killed a group of Colombian drug dealers, competitors for Frank's business, Frank announces to a table of his associates, both criminal and legitimate (including his lawyer girlfriend) that is he is "reformed" and that he wants to be mayor of New York. However, he has just told Jimmy that he feels no remorse over the deaths of the Colombians, and he shortly will kill an Italian American gang leader – another competitor – in cold blood. The Italian American gangster is angry about the deaths of the Colombians, with whom he says he has made a lot of money, and he especially resents Frank's willingness to use blacks in his gang, calling Frank a "nigger lover." Perhaps to create an ironic gloss on the demise of the Italian American gang, Ferrara flashes on the name of the restaurant where they are playing cards in the back room (and where Frank will shoot down the leader): Il Tramonto (Sunset). We now understand that Frank is set on eliminating all competition; he invites any and all thugs to join his gang including a trio of young blacks who attempt to hold him up while he is on the subway with his lawyer girlfriend, as well as the remaining members of the Italian American gang), but he will not tolerate anyone who challenges his push to control the entire drug trade in New York. Ferrara comments on Frank's ambition: "When Walken says, 'A nickel bag gets sold in the park, I want half,' what does that mean about the guy? It's the attitude that builds skyscrapers" (in Smith 23). Soon, Frank is talking to the leader of the Chinese gang, showing him around the South Bronx hospital for black chil-

dren, and urging him to join forces with him. The Chinese gangster tells Frank that he is "fucking crazy," and shortly thereafter
there is a violent shoot-out between Frank's gang and the Chinese,
the latter of whom are killed off. It seems that Frank is well on the
way to realizing his dream.

If both the gangs, and the rich lawyers and politicians are portrayed as corrupt, the force for good is embodied in the world-
weary police detective Bishop (Victor Argo). Ferrara has said that it
is all about what individuals do for others, since powerful institutions are ultimately built on and sustained by corruption. "To me,"
Ferrara says, "the King of New York is not Walken, but Argo.
That's my own private joke" (in Smith 22). Bishop (Argo) is truly
his brother's keeper, attempting to keep control of his wild, re-
vengeful young Irish American police associate (David Caruso)
while patiently stalking Walken. With his tired, hangdog face and
aging body, Argo does not at all present a heroic presence. He is
first seen right after Frank has shot the Italian American gangster to
death, seated in front of his computer in his darkly lit, plainly furnished apartment. Bishop is scanning the file of Francis White,
whom we learn was a foster child, and a long-time criminal with an
extensive record. Bishop shakes a pill from a prescription bottle, an
action he repeats at various times throughout the film. This soli-
tary, ailing, underpaid cop is indeed an odd "king," but his simple
words and actions define him as a profoundly good man who
eventually gives up his life in order to protect a hostage. The very
averageness of Bishop's everyday life and demeanor are in striking
contrast to his role as a representative of almost otherwordly Good
in the film. When Fishburne and others in Frank's gang are put in
jail on the testimony of a surviving Colombian, Caruso, Wesley
Snipes (Caruso's cop partner), and even Argo are triumphant, but
the killers are soon released when Frank pays their million dollar
bail. Bishop has already been seen striding into a luxurious restaurant and confronting one of Frank's fancy lawyers with photos of
the slaughtered Colombians, while he says: "How can you be a part
of this?" He also confronts Frank's lawyer girlfriend as she exits jail
with the released gang members, saying "Proud of yourself, coun-
selor?" He seeks to reach the conscience of these individuals who
are ostensibly on the side of law and order, but they are too caught

up in the wealth and power of Frank's and their own world to change. The film is not as overtly a social satire of the 1980s "me generation" as are the films *Wall Street* and the recent *American Psycho*, but it definitely evokes an era when "the fiscal grotesqueries of Milton Friedman, Margaret Thatcher, Donald Trump and other 80s icons became harder to stomach" (James 23). Frank's ambition to build an empire based on total control of the drug trade in New York is not that far from real-life, "legitimate" empire builders of corporate America, and his personal megalomania is very evocative of Trump's.

Frank is betrayed by a member of his gang, Joey (Gian Carlo Esposito), who serves as a go-between for the sale of Frank's drugs. His betrayal results in an unofficial police attack, led by Caruso, on Frank's gang's hideout during a drug and sex party, where Frank's two prostitute girlfriends are shot to death, as well as several other members of his gang. Frank and Jimmy (Fishburne) manage to escape in a car, and there follows a very well-filmed car chase scene, with Caruso, Snipes, and another very young cop whose wedding reception we have witnessed earlier, in hot pursuit of the criminals. Caruso's deep and personal hatred of Frank has already been established in a scene with him and Argo in a bar, which follows immediately after a scene at the Harlem Ballroom in which we see Frank and his wealthy politician and lawyer friends celebrating the successful campaign to save the black children's South Bronx hospital. This scene is nicely glossed by a black singer who is warbling "Dream on. We can make it paradise," and by a woman television reporter who is covering the event and who states to the camera: "This is a proud moment for the city." As Frank is basking in the glory of his success, Caruso is ranting to Argo in a crummy bar: "Frank is a movie star, the king of New York. His Park Avenue attorney gets Frank out in ten minutes. The system favors the scumbags, We get $36,500 [a year] to risk our lives and Frank gets rich killing people." Caruso furiously insists that there is only one way to get Frank (i.e., to shoot him down in a surprise raid); Argo responds: "You gonna shoot everybody you can't arrest? Do anything stupid and I'm coming after your ass." Driven by his rage, Caruso does not listen to his boss, and the car chase and shoot-out end in disaster, as the young cop is killed, and Caruso's partner

Tommy (Snipes) is then gunned down by a laughing Jimmy (Fishburne) after Snipes has pursued him in the driving rain to an abandoned spot under a bridge. Caruso's only satisfaction is in shooting to death the wounded Jimmy.

Frank will have his "Judas," Esposito, killed for his betrayal, and the slaughter has now risen to unprecedented heights: important members of Frank's gang are dead, his prostitute girlfriends are dead, rival gang leaders are dead, and two cops are dead. Frank still believes that he is invincible, however, and at the burial of Snipes and the young cop, he unabashedly drives by Caruso's car and shoots him dead as well. It is now a show-down between Bishop, the tired old cop, and the triumphant King of New York, Frank. The final scenes of the film concentrate on these two characters as they face off, first in Bishop's apartment where Frank waylays him, and then on the subway where Bishop stalks Frank in order to arrest (or perhaps simply to kill) him. In the cop's apartment, Frank seeks to explain himself to Bishop; he points out that the Colombians had thirteen-year-old girls hooking on the street, that the Chinese gang leader rented single rooms to Chinese immigrants for $800 a month, and that Artie, the Italian American gangster, had amassed thirteen million dollars. Frank says: "They were running the city into the ground. I never killed anybody who didn't deserve it." He further points out that he has a contract of a quarter of a million dollars out on all the people involved in trying to bring him to justice. Argo responds that, in spite of Frank's desire to do some good, he is in fact taking over drug cartels, to which Frank answers that people spend ten billion dollars a year in the United States getting high: "I'm not your problem, I'm just a businessman." Instead of killing Bishop, he leaves him handcuffed to a chair, teasingly pointing his finger at the cop and saying "Bang, bang" as he leaves the apartment. Bishop soon finds the key to the cuffs and frees himself, then pursues Frank onto the subway with his gun drawn. After running through several cars, he finds Frank calmly seated, goes up to him and says that it's over. Frank grabs a black woman as hostage, saying that he won't make it easy for Bishop; as the cop hesitates in his concern for the woman, Frank shoots him, but Bishop gets off a shot that hits Frank before Bishop expires on the floor of the subway car. Frank gets off the subway, and we see him walking along a very crowded street that is filled with stalled traffic. He gets into a cab and tells the cabby "Just drive," but the traffic jam is such that no movement is possible. As the slow, mournful Vivaldi once more plays over the cacophony of sirens and traffic noise, the cabby jumps out, indicates Frank to the many cops who have arrived in response to the subway shooting of Bishop, and we only then see that Frank has been shot in the stomach. As he sits looking out the cab window with his gun in his hand, his head drops back and he dies. Ferrara responds, when asked by Smith how he came up with the ending: "That came about on the spot. Walken said: 'it ends not with a bang, but a whimper.' This guy wasn't going to pull off some kind of operatic stunt; he thought he was going to make it to the end and escape. He thought, there are 9 million people, I'll just slip through the cracks and be gone." Smith comments that it is not the cops who get him but New York traffic, to which Ferrara responded: "Yes, the environment, the city. Plus he got shot in the stomach, which doesn't help." And thus ends the King.

Critic Liza Bear has commented on how good Ferrara is at conveying "the seductiveness of evil" (37). *King of New York* very clearly shows the allure of great power, and the illusion of indestructibility it creates, but it also shows the astoundingly high toll the attainment of such power takes on human lives, decency, and the overall social fabric. Frank White is a character who adds an important new dimension to the gangster genre due to his conflictual sense of good and evil. He wants to be his "brother's keeper," while exploiting one of the factors – drug addiction – that keep his brother down. The meaning of his character can be extended far beyond the limits of the overtly criminal world in which he makes his millions; his ambition and power are not so different either in cause or effect to the ambition and power of people involved in "legitimate" big business, Ferrara seems to suggest. The exploiters of others weaker than they are have been with us throughout history, and will be with us in the future. The gangster film genre thus modulates into a parable about power, a sort of "David and Goliath" story for today's world. Ferrara's emphasis on individual choice, idealistic as it may be, is ethically, even religiously, driven: there is the right thing and the wrong thing, he shows us, and each person must make the choice when faced with it. Frank tries to sit on the fence between right and wrong, but the evil ultimately far outweighs any good he might accomplish. Bishop knows the enormity of what he is up against, but he remains true to his sense of law and justice. Although he too dies in the end, he has not lost his "soul," while Frank's gangster soul had been lost long before his body died.

Body Snatchers: *Where Ya Gonna Go? Where Ya Gonna Run? Where Ya Gonna Hide?*

The 1956 film, *The Invasion of the Body Snatchers*, directed by Don Siegel, has become a cult classic of the Cold-War era. In it, an alien force takes over a small town in the United States, growing zombie-like pod people who replace the human citizens while they sleep. The film was remade under Philip Kaufman's direction in 1978, and Abel Ferrara's version, *Body Snatchers*, came out in 1993. At first consideration, this may seem to have been a striking departure from Ferrara's usual subject matter and genre preference, but upon further thought the issue of bodily invasion is not so far from the theme of addiction as seen in the earlier *Bad Lieutenant*. In *King of New York* as well, drugs are the mainstay of Frank White's empire. Bodies are "snatched" by addiction or illness in our real world, just as they are snatched by unnamed alien forces in Ferrara's allegorical film. The director himself makes the connection between invasive illness and alien appropriation of the body: "The parallel of Aids in the 90s is a much more frightening thought than communism in the 50s. Obviously, it's a metaphor for *something*, unless you're going to take the thing as a documentary and say, the Martians are here" (in Smith 23). By moving the story to a military base in the South where materials for chemical and biological warfare are stored, Ferrara is also able to suggest ties between both the institutionalized control of the military, and the ecological dangers of manmade products of war, and the alien takeover; and by concentrating on the struggle of young people to avoid being snatched as their more passive parents have been, a generational issue is implied as well.

With the usual collaboration of Joe Delia as music director and Nicholas St. John as co-screenwriter, Ferrara crafts a powerful –

and quite original – remake of the classic movie. One of the most striking departures for Ferrara is the setting, in the "pastoral" South, far from the mean streets of New York. The film opens with a shot of dark space filled with stars, which lends a vast, cosmic quality very unlike the typical claustrophobia of teeming city streets as seen in his earlier films. The camera then focuses on a car in which a family is traveling along a country road. A doctor (Terry Kenney), his young second wife (Meg Tilly), their son and his daughter from his first marriage (Gabrielle Anwar) are heading toward the military base where the doctor has been hired to check the safety of biological and chemical warfare materials. They stop at a gas station located in the midst of pastures in which cows are grazing, and Anwar goes off to the bathroom where she is confronted by a black man in military garb, who hysterically informs her: "They get you when you sleep." By the time she runs out of the bathroom and frantically informs her family that a crazy man is in there, he has disappeared. As the family continues on the road to the base, Anwar comments, in a voice-over, that we spend half our lives asleep. The pastoralism of the ambience is no longer as restful as it first appeared to be, and viewers will be less likely to step into gas station bathrooms with insouciance (just as viewers of Hitchcock's *Psycho* have a permanently altered sense of roadside motels and shower stalls).

Upon the family's arrival at their base home – a depressingly small, plain wooden house – it becomes clear that Anwar is an alienated teenager, resentful of her stepmother and of the necessary move to such sparse and restrictive surroundings. She soon meets the daughter of the Head of the base, a rebellious teenager whose mother is a stuporous alcoholic and whose father is a rigid, repressive military man. The two girls begin to spend time together, driving very fast around the base and frequenting the base's only bar where the bored soldiers hang out and get drunk. Meanwhile, Anwar's father has met the base's psychiatrist, Dr. Malone (Forest Whitaker), who is concerned that the chemicals stored on the base may be leaking out and affecting the sanity of the soldiers, many of whom seem to be delusional. They are afraid to go to sleep and insist that something is changing people around them, but Anwar's father assures the psychiatrist that there is nothing to worry about if the chemicals are stored safely and, moreover, that they could not in any case cause such delusions. Anwar soon meets an attractive young soldier (Billy Wirth) and falls in love with him, as they share their innermost thoughts and feelings.

A remake such as this one, based on a well-known plot, can surprise audiences only so much, since we are well aware that the "delusions" of the soldiers are in fact an accurate reflection of the alien takeover. Sure enough, the youngest member of the family, Anwar's small brother, is one of the first to report that something is seriously wrong. He hates going to daycare, where the strangely passive children all paint the exact same picture and where he is expected to go dutifully to sleep upon the command of his teacher. His father sees his unhappiness simply as a sign of adjustment problems, but things at home get a lot worse when the boy begins to insist that his mother (Meg Tilly) is not herself. We have in fact witnessed her transformation into a pod person, and we later see the attempted transformation of Anwar. While she is taking a bath, she dozes off and worm-like tentacles begin invading her body through her nose and mouth. She wakes up just in time to escape being changed into the eerily passive entity that her stepmother has become. The stepmother's mantra is: "Where ya gonna go? Where ya gonna run? Where ya gonna hide?" As the psychiatrist (Forest Whitaker) battles to stay awake with the aid of pills, Anwar's father realizes what has happened to his wife, and he hides his children in the storage room where the chemical warfare materials are stored while he seeks a way out of the base. The psychiatrist is confronted by a group of pod people, who tell him that unity is necessary and that he should give in to the inevitable, but he refuses, shouting that they will never get his soul just before he shoots himself to death. The father returns to hustle his children off to their car, but Anwar is deeply suspicious of him, and believes that he may already have been transformed. There is a showdown between the father and Anwar's young soldier boyfriend, who kills the father. He is a helicopter pilot, and decides that the way out of the base is to fly; he puts on the mask of passive conformity in front of his fellow soldiers who are guarding the helicopters, and manages, along with Anwar, to bluff his way among the by-now highly suspicious pod people who are swarming all over the base, looking for the remaining humans. When the pod people come across a human, they set up a blood-curdling, ululating cry that signals their find to the other aliens. Anwar's emotional concern for her little brother, whom she wishes to save, gives her away to her girlfriend, the general's daughter, who howls her discovery as the girl and her soldier boyfriend fly away, having pulled the little brother onto the helicopter at the last minute. The soldier realizes, however, that the boy has been transformed and forces Anwar to let go of him, as he then pushes the child out of the helicopter to his death below. They fly away over a scene of a long line of trucks, which are transporting the pod bodies, and it seems clear that the aliens are winning. The visuals thus come full circle, to a final shot from on high that echoes the perspective of the opening shot.

Ferrara makes of this well-known plot a multi-leveled allegory, which refers not only to pollution and illness (the chemicals stored for biological warfare; Aids), but also to addiction (the adults' recourse to alcohol), to conformity, and to the generational battle (rebellious teenagers versus complacent adults). The casting of Forest Whitaker as the courageous psychiatrist who would rather die by his own hand than give up his soul also introduces racial issues. In terms of Ferrara's typical preoccupations, this film highlights the horror of lack of free choice, as the invasive aliens determine the destinies of humans. The vision created in this film is of a post-theological world, in which God is either dead or simply indifferent to the fate of his human creatures, whose passivity, destructive militarism, and tendency to embrace thoughtless conformity have implicitly doomed them. Ferrara's comments on this story are rather unexpected, however. When asked by interviewer Gavin Smith, "What is your take on 'The Bodysnatchers'?" the director replied: "The greatest thing about that movie is the concept of it – that is, that the antagonists are *passive*. They're not eating you or shooting you, they're just saying, go to sleep and when you wake up, the world's going to be a better place. Plus, it's from an enemy you can't even see, because it's yourself. . .And the book is awesome, with an entirely different ending in which the aliens float off. The aliens' basic attitude is, hey you guys are such pricks we're leaving, we're offering you nirvana and you guys are so fucked up you can't even accept it, so we'll go somewhere where we're appreciated" (in Smith 23). These comments seem to imply that Ferrara was not so down on the aliens, whose goal was to "offer nirvana" to humans; yet his film ends up emphasizing very clearly the negativity of such "nirvana," which precludes free choice and self-determination. The remake is thought-provoking as well as engaging; most of the humans are not very attractive collectively, so we don't particularly mourn their transformation, yet the will to freedom of choice shown by the black psychiatrist and by the young lovers is fundamentally appealing, and I think that audiences end up hoping that Anwar and Wirth will somehow escape the spreading menace (or promise?) of a completely conformist, transformed world, in which strong emotions, war, pollution, and illness may be a thing of the past, but so will love, courage, and personal choice.

The Addiction: *Vampire Philosophy*

With this 1995 film, Ferrara moves into the horror genre, having already established his credentials as a masterful maker of crime, action, and science-fiction films. Independent film actress Lili Taylor plays the lead role in *The Addiction;* she portrays a young philosophy student in New York who is attacked one night by a weird woman (Annabella Sciorra) as she walks home. The woman turns out to be a vampire, who changes Kathleen (Taylor) into a vampire as well, via the time-honored method of sucking her blood. Kathleen's lust for blood leads her to attack her best friend, and she eventually sets up a party to celebrate the completion of her doctoral degree, to which she invites various professors, students, and vampires. The party turns into an orgy of blood-sucking and killing, until Kathleen herself (or, at least, her evil vampire side) is killed. Nicholas St. John, Ferrara's long-time collaborator and screenwriter, wrote the script unbeknownst to the director, who then filmed it exactly as St. John had written it. Called a "devout Catholic" by Ferrara, St. John's story appealed to the director because in it Kathleen "was getting to the point where she was asking, what is the intellect without the soul?. . .Intellect alone in this world is just going to leave you. . . addicted" (in Bear 38). Ferrara chose to film the movie in black and white, which contributes greatly to its noirish, stylized look and feel. Yet it also has very contemporary, realistic aspects, as when we see Kathleen in the classroom at the university, or when she is discussing philosophy with her fellow student and friend outside of class. Christopher Walken appears again in this film, playing a vampire who is very much a cynical, world-weary hipster. He seems to represent the lure of a purely bodily and intellectual approach to life, one that says to go for pleasure and to face up to the need for crutches be they addictive drugs, the study of philosophy, or blood-sucking. Kathleen fights against his view, but she is overwhelmed by her "addiction" to blood and her desire to wreak vengeance on her pompous professors and fellow students. Her blood lust is material as well as emotional, as both appetite and the desire for revenge push her to transgressive acts. The film has some strong performances, especially that of Lili Taylor, but it also skirts dangerously close to silly pretentiousness at times. However, the moral and social concerns that underlie Ferrara's films are also clearly present in *The Addiction*; the metaphor of vampirism works well in showing the torments of addiction, which bring people to act in ways that they would otherwise not act. It also underscores the spreading nature of addiction, which ensnares even the most unsuspecting of people and involves them in a downward spiral of degradation and violence. If an intelligent, diligent philosophy student can be taken over by extreme needs and a transgressive desire for blood, no one is immune. Once more, as in *Body Snatchers*, the battle between free choice, and internal pressures (addiction, desire) and external forces of evil (the aliens, the vampires) is illustrated in contemporary terms, although the battle itself is an ancient and abiding theme throughout history and art.

East of Eden

Abel Ferrara's films all take place in a post-lapsarian world that is populated by flawed, violent, weak, or simply evil people. His preferred setting is New York, a city filled with displaced persons, exiled souls, "strangers in a strange land." Yet, when pressed by interviewer Liza Bear about his preference for "characters who are depraved, decadent, or corrupt, or weak," Ferrara responds: "Like who?" Bear lists Frank White, the Lili Taylor vampire character, and Harvey Keitel's bad lieutenant, and Ferrara counters that Argo's cop character is good, the lieutenant gives the rapists a second chance at life just as their victim the nun, would wish, and only Taylor's evil side dies, and he summarizes: "I'm just seeing the world I live in. . . Are we making films about people who invent a cure for polio? We're making films about people caught in the grip of good and evil. Two sides to the coin. Where are you at and how do you deal with it. That's what the movies are about and that conflict is the fucking film" (in Bear 40). His apparent irritation at being defined as a filmmaker who focuses on bad people is due perhaps to the simplistic assumption that good and bad can easily be separated, while his self-declared interest is in the *conflict* between them within the same individual. The body is most often the locus of the effects of the conflict – primarily the bodily ravages of addiction – but the cause of the conflict is to be found in the soul of his characters. The personalized soulfulness (in all senses) of Ferrara's films links his art to the auteur strain in European art cinema; specifically we can see ties to Pasolini's goal of capturing a "certain realism" or to Godard's socio-political parables (and both are directors for whom Ferrara has professed a preference).[6] But Ferrara is, ultimately, a profoundly American filmmaker in terms not only of settings and stories but also in terms of his mastery of mainstream techniques that aim for entertaining general audiences, for creating narrative dynamism and exciting, action-filled spectacle.

Is Abel Ferrara an Italian American filmmaker, however? If by this is meant the ethnic background of a director, there is no question. If, however, the definition is more complicated, as it should be, then it is more difficult to categorize him as such simply on the basis of his family origin. Several of his films have Italian American settings, characters, or themes (*China Girl, The Funeral, Bad Lieutenant*), but just as many do not. I have suggested that it is his religious, even Catholic, sensibility that may serve to define him as

---

[6] Ferrara mentions in passing to Liza Bear that as a young man he liked to watch films by Joe Dallesandro, Pasolini, directors of Italian new realist cinema, and Godard (41). In talking with Gavin Smith about the issue of film violence causing real violence, Ferrara refers to Godard: "Violence is so much a metaphor; we're not making documentaries. I don't mean to sound like the Godard quotebook, but a gun going off in a movie is not a gun going off" (23). Referring to the effect of a low budget on a film, Ferrara again quotes Godard: "The economics of a film is the politics of a film" (in Forde, 29). For a probing analysis of Pasolini's ideas about the non-logical but necessary role of the body in knowing (the epistemological aspect of the bodily), about realism in the cinema, and about the clash of desire and reason (all concerns mirrored, if in different ways, in Ferrara's films), see Viano.

Italian American. Pasquale Verdicchio has made a similar argument in a recent essay in which he analyzes films by De Michiel, Savoca, Ferrara, and Scorsese. Verdicchio sees these filmmakers' unorthodox religiosity as stemming from their ethnicity, which alienated them both from orthodox Italian Catholicism and from mainstream American (read Northern European) Catholicism. The critic writes: "These films propose new ways of making spirituality and religiosity viable and available components of contemporary life, all the while paying heed and homage to the cultural heritage of the immigrant group itself, rather than to an institution external to it. The driving force behind these radical attempts appears to be an extended search for redemption. . ." (203). Verdicchio emphasizes the manner in which Ferrara, Scorsese, and the other filmmakers he discusses bring religion to the streets, to the interaction among family members; in short, to unconventionally everyday settings and stories. This tendency may be the result of an Italian American ethos, which is neither institutionally religious as is the Church-oriented Italian attitude, nor conventionally mainstream American, which is a Catholicism shaped more dominantly by Northern European antecedents. The maverick, independent quality of Ferrara's fables of transgression and redemption, centering as they do on the individual rather than on collectivities or institutions (which in his stories are more dangerous than supportive), may stem from his Italian American background, but may also simply reflect his very personal ethos.

Because Italian American cinema has long been linked to a preference for portrayals of the criminal world of the Mafia and of generalized gangsterism (see Casillo), Ferrara's attraction to stories about criminals, corruption, and transgression could be seen as entering into this line, thus providing another reason for calling him an "Italian American" director. His most overtly Italian American film, *The Funeral*, is discussed at length in an Italian critic's study of Italian American filmmaking, for example (see Casella). Ferrara himself describes the film as "the story of our [his and screenwriter Nicholas St. John's] families, of our blood. It was a way to go back to the real essence of our ancestors" (in Casella 369; this and subsequent quotations in my translation from the original Italian). The director is not worried about the fact that this is yet another story about a Mafia family, explaining that "this film doesn't represent all Italians, but only my family. In any case, the Mafia is a part of the experience of Italian Americans, and it's useless to deny it" (in Casella 432). More interestingly, I believe, he emphasizes that the "Mafia movie" is a cinematographic genre that is linked genealogically with the genre of the "Gangster movie," and that his film, *The Funeral*, is a "metaphor" constructed within the parameters of an established genre: "For this reason, we show a sequence at the beginning from *The Petrified Forest* with Humphrey Bogart, in order to make it clear that *The Funeral* is part of that tradition" (in Casella 433). The film was called *Fratelli* (Brothers) in Italy, and this title reflects well Ferrara's and St. John's intent, which was to show different levels of Italian American assimilation into mainstream American life via the three brothers, Johnny, Cesarino, and Ray. Ray (Walken), the oldest, represents the old tradition of *omertà* and *vendetta*; Johnny, the youngest who is a Communist activist, represents the future, and Cesarino is squarely between the two, literally driven crazy by his opposing allegiances and drives. It is the inner, emotional conflict inside of and among the brothers that most interested the director, and he asserted in summation: "The fundamental theme continues to be that of free will" (in Casella 430). To whom or what are we beholden for our actions? Ferrara's films ask us to consider this age-old ethical question. Is it to our community of ethnic "similars"? Is it to our families? Is it to a higher power? Or is it to ourselves as individuals with the power to choose? Moreover, do external forces, be they portrayed as the lures of drugs, power, money, aliens, or collective pressures to conform, ultimately shape us and bend us toward good or evil with more potency than some inner will? Does the weakness of the body override the strength of the spirit? Are we our "brother's keeper"? These issues are not limited to an Italian American world view, although many of the best filmmakers of this ethnicity have dealt with them, among whom Abel Ferrara, blood grandson of Esposito, cinematic "son" of Scorsese and Coppola, and "soul brother" of the Cains who wander in exile throughout our contemporary Land of Nod.

Works Consulted

Bear, Liza (interviewer). "Abel Ferrara." *BOMB* (Fall 1995): 37-41.

Boelhower, William and Rocco Pallone, ed. *Adjusting Sites: New Essays in Italian American Studies. Filibrary* 16 (Supplement to *Forum Italicum*). Stony Brook, New York, 1999.

Casella, Paola. *Hollywood Italian: Gli italiani nell'America di celluloide.* Milan: Baldini & Castoldi, 1998.

Casillo, Robert. "Moments in Italian-American Cinema: From Little Caesar to Coppola and Scorsese." Tamburri et. al. 374-96.

Cohan, Steven and Ina Mae Hark, ed. *Screening the Male: Exploring Masculinities in Hollywood Cinema.* London and New York: Routledge, 1993.

Cremonini, Zoraide. "The Damned Movie." *Vogue Italia* (November 1993): 38.

Fine, Marshall. *Harvey Keitel: The Art of Darkness. The Unauthorized Biography.* New York: Fromm International, 1998.

Forde, Noah (interviewer). "The Knight of Night: Abel Ferrara." *Venice: Los Angeles' Arts and Entertainment Magazine* 4.9 (January 1993): 29-30.

Giordano, Paolo A. and Anthony Julian Tamburri, eds. *Beyond the Margin: Readings in Italian Americana.* Madison, Teaneck: Fairleigh Dickinson UP; London: Associated University Presses, 1998.

James, Nick. "Sick City Boy." *Sight and Sound* (May 2000): 22-24.

Johnstone, Nick. *Abel Ferrara: The King of New York.* London, New York, Paris, Sydney: Omnibus Press, 1999.

Lehman, Peter. " 'Don't Blame This on a Girl': Female Rape-Revenge Films." Cohan and Hark 103-17.

Lilienfeld, Jane and Jeffrey Oxford, ed. *The Languages of Addiction.* New York: St. Martin's Press, 1999.

Smith, Gavin (interviewer). "The Gambler." *Sight and Sound* (February 1993): 21-23.

Tamburri, Anthony Julian, Paolo A. Giordano, and Fred L. Gardaphè, ed. *From the Margin: Writings in Italian Americana.* West Lafayette, Ind.: Purdue UP, 1991.

Verdicchio, Pasquale. "Unholy Manifestations: Cultural Transformation as Hereticism in the Films of De Michiel, Ferrara, Savoca, and Scorsese." Boelhower and Pallone 201-18.

Viano, Maurizio. *A Certain Realism: Making Use of Pasolini's Film Theory and Practice.* Berkeley and Los Angeles; London, England: U of California P, 1993.

West, Rebecca. "From Lapsed to Lost: Scorsese's Boy and Ferrara's Man." Giordano and Tamburri 198-222.

Different Voices, Different Tones

BIG NIGHT, SMALL DAYS

Anna Camaiti Hostert
LOYOLA UNIVERSITY ROME CENTER

And finally the big night has arrived! For the Italian immigrant brothers Primo (Tony Shalhoub) and Secondo (Stanley Tucci) in the film *Big Night*, opportunity arrives disguised as a jazz star. Their little restaurant, barely getting off the ground in an America still hostile to cultural and ethnic differences, is about to live its moment of glory: the famous jazz musician Louis Prima is coming for dinner, and with him the curiosity of the press and the new customers who will help them rescue their business from an uncertain fate. The big night will pay the ransom of all of the brothers' small days of struggle and humiliation.

Big Night, directed by Campbell Scott and Stanley Tucci (who plays one of the principle characters) is apparently very simple, a story like so many others. Two brothers, Primo (the cook-artist) and Secondo (restaurateur-business man), emigrate from Italy to New Jersey and open a little restaurant in hopes of finding fortune. The period dress and music tell us we are at the end of the Fifties or the beginning of the Sixties. In Italy the economic *boom* has only just begun, and, especially in the South where the brothers come from, there is still much hardship and unemployment. Departing for the American Dream is one of the few real possibilities for a better future.

To be Italian in America back then, however, was not at all glamorous. Italians were still called "wops," or "dagos," a still more pejorative and racist nickname, referring originally to the practice of the poorest immigrants to work "until the day goes," that is, day labor. *Poor devils.*

The two brothers try to import authentic Italian cuisine to the States. They come up against mainstream American taste which still tends, generally, to resist anything that appears too ethnic. Primo renders their situation still more difficult by refusing to give up on the fundamental tenets of the Italian culinary tradition. Not only does he butt his head against the wall of incomprehension of his own customers, but he also makes his brother Secondo's job of waiting tables and managing the finances of the restaurant nearly impossible.

Things go from bad to worse. The brothers are on the brink of financial ruin. This pits Secondo against obtuse and somewhat racist bank loan officers who not only doubt his ability to understand English, but also deny him further loans or extensions on his payments. They put him in such a state of prostration that he is forced to look elsewhere for help. He turns to Pascal, the owner of the pseudo-Italian restaurant across the street that he and his brother had on more than one occasion scoffed at for its daily slaughter of Italian culinary traditions with such "barbaric" American dishes as *spaghetti with meat balls*. "A Rape of Cuisine," Primo comments one day. But Pascal, a caricature of the successful Italian American, is successful precisely because he has yielded to American tastes. Pascal refuses the loan, proposing instead that Secondo and his brother come and work for him. Primo, however, would never do it; for the brothers, self-reliance is the cornerstone of the American Dream: "Isn't this the land of fucking opportunities?" says Secondo angrily. Success does not come right away. You have to have patience, Pascal suggests, and be able to adapt yourself to the tastes of your customers, "and later, but only later, you give them what you want."

Though Secondo refuses his offer, Pascal is apparently willing to help: he proposes to publicize their restaurant by inviting his friend and customer, the famous jazz musician Louis Prima. We observe the preparations for the big night, on which the two brothers spend all of what little money they have left. Watching this part of the film, one cannot help but think of *Babette's Feast*. In that film, the artistic talent of the great French chef is silent, oppressed by years of tasteless food and nauseating odors, but in the end, it explodes in all of its delicacy and creative power.

Though the dinner in *Big Night* will be a masterpiece of sight and taste, the brothers wait in vain for the big star to arrive. Pascal has swindled them not only in order to test the skill of the cook-artist, but also to ruin them, and force them to work for him. A true sucker punch from an unscrupulous businessman.

This is the basic plot. Into this are woven several other slight but complementary stories in which the two protagonists deal with love, sexuality, religion, and follow the customs of a culture that is not theirs and that often misinterprets or misunderstands their behavior.

I have chosen this film precisely because it tells, by means of food – an element considered marginal or better belonging to "low culture" – a story of Italian emigration. It shows us in images what it means to leave one's own country, customs, and history. A film about the dynamics of collective and individual identity, it makes us reflect on communication with the Other outside and inside of us. This is a theme of great significance in contemporary Italy. Waves of Africans, Asians, East Europeans, Albanian, and Kosovar war refugees force Italians, traditionally emigrants, and therefore used to thinking their alterity in environments different from their own, to confront their deeply repressed prejudices towards immigrants to Italy. This has been one of the most difficult lessons of emigration, because Italians are forced to realize that they are not automatically exempt from racism, homophobia, and other prejudices simply because they have their own painful history behind them. If they do not confront these issues, it is all too likely that, *in dark times*, their history of exclusion and violence will itself generate still more voracious and lethal monsters. Therefore an *illumination* is needed. But, as Hannah Arendt reminds us,

> even in the darkest of times we have the right to expect some illumination, and that such illumination may well come less from theories and concepts than from the uncertain, flickering and often weak light that some men and women, in their lives and their works, will kindle under almost all circumstances and shed over the time span that was given them on earth. (ix)

In this spirit I have chosen to write about cinema, which has always been considered in the academic field of humanities part of "low culture." Moreover, the choice of this film was not a casual one. I could have spoken about one of the many films of Martin Scorsese, who, in a certain sense, has made the theme of immigration his own. He has shown like no one else the individual and collective alienation that emigration has caused in the Italian-American community, and he has made us reflect on the formation and meaning of Italian-American identity. But, instead, I chose this film, because it rather subtly and unpretentiously takes food as its starting point, a theme very dear to Italians, in order to dismantle a series of stereotypes that mask the richness and diversity of Italian culture. Though things have changed much in recent years, liberation from still resistant stereotypes remains an important objective, which what calls itself "high culture" generally tends to undervalue, if not simply disregard. Breaking down the traditional boundaries between disciplines, by uniting the sacred and the profane – *high and low culture,* – will eliminate from the academic world a very provincial point of view, more concerned with internal games and power than intellectual interests. In doing so, it offers, I hope, a methodological *rigor* that keeps its distance from a certain *rigor mortis* that sometimes animates academic diatribes.

I also chose this film because food refers not only to the body – and everything we put in it – but also implicitly to the meaning of physical and cultural "incorporation," of becoming one body with the other. It therefore requires us to examine the barriers that this process of incorporation presents.

Moreover, food has represented, and in many ways still represents, a *topos* that locks women in the prison of the family. This movie, in fact, contributes to eliminating the stereotype of Italian women confined permanently to the kitchen, fixing meals for their husbands and sons.

Food was and still is a very important matter for Italians. The many regional types of Italian cuisine represent an important product of this culture. Italy, in the traditional international division of labor, was an agricultural country whose products, from grains to fish, vegetables and fruit, were exported all over Europe. Also, Italy has always been known for its delicacies. The numerous different recipes from all the regions, from North to South, are collected in one of the most famous artistic culinary book, known as *L' Artusi*, published at the end of the nineteenth century by Pellegrino Artusi. Here you can find the various and different ways of cooking pastas, meats, fish, and vegetables, and of making desserts or drinks, with a well-documented history of these recipes.

That history, however, is the product of a culture heavily contaminated by the frequent invasions of different armies and powers who ruled the numerous regions: it shows influences in the Italian cuisine that range from Arab to French, and Austrian to Slavic. The ones who preserved, improved, and repeatedly recreated artistically this patrimony were the women always present in the house. For centuries, women had a very conservative role in Italian society: they were only wives or mothers. They did not have a place outside the house. They were relegated to the role of what was called "angelo del focolare" (angel of the fireplace): their place was at home, cooking and taking care of the children. It is only in the last thirty years, thanks to the Italian women's movement, that women have left the house and have become public citizens.

Fixing meals at home and complaining about it, being jealous of their men outside the house, definitely constituted classical images of women for many years, and certainly still did during the Fifties.

In *Big Night*, the cook-artist is a man, while the three female characters are diversified and absolutely outside of the stereotypes (from both sides of the ocean) to which we are accustomed. There are no hysterical women, no scenes of jealousy or exaggerated theatrics, so typical of many female caricatures in Italian comedy or in classic films about Italian Americans. This omission is highly significant. Also there are no cold, eccentric or excessively strong American women looking down at Italian men. Secondo's Irish girlfriend Phyllis, for example, does not understand his hesitation about sex before marriage due to the necessity of achieving economic security before making their relationship official. But she accepts it and, without any paternalistic condescension, patiently waits. Once again, the stereotype of an Italian or an Italian American man whose wife-to-be has to be a virgin, following Catholic principles, as we see in Scorsese's *Who's That Knocking at my Door?*, is completely absent. The Italian Gabriella, a calm, sexy, and sarcastic Isabella Rossellini, Pascal's companion and Secondo's lover, accepts their clandestine situation *obtorto collo*, only because, in speaking her own language with Secondo, she finds some of the heat and passion she misses in her marriage. When Phyllis discovers the two kissing in the restaurant's bathroom, it is the wounded and jealous Anglo-Saxon girl who makes a scene and runs away.

Ann the florist, with whom Primo is in love but barely has the courage to talk to – yet another of the stereotypes of Italian machismo is undone – is able to overcome linguistic and cultural barriers and comprehend the tenderness and the talent of this timid and awkward man. Moreover, there are no melodramatic female characters, or scenes of crying and uproar. Last but not least, there are no scenes of excessive gesticulation, another extremely common American stereotype of Italians.

This is a small film about immigration that has larger cultural objectives. The principal theme is the authenticity of Italian cuisine compared to the hybrid served by Pascal's restaurant. By noting that in Italy *risotto* is not served with spaghetti and that *spaghetti and meat balls* is not – save a few restricted areas in Southern Italy where, by the way, it is mixed with other ingredients – a very popular creation in Italy, the film seems to imply a profound question, namely, what is the value of authenticity? What happens when it cannot be preserved? And what is the price of maintaining it in the presence of constant movements of people who produce a continual contamination and osmosis of habits and customs between those migrating and those remaining? How is all of this related to artistic talent and creativity? If this latter element is often a question of the capacity for experimentation, how does it fit with the rigidity of certain ethnic traditions? Does the abandonment of tradition constitute a betrayal of it?

The film, of course, has no intention of resolving these questions, nor do I, for that matter, but it seems to ask: How is an overly rigid sense of authenticity related to the recognition of artistic talent? By positing this as a value whose hybridization is the death of creativity, *Big Night* would seem implicitly to conclude that there exists a hierarchy in which faithfulness to one's origins and artistic creation come before the recognition of one's talent.

I am referring to the delicate and tender scene in which, after the discovery of Pascal's deception, the two brothers nearly come to blows on the beach. Primo, responding in Italian to his brother, who accuses him of not having learned anything during his time in the States, affirms: "You want me to sacrifice, don't you? No. My work dies if I sacrifice it. I'd rather die."

I am also alluding to the following scene, in which Secondo, returning to the restaurant, accuses Pascal of having ruined them because he discovered that Gabriella is his lover. But at the business man's negative response – he did it only as an act of respect, to save both of them from ruin, – Secondo replies that Primo will never work for him. Primo lives in a higher world than Pascal does: "What he has and what he is, it is rare, while you are nothing." Even if he is going to face financial ruin the creation of an artist, Secondo seems to be saying, is a way of feeling and living stronger and higher than any need for success or recognition of talent.

There is however an unanswered question in the film that would suggest a different interpretation. Not responding to the hostile question posed by Pascal: "What are you?" after he has said "I am a business man. I am anything I need to be at any time", Secondo leaves the question of his identity open. The success of new ideas in influencing tastes and social practices, the film seems to say, requires mental flexibility. The two brothers make peace right after their fight. In the concluding scene, Secondo makes scrambled eggs for two (symbolizing again, through food, a relationship of physical and emotional communication). Primo returns to the kitchen and they eat next to each other. At that point the film ends with an obviously very Italian overture to the importance of familial bonds. Secondo puts his arm around his brother, indicating a tie that cannot be broken by differences of opinion or economic ruin.

Throughout the entire film runs an implicit question regarding what is produced in the process of Americanization, taken as a symbol of contamination of the authenticity and purity of originary cultures. But is this such an irreversible and irredeemable evil? This seems to be the other side of the question that the authors of the movie are asking. The film, in fact, offers a double solution. If, on the one hand, Primo is the artist responsible for unique and unrepeatable creations, then, on the other hand, Secondo, who even in name follows his brother, a copy of him, is the one who seems more able to adapt, to evolve and to respond to the challenge of the American dream. Moreover, Primo and Secondo refer to the traditional first and second courses of any Italian meal. Obviously this order will be lost in the hybrid cuisine of the new world. What will come to dominate is the "primo" – that is, pasta, which will become *spaghetti with meat balls*.

But it is the less artistically gifted brother, the "stupid" replicant, who is destined to die, like the main character of *Blade Run-*

ner, which is the key to this film. He is in fact the one who does not want to look back, as if he were afraid to become a pillar of salt. He does not want to return to Italy and he does not want to remain attached to his roots if these keep him from following his dream of independence and self-affirmation. He certainly can defend his brother against the demeaning requests of Pascal, but like his brother, he does not want to give up his dreams either. The apparently more arrogant brother turns out to be the most humble. Perplexed and curious, Secondo listens to Pascal's advice against being too precipitous and arrogant in the free and immediate exercise of one's creativity. The film seems to be saying that the uncompromising imposition of one's own taste kills talent, and with it art, because its complete exposure to criticism and destruction does not allow it to survive. This is precisely the difference between countercultures and subcultures. For countercultures, the immediate appearance of all objectives makes them an easy target and therefore facilitates their elimination by the dominant culture. The oblique, indirect and, in a certain sense, invisible style of subcultures, on the other hand, contaminates and weakens the dominant culture. The attempt, on the part of countercultures – or, any new culture burdened by a voracious and invasive history – to undermine the dominant culture *here and now,* reveals a Will to Power incompatible with a broad diffusion of new concepts and social practices that is the essence of the Gramscian concept of hegemony.

The two brothers seem to represent a gap between the past and the future that the present is unable to fill. They represent two cultural attitudes. They appear trapped between the arrogance of history, burdened with the weight of the past, and the innocence and naïveté open to strange mixtures. This condition can be both dangerous and potentially exciting. The film seems to be saying that being attached to our origins to the point of not wanting to make changes of any sort is important, because it makes us what we are; that is, it gives us a more precise identity, but it keeps us from evolving and overcoming a more restricted, even if unique, point of view. It therefore prohibits us from having *multiple identities.* Above all, in some cases, it keeps talent from expressing and extending itself to a larger extent. Perhaps maintaining one's own roots should go hand in hand with the flexibility of experimentation.

But what then do the uniqueness and authenticity of the work of art mean in the age of its mechanical reproducibility? As Walter Benjamin has noted, arts such as photography and cinema have put the principle of uniqueness and authenticity in crisis. But Andy Warhol, among others, has shown us how to break with this principle and yet live happily ever after.

The anthropologist Arjun Appadurai tells us about the "diasporic spheres", Shangri-las that mass emigration and new media technologies have produced: fluctuating amorphous landscapes, navigated by individuals whose imagination is the product of a social-ethnic formation that extends as far beyond the boundaries of nation-states as does their own perception of what those landscapes offer. Reactions to "Americanization" are not only passive responses, but also interactions with local cultures. So the theme of *identity* in this film returns to the foreground with new and unusual characteristics that shatter the ideas of purity and authenticity of this concept, in its territory-bound, nineteenth-century formulation. This is thematized in the main course of the dinner in *Big Night*, a dish called a "timpano," composed of different and apparently unmixable ingredients – pasta, eggs, salami, and vegetables held together by a tomato sauce (naturally!) and wrapped up in a sheet of pasta (naturally!). This plate seems to be the final product of a contamination of different elements that amalgamate themselves so well as to become high art. And the irony is that it is considered authentic! Perhaps, on the strength of this image, we should approach new cultures with curiosity, with the intention of learning and trying previously unimagined combinations. Perhaps this dish can help us approach the Other more intimately and, at the same time, discover our most hidden Self.

BIBLIOGRAPHY

Appadurai, Arjun. *Modernity at Large: Cultural Dimension of Globalization.* Minneapolis: U of Minnesota P, 1998.

Arendt, Hannah. *Men in Dark Times.* San Diego: Harcourt Brace, 1968.

Artusi, Pellegrino. *La scienza in cucina e l'arte di mangiar bene.* Firenze: Landi, 1998. [*Science in the Kitchen and the Art of Eating Well.*] Torino: Marsilio. 1891.

Barolini, Helen. *Umbertina.* New York: Seaview, 1979.

Benjamin, Walter. *Illuminations.* New York: Schocken Books, 1985.

Brunette, Peter, ed. *Martin Scorsese: Interviews.* Jackson: UP of Mississipi, 1999.

Camaiti Hostert, Anna. *Passing: dissolvere le identità, superare le differenze.* Roma: Castelvecchi, 1996.

De Rosa, Tina. *Paper Fish.* New York: Feminist P at the City U of New York, 1996.

Deleuze, Gilles. *Cinema 1: The Movement-Image.* Minneapolis: U of Minnesota P, 1989.

_____. *Cinema 2: The Time Image.* Minneapolis: U of Minnesota P, 1989.

Di Prima, Diane. *Recollection of My Life as a Woman. The New York Years: A Memoir.* New York: Viking, 2001.

Gardaphè, Fred. "The Evolution of Italian/American Studies." *Italian American Review* 5.1 (1996): 23-35.

Gardaphè, Fred, Paolo Giordano, and Anthony J. Tamburri. *From the Margin: Writings in Italian Americana.* West Lafayette, Indiana: Purdue UP, 1991.

Hebdige, Dick. *Subculture: The Meaning of Style.* New York: Routledge, 1994.

Perniola, Mario. *Il sex appeal dell'inorganico.* Torino: Einaudi, 1994.

Tamburri, Anthony J. *To Hyphenate or not Hyphenate. The Italian/American Writer: An* Other *American.* Montreal: Guernica, 1991.

Viscusi, Robert. *Astoria: A Novel.* Toronto: Guernica, 1995.

_____. "Il futuro dell'italianità: Il Commonwealth italiano." *Altreitalie* 10 (July-Dec. 1993): 25-32.

THE QUEST FOR TRUE LOVE
ETHNICITY IN NANCY SAVOCA'S DOMESTIC FILM COMEDY

Edvige Giunta
NEW JERSEY CITY UNIVERSITY

In a poem entitled "Mafioso" Sandra Mortola Gilbert simultaneously links herself to and dissociates herself from two prevailing
images of her ethnicity in American culture – food and the mafia:
"Frank Costello eating spaghetti in a cell at San Quentin,/ Lucky
Luciano mixing up a mess of bullets and/calling for parmesan
cheese,/Al Capone baking a sawed-off shotgun into a/huge lasagna
– /are you my uncles, my/only uncles?" (*DB* 348).[1] As she engages
in the process of self-invention, the Italian/American woman artist
must consider in what ways her self-representation is shaped by her
ethnicity.[2] Such a process typically leads authors to question stereotypical images of Italian/American culture. Michele Linfante, for
example, entitles her play "Pizza," but transforms the expectations of cheer and conviviality associated with this celebrated
Italian food by delving into the protagonist's relationship with her
mother. While Italian/American male writers reveal a preoccu-
pation with their cultural tradition, Italian/American women
writers maintain an especially problematic relationship with that
tradition which defines women exclusively within the bounds of the
domestic imagination. As the space of female discourse, the domestic setting in both literature and film often functions as a metaphor for the ambivalent relationship of Italian/American women
to their ethnicity. Nancy Savoca's first film, *True Love* (1989),
depicts the domestic space as both nurturing and stifling. Within
this space, Savoca probes into the most elemental constructions of
ethnicity and gender in Italian/American culture.

The participation of women in the film industry as directors
and producers is a relatively new phenomenon. Film direction

---

[1] The author acknowledges *MELUS*, where this essay was first published in *MELUS* (22.2,
Summer 1997: 75-89). The following abbreviation will be used in parenthetical references:
DB: Helen Barolini, *The Dream Book*.
[2] On the use of the slash instead of the hyphen in Italian/American see Tamburri.

necessitates the conquest of one of the most male-centered indu-
stries, dominated by the values and laws of corporate America.[3]
The struggle Savoca faced while making *True Love* exemplifies
the kind of difficulties faced by a woman trying to enter the film
industry. Based on a script Savoca co-authored with her husband,
Richard Guay, the film was not made until seven years after they
conceived the idea because of their difficulties finding a producer.[4]
Savoca was told by the producers who refused to finance her film
that the script was "too regional, too ethnic" (Laurino 49). When
the film was finally made, it cost the producers only $750,000.
The cast was essentially made up of Italian/American unknowns –
it was Annabella Sciorra's feature-film debut – and Savoca, serving them "coffee and cake" in her home, taught them not to over-
play Italian/American stereotypes (Laurino 50). Savoca's film does
give the impression of a homemade movie: it is a domestic film in
form, content, and even budget. By dramatizing the conflicts
faced by its female protagonist as she attempts to author her life,
True Love self-consciously explores Nancy Savoca's emergence as
an Italian/American female director.

Reviews compared *True Love* to such films as *Mean Streets*,
Married to the Mob (Maslin C10), *Crossing Delancey*, and *Moonstruck* (Toumarkine 56). One critic called it a film on "young
urban ethnics in love" (Toumarkine 56), and another commented
on the "ethnic buoyancy of the images" (Hinson 7). It is an ethnic
comedy, suggested many reviewers, that utilizes conventions that
spectators will easily recognize from a popular genre in America
cinema – a safe, well-known world inhabited by characters who
speak a familiar language.[5] However, the writer/ director of *True*

---

[3] For a discussion of the role of women as directors and producers see Citron. For a history
of the emergence of women in the film industry see Heck-Rabi and Quart.

[4] Savoca and Guay invested $22,000 on a nine-minute trailer, shot in 1985, that they used
to convince would-be-producers to finance their film. On the production of *True Love* see
Cerone, van Gelder, and Laurino. Savoca has since made two films, *Dogfight* (1991) and
Household Saints (1993). In her last film, ethnicity is again on the forefront of the
narrative. Following a route which is often typical of ethnic authors, Savoca's cinema has
come full circle, starting from her ethnicity, moving away from it, and then returning to it.
On *Dogfight* see Giunta. For a discussion of the process of acculturation see Bonomo
Ahearn, "Definitions of Womanhood: Class, Acculturation, and Feminism," *DB* 126-39.

[5] See Sollors's discussion of ethnicity and comedy in "Ethnic Comedy and the Burlesque,"
Beyond Ethnicity: Consent and Descent in American Culture, 131-41, and Musser,

Love speaks an unusual language and tells an unusual story. The cozy kitchen of this Italian/American family functions as a claustrophobic setting that epitomizes women's entrapment within a pre-existing plot. As the embodiment of domestic ideology and mythology, the kitchen acts as the space in which all the crucial conflicts are enacted. By punctuating the plot with explosive conflicts between the two protagonists, Donna and Michael, Savoca questions the relationship between genders maintained within Italian/American culture. As the narrative unfolds in a seemingly comic tone, moving slowly but surely towards the central event motivating the action – the wedding itself – the inadequacy of the cultural roles becomes blatant. The characters in *True Love* struggle between the dream of romantic love – which according to the cultural norms of their community must lead to marriage – and the implicit belief that marriage denies and even kills romantic love. Donna's and Michael's expectations are shaped by gender roles they have so internalized that they re-enact them in a compulsive and grotesque manner.

Through a series of texts within the text, Savoca self-consciously examines "true love" and marriage, central fictions of Italian/American mythology. At the very beginning of the film, the videoclips and television screen that function as narrative frames establish the existence of the self-contained and fictionalized world Savoca is about to critique. The juxtaposition of the voices to the black image on the screen suggests a gap between language and image, while the interruptions, with the frequent rewinding and fast-forwarding of the videotape, anticipate the narrative's uneven flow. Moreover, since the voices one hears as the film begins are spoken by the characters watching themselves on video, from the start the film self-consciously focuses on the split between the characters and the parts they play.

With its celebration of food and "*la famiglia*," Norman Jewison's *Moonstruck* (1987) plays on the stereotypical images of Ital-

---

"Ethnicity, Role-playing, and American Film Comedy" in Friedman, 39-81. On representations of Italian Americans in American cinema see Ambrosini, Matera and Sanfilippo, Casillo, Cortés, Lordeaux, and Reich. See also Golden, "Pasta or Paradigm: the Place of Italian-American Women in Popular Film," in *The Italian Immigrant Woman in North America*, eds. Boyd Caroli et al., 350-57.

ian/American culture – even though the Mafia is absent. In the final scene of *Moonstruck*, set in the kitchen, after the awkward exchange of " *Ti amo*" between Loretta and her father,[6] Loretta is united to her "true love," the maimed Ronnie Cammareri, to the relief of Johnny Cammareri who can now reassure his jealous Sicilian mother that he will not marry Loretta. The Oedipal picture is complete. Capitalizing on the comic opportunities offered by stereotypes, Jewison feeds his audience the Italian/American "dream": "*la famiglia*" and its space, the kitchen, have triumphed. The reconciliation appropriately takes place in the kitchen with a general toast, "*alla famiglia.*" Then the camera moves out of the kitchen and focuses on the photographs of the family's ancestors, though one can still hear the voices from the kitchen: this gap between voice and picture on the screen, however, does not suggest a breach between language and image as it does in Savoca's film. There seems to be no conflict between past and present, older and younger generation, old and new world. Although she is a widow, and no longer in her prime, Loretta has found "true love," and of course it will be for life – Italian style. In this film, Italians prove they can manufacture old dreams even in the new country. Capitalist America has not invaded or destroyed the domestic haven of the ethnic family. Describing *True Love* as a "charming slice-of-pizza-life look at young Bronx Italian-Americans," a critic compares it to *Moonstruck* (Toumarkine 56).[7] But Savoca negates the domestic dream perpetuated by films like *Moonstruck*. Far from depicting the kitchen as a space of reconciliation, Savoca demolishes the domestic haven.

By naming her female protagonist "Donna" ("woman" in Italian), Savoca establishes her as the epitome of feminine ethnicity. Italian/American women must negotiate between the public and the private spheres, between the family and the individual, between self-denial and self-affirmation. The cult of the Virgin

---

[6] Are we witnessing an incestuous affair? "*Ti amo*" expresses unambiguous sexual love. "*Ti voglio bene*" is the appropriate expression for parental or filial love. Although *Moonstruck* tends towards self-parody, this mistake evidences the kind of inaccuracy that often results from treating Italian Americans as stereotypes.

[7] Stereotypes infiltrate critical language. Blinded by such interpretive trappings, the reviewer is unable to detect the director's defiance of stereotypes.

Mary that shapes definitions of femininity in Italian/American culture has had tremendous repercussions on external perceptions and self-representations of women.[8] Analyzing concepts of femininity among Italian immigrant families in Toronto, Harriet Perry argues that "the female Italian immigrant is defined primarily by means of a maternal metonym . . . [maternity is] the single key attribute . . . which enables them to achieve their fullest social recognition as women" (Boyd Caroli 223). The word "woman" thus assumes a very limited range of semantic possibilities, which in turn prevents women from imagining themselves outside the traditional feminine mythology. In *True Love* Donna's future seems spelled out as male characters joke with Michael about the pregnancy that supposedly will come soon after the wedding. The jokes suggest not only the complex ways in which feminine sexuality and maternity are intertwined, but also the control exercised by male ideology and language over definitions of femininity. Femininity is fully achieved, the cultural norm prescribes, only through maternity; at the same time, maternity seems to kill feminine sexuality. "You'd better look now, Michael. After the first kid, she's gonna blow up like a balloon," warns an old man. Maternity is simultaneously celebrated and denigrated by men – and sought and feared by women. As a mother, Donna will simultaneously become a woman and cease to be one.

The works of Italian/American women writers are haunted by mothers, aunts, and grandmothers, models of femininity that must be confronted, questioned and rewritten.[9] "I looked for you/

[8] For a discussion of the influence of the cult of the Virgin Mary on definitions of femininity and for an examination of motherhood as a cultural construct in Italian/American culture, see Perry, "The Metonymic Definition of the Female and the Concept of Honour Among Italian Immigrant families in Toronto," Smith, "Italian Mothers, American Daughters: Changes in Work and Family Roles," and Johnson, "The Maternal Role in the Contemporary Italian-American Family" in *The Italian Immigrant Woman in North America*, eds. Boyd Caroli et al., 225, 206-21, and 234-45.

[9] The following abbreviation will be used in parenthetical references: *UM*: Helen Barolini, *Umbertina*. Sandra M. Gilbert creates a series of haunting feminine figures who inhabit the poet's memory and shape her imagination in "The Grandmother Dream" (*DB* 350), "The Mothers at Seventy" (*Blood Pressure* 101), "For the Muses," "The Night Grandma Died," and "For My Aunt in Memorial Hospital" (*Emily's Bread* 17, 57-58). "Prayer to the Mothers" by Diane di Prima and "Bicentennial Anti-Poem for Italian-American Women" by Daniela Gioseffi (*DB* 369, 381-82) also consider how Italian/American women

spinning the wheel of my horoscope," Janine Veto writes in "Naturally, Mother" (*DB* 341), capturing the need for Italian/American women to acknowledge their bond with female ancestors in order to comprehend their present and create their future. In *Umbertina* Helen Barolini examines the contradictions faced by one of her characters who, as an adolescent, resents "that she was bound by men's notions of what women must be" (*UM* 34). Later, forgetting her own situation, she tells her daughter, who wishes to go to college, "No daughter of mine is going off to sleep out of town under strange roofs. Girls should be married" (*UM* 135). Women unwittingly participate in their own oppression by denying their daughters' voices and emerging individuality. A vicious cycle is thus perpetuated through generations. Sandra M. Gilbert and Susan Gubar identify the "anxiety of authorship" as the element hindering women's creativity, and argue that while the fear of artistic creativity is produced by a patriarchal power structure, such a fear is perpetuated through a

> matrilineal anxiety [that] ensures that even the maker of a text, when she is a woman, may feel imprisoned within texts – folded and "wrinkled" by their pages and thus trapped in their "perpetual seam[s]" which perpetually tell her how she *seems*. (52)

Analogously "trapped" by fictions and myths, Donna in *True Love* struggles between self-definition and cultural definition, and is ultimately unable to extricate herself from the "pages" of the old text.

The magazine clippings of happy beautiful brides on the refrigerator in the kitchen of Donna's mother, like the posters of sexy

---

must, through memory, free themselves from and reconcile themselves to powerful maternal figures. Barolini's *Umbertina* dramatizes even in its tripartite structure ("Umbertina," "Marguerite," and "Tina") how the struggle towards self-definition must take place on a journey into the past. The great-grandmother and the great-granddaughter are symbolically reunited when the unaware Tina sees Umbertina's bedspread in the Museum of Immigration: "Tina stood before the glass drinking in the beauty and warmth of the old spread. Its colors irradiated her spirit; the woven designs of grapes and tendrils and fig leaves and flowers and spreading acanthus spoke to her of Italy and the past and keeping it all together for the future. It was as if her old ancestor, the Umbertina she had fruitlessly sought in Castagna, had suddenly become manifest in the new World and spoken to her" (*UM* 407-8).

women in Michael's room, and a series of other fictions – from the monopoly game Michael and Donna play to the lively conversation Michael and his friends entertain with an ATM – enhance the fictitious quality of the lives of the characters and expose the precariousness of their myths. It is no coincidence that watching re-runs of *The Honeymooners* is Michael's favorite past-time, since he and Donna prepare to live their lives like "re-runs" of old stories. At the beginning of the film, scenes from the engagement party are shown in a repeated and frantic sequence, ominously anticipating the unfolding of the rest of the plot. As the hand on the remote control rewinds and fast-forwards the videotape, the characters move mechanically back and forth, appearing absurd and grotesque. Savoca renders the fracture between male and female worlds through the technique of cross-cutting: the two worlds are juxtaposed, but they hardly interact with each other. While the men watch a porno movie at Michael's bachelor party, the camera swiftly cuts to the kitchen where Donna's mother and friends joke about Donna's uncle, who hopes to realize in his bedroom the sexual exploits he has seen in *Last Tango in Paris* and *Deep Throat*. Donna's aunt describes her husband as a sexual animal, thus perpetuating yet another myth, that of the Italian/American male's sexual appetite and prowess.

In scene after scene, characters and audience are bombarded by fictional images that epitomize the way in which the ethnic group internalizes and responds to the values of Italian/American and mainstream American culture. On the night Michael interrupts what promises to be a romantic evening by going out with his friends, Donna stays home alone to satiate her frustration with potato chips and the video they had rented: one fiction replaces another.[10] When they are about to pick the wedding suit, the camera observes the characters from inside the shop-window, a symbolical screen/mirror that suggests both their fictitious roles and their entrapment within invisible yet impenetrable walls. The day before the wedding, as Donna angrily reminds Michael of all the commitments he has not kept, he ignores her, continuing to

---

[10] Also, American foods have replaced Italian foods. For the wedding reception, Michael and Donna choose a typically American menu of prime rib, baby peas and "blue" mashed potatoes. For a discussion of food in Italian/American culture see Russo, 263-4.

watch an episode of *The Honeymooners*. She responds by breaking the television, a gesture that represents the character's attempt to shatter the medium that figuratively contains her. When Michael vigorously objects to "blue mashed potatoes," exclaiming, "there's no such thing as blue food in *real* life," one of Donna's girlfriends reminds him: "this is *not* real life." And the manager of the restaurant where the wedding reception is to take place finally convinces him: "This is *your* day. And you should feel that anything is possible. A fantasy day." Yet there is nothing liberating or even escapist about the fantasy; in fact, Michael's and Donna's fictional experiences are unimaginative and imprisoning. Furthermore, this is one story neither Michael nor Donna is authoring. Although Donna and her female friends enthusiastically accept the idea of eating "unreal" food, the fictions of romance prove pernicious for women as well as for men.

While Donna can see the fulfillment of her destiny and her name – woman – only in marriage, Michael sees marriage as the denial of his masculine identity. Such a gap between male and female perceptions of marriage and "true love" is captured in several comic scenes. Donna comments on the exotic-looking display of sparklers the waiters carry while circling the newly weds: "It's like a fairy tale!" Michael retorts, "I don't know. It looks pretty fucking eerie to me." Both characters are aware of the heavily fictitious and contrived romantic mood, but while she is irresistibly drawn to it, he is frightened and repulsed by it. Gloria Nardini suggests that for Donna marriage represents

> the female odyssey. Like the lyrical, slow-motion love scene shot in a deep space series of dissolves in the kitchen, she thinks of Michael as romance, and she is shattered by his inattention to their wedding night. Michael, whose view of their wedding night is a more practical one – they have already had it, after all – just wants some more time "with the boys". . . . Men seem to be unable to understand the world of women. (15)

On the other hand, women are unable to understand the world of men, though their cultural roles make them more accepting and forgiving towards men. Yet Donna is dissatisfied with traditional female forgiveness. While she and other female characters live by conventional values, they also experience an increasing discomfort with those values. J.C. responds to Brian's marriage proposal at first by laughing; then she asks him whether *he* is ready for the responsibility of marriage. Later she adds that *she* is not ready to get married, and finally asserts her need for independence: "I have to do this by myself." She struggles before formulating an answer that focuses on and articulates her own desire.[11] J.C. represents a transitional figure between Donna and a different type of Italian/American woman. The fact that she is only a minor character signals the cultural constraints that hinder the full development of a new kind of woman character. The walls of the domestic space are still too strong to be torn down.

Scorsese and Coppola have suggested that the domestic space contains the possibility for a self-destructive violence.[12] Their "mafia" films often focus on the rituals and customs of the Italian/American family – which belong to a typically domestic and feminine realm. In an absurdly comic scene in *Goodfellas*, for example, Scorsese links food and death by having Tommy's mother serve an appetizing Italian meal for her son and his friends who, unknown to her, have just returned from trying to commit murder and have the still-living body in the trunk of the car parked outside her house. The kitchen knife, provided by the unaware mother, will be used later as a weapon to finish off the victim. Eating and killing are also linked in Coppola's *The Godfather I*, where Clemenza "crosses between worlds of family and business," alternating between cooking and killing (Russo 263). As John Paul Russo explains, in Coppola's film "the atmosphere of violence has seeped into the language and the images of plenitude" (264). Scenes of violence in

---

[11] Early in the film Kevin tells Brian that J.C. is "a little weird." This character somehow escapes the traditional feminine role: she is a cab driver, the head of her household (she looks after her twelve-year-old sister because her parents are alcoholics), and is less affected by notions of "true love" than her female friends. She warns them, "Let's not get domestic." The relationship between J.C. and Brian both mirrors and reverses that between Donna and Michael: it is the woman, not the man, who resists and even rejects marriage.

[12] Although Coppola and Scorsese have not directed domestic comedies, in their films they explore the implications of comic representation in connection with the domestic space. For a discussion of the role and representation of the family in Coppola see Ferraro, "Blood in the Marketplace: The Business of Family in the *Godfather* Narratives," *The Invention of Ethnicity*, ed. Sollors, 176-208.

Scorsese's and Coppola's films provide moments of grotesque comedy in which violence and domesticity merge. It is not always clear what space women occupy in such violent versions of the place that is traditionally allotted to them – the kitchen. Although kept in the dark, the women act as silent and acquiescent accomplices, and are thus contaminated by male-created violence.

Linking ethnicity and comedy, Savoca also explores the self-destructive forces within the domestic space. By having Donna's father use the videocamera, the director reveals the links between the creation of a film narrative and sexual power. According to the gender dichotomy between male/observer and female/observed in traditional narrative cinema, the gaze/camera functions as the instrument of power, the phallic symbol of cinema as a patriarchal apparatus.[13] If the camera empowers its user, the camera-like devices in Savoca's film clarify the extent to which women do not exercise any narrative power. Moreover, the videocamera also suggests that the ethnic frame controls the direction of the plot. The shots showing the seemingly innocent father circling Michael and Donna capture the power of the ethnic lens to mold the characters' parts. The role played by Donna's father foreshadows Michael's own role as a married man: although Michael is also limited by the images of masculinity in Italian/American culture which construct the identity of Donna's father, the power dynamics between the two genders clearly place Donna at a disadvantage. However, by inscribing her ethnicity in her film, Savoca authorizes both her experience as an Italian/American woman and her role as a female director. Thus telling this story of female powerlessness becomes the means by which Savoca can construct herself as an author and reverse the implications of the plot she narrates. The juxtaposition of images in color at the beginning of the film to those in black and white at the end signals the shattering of a dream that has lost its bright charm. At the same time, the juxtaposition allows the spectator to contemplate the

---

[13] Laura Mulvey theorized such a dichotomy in her seminal essay, "Visual pleasure and Narrative Cinema," first published in 1975. See also De Lauretis, *Alice Doesn't: Feminism, Semiotics, Cinema.* Althusser regards Education as the main Ideological State Apparatus, as opposed to the Repressive State Apparatus, of capitalist society, and considers the media – and thus film – among Education's main allies (159-61).

fictitious nature of two highly valued myths of Italian/American culture: true love and marriage. The images are in black and white because the spectator is looking literally into the viewfinder and seeing through the eye of Donna's father. By assigning the narratorial perspective and power to Donna's father, Savoca, the director in control of the other camera, exposes the role played by males in constructing the domestic dream.

Relying on Mieke Bal's discussion of "'the house. . . [as] fatherhood's synechdochic metaphor,'" Paula E. Geyh argues that "the house is at the center of an outwardly expanding sphere of patriarchal power which links the house of the father to the house as family . . . to the house of the nation, encompassing and collapsing the opposition between the public and private, the domestic and the political" (106-7). In *True Love* domesticity does not represent the autonomous and self-created space of female discourse. An all-powerful male gaze, even one as seemingly harmless as that of Donna's father, orchestrates the development of the plot. However, the black and white images from the video occupy only a part of the screen and are juxtaposed to the screen credits. Through yet another self-conscious device the director usurps the male's authorial space and claims it for herself.

Savoca's film suggests that while the patriarchal system victimizes primarily women, it also dooms men. This marriage will prove fateful to both Donna and Michael. The reflexivity of the film reveals to what extent the characters are enacting stereotypical roles, part of a cultural script over which they have little control. When Michael does not show up after his bachelor party, in an act of short-lived rebellion Donna goes with her female friends to see male strippers. Through the heavily fictitious atmosphere of the club, this scene epitomizes Donna's desire and struggle to create another space for self-expression, and also her inability to create such a space. She lets the male stripper drag her on stage (another dissatisfying male-centered fiction), but she cannot maintain that illusion either: with a phone call she gets back into her mother's kitchen, seeking news about Michael and consolation from her mother. In that same kitchen she and Michael will make love the night before the wedding. By breaking the tradition according to which the bride and groom should not see one other after midnight on the night before the wedding – and certainly not have sex – Donna expresses her dissatisfaction with that tradition: yet, even though she tries to alter its form, she cannot change its content. She will get married the next day, and her confused and contradictory feelings will not lead her to make any drastic decisions. As in the traditional plot, marriage and consummation take place – though the order is reversed – but no happy ending is likely to occur. Although Donna chooses to remain in the same plot, it has lost its seductive power: as the artifice is exposed, the romance fades away.

The video clip in the closing sequence shows the seemingly happy and sated guests, who after stuffing themselves with blue mashed potatoes, deliver their congratulations and good wishes to the couple. The disjointed shooting serves the purpose of realistic representation: after all, this is a home video. At the same time, it effectively translates into image the director's view of her characters. As the camera freezes the lost faces of Donna and Michael in two snapshots, the newlyweds turn away from the flash, hiding their faces in a vain attempt to shelter themselves from the deadly power of the camera to freeze their destinies. The contrast with the opening of the film is evident: the domestic comedy reveals its darker side as the dream of "true love" is shattered. The ambiguous closure forces even the spectators to confront their self-delusions and to question the origins of their narrative expectations.

The thick web of social roles that envelops the Italian/American community makes it impossible for the characters to articulate a narrative desire not legitimized by the community itself. The characters' desire must in no way question the expectations generated by their social roles. The Italian/American cultural milieu prevents Michael and Donna from exploring other avenues of self-realization outside marriage. Thus their work plays a very minor role in the narrative. Choosing the answer to a personality test called, "Do You Have the Perfect Match?" Michael answers question two, "Your dream house would be. . ." by creating a new option: "a two-family house in the Bronx." Donna agrees. Even when they try to escape traditional fictions, Michael and Donna fall victim to a domesticated imagination. After she asks J.C. whether or not she should marry Michael, Donna wonders about her alternatives. She would have to leave the neighborhood. She could move upstate and live by herself. The familiar, nurturing world of the Italian/American community promises no forgiveness to those who betray its myths and expose the emptiness of its rituals. On the way to the church, Donna's father asks whether she is sure about going through with the wedding. Donna's affirmative answer is undermined by the way in which father and daughter are framed and trapped in the limousine that is already driving them to the church: it is too late; they are dressed for their parts. One feels there is literally no way out. Donna chooses marriage not because she has found "true love," but because she lacks any sense of real or even imaginary alternatives to the wedding. She cannot *imagine* herself outside this fiction. She is the created rather than the creator. The American frontier has closed in on these characters: it does not go beyond New York State. Their story is contained within a videotape, the cheapened, domesticated version of cinema. Literal and symbolical meanings collapse together: the larger-than-life image of cinema is amputated by the confines of the television screen, while Donna and Michael are portrayed as puppet-like figures in a romantic plot that does not unfold as expected, but traps them nonetheless.

Donna's name emblematizes a social role that she strives to fulfill, mistaking it for her opportunity to achieve self-realization. If she is *Donna* as *Woman*, Michael is the tragicomic, domesticated counterpart of a powerful Italian/American "hero," Michael Corleone from Coppola's *Godfather* films. This Michael is neither angel nor demon, but a tamed, frightened and powerless overgrown adolescent. Savoca's film suggests in covert and yet forceful ways that reliance on cultural tradition is an anachronistic way to construe reality. The comic narrative tone thinly disguises the underlying tension. Rather than being solved, the conflicts that emerge for the couple are suppressed. Forced to identify with socially constructed notions of femininity and masculinity, Donna and Michael become victims of the contradictions entailed by those notions. They lack the tools and the space to articulate their desire. In this sense, Savoca's reliance on cliches and stereotypes in the dialogues implies the characters' difficulty for inventing new languages, new roles, and new narratives. "Let's talk." "O yeah?

About what?" "I don't know. . . About the wedding. . . getting married." As this brief exchange between Donna and Michael demonstrates, the wedding functions as an alienating and exclusive fiction that deprives the characters of any connection with other fictions – or realities for that matter – thus drastically limiting their possibilities for self-fashioning.

Donna's inability to cross the boundaries of the domestic imagination appears at first to be mirrored by Savoca's choice of the genre of the domestic comedy and her reliance on a non-experimental film narrative.[14] Savoca's film fits within the tradition of Italian/American cinema, especially the ethnic domestic comedy, but it also attacks that tradition and defies the conventions of that genre. Her approach is comparable to the revisionary strategies that, as Adrienne Rich argues, are crucial to the "survival" of the woman writer within a patriarchal culture (35). "Until we can understand the assumptions in which we are drenched," Rich writes, "we cannot know ourselves" (35). The impulse to romanticize and stereotype Italian/American culture is hard to resist.[15] Yet in demythologizing her culture, Savoca neither mortifies it nor elevates it to romantic heights. She defuses the threats of the tradition and the conventions she is working with by exploring their dynamics. Moreover, by "entering an old text from a new critical direction" (Rich 35), Savoca questions the position of women within narrative film.

Although Savoca may not be regarded as an avant-garde film director, her work does raise questions about what makes a feminist film. As Teresa De Lauretis argues in *Technologies of Gender,* "to ask whether there is a feminine or female aesthetic, or a specific language of women's cinema, is to remain caught in the master's house and . . . to legitimize the hidden agendas of a culture we badly need to change" (131). The emphasis placed by a number of feminist critics on the necessity of considering issues of

[14] On women and experimental film see De Lauretis, "Rethinking Women's Cinema: Aesthetics and Feminist Theory" in *Technologies of Gender,* 127-48.

[15] "Recently, there's been a real fascination with the Italian-American family, which has come to serve as an emotional outlet for presumably blander ancestries. Italians are regarded in love/hate extremes – either as narrow-minded racists who won't let anyone else (read: blacks) into their communities, or as hot-blooded Americans who are passionate about food and sex" (Laurino 49).

race, class, and ethnicity when formulating a feminist theory prompts us to read Savoca's work within the cultural paradigm that has produced her as a woman and an artist.[16] Savoca's exploration of issues of ethnicity and gender is bound up with her questioning of genre conventions and her reflection on power dynamics within the cinematic apparatus. The juxtaposition of camera and videocamera establishes the existence of multiple gazes, which in turn disrupts the dichotomy between male gaze and female as observed object. In Savoca's later *Dogfight* (1991), a film that also defies traditional genre definitions, ethnicity assumes a silent, suppressed and yet significant role – suggesting that there are unanswered questions and unsolved issues for this Italian/American woman director. With *True Love* Savoca has opened new avenues for the exploration of gender and ethnicity in Italian/American cinema.

Works Cited

Althusser, Louis. *Lenin, Philosophy and Other Essays.* Trans. Ben Brewster. London: New Left Books, 1971.

Ambrosini, R., V. Matera and M. Sanfilippo. "Tony Goes to Hollywood: Gli Italo-American e il cinema." *Il Velcro* 34 (May-August 1990): 373-87.

Barolini, Helen, ed. *The Dream Book: An Anthology of Writings by Italian American Women.* New York: Shocken, 1987.

_____. *Umbertina.* 1979. Salem, NH: Ayer, 1989. (Reprint: New York: Feminist Press, 1999.)

Boyd Caroli, Betty, Robert F. Hernia, and Lydio F. Tomasi, ed. *The Italian Immigrant Woman in North America.* Proceedings of the Tenth Annual Conference of the American Italian Historical Association, 1977. Toronto: The Multicultural History Society of Ontario, 1978.

Casillo, Robert. "Moments in Italian-American Cinema: From *Little Caesar* to Coppola and Scorsese." *From the Margin: Writings in Italian Americana.* Ed. Anthony Julian Tamburri, Paolo A. Giordano, and Fred L. Gardaphè. West Lafayette, IN: Purdue UP, 1991. 374-96.

Cerone, Daniel. "The Honeymoon Is Just Beginning for 'True Love' Director." *Los Angeles Times* (21 November 1989): F, col. 2.

[16] For a discussion of women's representation of ethnicity, see Dearborn.

Citron, Michelle. "Women's Film Production: Going Mainstream." *Female Spectators: Looking at Film and Television.* Ed. E. Deirdre Pribram. London: Verso, 1988. 45-63.

Cortés, Carlos E. "Italian-Americans in Film: From Immigrants to Icons." *MELUS* 14.3-4 (1987): 107-26.

Dearborn, Mary V. *Pocahontas's Daughters: Gender and Ethnicity in American Culture.* New York: Oxford UP, 1986.

De Lauretis, Teresa. *Alice Doesn't: Feminism, Semiotics, Cinema.* Bloomington: Indiana UP, 1984.

____. *Technologies of Gender: Essays on Theory, Film, and Fiction.* Bloomington: Indiana UP, 1987.

Friedman, Lester D., ed. *Unspeakable Images: Ethnicity and the American Cinema.* Chicago: U of Illinois P, 1991.

Geyh, Paula E. "Burning Down the House? Domestic Space and Feminine Subjectivity in Marylinne Robinson's *Housekeeping.*" *Contemporary Literature* 34 (Spring 1993): 103-22.

Gilbert, Sandra M. *Blood Pressure.* New York: Norton, 1988.

____. *Emily's Bread.* New York: Norton, 1984.

Gilbert, Sandra M. and Susan Gubar. *The Madwoman in the Attic: The Woman Writer and the Nineteenth-Century Literary Imagination.* New Haven: Yale UP, 1979.

Giunta, Edvige. "Narratives of Loss: Voices of Ethnicity in Agnes Rossi and Nancy Savoca." Special Issue on Italian American Culture. *Canadian Journal of Italian Studies* 19 (1996): 164-83.

The Godfather. Dir. Francis Ford Coppola. Paramount, 1972.

Goodfellas. Dir. Martin Scorsese. Warner Bros., 1990.

Heck-Rabi, Louise. *Women Filmmakers: A Critical Reception.* Metuchen, NJ: Scarecrow, 1984.

Hinson, Hal. "'True Love' With Warmth: Nancy Savoca's Graceful Comedy Debut." *The Washington Post* (September 15 1989): C7, col. 1.

Laurino, M. "That's (Not) Amore." *The Village Voice* 34 (31October 1989): 49-50.

Linfante, Michele. "Pizza." Barolini, *The Dream Book* 270-96.

Lourdeaux, Lee. *Italian and Irish Filmmakers in America: Ford, Capra, Coppola, and Scorsese.* Philadelphia: Temple UP, 1990.

Maslin, Janet. "'True Love' as It Is in the Italian Bronx." *The New York Times* (20 October 1989): C10.

Moonstruck. Dir. Norman Jewison. MGM, 1987.

Mulvey, Laura. "Visual Pleasure and Narrative Cinema." *Visual and Other Pleasures*. London: Macmillan, 1989. 14-26.

Nardini, Gloria. "Is it *True Love?* or Not? Patterns of Ethnicity and Gender in Nancy Savoca." *Voices in Italian Americana* 2.1 (Spring 1991): 9-17.

Quart, Barbara Koenig. *Women Directors: The Emergence of a New Cinema*. New York: Praeger, 1988.

Reich, Jacqueline. "Godfathers, Goodfellas and Madonnas: A Pedagogical Approach to the Representation of Italian Americans in Recent American Cinema." *Voices in Italian Americana* 4.1 (Spring 1993): 45-64.

Rich, Adrienne. *On Lies, Secrets and Silence: Selected Prose 1966-1978*. New York: Norton, 1979.

Russo, John Paul. "The Hidden Godfather: Plenitude and Absence in Francis Ford Coppola's *Godfather I* and *II.*" *Support and Struggle: Italians and Italian Americans in a Comparative Perspective*. Ed. Joseph L. Tropea, James E. Miller and Cheryl Beattie-Renetti. Staten Island, NY: American Italian Historical Association, 1986.

Savoca, Nancy, dir. *Dogfight*. Warner Bros., 1991.

____. *Household Saints*. 1993.

____. *True Love*. MGM/UA, 1990.

Sollors, Werner. *Beyond Ethnicity: Consent and Descent in American Culture*. New York: Oxford UP, 1986.

Sollors, Werner ed. *The Invention of Ethnicity*. Oxford: Oxford UP, 1989.

Tamburri, Anthony Julian. *To Hyphenate or Not To Hyphenate. The Italian/American Writer: An Other American*. Montreal: Guernica, 1991.

Toumarkine, Doris. "*True Love*." *Film Journal* 92 (October 1989): 56-57.

Van Gelder, Lawrence. "*True Love*: The Movie." *The New York Times* (24 November 1989): C10.

NEW JERSEY DRIVERS! @#%*!

Karen Pinkus
University of Southern California

I'll leave it to the ethnographers to flesh out what the viewer instinctively knows: That there is something brilliantly specific and authentic to the idiom and manners of Northern New Jersey Italian Americans in *The Sopranos*. In fact, a great deal of the pleasure associated with this unique program, broadcast in thirteen episodes per year (at this writing, the show has started its third year, and given the critical and public acclaim, it is likely to continue for years to come) derives from this particularity of location. Of notable interest is the way that the televisual apparatus (standing in for the filmic apparatus, for reasons that I justify below) constructs a spatial geography that is adjacent to The Cosmopolitan. Bridge-and-tunnelism, in other words. It is no accident that the series' opening credits roll over a carefully-edited car trip from The City (New York is simply The City) outward to the suburbs. Most of the shots are POV shots of the driver whom we come to identify as Tony Soprano (James Gandolfini), the father, central character, and virtual Boss of a New Jersey mafia clan.

From a narrative point of view, there is no reason why Tony's view should *not* be established as central and authoritative. The audio track, the song "Woke up this Morning," intersperses peppy lyrics ("Woke up this morning/got yourself a gun. Mama always said you'd be the chosen one...") with electronic pops. Although the music is heard over the visual sequence in which we identify Tony Soprano as the man in the driver's seat, the music actually seems at odds with the aesthetics of the house where Tony ends his journey. In other words, I don't actually hear this as Tony's theme music (he prefers Sinatra; and hard 70s rock at certain moments), but rather, the pseudo-hip music of the film's producers and writers, who can be presumed to inhabit The City. In essence, the song fits Tony's presence in the credits in relation to form (it has a peppy beat; you can drive to it), but not content.[1] Thus when the car pulls into the Soprano driveway, it is logical that the music ends. Through this combination of music and driving, the viewers have been eased into the narrative, situated along the peculiar spatio-temporal grid of the freeway, radiating out from center to periphery; a grid that provides some of the greatest pleasures the series has to offer (and that recalls the old quasi-joke, "Oh, you're from Jersey? What exit?").[2] The series of the credits/the car trip represents a moment of televisual transition, but not in the expected sense (transition enacted through commercial interruption or screen wipes). The viewer instinctively feels that this transition sequence, *is not like anything else on television.* In most television, the credit-sequence amounts to a banal repetition, a cue that the program is starting and it is time to get settled on the couch. Instead, *The Sopranos* credits seem fresh with each instance, and the viewer half expects something new to happen. This is because the credits truly inhabit the narrative (and to some degree, because the show's shortened season keeps it from boring viewers.)

In interviews, *The Sopranos'* creator and executive producer, David Chase, has noted that he first shopped around a feature-length film that would highlight the conflicts between a minor mobster and his aging mother. The conflicts would result in the intervention of a psychiatrist, a defiance of all cultural and ethnic expectations. The film would have set itself up as an Italian-American mobster genre film, only to subvert this genre. Chase was not able to find a studio to support this project. The fact that

[1] Tony wasn't born yesterday; he didn't wake up and get a gun; he's had a gun all of his life; rather, it is the viewer/writer/director who has only this morning taken up gun violence by participating in *The Sopranos.*

[2] In his meditation on urban and suburban space, *After the City* (Cambridge: MIT Press, 2000), Lars Lerup writes of the vast metropolis in terms of a loss of architecture. Even though they may seem "outside" or peripheral, suburban tracks or tract housing, radically shape The City. "It is asinine to suggest that the single-family house and its lot, agglomerated, have no consequence for urban form. They are the very cause of our daily commute. These agglomerations, or megaforms, are hard to visualize despite their molecular regimentation (house, lot, and street) because their horizons, their coherence as objects, are fuzzy and disjointed. The sorry news for architects is that the heroes of these consequential megaforms are the Levitts, the Eichlers, and more recently U.S.Homes, and thousands of lesser-known developers and builders who continue to house us" (25). In essence, the opening credit sequence of *The Sopranos* can be said to trace just such a megaform (whose consequences and sequences far outstrip the individual buildings of The City in importance).

the show was originally supposed to be contained to the format of a feature-length film accounts for many of its unique qualities, and that is why I have suggested above that in this particular case, the televisual apparatus may be understand to serve as a supplement to the filmic apparatus, a kind of extension or attenuation that is not normally characteristic of television (mini)series. The entire televisual apparatus of *The Sopranos* exhibits a quality of (amused and delighted) habituation to the North Jersey environment. It is as if no one really expected to find themselves *staying* in the place of the show's filming (and by no one, I mean to say the characters, the actors, the crew, but also the audience). This quality is perhaps exemplified by the evacuation of ethnicity from the name of the show's producer, David Chase. In his name we read a secret history. At some point his family aspired to get out of Jersey (to get out of the peripheral ghetto), so it is paradoxical that he (along with the crew, actors, audience, etc.) finds himself back there, but now in a position of mastery and self-reflexive irony.

A film lives or dies on authenticity. The authenticity of place must be established economically (in brief periods of time or through the use of clever perceptive codes), but with no expense spared. Details of set decoration are crucial to mob films like *Goodfellas* or *Donnie Brasco*, to say nothing of the *Godfather* sequence, frequently referenced by the characters in *The Sopranos*. As a television series, *The Sopranos* was shopped around to many of the networks before HBO "took the risk" (in its own self-aggrandizing campaigns, HBO affiliates itself with the danger of the mob). It flourishes on the tension between the televisual and the filmic (hence the frequent references to films, mob films in particular).

In the brilliant opening credit sequence seen each week, Tony's car floats past a series of found objects in the landscape such as the menacing fuel tanks of Elizabeth which read, "Drive Safely." Later, when the men hang out in front of Satriale's Pork Store or at the Bada-Bing Club, the viewer understands that no set designer could ever have invented these locales. In essence, then, a significant element in the series' success is this authentic on-location *quality*, a visual and aesthetic sense of pleasure, created above and before any theorization of authentic dwelling, habitation, heterotopias or "other spaces."[3] The sequence of opening credits is characterized by a somewhat jerky camera, hand-held shots of the kind pioneered by the television series *Homicide*, another "particular location" series set in Baltimore.[4] The camera also makes panned sweeps of the landscape, corresponding to the car culture of Jersey compared with (imagined) ambulatory trajectories of The City. The interiors may well be shot, we understand, on stages in the Silvercup studios in Queens, and that is why I refer to on-location "quality." But in many of the scenes, there is a sense of the (transported) presence of cast and crew in Jersey itself. Compare this with shows like *NYPD Blue* or *E.R.* which often begin with establishing shots on location (of New York or Chicago, respectively), but which give the viewer the sense that these shots have been captured by the B-team, disassociated absolutely from the stars who remain comfortably on an L.A. studio lot. Or *Seinfeld*, where the characters met in interior locations or cars and one had the sense that the camera went alone, or with a minor apprentice (flying coach, of course) to film the establishing shots of Jerry's building or Tom's Restaurant.

In essence, the three highly successful network shows mentioned above may revolve around a certain ethnic or regional specificity; they may well refer in the script to particular places; actors may develop local accents or idioms. But as spatio-temporal experiences, none of these three shows may be said to authentically inhabit their locations. Indeed, the success of these shows suggests that authenticity in the sense I have attributed to *The Sopranos* is not at all to be considered a necessary condition for television audiences. On the contrary, in these three shows it is character, and to much a lessor degree, narrative, that keeps audiences hooked on a weekly basis for a full broadcast season. The network shows are "timely" inasmuch as the characters react to and narrative is

---

[3] This reference is, of course, to a highly influential essay by Michel Foucault that is widely cited in much of the writing that could be classified as postmodern or "new" geographical thought.

[4] Although *Homocide* was not an Italian-American series, it did create a link between a certain "ethnic" feel and risky, handheld camera work, sharp dialogue, and most importantly, specificity of locale. Unlike most television shows, *Homicide* directors allowed their cameras to linger on the peculiar features of a building or a location, and in this sense I see the show as paving the way for *The Sopranos*.

driven by seasonal fluctuations and holidays. These shows work with a traditional calendar, reinforcing traditional historical notions of cyclicality. *The Sopranos*, in its postmodern, shortened season, often disregards such traditional cycles in favor of truncated, and at times, violent shifts in narrative. Most of the episodes appear to have been filmed in the summer, and the show does not bother with fake snow or heavy overcoats to create a *quality* of seasonality. A number of episodes in the second season highlighted Meadow Soprano's college applications, a process that normally takes place in December and January. Yet the viewer is not troubled by the fact that the characters move around in light jackets and no mention is made of Christmas. In essence, while watching the show, the viewer has other things to worry about. Ironically, the time of *The Sopranos* is actually more authentic than the (false and constructed) cyclicality of network shows (does anyone really believe that the *E.R.* actors are shivering as they stand on the reconstructed El tracks waiting for a train [in Burbank]?). *The Sopranos* time is like the ambiguous time of a psychoanalysis. There is no directional progress, nor do the characters engage in forms of labor where they are to be promoted, given raises, move ahead. The fact that the characters exist outside of forced work constraints makes them all the more heroic.[5] The fact that they exist outside of the law and conventional work, and yet they participate in suburban life in the details of its sublime banality, makes their autonomy all the more compelling. It is because Tony is home during the day that he can afford to have a vision of an Italian dental student visiting the Cusomano family next door, for instance. The time of *The Sopranos* is thus not like other televisual

[5] In a recent opinion piece on the show, an actual psychotherapist points out that an analyst in Dr. Melfi's position should not consider it her business to "cure" Tony of his professional socio-pathology, but only to treat the symptoms – anxiety, mental confusion, and depression – for which he initially sought treatment. Tony's unusual schedule, his quasi-heroic unoccupation is actually what gives him strength to overcome his pathology. "I do not recall Tony expressing a desire for help in developing a conscience or abstaining from criminal activity. On the contrary, criminal action is a valued activity in his life. Our disapproval notwithstanding, it brings Tony power, wealth, respect and prestige in his peer group. His criminal relationships constitute the fabric of his social structure, and are the source of his feelings of self-worth, power, and 'respect.' Without these sources of emotional gratification and support, Tony's life would be empty and intolerable." Marvin S. Beitner, "A Second Opinion on 'The Sopranos' Analysis," *The Los Angeles Times* (Monday, August 14, 2000): F3.

time. It distinguishes itself from television, echoing the cable channel's own slogan – "It's not television, it's HBO."

This might sound like a hollow promotion of the channel itself.
In fact, many people who do not normally subscribe to premium
cable channels are now getting HBO expressly in order to watch
the series.[6] Yet these same individuals derive pleasure from the
show because of its difference and independence from what they
might consider to be mainstream media productions. How does
The Sopranos manage to disassociate itself from the media conglomerate of which it is actually a part? The show is financed by
HBO, which is owned by Time Warner, now merged with AOL.
The possibility for corporate synergies are extraordinary, even if
these are dissimulated in the personalized colophon of the closing
seconds of film: The imprint of producer David Chase over a tra-
velling shot of a dirty iron bridge, a visual coda to the series' opening credits. What we might say, in essence, is that *The Sopranos*
does not have to hide its corporate ties because viewer loyalty pre-
dates such ties. This is not literally the case. It isn't that HBO used
to be independent and was suddenly swallowed up by big money.
But the executives at the cable channel have been very clever
about reinventing themselves and the series together as "groundbreaking." Put another way, it is precisely the on-location quality,
the found-objects and peculiar ethnic idioms that grant the show
its independent *credibility* in the face of the vast media machine
that makes it possible.

Indeed, the opening sequence of *The Sopranos* seems of fundamental importance to this reinvention process and it will be
worthwhile to examine it in detail. Roughly speaking, the sequence
begins with a rapid moving shot that we are able to identify as the
ceiling of the Lincoln Tunnel, only after the camera pans down to
give a broader perspective of the space. The director might have
chosen to include a shot of the tiled sign that divides New York
from New Jersey on the tunnel wall. Having myself been trans-

---

[6] In part, this observation is unscientific, but also see Josh Getlin, "HBO's Mobster Saga
Does New Jersey Proud," *The Los Angeles Times* (Thursday, April 6, 2000): A5, for an
indication of the kind of "grassroots" movement to watch cable TV generated by the show.
According to one report, HBO claims ten thousand new subscribers because of the series.
See, "Editor's Note," *The NIAF News* 16.4 (Fall 2000): 23.

planted from The City to Northern New Jersey at a crucial age, I have always fetishized that tiled dividing line and fantasized about its symbolic power. The tunnel aesthetic is not ultra- or postmodern. The tiles appear to date from an earlier era when the engineering feat of tunneling would still have been tinged with novelty. The tiled sign is what I would call a "public pool aesthetic" – it recalls bathhouses; an ethnic middle class. It's old school. Thus the driver to Jersey (or the viewer of the compelling credits) takes a journey that is the antithesis of futurity. The fact is that the infrastructure of the tunnel, like the locations of the transitional spaces between The City and the home, is crumbling. To actually show the dividing sign would be overkill, redundant, uneconomical. It would be the cheap equivalent of the establishing shot of the Sears Tower before an episode of *E.R.*. The point is that Tony does not need the sign to tell him he is returning back, home, and therefore the viewer does not need it.

After the vertiginous tiles, the viewer sees a POV shot from inside the car, as Tony drives out of the tunnel, into the light of day, taking the curve of the exit ramp where we have a splendid view of the Manhattan skyline. The camera pans up to the sign indicating the direction of the New Jersey Turnpike. In the side-view mirror is a view of the World Trade Center. The camera pulls back to reveal a partial profile of Tony Soprano with a giant cigar projecting from his mouth. He grabs his ticket (the gesture is the only truly violent one in the opening sequence, distinctly different from the smooth functional invisibility of the habitual commuter's E-Z Pass). Tony passes scenes of urban detritus, a crucial element in the landscape, especially as Tony tells his children and strangers that he's in "waste management." He passes the Statue of Liberty (here standing as the subject of a proprietary controversy between New York and New Jersey and not an inspirational or ideological embodiment of democratic freedom); a series of menacing fuel tanks bearing the words, "Drive Safely"; the Passaic River, with its sooty bridges and garbage dumps; a gigantic cut-out man holding a roll of carpet (cipher of the cheap shopping in Jersey); a highway-side grave yard; Satriale's pork market crowned with a pink pig sculpture; a Pizzaland shack; a series of lower middle class houses; then a series of nicer, middle class single-family dwellings; a tree-lined road. Finally, Tony pulls into his driveway and parks the car.

The Soprano home is visually coded as Italian-American. It has a brick retaining wall. It is yellow, with neatly-trimmed bushes and a bay window. It is a new house, and this is very important for the general economics of the show. That is, it is a house without much character, and without much history. "History" looms large only when Tony and his gang go to Italy during one episode shown in the second season. The Soprano's are more than likely the first occupants of their house. The house, at the visual cul-de-sac of a long itinerary from The City, was built for them, but they have not defaced it with too many personal details.[7] It is always immaculate, especially the kitchen (where Carmela produces endless baking pans filled with *manigott* or *rigott* pie). They occupy its premises like actors on a set. This is not to say that the directors have been sloppy about issues of continuity or lazy in their use of personal details. In fact, the viewer may well assume that the interiors are shot on a generic sound stage (Carmela's kitchen could be the set for any number of sitcoms or even for cooking shows), but this disassociation of exterior (or better, of the sequence leading from The City to the residence) from interior living space turns out to be pivotal to the construction of the family and its ethos.

Although the house is protected by its retaining wall and neat facade, it is rather permeable. One of the central driving devices of the show is the fact that the men must find "other" spaces (heterotopias?) in which to meet and talk business: At the Bada-Bing Club as nude dancers girate around poles; in a suburban detached whorehouse; at the nursing home where Tony parks his mother, Livia during the first season; at the doctor's office where Uncle Junior goes for his checkups; at a party supply store; but never at Satriale's, and never on the phone. Pussy meets his cop contact on a gravel lot on the banks of the Passaic. The two parties drive their late model American cars to the appointed spot. Pussy gets out. The camera follows him and shoots through the passenger side

---

[7] The question of ethnic coding on generic housing is potentially fascinating. For a suggestive discussion of how "decals" or "wrappings" might work in this context see Allan D. Wallis, *Wheel Estate. The Rise and Decline of Mobile Homes* (New York: Oxford Univ. Press, 1991) 162-5.

window as the two men do their business. One of the jokes is that the two cars are nearly indistinguishable. There's a thin line dividing them. Once they have finished, the gravel lot returns to being a non-place, a utopia (both non-existent as space, but also a potentially coveted place, a fantasy-land in that all land is scarce is this densist of metropolitan areas; to find a place where one can be alone is actually the fulfillment of a location scout's dream; yet it is the scout who has "created" this "other" space).[8]

To place this in a broader context, around the time of this writing, television cameras were allowed access to another "safe space," one configured "on the other side" – the actual dwelling for many years of Sicilian boss Totò Riina. As the cameras moved through the location, they inevitably followed the narrative and visual conventions of broadcasting, moving from public zones, through a series of increasingly hidden and private zones, mediated by intercoms. The Riina compound seemed remarkably like a Roman villa, with green atria and locations of "distraction" contained within outer protective walls. As narrated by the moving images, the compound confused interiority and exteriority, such that it was not possible to tell whether the occupant (the fugitive) was protected or trapped. Truly, the architecture or spatiality of the mafia is a potentially fascinating topic of discussion. What emerges from a brief comparison between the "genuine" compound of Totò Riina and the "safe spaces" of the Sopranos clan is that both are adaptations to the environment, and both are unknowable outside of the conventions and limitations of television's powerful form.

As much as possible, then, the Soprano house remains perfectly anesthetized. Of course, it becomes impossible for the spaces to remain uncontaminated. The kids end up searching for "mafia" on the web. Pussy wears a wire to Anthony Junior's Confirmation party. Hence the need to move business to other locations. But these displacements do not appear incidental to the life of the NJ

---

[8] Getlin, Op. Cit., writes: "During its first season, the show had difficulty convincing New Jersey property owners to let their sites be used, said location director Mark Kamine. But after its phenomenal success, the second season has been another story. 'People in New Jersey are practically begging us to use their diners and other sites,' he notes. 'One guy in an outdoors shop not only offered us his site – he handed us a long barbecue fork so that Tony Soprano could put somebody's eye out if we wanted to do that.'"

mobsters because the creativity they use to carve out these "safe" spaces actually comes to define them as non-traditional workers and brings them (to say nothing of the viewer) a degree of pleasure. What I mean by this is the kind of twinkle in the eyes of the protagonists as they reconfigure the NJ landscapes for their own purposes. This is intrinsically related to the notion of return and reinvention that I mentioned with regard to HBO's own success within the corporate landscape.

In terms of the relation between the New York mafia (only rarely discussed or seen on screen) and the NJ men, New York figures as the land over there where the Gottis, Genoveses and others operate their big-time operations. The City. *The Sopranos* could be said to inversely reference a whole series of gangster films set in The City, inasmuch as *for those City mobsters* (some real, some fictional; some minor, others mythical), New Jersey figures as a frontier to which agents may be sent to to do business. In any number of mafia stories set in The City, minor operatives have a vending machine route in Jersey; or a series of "pickups" in Jersey. But the capos and bosses themselves would never be seen out there; and the camera never goes there.

In the second season of *The Sopranos*, a new locale was introduced, namely, the pick-up lane at Newark Airport, a notoriously-policed street that passes in front of the unmistakably mundane modernist terminals. The shots are important since it would have been easy (and common) to film a generic "airport" scene on any number of prefabricated sound stages. The thought that the entire crew had to block off the flow of traffic at Newark in order to get in the authenticity and specificity of *that* airport where New Yorkers go to get flights out of the area, but which is hardly actually "in Jersey" is indicative of the kind of geographical rigor that I have been suggesting in this essay.

There is also a peculiar geography to the NJ towns of *The Sopranos*, moving from Nutley to Kearny, West Caldwell, Belleville, Montclair, Bloomfield. When one character wants to escape the Soprano clan, he hides out at the Pennsylvania border near "that George Washington slept-here-house." In the Jerseyspeak of the show, there is also "the other side." Not New York City which we have already discussed, but Italy. New Jersey is crumbling. Weehawken threatens to fall off the cliff into the river. The infrastructure isn't holding up, as we see in numerous gritty locales. But this is the point of showing the suburban exoskeletons so that they can stand in contrast to the hygienic sterility of the home. (The importance of this will be underscored when, on "the other side," Paulie will find himself unable to use the dirty bathroom in a fancy restaurant). The very nature of suburban space is its newness and cleanliness as opposed to the City. In the suburbs one is safe – this seems obvious – but there is also a kind of obliteration of labor. Growing up in the suburbs means (for most families) watching the father (and perhaps the mother) go off to work in The City. The children are kept safe at home until they are old enough to venture out. To cross the transitional spaces of bridges and tunnels. Of course, the Sopranos are a bit different since Tony doesn't go to The City often and he doesn't always work regular hours. Still, there are no signs of his labor at home. Instead, the house is immaculate. In an early episode we learned that Carmela takes Meadow once a year into The City for lunch at the Plaza, to participate in Real Class. But like all ventures into The City, this is just a temporary displacement. Thus the suburbs are like the spatio-temporal equivalent of waiting. The home is the center of everything – ethos – and outside of the home, there is only driving across interspaces to reach another home (another safe space, a shopping center, a restaurant, and so on). To some degree, this rhythm of dwelling (at home), and then moving to another interior by car mirrors the rhythm of television location shooting itself. This is not the case for the long-season network show, as mentioned earlier, which can rarely afford to inhabit a whole zone for weeks on end and must keep shooting off the set to a minimum (there are some notable exceptions such as *Law and Order*). Nor is this rhythm like the collapsed time of film production. In the format of the 13-week series, The *Sopranos* shooting schedule would be just long enough to disrupt the places inhabited by the crew and to actually change the landscape. In fact, *The Sopranos* has generated a geographical interest in the locations and created new ethnic, pop culture landmarks for Northern New Jersey.

Much of the exciting work in postmodern critical geographical studies has focused on the potential existence of a "third space."

Influenced by a brief, but remarkably lucid essay by Michel Foucault on "heterotopias," geographical thought has attempted to break free of the binaristic model of center-periphery, by positing and exploring an interstitial "other" space where traditional relations of power are evaded. Although I would not say that Northern New Jersey can simply be termed a "third" space since, as I have already suggested, it certainly exists in relation to the first space of The City, the fact that the Sopranos clan do not especially aspire to move to The City, and in fact, they don't often go there, thwarts any easy binary of exo- and endo-spatiality. But it isn't merely that the Sopranos clan are self-centered, since with respect to the narrative of the show, the viewers are themselves drawn into the Jersey setting, forced to see The City as the second, distant and murky space. This is perfectly set up by an episode from the second season when Tony's nephew Christopher is invited to a film set to meet hip independent filmmaker John Favreau, playing himself. Favreau and his co-writer, played by actress Alicia Witt, ask Christopher for a tour of the Jersey 'hoods and they pump him for argot and anecdotes for an upcoming project. For that brief moment before his knowledge becomes commodfied, Christopher is in the driver's seat – he's the New Jersey driver.

Rather than the model of the "third space," I believe that we can view the New Jersey of the series as a relatively vast space composed of a number of important Edge Cities, a term developed in the late 1980s by Joel Garreau. Garreau understood the notion of a city with tall buildings and a downtown, sidewalks and grids, as belonging essentially to a nineteenth-century conception of urban space. Instead, he reads Jersey as "suddenly being on the *right* side of the rivers." (Garreau 25). Thus the edge city might encompass a vast area that actually crosses over the boundaries designated for the purposes of electing city governments. And that is why it doesn't seem necessary for David Chase to state a precise designation for the specific town in which the Sopranos live. Edge cities that began to grow much more rapidly in the 1980s than older, established cities are based around a new and dynamic notion of entrepreneur-ship. They typically crop up along freeways, an idea that is so obvious it might be taken for granted. "Edge cities are most frequently located where beltway-like bypasses around an old downtown are crossed at right angles by freeways that lead out from the old center like spokes on a wheel" (Garreau 37). [9] The Edge City is also characterized by a changing ecology. The movement of this change is not all toward destruction or decima-tion. On the contrary, one of the most surprising things about life in the Edge City is the adaptability of animals to new configura-tions in the environment. Edge Cities on the East Coast, for exam-ple, are overrun with deer. Or in the specific case of the Sopranos, Tony's initial crisis is spurred by the appearance of a group of ducks in his pool. After instantiating themselves on his property, they leave suddenly. The ducks are a recurring motif in Tony's analysis, a sign of the centered-quality of the show's spatiality.

This essay does not seek to redeem the spaces of Northern New Jersey for feminists, Marxists, or other groups who have dedicated their attention to the field that is loosely called postmodern geog-raphy. This is not a question of correcting any forms of domination or oppression that may characterize Italian-Americanness. On the contrary, the mechanism of pleasure generated by *The Sopranos* is all about a continuation of politically repellent modes of speech and action, violence and Catholicism, offensive language and drugs. [10] The modern geographical movement traces its origins back

[9] Joel Garreau, *Edge City: Life on the New Frontier* (New York: Anchor Books, 1992) 37.

[10] In this sense, the various protests by Italian Americans against the show completely miss (or rather, make) the point. The protestors lack the capacity to derive pleasure from the very rigorous mechanisms of location and specificity that have made the series so popular. Their logic suggests that any specificity whatsoever is a form of stereotyping (that is to say, negative stereotyping). Groups such as NIAF (the National Italian American Foundation) have been actively lobbying against the show. In an editorial, the Chairman of this group wrote: "Equally disturbing is the way the American media has enthusiastically embraced this television show that casts Italian Americans as violent, immoral and foul-mouthed thugs with no thought to the effect it may have on millions of Italian Americans. We are profoundly offended by programs like "The Sopranos" that use authentic Italian American customs, traditions, values and even our religion to give dimension and credibility to otherwise ruthless characters and disgraceful acts." Frank J. Guarini, "From the NIAF Chairman," *NIAF NEWS* (Winter 2000): 4. The contradictions that emerge from this passage are overwhelming. First, Guarini blames the media for its support of the series, as if the media were somehow a separate and independent body. Next, he posits the ill-effects on real life of the diffusion of stereotypes. Finally, he admits that the series is actually quite authentic (including "Italian religion!") in its idiom and style, elements that are invested into the empty vessels of Italian American characters of ill-repute and narratives. Nothing could be more ludicrous than to suggest that those very elements of authenticity produced by and productive of the Northern New Jersey ethos ("Shame on Producer David Chase," read a poster carried by a protestor in Chicago), can somehow be separated off from the series like a layer of wrapping paper.

to the Marxist philosopher Henri Lefebvre, but also to Foucault who wrote about a series of spaces in contemporary culture that exhibit an apparent coherence and internal quality, spaces that might be understood as compensatory in relation to the messy real lived spaces of everyday life in the modern world. *The Sopranos* does *not* seem to perform this kind of ideological fantasizing like other television shows of a more conventional nature. Nor does the show grant an "authentic dwelling" to diasporic subjects, forced immigrants, or ethnic others. When the cameras move from The City to capture the found objects in an abject landscape, they also find pathos and beauty (Tony's ducks). One might view the whole enterprise cynically (capitalizing on his ethnic background, the cleansed David Chase returns home to unearth a whole culture for mass television audiences, funded by the world's largest media conglomerate), but this would be to overlook all of the genuine pleasures of location. Such pleasures seem to dominate the series' in all of its open-endedness; its lack of conventional narrative closure; and its refusal to make a wholesale deployment of ethnic stereotypes for easy identification. Rather, *The Sopranos* uniquely reflects the actual pleasure of presence *on location* back to the viewer. The characters inhabit their ethnicity authentically, just as they authentically inhabit the New Jersey landscape. In fact, during the summer of 2000, a casting call held in Harrison brought out thousands of aspiring extras for *The Sopranos*. The blitz of photos and resumes made the national news (on CNN, a Time Warner Corporation!). Driving to a working class "town square," these eager residents of New Jersey found themselves on location, always already inhabiting the spaces they had seen on the show, authentically productive of these spaces, and defying the boundaries that would seek to make any ethnic specificity a mode of confinement or abnegation.

WORKS CITED

Garreau, Joel. *Edge City: Life on the New Frontier.* New York: Anchor Books, 1992.

Lerup, Lars. *After the City.* Cambridge: MIT Press, 2000.

Peet, Richard. *Modern Geographical Thought.* Oxford: Blackwell, 1998.

Pinkus, Karen. "'Black' and 'Jew': Race and the Resistance to Psychoanalysis in Italy." *Annali d'Italianistica*. 16 (1998): 145-46.

Soja, Edward. *Postmodern Geographies: The Reassertion of Space in Critical Social Theory*. London: Verso, 1989.

_____. *Thirdspace*. Oxford: Blackwell, 1996.

Wallis, Allan D. *Wheel Estate: The Rise and Decline of Mobile Homes*. New York: Oxford UP, 1991.

Watson, Sophie and Katherine Gibson, eds. *Postmodern Cities and Spaces*. Oxford: Blackwell, 1995.

AN UNACKNOWLEDGED MASTERPIECE
CAPRA'S ITALIAN AMERICAN FILM

John Paul Russo

A Hole in the Head (1959), Frank Capra's first film with predominantly Italian American characters and subject matter, came at the end of his career, 38th of his 39 feature films, and 54th of 56 in terms of his complete film oeuvre.[1] Not that Italian American themes were absent from his earlier work. Among his silent films, *A Strong Man* (1926) includes a scene on Ellis Island of which Capra had personal memories, having passed through as a six-year-old from Bisacquino, Sicily in 1903. *The Younger Generation* (1929) treats immigrant assimilation and upward mobility in a Jewish family in New York.[2] An enormous plate of spaghetti looks as difficult to cut into as the Gordian Knot in a gag from *Rain or Shine* (1930), one of Capra's first talkies. "Notwithstanding their last name and Anglo-Saxon physiognomies," the Vanderhofs in *You Can't Take It With You* (1938) "recall on close inspection an Italian family: numerous, noisy, artistic, eccentric, hospitable, informal."[3] Martini (Bill Edmunds), the bar-owner in *It's a Wonderful Life* (1946), is evicted by the banker Potter (Lionel Barrymore) who scorns Italians as "a heap of garlic eaters."[4] Capra, underlining his identification with the Martinis, has them keep a goat (="*capra*") in their backyard, a symbol of the rural past. The sanctity of the Italian domus makes it the more significant that George Bailey (James Stewart), among his good deeds, helps the Martinis get a home, which is duly dedicated in a ceremony of wine, salt, and bread.[5]

---

[1] See Charles Wolfe, *Frank Capra: A Guide to References and Resources* (Boston: G.K. Hall, 1987).

[2] Victor Scherle and William Turner Levy, *The Films of Frank Capra* (Secaucus, NJ: Citadel Press, 1977) 74; Morris Goldfish/Maurice Gold "turns his back on the Jewishness of his parents and his ghetto origins."

[3] Paola Casella, *Hollywood Italian: Gli italiani nell'America di celluloide* (Milan: Baldini & Castoldi, 1998) 76.

[4] Casella, *Hollywood Italian*, 77. According to Casella, George Bailey, himself the son of an Irish immigrant, might more easily understand the Martinis' plight.

[5] One further avenue to be investigated is Capra's image of Italy in the seven *Why We Fight* documentaries (1942-45). Scherle and Levy print a chilling shot of an Italian soldier

In these films as in the political trilogy *Mr. Deeds Goes to Town* (1936), *Mr. Smith Goes to Washington* (1939), and *Meet John Doe* (1941), Capra invokes the time-honored values of his fellow islander Giovanni Verga: familism, the "religion of the home," hard work ("which sustains the home"[6]), endurance, and realism. To these values should be added an Italian's immanentist, non-legalistic Catholicism as well as the Marian virtues of suffering, compassion, and self-sacrifice.[7] When in the mid-1950s Capra wrote and directed science projects, his first two films treated the sun and blood, two topics in close symbolic association with Sicily.[8] Then, having engaged Italian American themes directly in *A Hole in the Head*, Capra proposed a second, more ambitious Italian American film, writing his own seventy-five page scenario on the rise of Jimmy Durante. But this project fell victim to the new Hollywood. Three co-producers (Sinatra, Dean Martin, Bing Crosby) and their legal teams had proven too much even for the pragmatic and amiable Capra.[9]

One silent film remains an intriguing mystery: John Antonio Moroso's manuscript short story "Hell's Kitchen" provided the scenario for Capra's seventy-five minute *For the Love of Mike* (1927).[10] It is unfortunate that neither the short story nor a film print has yet emerged, since the film bears on Capra's early attitude towards Italian ethnicity. According to Charles Wolfe, who has seen the Library of Congress copyright application, the film opens with the discovery of a baby on a tenement doorstep in Hell's Kitchen. A German delicatessen owner, a Jewish tailor, and an Irish street

---

teaching a small boy how to make the fascist salute (*Films of Frank Capra*, 199).

[6] The "centro ideale" of Giovanni Verga's *I Malavoglia* is the "religione della casa" (*I Malavoglia*, ed. Piero Nardi [Milan: Mondadori, 1964] 176; cf. 187, 204, 205, 280-81, 337, 344-45). The phrase "religione della casa" occurs in Verga's short story "Fantastichierie," from *Vita dei campi* (1880). Cf. Robert Anthony Orsi, *The Madonna of 115th Street: Faith and Community in Italian Harlem, 1880-1950* (New Haven: Yale UP, 1985) 75 ff.

[7] Lee Lourdeaux, *Italian and Irish Filmmakers in America: Ford, Capra, Coppola, and Scorsese* (Philadelphia: Temple UP, 1990) 130, 136.

[8] Capra was graduated from the Throop Institute, renamed California Institute of Technology (Caltech) in 1918, the year of his graduation. At one point in the mid-20s he thought of giving up directing and returning to Caltech to pursue a doctorate in astronomy.

[9] Frank Capra, *The Name above the Title* (New York: Macmillan, 1971) 465-66.

[10] Four stills may be found in Scherle and Levy, *Films of Frank Capra*, 47-49. It was Colbert's first film; seven years later, she received an Academy Award for Best Actress in Capra's *It Happened One Night* (1934).

cleaner decide to raise the boy whom they name simply "Mike."
When in high school Mike (Ben Lyon) wants to go to work, he is
persuaded to attend college by an Italian American girl, Mary
(Claudette Colbert). At Yale Mike is a social success, becoming
captain and stroke of the varsity crew. But when his multi-ethnic
godfathers arrange a banquet for his twenty-first birthday, he is
distracted by a young woman (Mabel Swor) who invites him to a
cocktail party in her apartment. Arriving late and drunk at his own
banquet, he insults the guests for having dined without him,
whereupon the Irishman knocks him out. Back at Yale, Mike turns
to gambling and falls into debt. Before the Harvard-Yale regatta, a
crooked gambler threatens to have Mike jailed unless he throws the
race. But not to disappoint Mary and the godfathers who are cheering him on, Mike rows Yale to victory. The men push the gambler
into the river (serviceable comeuppance and quintessential silent
film gag), and all ends happily with Mike reconciled to his godfathers and in love with Mary.[11]

Deliberately left vague are Mike's ethnicity and religion. To
attach him to any of the four ethnicities represented would have
been narratively and aesthetically redundant. That there are no less
than four ethnicities emphasizes the Melting Pot theme; besides,
two godfathers are Jewish and Irish Catholic, while the German is
probably a Protestant, thus underlining both religious diversity and
harmony, as they join together to raise the next generation. It
seems that Mike's last name is never revealed, but given Capra's
future films, one is tempted to think of him as the first in the long
line of Deedses, Smiths, and John Does – except that this is Every
Ethnic American. Mike is a foundling, no past, all future, like the
myth of America.[12] He ascends to the WASP elite by attending

---

[11] Wolfe, *Frank Capra,* 45-46; Robert Sklar, "A Leap into the Void: Frank Capra's Apprenticeship to Ideology," in Robert Sklar and Vito Zagarrio, eds., *Frank Capra: Authorship
and the Studio System* (Philadelphia: Temple UP, 1998) 51.
[12] In a letter to Dominic Candeloro, 22 Oct. 1978 (H-ITAM Digest, 16-17 July 2001,
Special Issue #2001-165, by permission), adopting a similarly mythicized, born-again stance,
Capra said he was a "10-90 [%] Italian-American": "I was so young (5) when my family
moved from Sicily to California that I remember practically nothing about my life before
coming to California. And since then I have had few contacts with Italian-Americans."
What could Capra mean by "few contacts" since the age of "5" (he was turning six on his
arrival in America)? What about his family and friends? What about Little Sicily in Los
Angeles where he grew up? It is as if "Italy" were a purely geographical entity, ending exactly

Yale and excelling at sports, in this case, an aristocratic sport, row-
ing, and a team sport at that. A fairy-tale quality pervades the
whole story, from its precarious beginnings, to the godfathers, the
good and bad swan princesses, and moral victory. Robert Sklar
argues that Mike can rise into the upper class while maintaining
early ethnic ties, "but only after those who love him also cross the
social barriers and assist him on the new territory he has pene-
trated."[13] Yet how could those who love him, themselves still in the
ghetto, join him in crossing the social barriers? And how could they
assist him? It hardly suffices for them to be cheering bystanders.
Moreover, marriage to Mary could be interpreted as a backward
step or compromise: while the family remains Italian (at least Mary
is Italian), the career will be mainstream. If Mike had wanted to
progress further into the mainstream, he would have married the
sister of one of his wealthy classmates.

For the Love of Mike anticipates A Hole in the Head. In both
films the integrity of the family is seriously threatened. In both, the
central character not only moves beyond the family circle and the
ethnic community, but faces a choice between a woman who will
become his future wife and a woman who tempts him to disgrace
or abandon his family. Gambling, a common Italian American
theme, nearly destroys both men. And both films end happily,
triumphantly affirming the values of the home.

Notwithstanding these similarities, the films have even more
considerable differences, chief of which are the temporal and spatial
distances from the immigrant starting-point: ca. 25 years vs. 50
years of assimilation; the Bronx in the mid 20s vs. Miami in the
late 50s. Unlike Mike, on the brink of manhood, the protagonist of
A Hole in the Head is on the brink of middle age and is a father.
His brother is a successful clothing merchant; his nephew, a Park
Avenue doctor. The climb out of the ghetto has been accomplished, but new problems arise in maneuvering the rapids of the
mainstream.

In A Hole in the Head, Tony Manetta (Frank Sinatra), a widower with an eleven-year-old son Ally (Eddie Hodges), is the pro-

where America began. Such thinking was not uncommon in Capra's generation (and since),
but his expression of it is certainly extreme.
[13] Sklar, "A Leap into the Void," in Sklar and Zagarrio, eds., Frank Capra, 52.

prietor of the Garden of Eden, a small hotel on Miami Beach. Neglecting his business, he has been living a fast life, currently with bongo-playing Shirl (Carolyn Jones), when an eviction notice forces him to telephone his brother Mario (Edward G. Robinson) in New York and ask for a loan. When Mario objects, Tony plays on his and his wife Sophie's (Thelma Ritter) sympathies by pretending that Ally is sick. Mario rightly suspects another "Tony trick," but Sophie swallows the bait and they fly down to Miami to assess the situation. Though Shirl cannot convince Tony to run away with her and leave Ally with the relatives, they enjoy a romantic evening which so distracts Tony that he fails to pick up Sophie and Mario at the airport. They arrive at the hotel to find Ally in perfect health. Already annoyed, Mario looks out the window and sees his brother kissing Shirl; he protests angrily at not being met and the family reunion begins on a sour note. Citing past experience, Mario refuses to offer any more financial help, and Sophie proposes that they take Ally home with them. As Tony will not hear of losing his son, she offers a compromise to which Mario reluctantly agrees: Mario will finance a five-and-dime store if Tony remarries and settles down. Sophie suggests the recently widowed Mrs. Rogers (Eleanor Parker), who is living in Miami. Tony, hoping to bamboozle his brother, agrees to meet with her.

While Mrs. Rogers wins Ally's affection, Mario clumsily airs his "business proposition." Mrs. Rogers walks out in dismay but, embarrassed at his brother's insensitivity, Tony invites her for coffee which leads to his having supper at her apartment. In the kitchen preparing dinner Tony and Mrs. Rogers discover their feelings for each other; they have both suffered terrible misfortune: the death of his young wife; a boating accident that claimed the lives of her husband and son. Tony confesses that he was trying to "use" her, but his candor appeals to her, and she goes along with the five-and-dime store ruse. When Tony tells Mario that he likes Mrs. Rogers and that they might get married, Mario does not fall for the trick. Tony learns that Shirl has left the hotel, breaking irrevocably with him. As Tony now has neither home, nor job, nor savings, Mario threatens to go to court to get custody of Ally.

At his wits' end for money, Tony tries to interest his old friend, Jerry Marx (Keenan Wynn), now a multi-millionaire promoter, in a Disneyland-type project. Marx invites him to the dogtrack and, to impress Marx, Tony sells his Cadillac convertible, his last tangible asset, and bets all his money. When he wins, he phones Ally to say he has the money, and Ally joyfully arranges for a party. However, to keep up with Marx, he bets his winnings and loses. Insulted at having been toyed with over the Disneyland project, Tony confronts Marx, one of whose bodyguards slugs him. He returns in disgrace to the hotel where everyone awaits him. As the party collapses, Tony admits that he has been a poor father and, breaking his promise to Ally never to send him away, tells him he must live with Mario and Sophie. When Ally refuses, to everyone's shock Tony slaps him. The next morning, taking Ally to the airport, Mario has a change of heart: as head of the family, he will help his brother financially and will not separate father and son. He lets Ally out of the cab to rush back and find his father. Mrs. Rogers, who had come to say goodbye, invites Tony and Ally to dinner. Deciding to take their first vacation in years, Mario and Sophie rush to join Tony, Ally, and Mrs. Rogers as they run happily up the Beach.

Though *A Hole in the Head* enjoyed popular success (eleventh in box-office receipts in 1959), it has fared poorly with the academics. For Donald C. Willis, the film is full of "hot air and self-pity," "sentimental, in a cheerless, gloomy way." [14] After *It's a Wonderful Life*, according to Raymond Carney, "Capra's spirit failed": *Here Comes the Groom* and *A Hole in the Head* "internalize the Eisenhower Era's unequivocal affirmation of the social integration and familial 'placement of the individual'"; the vision of the film is that of "happy marriageability, cozy domesticity, endless child rearing, and staying in one's place, snugly at home" – strange commentary for a film about a single parent. Carney mistakenly refers to the film as a "musical comedy" although it has only two songs: *All My Tomorrows*, which is sung during the credits, and *High Hopes*, which is well-integrated both structurally and thematically (it won the 1959 Academy Award for Best Song).[15] Capra's critics "pay scant attention to his Italian background," Lee Lourdeaux complains, but, as if to confirm his own point, he treats

---

[14] Donald C. Willis, *The Films of Frank Capra* (Metuchen, NJ: Scarecrow Press, 1974) 122.
[15] Raymond Carney, *American Vision: The Films of Frank Capra* (Cambridge, Eng.: Cambridge UP, 1986) 484, 485, 488, 489.

Capra's one specifically Italian American film in just half a sentence: "[Capra] could spin a saccharine father/son story."[16] Where could Lourdeaux have found stronger evidence for his own thesis? "Seeing two of Capra's last films" (*Here Comes the Groom, A Hole in the Head*), was for Barbara Bowman, "an extremely depressing experience."[17] "Not one of Capra's more important films" is the best Charles J. Maland can say, while Paola Casella ignores it.[18]

Capra's career has been most frequently mapped in terms of a triangle, rising slowly to the apex at *It's a Wonderful Life*, then falling steeply, as if Capra failed to go out "on top," as did Ford with *The Man Who Shot Liberty Valance* and Fellini with *The Voice of the Moon*. Since the great majority of Capra's films precede the apex, critics typically expend their energies on explicating those works and quickly dismiss the late period in terms of decline, loss of artistic control, and rehash of earlier themes. Even the respectful Leland Poague refers to Capra's "retrospection period," a self-reflective assessment of his career that began with *It's a Wonderful Life* (and its many flashbacks), though Poague's notion of retrospection does not include Capra's personal attitude towards his ethnicity in *A Hole in the Head*.[19] But a director on the order of Capra – and Andrew Sarris in his most recent estimation (1979) placed him in the Pantheon of American directors – keeps experimenting and developing from the beginning of his career to the end. Genius, wrote Samuel Johnson, "is active, ambitious, adventurous, always investigating, always aspiring; in its widest searches still longing to go forward; in its highest flights still wishing to be higher."[20] *A Hole in the Head* is Capra's first color and first widescreen film. Thematically, it moves beyond the young family of *It's a Wonderful Life*, to a single-parent household; beyond marriage, to the problems of a widow and a widower; beyond sibling rivalry to

[16] Lourdeaux, *Italian and Irish Filmmakers*, 131, 162.

[17] Barbara Bowman, *Master Space: Film Images of Capra, Lubitsch, Sternberg, and Wyler* (Westport, CT; Greenwood Press, 1992) 47.

[18] Charles J. Maland, *Frank Capra* (Boston: Twayne, 1980) 167 ("What probably attracted Capra to the material," writes Maland in a pathetic observation, "was the notion that humans need other humans for a satisfying life" [168]); Casella, *Hollywood Italian* 78 ("But the merit, if we wish to define it so, is Frank Sinatra . . .").

[19] Leland Poague, *The Cinema of Frank Capra: An Approach to Film Comedy* (South Brunswick and New York: A.S. Barnes and Co., 1975) 61.

[20] *Life of Pope.*

sibling understanding and forgiveness. Moreover, no critic has studied the film from the perspective of its ethnic subject matter, the chief feature by which it immediately distinguishes itself from all previous Capra sound films.

The film began its life as Arnold Schulman's one-act play *My Fiddle's Got Three Strings* (1950); this was adapted for television as *The Heart's a Forgotten Hotel*, directed by Arthur Penn (1955), and subsequently made into the three-act play *A Hole in the Head* (1957), directed by Garson Kanin and enjoying a modest success (157 performances).[21] Frank Sinatra purchased the film rights and asked Capra to change the Jewish characters to Italian Americans and to direct it. Though Sinatra coproduced the film, he left Capra in total control of production, which included casting decisions.

But would Schulman cooperate with script additions and other changes? In his autobiography Capra recalls Schulman's arrival at his California farm. "You wanted to change the characters from Jewish to Italian, maybe because you're Italian," Schulman said to Capra who had just opened the door; "Well, I'm a Jew and I'm proud of it. My characters are Jews, and they're proud of it. And they'll remain Jews. And lastly, if I write the script, I will *not* end the story with the usual Hollywood hackneyed, stale, bromidic, banal, obsolete, senile happy ending. No critics are going to accuse me of going Hollywood and putting buttered Capra-corn in my show."[22] Capra always admired people who could stand up to the Establishment – even when the Establishement was now Capra himself. As it happened, Schulman got along well with Capra, who was famous for his ability to work with the more temperamental actors and actresses. Schulman made the necessary alterations, strengthening the design, characterization, and language. However, Capra retained over half of the original play, and so Jewish and Italian American elements are joined together – at times, to a careful eye, not seamlessly.

The strongest Jewish components of both the play and the film are linguistic richness and intellectual sophistication: self-conscious wordplay, quick repartee, pointed humor. The play and film

---

[21] Arnold Schulman, *A Hole in the Head* (New York: Random House, 1957). Unless otherwise stated, quotations will be taken from Schulman's longer filmscript, not the play.
[22] Capra, *Name Above the Title*, 452.

abound in what Leo Rosten elsewhere describes as colloquial English uses of Yiddish Linguistic Devices,[23] among which he numbers: "sarcasm via innocuous diction": in the film *Hole in the Head* (*HH*) one has the examples: "Even when he's *lying*, he's lying"; "What do you think, we're going to let the boy live here like a bum with hot dogs?"; "You want him? Take him. From now on. *She's* your brother." Rosten: "Scorn through reversed word order"; *HH*: "*Me* he calls a bum"(=he's the real bum); "*Everything* he knows, my son" (=my son is stupid). Rosten: "derisive dismissal disguised as innocent interrogation"; *HH*: "Easy Street? *I'll* tell you who lives on Easy Street. *Nobody*." Rosten: "politeness expedited by truncated verbs and eliminated propositions"; *HH*: "*Everything* she cries [about]." "A dollar and a quarter [for] a cup of coffee – at least they could throw in a *schnick*." "They all look at me [as if] I did something terrible." Rosten: "Contempt via affirmation"; *HH*: "You got so much money you don't need a dime," says Mario to a cab-driver who spurns his tip; "well, I need a dime and I've got more money than you." Rosten: "fearful curses sanctioned by nominal cancellation"; *HH*: "so help me [God] – I should drop dead" (i.e., I should drop dead, but may God prevent it). Rosten: "Use of a question to answer a question to which the answer is so self-evident. That the use of the first question (by you) constitutes an affront (to me) is best erased either by (a) repeating the original question or (b) retorting with a question of comparable asinine self-answeringness"; *HH*: "If I could give you a reason, would I give you a reason?"; "*Why* I know. How much?"[24]

Other aspects of the film call attention to the play's original ethnic and cultural context. South Miami Beach in the 1950s had a large Jewish population, not an Italian American one. In both the play and film Sidney/Tony recalls how Max/Mario as a youngster used to enjoy the Turkish baths.[25] According to Rosten, "when the

---

[23] Leo Rosten, *The Joys of Yiddish* (New York: McGraw-Hill, 1968) xiv.

[24] Many of these lines are delivered by Edward G. Robinson, who was Jewish, but who as Mario was playing his twelfth Italian American. He modulates perfectly between the Jewish and Italian American characters. Because Robinson died before completing his discerning autobiography, *All My Yesterdays* (1973), which concludes in the early 50s, he was unable to give us what would doubtless be his highly interesting observations on Mario's character.

[25] At first Mario (who has not swum in twenty years) replies prosaically why he will not swim on Miami Beach: "You sit there. You get hot. You go in the water. You get cold. You

Jews came to America, one of the first communal institutions they required was a *svitzbud*. 'Turkish baths' were enormously popular on New York's Lower East Side."[26] However, they were never popular among Italian American immigrants, who did not have them in Italy. Rosten lists "I need it like a hole in the head" among expressions that "probably owe their presence in English to Jewish influence."[27] To be sure, many of the Jewish references could equally be Italian American: "a hole in the head" itself had passed into common American usage. Still, if Capra had wanted an Italian American film "inside out," he would have had to write or adapt a script about Italian Americans, with their own idioms, speech patterns, references – his procedure, as far as we know, in the Durante scenario. But *A Hole in the Head* is what Sinatra had to offer, and not having made a film in eight years and eager to direct again, Capra bowed to necessity, worked with the materials at hand, and in the process added to and transformed them.

Capra's italianization of the play began with simple name changes: Sidney to Tony, Max to Mario, both generic Italian names. Louis "Bender's" becomes Louis "Bendi's." Unchanged from the play is Sophie's name, which is not a common Italian American first name. However, since the name means "wise" and since Sophie possesses common sense and a good heart, Capra may have decided to keep it. Besides, Sofia, which *is* a common Italian name, might have suggested the "irrelevant association" of Sofia Loren whose American career was then rising rapidly. As for specific Italian American themes new to the film, Tony gives lengthy advice to his son on the subject of *bella figura*. Food is a central Italian American symbol for plenitude and the family: there is no "kitchen scene" in the play[28]; in the film Tony and Mrs. Rogers together prepare a dinner of spaghetti, and one of the film's last lines is an invitation to dinner. Capra emphasizes religion among women and children – a southern Italian theme. Mrs. Rogers con-

---

come out. You get hot again. You call this pleasure?" After Tony's reminder of the Turkish baths, Mario comments thoughtfully, even cheerfully: "That's different. You go to the baths, you take off your clothes, you meet people!"

[26] Rosten, *Joys of Yiddish*, 378.

[27] Rosten, *Joys of Yiddish*, xv.

[28] Popular in the genre of "kitchen drama" of the 1930s, kitchen scenes were a staple of ethnic drama surviving into the television era, e.g., Jackie Gleason's *The Honeymooners*.

siders herself "religious"; Ally says his prayers, goes to church, and lights a candle, which appeals strongly to Sophie. Tony says his wife was "very religious" and wishes he were; he prays for Ally, and he prays to "Jesus" to let him win at the dogtrack.

The film chiefly departs from the play in its second half where Capra introduces his major new scenes (kitchen, Hotel Fountainbleau, dogtrack, Tony's confession, the ending on the Beach) and new character (Jerry Marx), and stresses two Italian American themes: gambling (or luck) and secularized redemption through familial love. As for gambling, the play had several exchanges mockingly imitating the game-shows of the 50s: "for one million dollars, who won the 1931 lightweight boxing title?" In the film, besides even more numerous game-show references, Tony gambles recklessly. "You'll never understand me," he tells Mario, "because I go on hunches." The southern Italian penchant for gambling derives from a belief in luck, providence, *fortuna*; since these scarcity-driven people did not have a sufficiently large measure of control over their lives, they placed their hope in a force, variously named, beyond themselves.[29] As Paul Giles writes on Martin Scorsese, where the "early American Puritans regarded gambling as sacrilegious and believed that God allotted worldly reward and punishment according to his predestined plan of the elect and the damned," for Scorsese (among other Catholic artists), "it is luck, and the cultivation of skill to make that luck count, which is one of the sacred ideas capable of saving his heroes from the poverty of their native environment."[30] Tony shuns self-criticism by blaming his luck; and he calls his son, ironically, "Lucky Ally," because his mother died and because his father is so unsuccessful. Despite his misfortunes, however, Tony prides himself on his "hunches" ("when I'm hot, I'm red-hot") and bets everything at the track. "Lucky Ally" is the name of the dog that loses Tony's big race – a sure sign on Capra's part that Tony was wrong to "bet" or risk the family. Nothing diminishes Tony more than his foolish risk-taking, which partly accounts for his diminutive name "Manetta" (="handcuff"); gambling enchains him. But an equally strong rea-

[29] See Robert Casillo's essay on Scorsese's "*Casino*" in this volume.
[30] Paul Giles, *American Catholic Arts and Fictions: Culture, Ideology, Aesthetics* (Cambridge: Cambridge UP, 1992) 338-39.

son for the name is his feeling of being trapped by responsibility.

As for redemption through familial love, in circular fashion Schulman's play ends almost where it began, with Sidney and Ally together, happy to receive some money from Uncle Max – less than a third of what they need – to put off the landlord for a few months, whereupon they will be back where they started. This lack of dramatic development is the play's major weakness. In the film, on the contrary, every major adult character undergoes a trial of conscience in which love plays a motivating role: parent and child, brother and brother, man and woman. Tony undergoes a trial in all three categories, as father, brother, and lover. The scene in which Sidney/Tony slaps his son is the climax of both the play and the film. But in the play, Sidney merely goes for an all-night walk and no change in his character or conduct follows. In the film, all of Tony's frustrations culminate in this action, directed at the person he loves: he has just lost his money and his car, he has been punched by the bodyguard, his girlfriend has left him, he has broken his promise to his son never to give him up. In the play, whether Shirl will remain with Tony depends on the toss of a coin. In the film she realizes that he will not leave his son, suffers brief pangs of self-pity, then cheerfully takes off to "Zamboanga" ("Where's Zamboanga?" "Oh, who cares?"[31]). Married at fifteen and divorced, now in her twenties, she will not be tied down to a family.

In the play Mrs. Rogers is a complicating device; as a character she never develops: in the end, as Sidney says, "we're just not right for each other." In the film, Mrs. Rogers and Tony fall in love and will eventually marry. As a rounded character, Mrs. Rogers passes through a final stage of grief over the loss of her husband and son in the drowning accident two years before; but there is no son in the play, so Capra has intensified her pathos (a character's losing a husband is one thing, a husband and child quite another). She invites Tony to her apartment – the first man to have been there – and cooks him dinner; she appears at the hotel to welcome him back from the dogtrack and figures prominently in the ending.

Mario, too, undergoes a conversion in the film that does not

---

[31] It is in the Phillipines.

occur in the play: he not only agrees to pay the entire back rent, but helps Tony for the first time with a measure of grace, realizing the imbalance in his own life as well as his responsibility for his own family problems. Mario's reward for his self-discovery is his first vacation in years.

Schulman's filmscript is both darker than his play and also more optimistic; and it takes risks in its commitment to the possibility of change. That the filmscript takes these risks and ends on a salvific note is doubtless the influence of Capra whose artistic vision reveals itself fully in the transformation of the script from play to film. It should also be said that the film is a triumph of ensemble acting; there is no weak link anywhere among the performers.

So organically unified is the film that the credits announce its central themes. The film's title *A Hole in the Head* and the names of its cast members are bannered as aerial advertisements attached in a row to the tail of a Goodyear blimp. We are at once lifted to – or plunged into – a world of promotion, the fast deal, and the south Floridian ambience. Carl Fisher's promotional feat, Miami Beach rescued from mudflats in 1915-21, unfolds below. One looks at the banners from above and beyond them, with Miami Beach in the bottom background: the viewer is "flying," from north to south. If one knows what to look for, one can see the then new Hotel Fountainbleau. As the credits come to an end, one arrives, like a tourist, at Tony's hotel at the southern end of the Beach, and the action proper begins.

To have a "hole in the head" means to be crazy or stupid, or to have big ideas that come to nothing, to be a loser in a town of winners. In the course of the film, Capra adds other meanings to the expression. It can be the space or void in the mind or soul waiting to be filled with joy and love. It also signifies creative imagination or creation *ex nihilo*, as when Shakespeare writes in *A Midsummer's Night's Dream* (V.i, ii) that "strong imagination" gives to "airy nothing" a "local habitation and a name," and that the "lunatic, the lover, and the poet/Are of imagination all compact." Besides the title, the expression "hole in the head" occurs three times in the film, at the beginning, exact middle, and end, and is alluded to once elsewhere. Also, several props convey the notion of the hole. Both Julius and Ally practice the hula hoop (which had just been an entrepreneurial bonanza for its "lucky" inventor), reinforcing the idea of play. As he holds a piece of ice to the light, Mario asks why Miami is the only place in the world where ice has a hole in it. Shouldn't hot Miami need all the ice it can get? For Mario, only doughnuts are supposed to have holes. Jerry Marx uses the phrase "in and out," in reference to getting into a hole and out of it – or good luck.

The credits convey one of the film's recurrent metaphors for imagination, that of high flying, which Tony, who sees his son as a rocket scientist, possesses in both its creative and self-destructive forms. Shirl, who likens herself to a "wild bird," ridicules Tony for being a "kiwi bird" that cannot leave the ground (he is tied to his son); in lipstick on her hotel bedroom mirror, she draws a wild bird flying away as her parting message. Mario and Sophie take their first plane ride; down-to-earth Mario, as one would expect, is terrified by flying, but in the end the trip liberates him. Mrs. Rogers has a toy airplane in her house, once perhaps belonging to her son. Tony starts playing with it. (One recalls Capra's interest in astronomy and the plane crash in *Lost Horizon* that "liberates" the occupants in Shangri-La.) A "gas" and "gasser" – fizzy air that makes for lightheadedness – are slang words for fun spoken by several characters. Mario is not amused by his wife's being called a "gasser," since she does not seem so to him. "High apple pie in the sky" is how one characterizes the hopes in the signature song *High Hopes*.

Under the credits Sinatra sings Sammy Cahn and James Van Heusen's *All My Tomorrows*, a few bars of which Tony hums during the film.[32] Time in this song involves a sad, lonely present, but a future filled potentially with love: Tony's son, Mrs. Rogers as his future spouse, even a new relation with his brother. This idea of time is opposed by another, future-less time: in Shirl's words, "no tomorrow," i.e., immediate pleasure. Tony's problem is how to balance the two kinds of time and combine both imagination and responsibility; and he must learn the difference between good imagination and mere "promotion." His inability to resolve these conflicts sets the plot in motion.

At the outset of the film, in a voice-over, Tony describes a

---

[32]For a time *All My Tomorrows* was considered as a title for the film.

twenty-year-old photograph of three young men on Miami Beach: "Once upon a time . . . ," he begins, then pauses, as if to ironize the fairy-tale motif. In their early 20s, the hitch-hikers came down from the Bronx to seek their fortunes, bought a cab, and were in business. Jerry Marx became an enormously wealthy promoter; Mendy still drives a cab; and, as he stands in the photograph, Tony remains "in the middle," trying to make his first million in the hotel business. In a night shot of the Garden of Eden hotel, Tony confesses his weakness for Eves; beautiful women appear dancing with him in night clubs, down to the latest, Shirl, who "would make the serpent eat the apple." As his convertible glides down Ocean Drive, she stands up and gives a rebel yell. "If anyone thinks I'm a well-heeled bigshot on a spree," Tony interjects, "they've got a hole in the head. The truth is, I'm busted." Yet his carefree voice betrays that fact that his situation has neither depressed nor enlightened him. The time is night, the scenes are night clubs, the sounds are jazzy, loud, and brassy, and pastel convertibles drive up and down the strip. Camera action is frenetic. Then, with a final sentence and shot that counterbalance all that has been said and seen thus far, the mood changes with a shot of a hotel room in peaceful, morning light, and silence, with a gentle breeze blowing through it: a separate world. "Oh, I almost forgot, I've got a son, how about that." The camera discovers Ally asleep with his head on the arm of a chair; half his body is in a horizontal position, adding to the peacefulness, in contrast to the vertical dancers. Almost an after-thought, the words are perfectly complemented by the shot's formal qualities. Both the words and duration of the shot are brief in contrast to the previous scenes, while "almost forgot" adumbrates Tony's negligence (though, at the same time, one feels he just may be saving the mention of his most important concern for last).

Strengthening the contrast in these voice-over scenes are the colors, which bear out Leland Poague's comment on *A Hole in the Head*: "warm colors (reds, oranges, browns)" express the "virtues of the family" as opposed to "cold and hard colors (dark green, steel blue) that come to stand for insensitive self-centeredness."[33] The

---

[33] Poague, *Cinema of Frank Capra*, 116. This is a far cry from Joseph McBride's astonishing

neon hotel sign "The Garden of Eden" is pale blue, as is his pale blue Cadillac with a blue interior. The women in the nightclubs wear cool, silvery linens. Shirl is clad in a tight-fitting turquoise dress; it conceals a bathing suit, of the same color. The moonlit ocean looks vaguely menacing, alluring and strangely cold, and when Shirl takes her 4 a.m. swim and rides in on her surfboard, shrieking with delight, she appears in silhouette like a demonic Venus Rising from Sea. Cursing references to "turning blue" (Tony to Mario) underline the connection between blue and death. Capra's own primal association with the sea had been profoundly negative. When as a six-year-old he arrived in Los Angeles and was welcomed by his older brother, instead of greeting him with a hug, Capra kicked him, so difficult had been the ocean and transcontinental voyage. Then, too, as Leonardo Sciascia writes of the Sicilians, "How could such an insular people love the sea, which is only good for carrying away emigrants and bringing ashore invaders."[34]

The colors change dramatically when the camera shifts in the opening voice-over from the night club scene to the family world. A warm morning light bathes the room in which Ally is sleeping in the chair. A redhead, he wears a bright yellow bathrobe. From this end of the spectrum will come colors associated with the family: Ally's light brown shirt and tan trousers, Tony's red shirt, Mrs. Roger's red hair and orange dress suit, the golden spaghetti, the tawny-colored beach sand at the end of the film. The hotel's kindly desk clerk is nicknamed "Red." The winning dog that Dorine chooses is "red" ("she has a thing about red dogs").[35] Stalwart representative of the family, Mario wears brown and does not like the sea or swimming. Worth noting is the fact that, even in his black-and-white films, Capra thought in terms of a film's particular color range: *The Bitter Tea of General Yen* (1933) "had a cool, blue tinge"; "the other end of the story spectrum – the warmer red end"

---

remark, apropos this film, that Capra "had no sense of how to use color dramatically or aesthetically" (*Frank Capra: The Catastrophe of Success* [New York: Simon & Schuster, 1992], 630).

[34] Leonardo Sciascia, *Sicily as Metaphor*, trans. James Marcus (Marlboro, VT: Marlboro Press, 1994), 25. Sicilians, like other Italians, prefer the towns. When one of Capra's older brothers first saw the sea in Palermo, he wanted to return home, fearing that such an enormous body of water could never be crossed.

[35] A curious exception is the rust-red linen jacket worn by Jerry Marx.

would be used in *Lady for a Day* (1934).[36]

Not from laziness, Ally sleeps late because he keeps irregular hours helping out at the hotel in his father's frequent absences. The very day the eviction notice arrives, Ally cannot find his father "all afternoon." Ally's knowledge of the lease's "fine print" typifies his intelligence and dutifulness; he is seen reading, discussing his zoology book, correcting his father's mispronunciation of "dinosaurs," keeping the hotel books, answering the receptionist phone with dispatch, greeting hotel guests politely, etc. By no means as bright as Ally, Tony disparages his "crazy" books, but in this film "crazy" has a way of meaning imaginative, bold, or insightful, and Mrs. Rogers looks at the same book and compliments Ally on his being "smart." Good at his job, Ally nonetheless dislikes the hotel business; two years after Sputnik, he dreams of being a rocket scientist, which implies a desire to "fly high." Thus, Ally's thirst for knowledge combines with imagination. The child theme in Italian American culture is extremely important; the character of Ally (in Hodges' performance) is one of the theme's finer expressions.[37]

With the eviction notice weighing heavily on his young mind, Ally has waited up for Tony until 4 a.m. (they share a hotel room) Father and son are a study in contrast. The boy quit playing after school to work at the hotel; the father has quit work to play. Ally is already old enough to realize that he must defer gratification to achieve a goal. Yet his father mocks his maturity, calling him a "nag," "a bigshot corporate lawyer," an "old man with a beard," even though Ally assumes adult responsibilities only because of his father's laxity. As Sophie observes, Ally at 11 is more mature than his father at 41. The boy certainly possesses a greater sense of responsibility and more poise than Sophie's son Julius, married in his 20s. When Ally discusses the lease with Tony, the son is the realist, and the father, the dreamer. Tony pretends he owes only one month's rent; Ally responds with precision, "five months." Tony thinks of asking his "friend" at the bank for a loan – the kind

---

[36] Capra, *Name above the Title*, 144.

[37] In Ally, Capra directed one of the best child performances in post-war film. Capra had been much impressed by Hodges as Winthrop Paroo in the original Broadway production of Meredith Willson's *The Music Man* (1957). By the time Willson's musical was made into a film (1962), Hodges was too old for the part, which went to Ronny (Ron) Howard.

of old-fashioned personalism that is getting him nowhere in the business world; Ally reminds him that he had tried and failed the previous month. Tony plays the quiz-show host with Ally as a contestant; Ally knows all the answers. For distraction, Tony wants to play gin rummy at 4 a.m.; Ally just wants to go to sleep. But when they play, the boy keeps his mind on the game, and wins.

The scene concludes with their reminiscences of the wife and mother, and the closeness of father and son comes through powerfully. The father wants to become rich so that he can provide Ally with things he never had, chiefly, a good education. Somewhat naively, Tony thinks of building Ally a rocket science center; then, he suggests that Ally should first do something practical and "solid," like being a bank president. The mind that darts about so fancifully captures Ally whose initial attempts at deflating his father's hopes give way to exuberance (In those scenes where they are rough-housing together, the imaginative child in Tony comes to his aid, as when Tony says eagerly to Ally, "let's go and take a drive because all the nines [of the speedometer] are about to turn." This is the kind of spontaneous game that would appeal to an eleven-year-old, and Tony will probably have as much fun as his son. Is it also a sign that Tony's number is coming in?) Then Tony says abruptly, "knock off" (go to sleep). Two voice-overs follow: one in which the son prays for his father, and the second in which the father prays for his son. Whatever Tony's failings as a parental model, he loves his child and knows how to express his love. The strong bond between Tony and Ally continues a trend in Capra's films, which present healthy father-son relations, like Capra's to his father.[38] What never fails in the film is the reality of these two central characters and of Capra's involvement with them.

Singing and dancing outside the window of the hotel room at 4 a.m., Shirl tempts Tony to come away with her; in the semi-darkness her appearance is vampire-like. Tony rejects her enticements by shouting "knock off." Said to both Shirl and Ally in similarly curt fashion, "knock off" indicates Tony's desire to clear a space for himself by, temporarily, pushing both away. In response Shirl sneers that "the landlord is a kook," but Ally smiles, pleased that his

[38] Capra's father insisted, against everyone else in the family, that young Frank go to college.

father has chosen to stay with him. The last shot shows Tony's grim expression; he must find a way out of the growing problems.

Mario's up-scale lady's clothing boutique in New York contrasts with Tony's hotel lobby. The boutique is elegantly appointed, well-organized, prosperously up-scale, and quiet (people talk in whispers); the hotel lobby is somewhat shabby, with racy pictures on the walls, and noisy guests. Mario sells highly erotic lingerie such as garter-belts and silk gloves, which serves only to emphasize the low ebb of his own eroticism, unlike his brother's in the Garden of Eden. A mannequin hand wears a glove, in chillingly iridescent blue, on a display case in the foreground, beckoning to the viewer throughout the scene.

Mario is attending to a customer when the telephone rings, so he asks Julius to answer it (what Ally would have done without so much as being asked). Julius replies airily, "Why? It's not for me." Thinking it might be business, Mario urges him to answer, but Julius flatly says, "Nobody would call me here," to which the thoroughly annoyed Mario replies nastily, "Nobody would call you anywhere." Mario's poor relations with his son, based largely on neglect, are expressed in the language of disease, bodily functions, and idiocy. Sophie steps in to defend Julius with "he's your son," but Mario responds sharply, "In the house he's my son, in the store he's a tumor." When a customer comes in the store, explains Mario to Mrs. Rogers, Julius "runs in the toilet"; "I've got a stupid son." The awkward Julius, trying to get the hang of the hula hoop, asks his father to look at him as if he were a young child in need of attention. "Genius!" says Mario. (In a subsequent scene, the naturally coordinated Ally has no trouble doing the hula hoop.) One cannot imagine Mario horsing around with Julius as Tony does with Ally. The patriarch of the family has serious family problems of his own.

In the phone call in which Tony asks Mario for money, Tony says that Ally is sick. But all bodily discomforts lie on Mario's side of the family. When Tony asks how Sophie feels, Mario responds, "terrible"; he is exaggerating because he senses at once that he will be pressed for money. Later Mario says Sophie has a sore back. He himself has bad feet, a problem that his son, a doctor, reportedly believes is psychosomatic. After eating hot pastrami for breakfast,

Mario has a bad stomach. Sophie tells him to stay off cola and drink water; Mario says, disparagingly, that Sophie is "in love with plain water." The generous, party-loving Tony wants to open a bottle of wine in the scene welcoming Mrs. Rogers; but under stern-faced Mario, he settles for what, unselfconsciously, he calls "a water" (as if he were ordering at a bar). Mario thinks in terms of disease, as when he says that Tony has a "disease": he is "happiness crazy." When Mario worries himself sick that a "stranger," that is, a non-family member, will rob him of his chance to save his brother, an exasperated Sophie says, "For heaven's sake, take your bicarbonate." According to Mario, his doctor son could make a living off the family alone.

The square oldest brother with a deep sense of responsibility, Mario heads a large, extended family and, though second generation, he remains closest to his parents' generation in mind-set: bossy, hard-working, worried about money, self-sacrificing. Since he helped raise his younger brothers and sisters, he probably had little time to be a child himself or to learn how to enjoy himself. In a defensive way, his own deficiency becomes a source of pride, as he brags that he has never had a vacation. Tony, on the other hand, is the much-beloved, pampered younger brother, perhaps ten to fifteen years Mario's junior. Psychologically and culturally, he is more allied to third-generation Italian Americans, and his expectations differ from Mario's accordingly. The generational difference may also help explain what appears to be another deficiency in Mario: he never played with his two sons, whereas Tony plays with Ally. Mario's father, the immigrant ca. 1890-1914, would not have been expected to play with his children. By the 1950s, however, American fathers were expected to do so. Thus, though Mario and Tony are both second-generation Italian Americans, Mario is closer to the first, Tony to the third.

Arriving at the hotel in the early morning hours, Mario paces about the lobby in a disgruntled mood, while Sophie casts a censorious eye on the scantily clad women in the pictures on the walls: a bad place for Ally, she surmises. Then, to their consternation, Miss Wexler (Connie Sawyer), a middle-aged hotel guest, staggers in drunk and starts banging wildly on the desk bell for her room key. Twice in the film, she leaves sober and returns cheerfully drunk. An important detail, only in the film, is that her mother is lodged with her at the hotel. A person can and should be responsible for the family, implies Capra, but can also enjoy life. Miss Wexler wears a cocktail dress of green and yellow silk, colors that combine both the family and the escape or outsider themes. Unable to fathom the situation, Sophie says bluntly that the hotel is filled with tramps, drunks, and dope fiends.

According to an old Italian saying, brothers who fight when young are close as adults, and those who do not fight when young will lack close ties in later life. Tony and Mario, who argue incessantly, appear to have been fighting all their lives, and, in this sense, both of them have yet to grow up. They know their roles all too well: the dreamer (and upholder of *bella figura*) vs. the dogged, practical man. Mario attacks Tony's business sense, such as running a hotel in the poor end of town; and he disapproves of Tony's lavish lifestyle of expensive clothes, a fancy car, and "tramps." When Tony counterattacks Mario for having "no imagination," the kind that made Jerry Marx "a millionaire," Mario replies sarcastically, "You've got imagination; I don't have any. You've got it and you're poor." Putting a price tag on imagination is an error that will be corrected, for both men, in very different ways, but Tony at least has a sense of one right meaning. "No," he replies, "broke many times, but never poor. You'd never understand that." Although their argument becomes heated, they always manage to keep talking, and Mario's acerbic wit as well as the sight gag of a Recalcitrant Chair lightens the mood. Grumpy Mario is "bounced" five times by an ultra-modern chair that does not work properly, a mild satiric punishment for his ill-temper; when the charmed Tony sits in it, to Mario's amazement, the chair does not move. The loyal Mario will come again to Tony's aid, but this time he intends to set "conditions," which prove insurmountable. In their exchanges the word "bum" is thrown about so frequently that it takes on a linguistic life of its own, echoing in a staccato rhythm: "Bum." "Bum?" "BUM! Bum." Listening behind the door, Ally breaks in to defend his father, protesting that "he is not a bum, he's a champ." Sophie tells him not to be upset about their fighting: "they're just brothers."

The conflict between imagination and responsibility is further developed in brief, tense scenes between Tony and Shirl. To her ex-husband's family which pestered her continually to have a baby, her response was, "Why, I'm a baby myself." Extolling the freedom of the young divorcee, she surprises Tony by asking him to marry her. In an elaborate metaphor she explains that as opposed to her being a "wild bird," he is a "kiwi bird," not "selfish enough" to be a wild bird. His comment, that he is "the most selfish guy in the world," elicits her pointed reply: "Would you leave your kid?" His silence is an admission that he cannot, but he does protest that he wants to "take off . . . anywhere . . . Africa," a faraway land of wildness and freedom from responsibility, his own version of Zamboanga. In love with Tony, Shirl is intensely jealous and suspicious that, ruse or no ruse, he even thinks of meeting a Mrs. Rogers.

On the beach Tony and Ally ponder their uncertain future. Unwilling to live with his relatives, Ally wants the meeting with Mrs. Rogers to go well in order to mollify Uncle Mario, get some money, and so stay together.[39] Tony sympathizes with his son and accuses himself of being a poor father, incapable of providing a stable home and regular meals. He tries to comfort the "worrier" by the promise of a new refrigerator and frozen foods, but Ally knows they have no money. Tony's mood darkens: "You must have been standing behind a pole or something the day they gave out the daddies." Not many fathers can talk so candidly to their sons. Tony continues in this vein. "I could touch a piece of solid gold. Pssst. Spaghetti, right in front of my eyes." At either end of the spectrum of value, the valences on gold and spaghetti can reverse themselves, because spaghetti is one of the totemic foods of the Italian Americans. Ally looks at his father and smiles, "Pop, you've got a hole in the head." Their mood changes, and with an upsurge of imagination ("a hole in the head"), Tony regains his buoyancy and cheers up Ally in a way that he (Sinatra) can cheer up anyone, by singing. First Tony with one stanza, then Ally with the next, they sing *High Hopes*, which is about achieving the impossible by constancy, pluck, and imagination. An ant moves a huge rubber tree plant, bit by bit; a ram knocks down a million-kilowatt dam, piece by piece.

---

[39] Only Sophie seems to grasp that Ally, having lost one parent, is especially fearful of being separated from the other.

The song refers often to height: "high apple-pie in the sky hopes." As they return to the hotel, Ally reminds his father quite rationally that it is not only a question of his liking Mrs. Rogers, but *her* liking him. Such a thought – being undesirable to a woman – has never crossed Tony's mind, so he starts playfully trying to beat up on his son for even suggesting the possibility, and a scene which began so sadly ends in squeals of laughter.

After Mario ruins the meeting with Mrs. Rogers by improperly treating her and his brother as merchandise on sale, Tony by apology invites her for coffee and they end up at her apartment. The film will hinge on the kitchen scene, a superb example of Capra's emotional depth and artistic economy.[40] The scene almost does not occur, because on her walk with Tony, Mrs. Rogers reveals extreme nervousness over Tony's relaxed, innocent comments. She is rushing away from him when Mendy the cab-driver, one of the original trio, happens to drive past and wave to both. Mendy's cab is a known quantity, not unusual for the small town that Miami Beach was in mid-summer, i.e. off-season, in the 50s. Mendy's playfully teasing "Watch out for him, Mrs. Rogers, he's a tiger!" enables her temporarily to overcome her jumpiness. As it were providentially, a moment of secular grace in the form of a friendly word guides the outcome. That this is Mendy's only scene (and it takes but a few seconds) serves to heighten its importance, its indispensability to the action of plot.

By the time Mrs. Rogers and Tony arrive at her apartment, they are already sorting out their lives and sympathizing with each other for their separate, but strangely parallel tragedies. Never having invited a man to her apartment, Mrs. Rogers is still nervous and spills water on Tony as she makes his drink, but his graciousness eventually puts her at ease. She admits to walking around in a daze in Miami to which she came after her husband's death two years before. Sometimes she does not talk to anyone for days. Her response to tragedy, withdrawal, is the exact opposite from Tony's, a frenetic socializing. Yet they can understand each other's predicament, and for the first time she can express her feelings of empti-

---

[40] Even Willis makes an exception of this scene from his general condemnation (*Films of Frank Capra*, 123). Parker and Sinatra are at their finest.

ness and the fact that she is "not needed by anybody." Quite spon-
taneously, and against his protest, she agrees to help him trick
Mario, as she says, "to be useful for something." As Tony helps
with final preparations for dinner, they stand over the stove, each
holding a handful of golden spaghetti ready to be dropped in the
boiling water. Where previously he had contrasted a block of gold
and flimsy spaghetti, now the block of gold *is* the spaghetti, that is,
a symbol of the family, plenitude, and, as it happens, the future
with Mrs. Rogers. Capra has infused one of the commonest symbols of Italian America with fresh life, totally prepared by what has
happened previously in the film. Its gleaming burnished gold fits
within the symbolic color scheme of the film as a whole.

Mario and Sophie eagerly await Tony and are delighted that he
is going to get married. But when Tony asks Mario for a few
thousand dollars to tide him over, Mario will not be fooled.
Predictably they argue, and Tony's stress is exacerbated by his
discovery of Shirl's sudden departure. She has scrawled in lipstick,
on her hotel room mirror, a message for her grounded kiwi bird,
reminding him of his familial obligations, while a wild bird is
depicted at the top of the mirror as flying away. Enraged, Tony
runs back to Mario's room and lunges into his brother in the film's
most negative line: "You can take your sanctimonious act back to
New York and turn blue." The curse on a family member takes its
color, blue for death, from the opposite end of the spectrum
associated with the family, red for life.

In contrast to the modest, family enterprise of the Garden of
Eden, the Fountainbleau Hotel and dogtrack epitomize another
side of the Floridian ambience: the world of big money, resorts,
advertising hype, lavish shows and entertainment, something that
would be perfected a decade or two later in Las Vegas.[41] The center
of this world is the promoter Jerry Marx, "Mr. Fabulous," whom
Keenan Wynn portrays in a brilliant satiric study.[42]

[41] Capra captures the color and the tone of south Florida, from the small hotel to the big-
time resort. One will forgive such minor out-of-towner's errors as the Garden of Eden's
concierge telling Eddie to get the New Year's decorations "in the basement." Given the water
table, no Miami Beach hotel (or South Florida home, for that matter) has a "basement."
[42] In a way he has some of the "hustling, risk taking" that Capra and Columbia Studios head
Harry Cohn are described as having in their early years at Columbia. Each "harbored a desire
for success on his own terms and for acceptance within the Hollywood elite" (Thomas

He is one of the original hitch-hikers in the photograph; now, twenty years later, he is stepping out of his own plane, 50s-style, surrounded by gorgeous women and papparazzi. As he stands up in a car to wave flamboyantly to passers-by, he accidentally drops his cigar ash on Dorine (Joy Lansing); it is typical of his inattentiveness to others and associates him with death. The cigar ash is a symbol of his sterility; Dorine (from d'or, of gold; or Doris, a Greek sea nymph) sounds like a false advertising name. He has no connection (and no chemistry) with her except propinquity; she is another promoter's prop, a secretary disguised as a mistress. Beautiful women surrounded Tony in the opening scene, too, but for his genuine love of pleasure, not for his money and power. A Marilyn Monroe look-alike, Dorine constantly reminds Marx of his many appointments, of his being behind schedule; using her for this unpleasant task, Marx barks at her or makes fun of her voice. Their relationship is a business deal. Shirl, on the contrary, loves Tony and encourages just the opposite, no schedule, just fun; and Mrs. Rogers is actually compared to Marilyn Monroe – in other words, Tony has what money cannot buy: a woman's love.

For the insincere Marx, Tony at one moment is his "best" and "oldest buddy"; in the next, "I didn't know you were alive." He cannot remember that Tony is not on vacation in Miami Beach, but lives there. He forgets – or more likely, pretends to forget – Tony's "Disneyland" project on South Beach. Marx speaks in nonstop cliches: "cabbage" and "dough" (for money), "take a load off," "let her ride." "it's a gas," "I don't know what I'd do without her" (for someone who is utterly expendable), and so forth. He always has a degrading or diminutive name for someone: a waiter is "Peanuts," Tony is "Meatball" (an Italian American slur), his girlfriend is "Kiddy," his bodyguard is "Buddy." Once he turns to someone off camera to tell him that Tony is a "wonderful guy" (more hype): "You weren't listening, were you?" he says to the man off camera, as if everyone should be hanging on his every word. Flashy and vulgar, he pulls his rib flesh and complains about getting fat; he asks Tony, thin as a rail, if he has such problems, at which Tony

Schatz, "Anatomy of a House Director," in Robert Sklar and Vito Zagarrio, eds., *Frank Capra*, 26).

stares uncomprehendingly. He brags about his wealth, "I need 'em [extra hotels] like I need a . . . another foot." From his hesitation, and the fact that we have already heard the phrase "hole in the head" twice, the viewer knows that Marx was about to say "like I need a hole in the head." Capra will not permit him to say the magic words, as if he were out of the charmed circle. Or rather, his kind of imagination is of a low-order speculation and media promotion, not the kind of "hole in the head" that Tony and Ally share. Interestingly, Marx's simile is from the opposite end of the body: the foor. He is the film's negative pole.

Jerry Marx represents a real menace – he would not have arrived where he is without it. In many respects, Marx is what Tony would like to be, rich, powerful, in the spotlight; only Tony lacks the low cunning, the persistence, the ability to manipulate other people, and perhaps the luck. Tony's ecstatic pleasure over winning so much money in the first dog race does not go unnoticed by Marx, a shrewd operator, who knows that such joy over a (for him) relatively small amount of money ($5000) must mean that Tony is not the promoter he pretends to be. Almost cruelly, Marx encourages Tony to bet all his winnings on the second dog race ("That's the old confidence," he says). Having just phoned Ally to say he had the money for the back rent, Tony is shocked and scared after losing the second race. As Marx hurries to leave, Tony presses him for a loan to float the Disneyland project (and use some of the money for the rent). Marx puts him off: "That's a great project – for Disney." Angry at having been led on by Marx (who had pretended he was going to call Walt Disney), Tony accuses him of lying to an old friend. At this point Marx says bluntly, "Never try to promote a promoter. You don't have the knack for it." He thereupon gives Tony a few bills to "go and buy yourself a cigar," i.e. get lost (one recalls the falling cigar ashes in Marx's first scene). When Tony throws the money back in his face, a bodyguard steps in and slugs Tony so hard that he runs into the men's room. The scene ends with a shot of the door. One does not see Tony's degradation – with his love for character, Capra shows great tact and discretion in such matters. By contrast, a contemporary director would have dragged us through the bathroom.

Jerry Marx with his "fabulous" wealth and the dogtrack scene together highlight Capra's choice of the number 5 to set up a system of proportionality and value in the film. Tony is behind five months on his rent and asks Mario for a loan of $5000. Mario proposes a *five*-and-dime store for Tony and his future wife, and is bounced ungracefully five times by the Recalcitrant Chair. Tony sells his Cadillac for $500, not $600, which he wants.[43] He bets this $500 and wins $5000 at the track on the no. 6 dog, then bets it all on no. 5 ("Lucky Ally") and loses. Tony's Disneyland proposal needs five million to attract investors. Marx pays five million in taxes per year. Then, there are multiples of five. Mario at the outset gives a dime to a cab-driver, and thinks it is a worthy tip; at the end of the film, he will not fret over his money because he can buy a "100" meters.[44] Julius says that it would take 10,000 garter-belt sales to pay out $5000 for Tony's back rent. All the 9s are about to turn on Tony's speedometer. The very last figure mentioned in the film is "ten million," what Tony will give Ally if he knows who won the lightweight championship of the world three times. Ally "wins" the money with "Greta Garbo" (a private joke between them). By the use of five and its multiples, Capra exerts aesthetic control over numbers, giving them an air of providentiality. Tony is usually at the low end of the figures, but by losing at the track, he provokes the family crisis and actually "wins," whereas if he had won at the track, he would only have put off solving his problems and eventually have lost again, and the cycle of his addiction would have continued.

The Jerry Marx scenes also show Capra's extraordinary ear for slang and local idiom. In a film about a "kid" and kid-like behavior in adults, the word "kid" "kiddy," etc. recur frequently, reaching a climax at the dogtrack. To begin with, the "kid" is Ally, who says that he does not want to be called "kid": "a kid is a goat," he says, with denotative precision. He wants to be respected as an adult. In-

---

[43] There could hardly be a finer example of Capra's economy of artistic means than the scene in which Tony sells his Cadillac. In less than ten seconds an entire ethos is summoned up. Used Car Dealer: "Five hundred, take it or leave it." Tony: "Six." Used Car Dealer: "Five." Tony, accepting the deal: "Louse."

[44] There are, in all, three cab scenes: these two at the beginning and end of the film, and the providential Mendy talking to Tony and Mrs. Rogers in the middle of the film. In each case, Capra has not just used a cab as a conveyance, but has made the cab or cab-driver an element within the film's thematic structure.

deed, this "kid" is going to sing the stanza in the song *High Hopes* about an adult kid, that is, a ram, who by persistence knocks down a million-kilowatt dam. Tony bets on Lucky Ally because he has a "kid" named Ally; Marx replies, "no kidding." A moment later, Marx addresses Dorine and Tony both as "kid." After he tries to brush off Tony, the word (or forms of it) reappears in a bitter key: "kid," "no kidding," and "listen, kiddy."

Since Ally informs everyone that his father has saved the hotel, virtually the entire cast is assembled for a celebration, touched off by its choric recital of "For He's a Jolly Good Fellow." Tony's depression is apparent to all but the self-important Mario, who still believes that a triumphant Tony has been rescued by a "stranger" instead of himself and who prepares himself for Tony's curse of "turning blue." Sophie criticizes her husband severely for acting like "god" in dispensing his favors. Under her sympathetic questioning, Tony confesses that, having lost the money, "I'm nothing but a bum." Mario is full of conflicting emotions: worried that Tony "doesn't need his brother any more"; angry that Tony has again squandered his money; proud at being reinstated as the patriarchal provider of delinquent family members; "crazy" that his brother calls himself a bum, which reflects badly on the family. He pleads with Tony that he has always helped out, only setting conditions so that Tony will "be somebody." Proud that no one in the family is a "bum," Mario invokes the memory of their immigrant parents, the model of familial pride and perseverance against great odds: "Now Momma and Poppa, when they came here, what did they have? I'll tell you: *rags on their backs.* But they worked hard, and made good. And you're a *part* of them, you're a part of *me.*" With this declaration, Mario agrees to pay the back rent.

The difference between this bail-out and previous occasions lies in the fact that it is now no comfort whatsoever to Tony who, for the first time, admits to his family and to himself that his problems are not essentially of money or luck but of character. Only the risk of losing his son has pushed him to this level of understanding. Hence his self-hatred deepens when he must commit what Don De Lillo in *Underworld* calls the "unthinkable Italian crime," so terrible that Italians "don't even have a name for this": abandonment of the family.[45] Telling Ally that he can no longer afford to care for him, he breaks his promise and says he must go with his aunt and uncle. Ally protests tearfully: "they don't need me, you need me." As the third reference to "need," in addition to Mrs. Rogers' and Mario's, Ally's words reveal extraordinary insight and maturity, though not beyond what he has shown himself capable of. To make Ally angry with him and therefore more likely to leave with his uncle and aunt, Tony pretends not to "need" Ally at all; it is another expression of self-abasement, and painful to watch. As Tony remarks, Ally has been a hindrance to his business "operations" (the word has a terribly metallic, unfeeling sound on his lips): "I need you like I need a hole in the head." The third and last quotation of the film's title is the most dramatic. Ironically, Tony does need his son – and needs him like a hole in the head, the space filled by hope, love, and creative imagination. After such a rebuke, Ally agrees to go, "but not with them," implying that he will run away from home. At this, Tony slaps him, an action that shocks Mario, Sophie, and Mrs. Rogers. Just as the bodyguard had slugged Tony in the first climax, Tony intensifies his self-hatred by transferring that blow to the person whom he most loves in this second, and greater climax.

Outside the hotel, Mario, Sophie and Ally prepare to enter the cab for the airport when Mrs. Rogers arrives asking for Tony. Mario points with his head to the palms across the street: a distraught Tony looks on at events taking place without him. In the backseat of the cab, Sophie asks innocently why Tony did not say goodbye. Himself at the breaking-point, and moving toward his own catharsis, Mario bursts out: "Goodbye to what? Did you see him back there, Tony, my bigshot brother, behind the tree like a crazy man watching his son leave? What's going to happen to *him*?"

From his question unfolds one of the most inspired scenes in all of Capra's work, which is to say in American cinema.[46] One

---

[45] Don De Lillo, *Underworld* (New York: Scribner, 1997), 204, ctd in Federico Moramarco, "Remembering Arthur Avenue: De Lillo's Italian American Identity," forthcoming in the Proceedings of the XV Congresso di Associazione Italiana di Studi Nord-Americani (AISNA), Siracusa, Nov., 1999.

[46] One can only disagree most strenuously with Donald Willis's comment that "the nadir of *A Hole in the Head* is the ending" (*Films of Frank Capra*, 123). One of the first errors of criticism, flush with itself, is that it cannot tell the difference between the true voice of feel-

hears Ally, as yet unseen, shouting for his father from a great distance, up the long avenue between the hotels and the beach. Most likely at Sophie's urging, Mario has had a change of heart and has let Ally go back. As the shouts get louder, Ally comes into the picture running down the center of the street, and commanding the entire screen, where at the beginning of the film Shirl stood up in Tony's convertible and gave her rebel yell. Ally finds his father on the beach, they hug each other, and fall into the shallow surf, while Ally gleefully implores Mrs. Rogers, who has been waiting tentatively among the palms, to "save me," thereby bringing her back into the scene. Mario and Sophie return in the cab to find father and son playing, fully clad, in the surf. What, wonders Mario, could they be doing? It seems so crazy. "How would you know," Sophie reproaches him, "did you ever play with your sons one day in your entire life?" Mario responds, "Julius," as if to say, "Preposterous, who would want to play with him?" But the answer falls lamely, without the bite it would have had earlier. "They're so happy and so poor," says Sophie. Echoing his brother's comment, to the effect that he would never understand the difference between being broke and being poor, Mario replies in full awareness: "No, Sophie. Broke, yes, but they're not poor. *We're* poor." He turns to re-enter the cab because "the meter's running," but stops suddenly to ask, what *does* it matter? he could buy a "100" meters. He and Sophie will remain in Miami for a vacation. Grabbing her arm and shouting "Geronimo!" he leads her onto the beach in order to catch up with Tony, Ally (riding piggyback on his father), and Mrs. Rogers.[47] Not only has the family survived the crisis, it has been enlarged and strengthened.

The last shot shows them all running jubilantly up the beach, becoming smaller and smaller in the distance. Where during the opening credits the viewer moved from north to south above Miami Beach, now one follows the family group from south to north, thereby effecting a formal closure. To counterpoint the sad mood

---

ing and sentimentality.

[47] "Geronimo" had earlier been explained to Miss Wexler as meaning "Have a good time." But this is a toned-down interpretation of the World War II parachutist jump call which became a slang term for "Let it rip!" In De Lillo's *Underworld* (12), in order to get into the 1951 Dodgers-Giants playoff game, the boys crash through the turnstiles with the signal *Geronimo!*

of *All My Tomorrows*, the song sung by Sinatra as the credits were shown, the concluding music of *High Hopes* points forward with its playful optimism, particularly refreshing because it is the song's only reprise in the film. As the camera pulls back slowly and mounts higher, and as the tiny figures are farther and farther up the beach, the viewer observes the scene from a great height, until the real sand, sea, and sky change imperceptibly to painted sand, sea, and sky. "Once upon a time," Tony had begun his voice-over; again, the realism gives way to aesthetic space. One is seeing not with the visual, but the mind's eye, from the point of view of "flying high," that is, of a hole in the head. Neither the riches nor the luck of a Mr. Fabulous, Capra celebrates the far greater wealth of the family and of fable.

Spectacular Imagery in Italian/American Short Films[1]
Race as Stage-display Pageantry

Anthony Julian Tamburri
Florida Atlantic University

Preliminary Comments

The short film is a cultural production that, until three decades or so ago, enjoyed a fairly good fortune with respect to being shown in many movie houses.[2] Until the late sixties and early seventies especially, when one went to the movies, there was often a short film of some sort, animated or real, that preceded the main attraction, thus providing numerous possible fora for such short narratives. This, I would suggest, is not the case today; for it is rare to go to a mainstream movie house and enjoy a prefatory short to the feature presentation. Today, very much in tune with the times, we are assailed by anywhere from five to fifteen minutes of trailers, with a commercial now and then mixed among them, these trailers themselves a commercial venture in their own right. Indeed, in some theaters the various trailers may take up to twenty minutes. With tongue only half in cheek, one wonders if the trailers might not some day become their own form of art, as some critics have dared, though be it sarcastically, compared the trailer to its feature-length product. In this regard, I would remind the reader of an article in *Newsweek*, where we read that one-third of the "500-person audience opted *not* to" stay for the film, viewing only the two-minute trailer of the then forthcoming *Stars Wars: Episode I–The Phantom Menace*.[3] All this, of course, also has some practical rami-

---

[1]For my use of the slash (/) instead of the hyphen (-), see my *A Semiotic of Ethnicity: In (Re)cognition of the Italian/American Writer* (Albany, NY: SUNY P, 1998).

    A modified version of this essay was delivered at the annual symposium of the Center for Italian Studies of SUNY Stony Brook, *Spectacle in Italian and Italian American Life*, 22-23 October 1999, and consists of various parts from different chapters in my *Italian/American Briefs: A Semiotic Reading of Short Films & Videos* (West Lafayette: Purdue UP, 2001), where I also include discussions of three other films: Joseph Greco's *Lena's Spaghetti* (fiction), Madonna's *Justify My Love* (music video), and Will Parrinello's *Little Italy* (documentary).

[2]I refer to that type of film under sixty minutes in length, be it a narrative fiction, or documentary.

[3]Kendall Hamilton, "The Second Coming." *Newsweek* 132.22 (30 November 1998): 84.

fications; for one often wonders when exactly the feature film is to begin and how the actual beginning time of the film jibes either with what one sees in the papers or, when checking on starting times, with what one is told over the phone.

The desire to deal with the Italian/American short may, among other things, help create a forum specifically for the Italian/American short visual narrative, be that which we would readily consider an account of fiction, a music video, which may also be a fiction, or a documentary – this too a potential fiction, be it only by virtue of the means with which we examine either genre (fiction or documentary), if not also by some narratological aspect of the nature of a text based on fact, documentary, or autobiography. Such notions we find in recent work on autobiography, as Graziella Parati reminds us in her study of woman's autobiography, or in a more classic study that is Philippe Lejeune's. Lejuene reminds us of what he had stated earlier about the actual task of reading (i.e., analyzing) fictional and autobiographical texts: "We must admit that, if we remain on the level of analysis within the text, there is no *difference*. All the methods that autobiography uses to convince us of the authenticity of its narrative can be imitated by the novel, and often have been imitated" (13; emphasis textual).[4]

In spite of the lack of venues for the short film, it seems still to be very much in vogue. To be sure, unless the short film is commissioned for something special such as an anthology of sorts that will run as a feature presentation (e.g., *Boccaccio '70* [1970], *New York Stories* [1986], *Boy's Life II* [1998]), it is often the young filmmaker at the helm of the project; this is particularly true for the young filmmaker who cuts her/his teeth on this timely production for an array of reasons, at the head of which we must list most obviously the economic factor. Indeed, numerous are the directors of short films, finished products which are often shown in small

---

[4]See his, *On Autobiography*. Forward by Paul John Eakin, translated by Katherine Leary (Minneapolis: U of Minnesota P, 1989). For Parati, in turn, autobiography becomes something more than the "metaphor of truth" (1) ... it is, she tells us, a "fiction, [...] a narrative in which the author carefully selects and constructs the characters, events, and aspects of the self she or he wants to make public in order to convey a specific message about her or his past and present identity" (4). See her *Public History Private Stories. Italian Women's Autobiography* (U of Minnesota P, 1996).

movie houses, off-beat theaters, and university theaters, if not also at the more competitive film festivals, be they regional, national, or international.

This last forum of the film festival was in fact my introduction to the first of three films in this essay, *Nunzio's Second Cousin*. I met the director at the screening of his film at the 1994 Telluride Film Festival.[5] An analogous sort of meeting took place with regard to *Uncovering*; I first meet Mariarosy Calleri at a conference sponsored by the John D. Calandra Italian-American Institute on the lost world of Italian/American radicals, which took place in May 1997 at the CUNY Graduate Center. Madonna's video took a much more commercial route; I saw it, like everyone else for the first time, on MTV.

So much has been written on film in general. One need only peruse the innumerable bibliographic listings in any study to see how exhaustive the critical and theoretical production has been to date. However, with specific regard to the short film, the terrain is, for lack of a better word, quite barren indeed. Whereas in literary studies short fiction has enjoyed a good deal of critical and theoretical success,[6] the short films seem to be a target of study only within the more specific and specialized studies of the so-called avant-garde cinema or the documentary. Yet, even here, careful attention to the brevity of discourse takes second-stage, and notions of something we might consider to be specifically a narrative strategy of the short film is left for us to ponder. Thus, while I shall, to some extent, refrain herein from theorizing specifically about the short film, my hopes are that the actual fact of discussing Italian/American shorts will at least figure as some sort of first step, so we may, in our studies of visual Italian America, include as a necessary topic of investigation those shorts that have so often gone unexamined for an array of reasons the least of which is aesthetic quality. Along with the likes of Dina Ciraulo, whom I mentioned ear-

---

[5]At the same festival I also met Joseph Greco (*Lena's Spaghetti*). At the 1995 Telluride Festival, I then met Dina Ciraulo, another Italian American whose film, *Touch*, was also screened in the session of student films. She, too, proved equally gracious in providing me a copy.

[6]I would state, *en passant*, that here, too, one might have a legitimate complaint vis-à-vis how much has been written instead on the long narrative.

lier, certain other names indeed come to the fore. Louis Antonelli's extensive award-winning experience with the short film is unknown to the majority of Italian Americans be they members of the public at large or actual scholars of the artistic world of Italian America; his films have won countless prizes both in the United States and abroad. A second case involves the work of Helen De Michiel: now having ventured into the feature-length world of cinema with *Tarantella* (1995), De Michel is another filmmaker who has proven to be most articulate with the short format. In addition, short documentaries both in the United States and in Canada about the numerous Little Italies, if not the villages in Italy of the parents and grandparents of the filmmaker, abound: Santo Barbiere, Anthony Fragola, and Patrizia Fogliato are just three of the many names that come to mind in this category.

To be sure, the brevity and conciseness of the short film constitute some of its very appealing characteristics. Like the short-story writer, I would suggest, the ability of the short-film filmmaker to be both concise and inclusive is what draws the viewer to the text and ultimately satisfies his/her curiosity. This, of course, would include the filmmaker's capacity of some semblance of character-development which would prove essential in maintaining the viewer's interest. Thus, the short-film filmmaker needs to develop a narrative strategy that is both economic in length and comprehensive in description, much in the same way any celebrated, short-story writer succeeds in writing in such a mode. Such narrative success is evidenced by the three films included herein. Each in its own way, especially the first two films, offers a story-line albeit brief that, while asking questions of its viewer, does not leave him/her hanging vis-à-vis information that might otherwise be considered fundamental to said story-line. Finally, the short-film filmmaker, like the short-story writer, often offers his/her viewer some sort of attention-getting ingredient that will grasp and maintain the viewer's attention. Be this related to character or plot, it is this aspect of the film that we might consider, for out purposes here vis-à-vis the notion of *spectacle*, that which would fall into the category of the "remarkable," the "foolish," the "improper," the "curious," or the "contemptuous," not to mention – in some cases, perhaps –

the "marvelous" or the "admirable," as has been so defined. Or, in a more jargonesque parlance, *up front and in your face*.

Spectacle, Luigi Barzini tells us,[7] is "*extraordinary* animation" (58; my emphasis), where "everything is displayed everywhere, in *dramatic* and artistic *disorder*" (59; my emphasis). He underscores, later in the same chapter, the public aspect of Italian spectacle:

> The extraordinary animation, the vivid colors, the disorderly abundance of all God's things, the military uniforms and clerical robes, the impressive faces, the revealing gesticulation, the noise: these are among everybody's first superficial impressions in Italy, anywhere in Italy, in the north as well as the south, in big cities as well as in decrepit and miserable hamlets forgotten by Italy. (66)

We find similar notions in more quotidian outlets such as *Webster's New World Dictionary* or the *Oxford English Dictionary*. In the first case, we read:

> *Spectacle*: 1. something to look at, esp. some strange or remarkable sight; unusual display 2. a public show or exhibition on a grand scale. . . *make a spectacle of oneself* to behave foolishly or improperly in public.
> *Webster's New World Dictionary*, 2nd edition, s.v.

In the second case, a tad bit more intriguing, we find two entries for the noun "spectacle":

> *Spectacle*: 1. A specially prepared or arranged display of a more or less public nature (esp. one on a large scale), forming an impressive or interesting show or entertainment for those viewing it. . . . 2. A person or thing exhibited to, or set before, the public gaze as an object either *(a)* of curiosity or contempt, or *(b)* of marvel or admiration. . . . 3. A thing seen or being seen; something presented to the view, especially of a striking or unusual character; a sight. . . .
> *Oxford English Dictionary*, s.v.

> *Spectacle*: 1. A piece of stage-display or pageantry, as contrasted with real drama. . . .
> *Oxford English Dictionary*, s.v.

The various descriptions we find above, I would submit, manifest themselves in the films we shall examine herein. They each deal

---

[7]Luigi Barzini, "The Importance of Spectacle," *The Italians. A Full-length Portrait Featuring Their Manners and Morals* (New York: Atheneum, 1983 [1964]): 58-73.

with provocative and eyebrow-raising issues that constitute, to borrow again from above, an "unusual display . . . on a grand scale."

Three Readings
1. Nunzio's Second Cousin

One of six shorts chosen for the "Resume Films" session at the Telluride Film Festival, *Nunzio's Second Cousin* was an instant hit with the audience for its up-front and in-your-face manner of dealing with sensitive and controversial issues. In his film, Tom DeCerchio confronts the questions of race and homosexuality, two seemingly taboo issues in the general community of Italian America, thus forming a triangle of issues of race, sexual orientation, and ethnicity. From the opening parking-lot scene, sexuality and race constitute both prominent and problematic themes in the film. The initial confrontation between the racially mixed gay male couple and the gay-bashing group of suburban boys sets the stage for these conflictual themes. Anthony, the police officer, and his black "date"[8] exit a bar and are on their way to what we assume is to be a delightful dinner when they are spotted by some prospective gay-bashers from Cicero, Illinois who immediately run to attack them.[9]

On a more general scale, we witness the confrontation of two different sets of sign systems. The traditional, Italian/American sign system of white heterosexuality clashes head-on with an Italian/American sign system that has now been altered according to the gay police officer's individual life situation: biracial homosexuality. Such polyvalence – or better, rhetorical malleability of signs – is evidenced in a number of ways. Through a few seemingly insignificant transitional scenes, the clash between a traditional Italian/American sign system and a second having undergone a more radical modification also comes to the fore. While Cicero is already marked by an Italian Americanness, in that it is well known as an

---

[8]"Date" is the word Anthony uses when he refers to him in his conversation with the boys from Cicero.

[9]For those who know the reputation of Cicero, Illinois vis-à-vis racial awareness, one can only ascribe a keen sense of irony, as well as a strong dose of parody, to DeCerchio's use of this Chicago suburb as the main characters' home town. As such, it thus figures as the geo-ideological analogue to Queens's Howard Beach and New York's Bensonhurst.

Italian enclave, DeCerchio also invests ethnic signs early on in the film when – after having literally stopped the young men in their tracks by pulling out his gun – Anthony has the boys recite an apology to "all the fags in the world," that "gay people are good people"; for he also has them repeat that "Michelangelo was gay and he's a freaking genius." And he does so just as, shortly after, he has Anthony and his "date" kiss openly in front of the now disarmed gay-bashers. At this point, Anthony's statement reflects, in disaccord with that of the would-be bashers, a new Italian/ American sign system that adds biracial homosexuality as an accepted characteristic. But the collision of two worlds continues to manifest itself; once Anthony goes back to the old neighborhood, he confronts the cancer of racism that seems to permeate some white, working-class ethnic enclaves. We see in his conversation with Mr P:

> Mr. P: "It's always nice to have a cop around. You know what they say:
> 'A cop a day keeps the niggers away!'"
> Anthony: "Yeah. Well, I wish they wouldn't say that."

The clash between the old world and the new world is exhibited in two ways. First, Anthony responds in disagreement: "Well, I wish they wouldn't say that." Then, in another sign of disagreement – this time not verbal – Mr. P exhibits puzzlement at Anthony's reaction to his – unbeknownst to himself – racist comment. All this is then furthur underscored by the irony in the fact that Anthony's *date* of the night before was a black man.

Race is further underscored when Anthony comes to greet Jimmy at the door and proceeds to tell him what is in store for him after dinner. In a scene couching the threat of violence in comedy, the taller and stockier Anthony puts his arm around Jimmy and, while first tapping on his chest and then waving back and forth in his face a long, thick salame, states: "I bet you thought I invited you here to fuck you in the ass." Pausing, he then continues, "No. I'm gonna wait until after dinner." Then, after pushing Jimmy into the house, he closes the door behind them. Here, of course, we see DeCerchio's blatant use of phallic imagery in the form of the salame, further exaggerated in, let us say, its physical abundance. It is, first of all, a sign of threatening force that, at the same time, refers to the legendary attribute of genital abundance often imputed to Italian men. Yet, it goes one step further in its semiotic function; for one other potentially significant marker is the salame's color – dark brown; let us not forget Anthony's date of the evening before, the black man in leather pants and chest-ware. The legendary large penis is also an attribute imputed to Black men, for which another form of identity may seem to rise to the surface. Let us not forget that Italians, Southern Italians in particular, were often considered people of color; this was especially true of the opinion of early sociologists – as well as some governmental agencies – who looked upon most immigrant groups as non-white.[10] There is a final, comical element at the dinner table that continues to remind us of the race issue in this film. When Anthony's mother informs him that she has bought cannoli, with "nuts on top," they way he likes them, she adds, he then asks, "with *chocolate* nuts on top?" (my emphasis).

Indeed, here, semiotically speaking, we are again in the realm of *secondary signs*, something that, in the words of a Roland Barthes, instead of being, let us say, the cardinal functions/nuclei or catalysers, would be, instead, something in the line of the indices or informants: those secondary and tertiary signs that seem to have no constitutive function in the production of meaning yet, when all is said and done, figure significantly.[11] Thus, as viewers, we are again reminded of the race issue, introduced at the beginning by

[10]I would also add that this attribution of non-whiteness is now a voluntary characteristic a number of contemporary Italian Americans of southern Italian descent have adopted. See, for instance, Rose Romano's "Coming Out Olive," in *Literary History and Social Pluralism*. Edited by Francesco Loriggio (Toronto: Cuernica, 1996) 161-75; and Rudolph J. Vecoli's "Are Italian Americans Just White Folks?" *Through the Looking Glass: Italian & Italian/American Images In The Media*. Eds. Mary Jo Bona and Anthony Julian Tamburri (Staten Island, NY: AIHA, 1996) 3-17.

[11]I refer the reader to Roland Barthes's notions of functions, neclei, catalysers, and the like. Functions, for Barthes, are units of content that drive the narrative. The essence of the function, according to Barthes, "is the seed that it sows in the narrative, planting an element that will come to fruition later – either on the same level or elsewhere, on another level" (89). Catalysers, instead, fill up space between the cardinal functions. In turn, indices index character, feeling, atmosphere, and philosophy; and, in addition, informants serve to authenticate, they are pure data of immediate and, I would add local, signification. For more on Barthes notion of narrative, see his seminal strucutralist essay "Introduction to the Structural Analysis of Narratives" (1966) in *Image Music Text*, trans. Stephen Heath (New York: Hill and Wang, 1977) 79-124.

Anthony's "date," which has now seemed to fall by the wayside: both Mr. P's rewritten racist proverb of a "nigger a day" and the dark salame do keep race, albeit seemingly in the background, as part of the general semiotic of the filmic text.

2. Like a Prayer

While sexuality constitutes both a prominent and problematic theme of Madonna's music/performance, religion and race play equally important and integral parts in her videos. In *Like a Prayer*, all three themes reoccur. In fact, together, they serve as integral components of Madonna's *visione del mondo* and figure, at the same time, as reasons for which some of her videos have ruffled, to say the least, the dominant culture's feathers.[12] Thus, it is that sexuality and religion combine with race to form a radically different *visione del mondo* which now surpasses in its provocative nature most of the so-called *mainstream* videos which had thus far appeared.[13]

Like a Prayer opens with a type of prologue. There are four quick shots that announce the major theme of the racial dilemma depicted in the video. There is a burning cross à la KKK, a quick shot of one of the white muggers, another quick shot of a black man being escorted by a white policeman, and *Madonna* who takes refuge in a church where she immediately finds a statue of a black Christ, behind bars.[14] Before anything else takes place, *Madonna* lies down on a pew and enters a dream state, as the lyrics readily imply:

> I hear your voice, it's like an angel sighing
> I have no choice, I hear your voice

[12]Today, to be sure, the notion of "dominant culture" or "canon," as we knew it until not so long ago, may now be placed into question: Who are the members of the dominant culture? What constitutes the canon today as opposed to ten or twenty years ago? These questions notwithstanding, I shall use these terms as aesthetic points of comparison in so far as for "dominant culture" or "canon" I understand that which is considered *correct, right, artistic*, etc. by that community of people that has the power to decide (read, impose?) such issues.

[13]I use the word "mainstream" here since it was Madonna herself who characterized her "art" as such during her *Nightline* interview December 3, 1990.

[14]When I say *Madonna*, in italics, I refer to the character in the video, not the flesh and bones singer/actress.

Feels like flying
I close my eyes, Oh God I think I'm falling
Out of the sky, I close my eyes
Heaven help me.

Almost as if she were on the very edge of the beginning of the video's dream world, she first encounters a black woman who literally thrusts her into her dream state in which *Madonna* will immediately liberate the black Christ. Once *Madonna* opens the barred, prison-like barricade, the black Christ statue comes to life, whispers something in her ear, kisses her good-bye on the forehead, and exits the church.

Throughout the video there is a succession of images that constantly underscore the racial element in their many possible significations. One of the more dramatic – read, spectacular – successions of inter-changing scenes underscores the presence of the blacks and ultimately situates them in an equal if not more significant position of empowerment in Madonna's *sui generis* church. The black woman who occupies center stage in the choir scene is a type of priestess in front of whom *Madonna* eventually kneels – a recollection of the typical ancient baptism scene, this time, however, without the baptismal urn. As the scene progresses, the video switches to a close-up of the black Christ and *Madonna* about to kiss. But a sudden switch back to the previous scene momentarily interrupts, as if to remind the viewer of the church setting. Once the kiss takes place, the screen is filled with a close-up of the two faces, one black the other white, and what follows is a series of six quick scenes underscoring a collision of diametrically opposed racial ideologies. As the camera scans upward above the black Christ's head, the following images quickly succeed one another: 1) one large burning cross; 2) *Madonna* dancing; 3) a field of burning crosses; 4) a quick, frontal close-up of Madonna with both hands to her mouth – too quick at regular speed to be sure if she is happy or anguished; 5) a quick, frontal close-up of the wooden Christ statue's face crying – this time tears of blood; and 6) the black man being taken away by the police.

What Madonna eventually does in this video is layer her narrative text to the extent that it consists not only of the reality of a narrative text and therefore includes the fictive reality one readily assumes the narrative text represents, but she adds to this the dream sequence. To further complicate matters, her dream sequence is consistently interrupted by scenes from the fictive reality, and the boundaries between the one and the other are ultimately blurred. This blurring of textual boundaries is consonant with her over-riding theme of the necessity to blur social boundaries – here specifically, racial – that Madonna seems to so readily transcend in most of her videos. The black Christ *Madonna* frees is, in her fictive reality, the falsely accused black man – a parallel too striking to ignore which, here, is underscored by the fact that one actor plays both roles. Madonna's twentieth-century, secular Christ, this black man – an obvious outsider in this video who is falsely accused of committing a crime perpetrated on a white woman by three white men – reifies the false accusations launched against the biblical Christ, also an outsider in his own time, whose *otherness*, in this video, is now represented by, among other things, his skin color.

3. Uncovering: *An Experimental Documentary*

Mariarosy Calleri's *Uncovering* is no less "extraordinary" or "dramatic," to echo Barzini's adjectives. Indeed, like *Nunzio's Second Cousin* and *Like a Prayer*, *Uncovering* is a provocative short film that demonstrates among other things how members of a post-1980s generation deals with issues of intolerance, be such intolerance steeped in gender, sexuality, or, for our purposes here, race. I specifically use the label post-1980s as a marker precisely because of the decade's association with what has now become known as the *me generation of the Reagan era*, when government itself was considered by many, in its own way, not to be sensitive to issues of civil intolerance. I would further add that, from the specific view-point of ethnicity, these films figure also as significant markers of how the Italian American (DeCerchio and Madonna) and [im]migrant Italian living in the United States (Calleri) may perceive the import and impact of such issues in the United States in the mid-1990s.

What we thus find in this experimental documentary is that the Italian/American female occupies a space contrary to the stereotype. No longer at home in the kitchen nor an appendage to her male partner, she sheds all and any sort of prudery both in her physical expression and her male preferences. Throughout a good deal of the film we bear witness to the naked body of the Italian woman. In a caress during the middle minutes of the film, she and a naked African/American male constitute the visual "backdrop" for a long series of answers to the first of three questions: "What characterizes an Italian woman?" She metamorphoses, we come to see, from that of a woman with, we are told, a "great body and an accent, . . . very warm, very family oriented, [and] a great cook," to "sexy, beautiful," with "a lot of attitude, . . . a lot of umph, very sensual, . . . a very powerful woman," to "sophisticated." The image of black and white persons occupying the entire screen was already present in DeCerchio's *Nunzio's Second Cousin* and Madonna's *Like a Prayer*. In both cases a kiss occupies the entire screen: in the first, Anthony and his black male date fill the screen as they kiss; in the second, the black Christ and Madonna kiss.

Such a metamorphosis of the female is signaled in a most articulate manner. Our very first image of woman appears at the opening of the film: she is "woman with camera," as the credits tell us, an obvious allusion, we may assume, to the process of filmmaking itself. But once the series of questions and answers begins, that which we may characterize the heart of the documentary's narrative, our next image of woman is a mannequin in a store window dressed in a bride's gown. This is then juxtaposed to the biracial couple which has been set off from the previous image by a few moments of a blank screen framed in black, another sign clamoring quite loudly in what, it becomes apparent, is, from a traditional view-point, a cacophony of signs and sign-functions.

The mannequin dressed as a bride, indeed a *simulacrum*, we might say, is the sign par excellence of the traditional Italian female who is now placed under erasure, to a certain degree, as she is shadowed by the less traditional figures of the Italian woman. For let us also not forget that the mannequin *qua simulacrum* is the typical ectomorph we see in many shop windows, advertisements, and other public fora that have obscured a healthy view of the female. More anorexic than not, these svelte figures may often impact negatively on a young woman's sense of self, as some studies have already shown.[15] Calleri's female, instead, is the opposite. Beginning with the female half of the biracial couple, it is clear we are dealing with a woman who clearly falls into the category of the endomorph. By no means overweight in a general sense, but surely heavier than the ectomorphs we're accustomed to seeing, this woman is the descendent, we might say, of the female models of Titian, Ruben, and the like.

Let us also not lose the irony in Calleri's use of the mannequin as a counterpoint; for the mannequin may surely represent a sort of automatism which, in a male-female relationship in a male-centered context, can easily be translated into excessive obedience on the female's part. Thus all of the above, I would submit, leads us to yet another significant aspect of the biracial couple. For as the voice-over accompanies most of the above-mentioned scenes of the white female and black male caressing, we see their bodies but not their faces. In fact, we only see the woman's face toward the end of the film, underscoring, I would suggest, each one's every*person*ness, signifying thereby not so much their individuality of personhood but rather their generality of gender, ethnicity, and race, which here clamors much more loudly given the broad spectrum these signs must re-present.

The remaining two questions in *Uncovering* are: "How would you describe an Italian woman?" and "What makes her different from an American woman?," to which an array of responses flow. With regard to the second of our three questions, two of the more significant responses are: a) "Brunette, that's all I can think of"; and b) "Olive skin, dark hair, attractive as far as dark eyes, wilder, southerner."[16] Both responses call to mind the notion of Italians, especially Southern Italians, as people of color. All this is then

---

[15]For more on the representation of women in cultural productions, see Susan Bordo, *Unbearable Weight: Feminism, Western Culture, and the Body* (Berkeley: U of California P, 1993) and Mary Russo, *The Female Grotesque: Risk, Excess, and Modernity* (New York: Routledge, 1995).

[16]Given the Italian context in which Calleri has and continues to work, this description of the Italian woman may seem to have a strange intertext for the non-Italian. It is rather consonant with a general description that calls to mind one of Italian literature's most controversial female characters: Giovanni Verga's La Lupa of the eponymous short story.

underscored in one of the answers to the third question, when the man responds:[17]

> More white women or American women are just very passive, an Italian or Hispanic woman would more or less take that extra mile, you know, just to get what she wants.

We find the formula "white = American" juxtaposed to one of "Italian = Hispanic," so that the Italian is indeed part and parcel of a category that we might readily establish as one of color. It is also at this point that the notion of difference is finally punctuated both verbally and visually. In the responses we have seen thus far, we see the Italian woman situated in the realm of colorness. In this final list of responses, yet another one underscores the general notion of difference:

> You can't generalize, the good thing about Italian women, like all Italians, it's that they are so different, you know. [...] They are all different, yah. Italian women are not the same, are they?

This response is curiously significant, indeed, and in its own way it is nicely ambiguous. The key words here are, of course, *generalize* and *different*, both of which underscore plurality; and I would include the adverbial *so*, which can only emphasize the Italian woman's distinction among women. We see also that the notion of difference is extended to Italians in general; so that while Calleri's film is mostly concerned with the position of the Italian woman, she momentarily takes advantage of the situation here to include in her praise of distinction and singularity also the Italian female's brother, so to speak.

To be sure, Calleri's *Uncovering* ultimately proposes a new way of viewing the Italian female and her body, physically and conceptually, in her relationship to gender, sexuality, and, here too, race. On the screen, that is, Calleri uncovers woman, both literally

---

[17]Let us not forget that this is not so foreign a notion among a good number of Italian Americans. I remind the reader of various essays and creative works of the following: e.g., Lucia Chiavola Birnbaum, Mary Bucci Bush, Jerome Krase, Rose Romano, Pasquale Verdicchio, Maurizio Viano, and Robert Viscusi. I would especially underscore Matthew Jacobson's *Whiteness of Another Color. European Immigrants and the Alchemy of Race* (Cambridge, MA: Harvard UP, 1998).

and metaphorically, vis-à-vis her relationship to man, accented here by *her* ethnicity and *his* race. Calleri, thus, I would suggest, also uncovers her viewer's relationship to this triad of gender, race, and ethnicity, as her viewer is left to ponder the thirteen minutes of experimental narrative that exudes such an ideologically charged semiotic.

Concluding Comments

In what may seem to have been a rare move among social scientists of Italian America, Patrick Gallo closed his 1974 study with a type of call-to-arms for which Italian Americans and blacks should form the ethnic coalition that would figure as the nucleus of an inter-ethnic response to the WASP dominant power structure. "What is needed," Patrick Gallo wrote at the end of his study, "is an alliance of whites and Blacks, white-collar and blue-collar workers, based on mutual need and interdependence and hence an alliance of political participation." Namely, the notion of *us and them*, not *us against them*. "But," Gallo continues, "before this can realistically come to pass, a number of ethnic groups have to de-velop in-group organization, identity, and unity." And here Viscusi's notion of the "group narrative" comes to mind, which he so eloquently rehearsed in his "Breaking the Silence" (1990).[18] Finally, Gallo states, "[t]he Italian-Americans may prove to be a vital ingredient in not only forging that alliance but in serving as the cement that will hold our urban centers together."[19] Gallo, we see, anticipates what Stuart Hall was to state years later with regard to Cultural Studies, reminding us that we must learn not to speak in terms of racism or prejudice in the singular, "but of *racisms* [as also prejudices] in the plural" (11).[20]

[18] *Voices in Italian Americana* 1.1 (1990): 1-13.

[19] Patrick J. Gallo, *Ethnic Alienation. The Italian-Americans* (Fairleigh Dickinson UP, 1974) 209.

[20] See his "Race, Culture, and Communications: Looking Backward and Forward at Cultural Studies," *Rethinking Marxism* 5.1 (1992): 10-18.

While the older generations concentrated more on the by-now, well-known thematics of immigration and organized crime, as well as the debunking thereof, these younger artists/performers of short films have added to the general theme of heritage, and at various degrees, that of gender, sexuality, and race.[21]

Race, indeed, constitutes a significant issue in these short films. And while it is true that films such as *The Godfather* and *Mean Streets* have shown the deplorable racist behavior of those individuals who populate such films, no prominent, Italian/American director has truly dealt up-front and in-depth with the issue of race-crossing in a positive light in a feature-length film.[22] Instead, all three films – a fictional narrative, a music video, and a documentary – question the status quo of the relationship between whites (read, Italian Americans) and blacks. Race, that which has become to some degree an ugly stain in Italian/American history,[23]

---

[21]Indeed, we should not ignore other Italian Americans in between these two generations who have reworked the thematics of crime in general if not, specifically, organized crime. I have in mind Abel Ferrara's *The Bad Lieutenant* and *The Funeral*.

[22]The only filmmaker to deal critically thus far with the issue of race and Italian Americans has been Spike Lee, especially in his *Do The Right Thing* (1989) and *Jungle Fever* (1991).

[23]In addition to the two infamous, tragic episodes of Howard Beach (1987) and Bensonhurst (1989), I would remind the reader of two more insidious cases of bigotry that have made the news: Alfonse D'Amato and John Lombardi. Then senator Alfonse D'Amato made the headlines for his outrageous imitation of Lance Ito, presiding judge in the O. J. Simpson Trial, on nationally syndicated radio. On April 5, 1995, being interviewed by Don Imus, in a mock Japanese accent D'Amato launched into his imitation of "little" Judge Ito, while discussing the re-opening of the Senate Banking Committee hearings on the Clinton's involvement with Whitewater. Imus suggested that D'Amato and his committee wouldn't attract as large an audience as long as the O. J. Simpson trial continued on TV. "Judge Ito will never let it end," D'Amato said in a fake accent. "Judge Ito loves the limelight. He is making a disgrace of the judicial system. Little Judge Ito will keep us from getting television for the next year." The remarks in themselves are ridiculous and would have gone unnoticed but for the fact that this man dared to make fun of a people by stereotyping and deriding the way they supposedly pronounce the English language. The fake Japanese accent used by D'Amato makes those remarks offensive to all people who are concerned about bigotry and racism in the United States. All Italian immigrants, especially those who learned to speak English in grade school, and their progeny should take special offense at Mr. D'Amato's racist behavior. As children, many immigrants were the recipients of such racism because they did not speak English well, or because they had, as many Italian Americans did, the "oily brown lunch bag," or for whatever other reason that differentiated them from their classmates.

Equally offensive, in January 1998, we read about John Lombardi's ignorance of not knowing his *biscotti* from his cookies when, in wanting to compliment, as he stated afterwards, his new boss, he referred to him as an "oreo," since the new chancellor, black, to our chagrin, is here redefined. In tune with Patrick Gallo's perspective, these three filmmakers examine the race issue through a similar lens: eschewing the argument of *us against them*, their films underscore instead the hopes and necessity of *us and them*.

All three films transgress to one degree or another those traditional narrative formats we might readily associate with a more conformist discourse of the Italian/American filmmaker. What each film has surely succeeded in doing is to offer its viewer a new way of seeing Italian America and its many facets. In the end, each film uncovers its viewer's relationship to the internal and external dynamics of all the Little Italies as notions of race, gender, sexuality, companionship, family, and other issues come to the fore. In this sense, newness becomes the operative word as these filmmakers, each in his/her own way, have succeeded, at these various stages in their careers, in maintaining an artistic freedom that has allowed them to engage in different forms of a *sui generis* creativity. They have indeed done so in a manner in which the traditionalist might consider — and again I hark back to the definitions of *spectacle* listed at the outset — "curious," "unusual," "strange," if not "contemptuous." Yet, notwithstanding these or other categorizations, they have, in so doing, avoided at all costs falling victim to the shackles of both a thematic and formalistic tradition, appropriating, as we have now seen, a more liberating and expansive discourse.

---

according to Lombardi, knows how to deal with the white powerbrokers of the academic world.

Also disappointing is the fact that there has been no overt denunciation of Mr. D'Amato's actions by Italian/American foundations and organizations, especially from those groups that, whenever possible, complain about the image of Italian Americans portrayed by the media. The same silence from the Italian/American community also manifested itself after the Lombardi comment, which was reported by the national wire services.

UNA CHIACCHIERATA

Annabella Sciorra & Joseph Sciorra

Annabella and I have long talked about doing some kind of interview around our respective work with Italian-American cultural production. Annabella has played Italian-American characters in films and television programs such as the television adaptation of Mario Puzo's *The Fortunate Pilgrim*, Nancy Savoca's "True Love," Spike Lee's "Jungle Fever," and HBO's "The Sopranos." As a folklorist, I have researched and written about the vernacular cultural expressions of Italian Americans, ranging from religious *feste* to yard shrines, from Christmas *presepi* (crèches) to Sicilian oral poetry. In the summer of 2001, we reclaimed our Italian citizenship.

Anthony Tamburri and Anna Camaiti Hostert invited us to participate in this publication and suggested that we not conduct a turn-taking, question-and-answer interview but a free-flowing *chiacchierata*, or chat. On April 27, 2001, I met Annabella at her apartment for a late dinner of pasta with zucchini that ended around 3 AM. But a casual conversation came with its own set of problems as I discovered when I listened to the tapes. We talked about everything from hip-hop to a bicycle accident under the Brooklyn Bridge. As siblings, we engaged in our familial style of speech: we interrupted each other, finished each other's sentences, and communicated non-verbally. And we cursed a lot, especially as we got progressively drunk.

Anthony selected an excerpt from a partial transcription, totaling three and a half hours of conversation, which I in turn transcribed in detail. Annabella and I then edited and rewrote it for legibility and clarity.

I am indebted to Francisca Vieira of the John D. Calandra Italian American Institute, Queens College (CUNY), for her work on the initial transcription.

— Joseph Sciorra

Fade In

JS: I think things are happening, at least in the city. I don't know what's going on in the rest of the country.

AS: Umm, this pasta is good.

JS: Yea, it's great. There are some really exciting things happening that are not inspired by "The Sopranos" and other mob movies. Folks that are into that are never going to get into the Collective's Malafemmina film festival.[1] And, of course, the Collective is never going to get the kind of exposure that "The Sopranos" gets. They're not going to get a write up in *The New York Times*. There are other events, like Karen Guancione's *malocchio* exhibit and IAWA's monthly readings at the Cornelia Street Café.[2] There's so much going on. I really think there's a kind of mini revolution going on.

These are really good olives.

But we just keep on getting the same old mafia shit over and over. Meanwhile, there are people who are not only into being Italian American, but they're creating new ways of being Italian American, new cultural expressions, that are not your oldfashioned ethnic politics. You know, the Columbus Day Parade, Italian flag waving, Lee Iacocca. These are very political ways at being Italian American. But there are new ways, cultural ways of being Italian American, whether the focus is women, literature, film, what have you. There are exciting things going on. But the media is not picking up on it for one reason or another. Now that I've returned to the fold by working at the Calandra Institute, I see all this programming – lectures and conferences – going on. You just got to keep your ear to the ground. All this amazing stuff is happening.

[1] The Collective of Italian American Women and Casa Italiana Zerilli-Marimò at New York University's film festival "Malafemmina: A Celebration of the Cinema of Italian American Women," May 17-20 2001.
[2] "Contro il malocchio/Against the Evil Eye," mixed media installation, Maass Gallery, Purchase College, May 1-June 3, 2001. IAWA stands for Italian American Writers Association.

AS: I really want to call that woman I told you about, Joy Behar.[3]

JS: Yeah, I'm curious to know who she is. I'm not familiar with her. I didn't even know about the show.

AS: She's got Bette Midler's sense of comedy and timing.

JS: Kind of brassy?

AS: But really smart and not afraid to be like (with a New York accent), "Oh, Barbara, please." (Laughing.)

JS: So, what did she do before this show?

AS: Mommy said she was a standup comic. I didn't know that.

JS: Huh! And so she went from being a standup comic to going on this show and that's it?

AS: I don't know. I think so.

JS: So who is she?

AS: Joy Behar.

JS: So who the hell is she?

AS: (Laughing.)

JS: You should call her and see what's going on.

AS: I really want to call her. Mommy called me after the interview. Did I tell you this? She left a message on the machine. She said, "I thought you were fabulous! Fabulous!" So I called her up and . . .

---

[3] Calabrian American, comedian, and co-host of the television program "The View." Annabella was a guest on April 25, 2001.

JS: Maybe because it's her program.

AS: You mean, that she likes the program?

JS: Yea. Or maybe she identifies with it.

AS: Yeah, could be. I think she likes it. I think a lot of women like it. A lot of women watch it because it's like being in somebody's kitchen. They all have cups of coffee. (with a New York accent) "Oh, did you read in the paper what it said about our kids not being schooled properly and it says that if you send your kids to preschool they're more likely to have problems and be violent in public schools when they get older." And then somebody answers, "Oh, please, I think that's ridiculous because that's like saying, like, you know, people ..." (Laughing.)

JS: (Laughing.)

AS: And then one of the other women will say (in a soft, mild-mannered voice), "No, I really think that it's true because I know my friend said that her child went to..." It's like waking up and seeing mommy, Chickie, and Angie having coffee with the Entenmanns cake (laughing), with the knife in it permanently.

JS: (Laughing.) Right.

AS: It's just like that. It's got that kind of feeling. And they all have very different points of view. Joy knows who she is, she knows her opinion, and she's very willing to come out with them, and she doesn't really care if anyone has a problem with it.

JS: Right.

AS: All the women are smart, but I related to her really quickly. So, like I was saying, I called mommy and I said, "You left a message?" And she goes, "Yeah. That was really funny! You could see that you gave her *la confidenza* backstage." And I was like, "How did you know that?" And she said, "You can just see." You know what that means? When you give someone permission to be friendly, to be casual. And I said, "How did you know?" She goes, "You can just tell." And it's true.

Joy came looking for me backstage because she wanted to say hi and talk about stuff and "The Sopranos." And like I said before, we had a little chat about "The Sopranos." She told me she wouldn't bring up anything about anti-defamation and the show, because it's talked about so much right now. I've been asked in every interview, "So what do you think about the fact that the Italian American anti-defamation league from Chicago . . . blah, blah, blah." I don't know who it is exactly. I would like to know. Who are they suing? HBO or "The Sopranos" production?

JS: I think they're suing HBO.

AS: Joy seemed to know a lot about the different Italian-American organizations out there, where they come from, how they got started. She was very knowledgeable about it.

JS: Well, you wonder how plugged into the whole Italian-American community she is, like the leadership, quote, unquote.

AS: She's part of this Italian-American women's organization. I can't remember what it was. They were calling her back to the stage.

JS: N.O.I.A.W.?

AS: I think that might be it.

JS: National Organization of Italian American Women. Like I said, I'm back into this kind of thing, you know, being a sort of a "professional ethnic." I'm learning all about these different groups.

Did you see the Sunday paper? Two articles on "The Sopranos." One about Bob Viscusi and the Italian American Writers Association. It was about the group's upcoming book fair in Westchester soon.[4] Of course, the article is totally framed by "The Sopranos." And then there was Maureen Dowd's Op-Ed piece.[5] Andrew Cuomo, who's running for governor of New York, came out against "The Sopranos."

AS: Is he running?

JS: Yeah, he's running. So the headline for that article was "Sopranos vs. Cuomos." Everything centers around "The Sopranos." Viscusi, this professor who's part of the Italian American Writers Organization, said in a recent newsletter that we're at a point of crisis in regards to Italian-American representation, because anything and everything about Italian Americans is being defined around "The Sopranos."[6] Either you're for it or you're against it. It's become the point around which we all communicate now. Ten years ago, it was Yusuf Hawkins and the killing in Bensonhurst. Maybe because it's this pivotal thing that everybody is ranting and raving about, or defending or dismissing. And so you have to have some kind of response to it. It has this incredible power. Like you said before, you don't give a damn what people think about the show because you're playing this hot character in the hottest show that's out there.

AS: Honestly, if I never act again, it's the best character that anybody has ever written for me, that I ever gotten my hands on. And it happens to be on "The Sopranos." My character, Gloria, has nothing to do with Tony Soprano's business. She's a Mercedes car dealer. I think the characters are written incredibly well. The issues the characters deal with are complex and exciting. And I think the acting is brilliant. Edie Falco is fuckin' amazing.

JS: The show is amazing.

---

[4] Felicia R. Lee, "Italian Stories, Without Bullets," *The New York Times*, April 22, 2001, City section, p. 1.
[5] "Cuomos vs. Sopranos," *The New York Times*, April 22, 2001, Weekend section, p. 17.
[6] "Why IAWA?" Newsletter, "Reading and Civic Virtue," Episode 35, April 2001.

AS: It's really interesting because since "The Sopranos" has been on, I have seen other scripts that deal with Italian Americans where they're actually talking differently, like, "Do you want some *lenticchie* (lentils)?" On TV! For a TV show!

JS: Right, right.

AS: I read this script for a show about an Italian-American mayor, a female mayor in Massachusetts. Before "The Sopranos," it wouldn't have been written like that. It would've been, "Do you want some more macaronis?"

JS: Right.

AS: You know what I mean? And suddenly we're allowed to be much more real about being Italian American and exploring different kinds of Italian-American existence. And this is happening at the same time where I'm still too ethnic for some parts.

JS: Like what parts?

AS: One was to play a frontier woman and the part was offered to another woman who's the same color as I am but she has a French name. We could be sisters.

JS: Right.

AS: And the other role, and this was really interesting, because the other role was on a show about an Italian-American family. And the character was somebody one of the leads in the show meets. The studio said, "No. We want a white, more blonde kind of person to play that part." And she's described as being the "most beautiful woman in the world." And the lead actor, the guy who's producing it, is Italian American and he's definitely not the kind of person who thinks you only have to play your ethnicity. He knows we're all different. But the studio is, "No. That needs to be somebody more American." They don't say it like that. They say, "That's not the way we're going on this." And so I called the producer and I said, "I want you to be honest with me. Is this an ethnicity thing?" And he said, "Yea." And then, on the other hand, there's the Latino community saying I can't play a Puerto Rican. So what am I suppose to play?

JS: Right.

AS: I'm only going to play Italian Americans? That's bullshit. And that's a struggle that just keeps going on and on and on. We're all actors.

JS: Right.

AS: Go ahead. I'm sorry.

JS: I think this is the kind of thing the activists who oppose "The Sopranos" refuse to understand. Actors need to work.

I'm on the American Italian Historical Association list-serve and it's been hijacked by these activists. It's a scholarly organization. And the list-serve has been hijacked by these anti-defamation, anti-Sopranos, anti-mafia movie activists.[7] And they've used the terminology to describe Italian-American actors, producers, directors who do mafia movies as "traitors," as "Uncle Doms." It's a phrase Bill Tonelli picked up in the *Times* article a couple weeks ago.[8] Uncle Doms. No different, they say, than Jews who sold out other Jews in occupied Poland, like those who rounded up Jews and handed them over to the Nazis. Some one actually wrote this about Italian-American actors! It's incredible! This is hysterical, ahistorical, insane, over-the-top language, with no consideration for the fact that we're not living in fucking Nazi Germany or Nazi-occupied Poland. We're living in the United States, where people have to eat and pay their rent. These people are not creating films and TV programs. You want to do the Joe DiMaggio story or the Connie Francis story? Go ahead! Do it. None of these organizations and none of these people are writing the screenplays,

[7] Since this interview took place, the list-serve has acquired a new editor. [Editor's note]
[8] "A 'Sopranos' Secret: Given the Choice, We'd All Be Mobsters," *The New York Times*, March 4, 2001, Arts and Leisure, p. 21, 25.

producing them, getting their hands dirty in all the things that it takes to produce shows in Hollywood and on TV. They're not doing it. Besides, where are the roles? I hear you. You can't play the pioneer lady. You can't play Latinas. You can only play Italians? That's crazy. And I don't think these folks are really interested in doing some of the great Italian-American stories. I don't think they really want to do the Connie Francis story, the Tina Modotti story.[9]

AS: I do. I can't get anybody interested in helping me.

JS: I'm also talking about all those people who have the money, the directors, everybody else, and the machinery behind it to make it happen. I keep hearing that Pacino was supposed to have played Vito Marcantonio, who was a radical politician from East Harlem in the 1940s and 1950s, who defended W.E.B. Dubois and Pedro Albizu Campos, who was friends with Paul Robeson.

AS: Wow.

JS: He was this incredibly popular radical, loved by his constituency. I don't know the details of it but supposedly there was this screenplay out there and it never got produced. Pacino was supposed to play Marcantonio. I don't know anything else other than that. That would be a great fuckin' story!

AS: Yeah.

JS: And this story about Peter Panto that Arthur Miller wrote.[10] Nobody knows about it. He wrote about it in his autobiography. I wrote to him and he responded.

AS: Arthur Miller?

[9] Modotti (1896-1942) was a photographer and Communist activist working in Mexico.
[10] Panto (1911-1939) was a Brooklyn longshoreman who led a rank-and-file revolt against a corrupt union and was killed allegedly on orders of crime boss Albert Anastasia. Miller wrote a screenplay based on Panto entitled "The Hook." Miller discusses Panto and "The Hook" in his autobiography *Timebends: A Life*. Grove Press, 1987.

JS: Yeah. I invited him to this event that we're doing on Peter Panto and Italians on the waterfront.[11] He said that he couldn't attend. And I also asked, "Would it be possible to get a copy of your screenplay?" He said he didn't think the screenplay was good enough to circulate. So, I guess we'll get to see it after he donates his papers to some library. But I don't think the Italian-American community or should I say, the people who speak for the Italian-American community, are interested in telling the story of Tina Modotti or Peter Panto, people who fought against the mafia, against fascism. They're not interested in those stories. They want these heroic, mainstream stories. They want the Yogi Berra story, the Joe DiMaggio story. Which are all great stories but that's the only stories they seem to be interested in. And they'd tell them in this celebratory manner, you know, "Italian American pulls himself up by the bootstraps and becomes a great and famous, you fill in the blank." That's the only story they're really interested in.

AS: They're all great stories.

JS: But those are not even getting done. And the way they want to tell those stories is really uncreative.

AS: And corny.

JS: Really corny.

AS: Like a TV movie.

JS: Exactly. So these things are not getting done and if they do get done they're hokey.

AS: And then if they make a story with Italian-American actors playing non-Italians, they say, "Oh, now we gotta have spaghetti." I think that's how people think [laughs]. It happened to me. I was

---

[11] "Italians on the New York Waterfront: A Tribute to Peter Panto," a conference sponsored by the John D. Calandra Italian American Institute, October 13, 2001.

doing this movie and they were casting the male lead. I suggested Anthony La Paglia, this great Italian-Australian actor. But the studio literally told me, "But if we have you and him playing a normal American couple then we're gonna have to have you both eating spaghetti." And I think they think the story becomes an "Italian" story if the actors are Italian Americans.

Fast Forward

JS: So, what does that mean you trained not to be an Italian American?

AS: When I was growing up I was really infatuated with British actors because they worked in ways that I found to be creative and interesting. They worked from the outside in. In other words, they worked on accents, they used their bodies, costumes, makeup. They built characters. For me, if you say, (using a nasal voice), "This is my character" (laughs), then you're going to have a reaction. I'll have a reaction, as the actor. It'll make me feel a certain way. But most of the classes I took here in New York used a type of method acting that called up real events from your life that the actor used, that were considered to be more real, quote unquote. For me that was too complicated because I saw acting as a simpler process. You don't have to call upon your "real" feelings, your real feelings are going to come up, period. There is no character; it's just you and a bunch of words on a page. If you say, "I feel silly," you're gonna feel silly. If you say, "I feel sad," you're gonna feel sad. It's just human nature. It's how kids make believe, how they play. It's the easiest thing in the world.

There was an acting technique I was introduced to that believed that if you recall, for example, your grandmother touching your hair when you were five years old, you can recreate that situation and use that emotion for a moment, for a scene. So, then you have actors in the middle of a scene, on the movie set, who are trying to recall some smell from their mother's kitchen (laughing), recreating internally some memory from their past. Meanwhile, everybody is waiting on the set to move on. By the time I studied acting, I was a getting a fourth generation interpretation of that technique. But there were some really great actors who came from that school of acting: Marlon Brando, Al Pacino, Robert DeNiro, Harvey Keitel.

I was more attracted to the school of acting that concentrated on body language, gesture, costume, and accents. And that was more interesting to me because it made me feel different and react differently than who I was normally. I use to dress up as characters when I was little, all the time. I remember once getting dressed with a cape, with my hair in braids, and I limped, and took the bus from one end of Brooklyn to the other, making believe I was this character I had created.

JS: So, there's a difference in getting in touch with this kind of primal feeling versus being an actor and dressing up and embodying a character?

AS: Yea. People describe it as working from the inside out, which is the more American method, which really took off in the 1950s. Working from the outside is a more British style of acting. When I was going to school, everybody wanted to be Robert De Niro and Al Pacino, so they would mumble, thinking that was "more real." But you couldn't understand what they were saying. I wanted to learn how to speak differently than the way I grew up speaking. I wanted to learn how to be able to change the tenor and timber of my voice. I wanted to learn different accents. I wanted to learn how to use my body in different ways. I was lucky because I was a dancer.

For example, my character Gloria on "The Sopranos" is not how I walk. Gloria walks like Gloria. That's not the way I walk. There's a scene in the next episode with Van Morrison singing "Gloria." You know? (sings) "G-L-O-R-I-A. GLOOORIA!" It's really hot! And I pull up in the Mercedes, get out, and I walk down the pier to the boat. The only problem is that there all these holes in the pier and I'm in four inch heels. So, I couldn't do my Gloria walk. It was upsetting since I worked on that walk, and here she was with this hot outfit and Van Morrison singing "Gloria," and she couldn't walk her walk.

JS: This is a side of acting I wasn't familiar with, the art of the craft. I didn't know about the differences between British and American techniques.

AS: I never really understood method acting, at least as it was taught to me. I never got it. I thought some of the exercises were bullshit. I remember once being asked to lay on the floor and go, "Mommy. Mommy." And I was like, "I'm not fuckin' doing that. (laughing) That's stupid. I'm not going to do it." My emotional life was so heighten anyway because of who I was, because of what I saw growing up, because of my cultural experience. Whether it was because I'm a New Yorker or Italian American, I don't know. The point is I didn't need to heighten my emotional life. What I needed was technique. How do I get from here to there every night on stage, eight performances a week? That's what I wanted to learn. For me, it was easier to get very technical and then take all that technique and throw it in the garbage and just go out and have a good time and play with it.

Fade Out

NAME INDEX

Abbandando, Frank 86
Abrahamsen, David 22
Abt, Vicky et al. 171
Adonis, Joe 83, 86
Aiello, Danny 129
Allen, Woody 137, 145 n.2
Althusser, Louis 32, 33, 268 n.13
Altman, Robert 200
Anastasia, Albert 86
Annotico, Richard 76 n.10
Antonelli, Louis 325
Anwar, Gabrielle 237-240
Appadurai, Arjun 257
Ardizzone, Tony 58
Arendt, Hanna 251
Argento, Asia 227
Argento, Dario 217, 227
Argo, Victor 232-236, 242
Aristotle 55
Arquette, Rosanna 201
Artusi, Pellegrino 252
Autry, Gene 81 n.15
Avalon, Frankie 74
Azpadu, Dodici 9 n.15

Bacarella, Michael 76 n.10, 79
Badham, John 127
Bal, Mieke 269
Barbera, Joseph 87
Barbiere, Santo 325
Barolini, Helen 11 n.21, 259 n.1,
    263 n.9, 264
Barrymore, John 173
Barthes, Roland 329
Barzini, Luigi 326
Baxter, Nicky 16 n.25
Bazelli, Bojan 229-230
Bazin, Andrè ii, 98, 99
Bear, Lisa 235, 240, 241
Beckett, Samuel 199-200
Behar, Joy 340-343
Belmonte, Thomas 69 n.1
Benjamin, Walter ii, 116, 205, 257
Bergson, Henri 205
Bernardi, Sandro 98
Berra, Yogi 348
Bertolucci, Bernardo 112, 135, 142

Bhabba, Homi 19
Bidney, David 58
Billitteri, Salvatore 17, 17-18 n.30
Bioff, Willy 84, 85
Birnbaum, Lucia Chiavola 334
    n.17
Blasetti, Alessandro 131
Boetticher, Budd 198
Bogart, Humphrey 244
Bogle, Donald 11, 81 n.15 n.16
Bona, Mary Jo 9 n.15, 34
Bonanno family 88
Bonanno, Joe 86
Bowman, Barbara 297
Boyd Caroli, Betty 263
Braidotti, Rosie 220
Brando, Marlon 136, 203, 349
Bridges, Jeff 139
Brill, Steven 160
Brown, George 84, 85
Brown, Jim 81 n.16
Brown, Norman O. 54, 55
Brunetta, Gian Piero 131
Bruno, Edoardo 113, 116
Bush, Mary Bucci 334 n.17

Cage, Nicholas 104
Cagney, James 80
Cahn, Sammy 304
Caillois, Roger 162, 164, 165, 172,
    173
Calleri, Mariarosy 324, 332-336
Camerini, Mario 131
Campos, Pedro Albizu 347
Canetti, Elias 113
Capone, Al (Alphonse) 49, 52, 53,
    60, 70, 80, 86 n.19, 169, 216,
    259
Capone, James Vincenzo (Richard
    Hart) 87 n.19
Capone, Louis 86
Capozzola, Richard A. 49
Cappabianca, Alessandro 117, 123
Capra, Frank v, 51, 96, 130-142,
    192, 291-321
Carpenter, John 203
Carradine, David 82 n.18